All Played Out

Also by Pete Davies

The Last Election
Dollarville

All Played Out

The full story of Italia '90

PETE DAVIES

HEINEMANN : LONDON

For Joe

**who at the age of eight months
just got his first football**

William Heinemann Ltd
Michelin House, 81 Fulham Road, London SW3 6RB

LONDON MELBOURNE AUCKLAND

First published 1990
Copyright © Pete Davies 1990

Reprinted 1990 (twice)

A CIP catalogue record for this book
is available from the British Library
ISBN 0 434 17908 6

Printed in England by Clays Ltd, St Ives plc

Contents

Acknowledgements

This book could not have been written without the extensive and generous co-operation of many of the English footballers who went to Italy in the summer of 1990.

Above all, it could not have been written without the help and time given me by their manager, Bobby Robson – help and time that was always courteously given, even when he certainly had better things to do than talk to me about, for example, 4–4–2: to 4–4–2, or not to 4–4–2 . . .

I doubt they'll like everything in this book – but I hope, in the end, they'll believe it to be fair. And speaking of fairness – given the common image of footballers as dim and greedy individuals – I must stress that in the months leading up to and during the World Cup, no player ever asked for money from this book.

I must also thank those people at the FA who always answered my many questions and requests so politely – in particular Glen Kirton, David Bloomfield, and Michelle Rogers. And I must give special thanks to Jane Nottage of Italia '90, without whom my weeks chasing football round Italy would have been mightily more awkward and uncomfortable.

Finally, my thanks to Rebecca, who may well have thought it was daft to begin with – but who, like thirty million others, ended cheering England on, as their cruel and brave finale unfolded in Turin.

Introduction

As I rode the glass lift down the outside of the vast grey bulk of the San Siro, hordes of jubilant people spilled round the squat spiral walkways to either side of me. They were mostly Milanese, but they'd become, for a day, honorary citizens of an African country whose national gold reserves are smaller than the personal wealth of Diego Maradona.

At the foot of one of the pillars, an enormously tall rasta, naked to the waist, knelt among a throng of photographers on the red, yellow, and green flag of Cameroon; he repeatedly bowed his head to the Tarmac, arms outstretched before him in exultant triumph and amazement.

In the parking lot, another man stood with his wife and two small sons – all four were dressed from head to foot in the blue and white of Argentina. The man raised his hands above his head and chanted at a TV crew, with a frantic and lonely grin, 'Ar-gen-tina! Ar-gen-tina!' – and he tried to get his family to join in.

But the wife and the kids looked embarrassed and miserable; they knew who'd won, and they knew that their father looked ridiculous. Argentina 0, Cameroon 1. It was the most sensational opener in the history of the World Cup – and one of the wackiest afternoons I ever had in my life.

And I felt thrilled to the core – because in Cagliari and Rome, in Naples and Turin, there was so much more to come . . .

This book is not exclusively for people who love football.

People who do love football will, I hope, enjoy vehemently

disagreeing with at least half of what's said in it, since that's at least half of what being a fan is all about.

We all picked our own teams – then we thought the manager was a wart when he picked someone else. We all thought Brazil were either brilliant, or terrible – what are the artists doing, we cried, playing this defensively dreary Euro-formation? And we all thought England were either lucky, or magnificent – at last, we cried, the yeomen are playing that fluid and flexible Euro-formation . . .

A lot of us probably thought, at one time or another, that Brazil and England, to stick with those two, were brilliant, terrible, lucky, magnificent, so unlucky it's daylight robbery, the best team in the world, the worst team in the world, Sodbury Mechanicals could put a hatful past 'em with a hangover on a Sunday morning . . . it all depends on where you're sitting.

Chris Waddle said on the eve of the Belgium game in Bologna – suddenly giving up on a detailed criticism of the way England had traditionally played football, and the way that had tended to limit his contribution – 'But who's to say I'm right? Every system's there to be beat, and it's all opinions, isn't it? That's why it's such a great game.'

With football at its peak, these opinions – this turbulent Babel over whether this man should play instead of that, over whether our system works better than theirs, over whether this team's a bunch of cheating slime, or whether that other team has eleven heroes, when last month you thought they were all playing in diving boots – all these opinions, when football's at its peak, have about them a passion that no other sport can generate with such intensity, for so long, among so many.

In the reception at Anfield, a couple of days after Liverpool were beaten by Crystal Palace in the FA Cup semi-final, I watched two angered and grieving men come close to blows as they discussed the merits or otherwise of Dalglish's team selection . . . Why? Why does it matter so much? Why, at Italia '90, were some games seen by forty per cent of all the people on this earth? And why did a total of thirty billion people tune in, at some point, to those fifty-two games?

For those who'd not normally think of themselves as 'people

who love football' I hope this book might go some way towards answering those questions.

In England, thirty million people watched the semi-final against West Germany in Turin on 4 July 1990 – the biggest TV audience in the country's history for any single sporting event, and not far short of twice the previous record held by the Tyson–Bruno fight.

Among those thirty million were many who'd never been to a League match in their lives; and many more like my wife who, when she was a kid, went to watch her local side a few times, but who's never bothered much since. Given that the side in question was Huddersfield Town, there'll be cruel souls who'll say, no wonder she stopped bothering – but she enjoyed it. She just wasn't interested enough to keep going as she grew older.

When it came to the World Cup she, and her parents, and millions more, all got interested again. Everyone likes to watch the people who are best in the world do their thing – but doubly so when the people who are best in the world suddenly turn out to include your own team.

So this book is for those people too, in the hope that some will stay interested now, and start going again to a game that's been much traduced, has many failings, and is under greater threat than ever from greed and TV – but which still remains, for the moment, the most thrilling and beautiful game ever played.

This is not a disinterested hope. For many Brazilians it may have been heresy to play a European defence – three in the centre, two pushing up wide. But when England did this, it was progress – what we might call a leap into the present – and it worked. The players certainly liked it – and, in theory, it encourages a more open and more skilful game than our traditional congested midfield, with the ball hoofed biff-bang-wallop over the top to avoid the jam.

As English grounds (far too slowly) become safer and more sanitary, attendances have been rising for several years. With the success in Italy, and the return of English clubs into Europe, it's a sound bet they'll rise even further. But the new spectators will expect our clubs to strive for the new standards set by the national side. If they don't, the new spectators won't stay — and the success in Italy will have been a hollow gesture for everyone, barring only the twenty-two men and their manager who achieved it.

As for Italy it was, certainly, often thrilling and beautiful to be there; and it was many other things besides. The World Cup's grown so big (some would say, so bloated) that it's become a whole alternative world unto itself: Planet Football, an un-reality zone of media and marketing mayhem, a land of hysterical fantasy.

So in one way I didn't go to Italy at all. I got there and found that the country had turned into a logo, and the game into a cross between epic saga, operatic flourish, organised intelligence, and sheer brute war.

But then, Planet Football — it's a place where the simple dreams of boys kicking a ball between coats on the ground are force-nurtured, under floodlights and cameras, to the most mutant and enormous dimensions.

The harvest of this strange place, this sporting greenhouse, is soul food for billions — a kind of particle accelerator for the emotions of the world. People hunch intent with their drinks before jabbering screens in Dublin and Douala, Moscow and Medellin, São Paulo and Seoul. They watch the dramas far away; their spirits go speeding down the tunnel of the game and, smashing, release subatomic primal frenzies of hope, joy and despair on to the streets of the world.

Because you're in a territory now that excites alarm and exhilaration in the hearts of those who travel it. You creep under outcrops of rage, cross ridges of desire, and fall lost in wide plains of desolation; you stumble past fleeting vistas of sublimity, and mire in bogs of failure.

At the core of this crazed landscape, the great stadiums wait — the stills in which men and their nations are boiled down to the essence of what they are.

So this is a ride round the fourteenth World Cup — a trip to Planet Football. I got there via Stockholm and Poland, then, when I arrived, I went to twelve different matches between thirteen different countries in six different cities in twenty-seven days . . . and this is how it was.

1   Sardinian Cavalcades

Welcome to Cagliari

Mario Mariosardara, known to one and all simply as Marius, is a slightly stout, bow-legged, and cheerful man, looking very well indeed on his sixty-odd years. He's the chairman of the Cagliari supporter's club, and his bar – the Bar Marius on the junction of Viale Trieste and Viale Trento – is a shrine, a veritable temple to the great and good god Football.

We met in April, at a conference called 'Arrivano Gli Inglese': 'The English Are Coming'. It had been called to consider how Cagliari might best prepare itself for the most feared fans in the Mondiale – but as far as Marius was concerned, the English were welcome. He had a big banner put up in his bar to say so; and among the pictures of his local heroes on the shelf behind the chrome counter, he added for the occasion a signed photograph of Gary Lineker.

After the conference, the British Council gave us dinner at Il Corsaro, on Viale Regina Margherita. I sat on Marius' right, and on his left was Tom Finney. Marius talked about the weather – a serious business in Sardinia, where it had pretty much given up raining for three years, so that farmers had dire troubles, and in my *pensione* you could only shower in the mornings – and we talked about football, and fans, and about life in general.

But with metronomic regularity, Marius's conversation was punctuated at ten-minute intervals with sudden happy little sighs of disbelief: 'I can't believe I'm sitting next to the great Tom Finney.' He'd smile a little smile, like he'd just woken up in heaven and decided, after due deliberation, that he liked it, he liked it very much; he'd then say quietly again, 'The great Tom Finney . . .'

Finney at the conference told a nice little story. Back when £12 a week was the maximum wage, the manager at his club (Preston North End) called him in at the end of the season and said, as always, that they'd like to keep him – and the wage would be, as always, £12 a week, with £10 a week in the summer. Next in was Tommy Docherty, and the manager said he too would have £12 a week – but only £8 a week in the summer.

'No,' says Docherty, 'I want what Finney's getting.'

'But Finney's a better player than you.'

'Not in the summer he's not.'

Tom Finney . . . third equal with thirty goals on the England all-time scoring list with Nat Lofthouse and, since his goal against Brazil a month earlier, who else but Gary Lineker. Marius, an absolute fan, sat and smiled through the multi-course spectacular, and said over and over how he couldn't believe he was sitting next to the great Tom Finney.

Gary Lineker, of course, makes a bit more than £12 a week.

Bobby Robson ate in Il Corsaro some months before the draw for the World Cup in Rome on 9 December 1989 . . . In their qualifying group, England at that time still needed two points from away games in Stockholm and Katowice – but the Italians knew where they'd be sending the English if they got those two points: Quarantine Camp Cagliari. The secretary of the local organising committee, Roberto Pappalardo, whose family owned most of the cinemas on Sardinia, told me it had been known for six months in advance of the draw that if they qualified, then England would be there.

Because these were not the glory days of Tom Finney. These, it seemed, were the new horror days of a nation that was all played out, a nation of riot and yobbery, a nation whose football was oafish and whose fans were louts, a nation with a ridiculous government, an economy in a tailspin, food you daren't eat and weather you daren't go out in . . . England, England, whatever the hell happened to England? The arrival of its team and their brute following would have to be planned for a year in advance – though as we shall see, advance preparation in Italy's not a thing that runs to any fixed or recognisable schedule . . .

Marius didn't see it that way. At the conference he said that he'd been following football for fifty years, and if there was a great deal of alarm developing over England's presence on the island, himself, he could see little reason for that. And – despite the shrill fear and loathing of their newspapers, banging on and on about hooligans until the very word became synonymous with English – a sizeable proportion of the other good people of Cagliari seemed to feel the same way. English football is held in higher esteem abroad than it is at home; for Marius, and for many others, England playing three World Cup matches in Cagliari was just *great*. It was, I'd estimate, the fourth best thing in Marius's life as a fan.

The third best thing would have been Italy winning the World Cup in Spain in 1982 – a moment when, some say, Italy felt truly united as a nation for the first time in its 130-year history, with the much-loved then-President Sandro Pertini leaping to his feet in ecstasy and abandon beside King Juan Carlos in the VIP box. (I'm reckoning that as the titles of '34 and '38 occurred during the forced unity of the Mussolini time, they can't be held to count in the same way.)

But I don't doubt that the first best thing for Marius would have been when Cagliari won the national league championship in 1970. It was in honour of this triumph that the Bar Marius had been made into a shrine, with many huge, grainy, black-and-white photos, and even a statue, of the winning side's great man Gigi Riva, along with flags and pennants, and every other imaginable kind of memento.

It was after this victory that the Stadio Sant'Elia was built, to accommodate the club's new ambitions. But unfortunately, things didn't work out the way the people of Cagliari had hoped; in the following years they slipped back into grief and relegation. In 1971 Italy played Spain in Cagliari, and made the enormously tactless blunder of not selecting any members of the previous year's championship winners; in the Great Orange Riot, the national side was harried off the field by furious Outspan-hurling locals.

No more internationals were played in Cagliari for the next eighteen years – until, on 21 December 1989, Italy came back to the forgotten island, and drew a friendly 0–0 with Argentina. By all accounts this match was so dreary, the Sards could probably have done without it – even Bobby Robson, congenitally cautious in public, said the game was 'very disappointing' – but it did mark an important return to recognition for Cagliari. And with the World Cup coming their way, they were halfway through a season whose end would bring the second best thing in Marius's life as a fan: promotion back into Serie A, the Italian First Division.

It was a very fine way to kick off your World Cup, and on 3 June 1990, it was to celebrate this that we gathered at the Bar Marius.

The bar itself was theoretically shut, though a handful of us did limbo our way under the door grille that was levered up a metre off the floor, to get ourselves a preliminary beer or two. I snatched a glance at a triumphal edition of one of the local papers, *L'Unione Sarda*: 'Cagliari In A', cried the headline, 'Back To The Future!' Now, from the pit of C, from years of suffering and humiliation as in Dante's *Inferno*, a return to the celestial music of A – it was new life, it was renaissance, it was joy unconfined and unending . . .

Cagliari are the *rossoblu*, the red and blues – and every one of the cars gathering outside was either covered in flags in those colours, or simply painted in them for good. There were two flatbeds to head the procession, both trailers crammed with crazy souls with their faces made up in *rossoblu*, wearing *rossoblu* ostrich-feather headgear. They had drums and hooters, cymbals and horns. There were guys with wonderfully hideous red spangly jackets, and equally awful gold spangly top hats; there were guys with blacked faces wearing garish gauze *rossoblu* dresses, and girls of a positively unearthly beauty riding the bonnets of cars in *rossoblu* pixie suits. There were *rossoblu* caps, seed hats, headbands and scarves. Pictures of the team were taped to car doors and windows; makeshift wooden 'A's painted *rossoblu* stood proud on the roofs of this motley vehicle jamboree, and big 'A's were sewn on to the shirts of the girls. There were women and kids everywhere among the boys, the *rossoblu ragazzi*; and there were police cars and bikes, ready to shepherd the hooting convoy on its way all round town.

I rode in the cab of the lead truck, and when we began there were maybe thirty cars; but that number grew until they stretched as far back as I could see, and then further. Listening to snatches of commentary on the radio from Cagliari's last game, away to Messina – not that the result mattered any more – we set off at a crawl in a cloud of *rossoblu* confetti, past a babe in her mother's arms waving a *rossoblu* pennant, west on to Viale Sant'Avendrace.

A man in an orange and white lace skirt yelled from the trailer behind me for regular updates from Messina. We tossed little tags of paper out the windows that fluttered up and away in the wind on to the streets, the tags printed on one side with the name of the club president, and on the other with the name of a brand of coffee. A three-wheeler van cruised alongside us, sporting custom-made *rossoblu* skirts. We forked right on to the climb up Via San Michele, and looped back towards the heart of the town along Via Is Mirrionis. People threw plastic *rossoblu* pennants off the flatbeds to all the children who scampered beside us as we went on our deafening drumming way, and, clutching footballs and flags, they ran cheering beside us until their mothers scooped them up. Pairs of boys on scooters raced back and forth around and between the cars, one steering (if you can call it that) while the pillion riders waved vast banners. In windows and on balconies people called out and applauded, and were clapped back in return.

And so we made our way across the back of the intricate medieval centre, perched around the Arsenal and the Castello with their views over the broad bay, the Gulf of Angels. Cagliari – Italy's seventh biggest port, and the principal port and city of Sardinia – sprawls as a peculiar agglomerate of ill-connected districts, many sprung up since the town was bombed heavily in the war. The city's quarter of a million people now find space to build wherever the hard geography of rock and brackish marsh will let them. It's not the prettiest place on earth – it's an unpretentious working port, with the ready humour such towns tend to have – but it's far from being the ugliest, and if you treat it right it's friendly and warm. And it does like its football . . .

We passed under the enormous and imposing San Remy Bastion, through the twisty old shopping district – Via Manno had (of course) a World Cup promotion going on, with a large model of the mascot, Ciao, mysteriously suspended in a perspex globe – and then we came to the sea down the wide slope of Largo Carlo Felice, under the walls of the medieval

9

heart, and the heavy mass of the Elephant Tower. We turned left on Via Roma, the grand harbour-front avenue, with ferries from the mainland, and Korean and Yugoslavian freighters, all wedged together under the cranes to our right.

To our left, under the solid and shuttered four-storey facades painted, eclectically, lilac and cream, mauve and maroon, ran the long arcade with the Caffe Torino and the Caffe Roma – places that would soon be gathering points for the more visible variety of England fan. Along this arcade, too, stroll the youth of Cagliari – hardly a gilded lot, but graced, certainly, with some of the best-looking girls I ever saw in my life. The guy driving my truck kept leaning out and calling to them, 'Hey, wanna ride? Wanna ride in my cab? Wanna sample some English cock I got in here?'

We were *en route* to the stadium now, the last stretch of our two-hour Sardinian cavalcade. By the time we were passing the Stadio Amsicora – Cagliari's previous ground, now home to a successful hockey side – the procession involved literally hundreds of cars, packed three wide so the main road out of town was blocked solid by a hooting, parping, gear-grinding mass, the whole thing stretching back hundreds and hundreds of metres under an ocean of flags. It can't have done much good for the greenhouse effect – but it was certainly fun.

Then everyone unfurled off the road into chaos in a vast parking lot; the armada broke up, some headed for the beach at Poetto, and others back home. I got out and stumbled around among the celebrants, bewildered and grinning. I said to one guy I vaguely knew, 'That was great.'

'Oh,' he said, 'that was nothing, that was tiny. You should have seen us last week when we were playing at home.'

I thought, if this is what happens when they get promoted to Serie A – what happens if they win the World Cup?

And what happens *if they lose*?

The Sunday before, Bobby Robson went to Cagliari's last home game, against Triestina.

I'd watched Cagliari at the Sant'Elia myself, back in April – they beat Padova 1–0. In England, obviously, you'd need to stick a roof on the place – not being rich in rain, Cagliari has little need of one – but apart from that, I can't think of many

First Division clubs that wouldn't swap everything in an instant for a home like this ground (if they had any sense, which is, of course, not a definite assumption). But it is, anyhow, a simple two-tiered bowl, it seats 40,000, and it's splendid.

Even with only 15,000 in it for the Padova game, it was still a sight more lively than most Second Division fixtures you could think of in England. The cheap seats in the upper tier of the Curva Nord where the lads, the *ragazzi*, all sit, was a packed throng of *rossoblu*, with their banners strung the whole length of the rim of the tier. The banners read, FUR-IOSI, EAGLES, ULTRA CAGLIARI, BRIGATA S. ELIA, CRAZY BOYS, BUNKER SKiN, and SCONVOLTS – for which an appromixate slang translation would be, HEAD-CASES. And when the team came out, so did a torrent of *rossoblu* smoke flares.

Equally different was the quality of the play – notably in defence, where the ball was never hoofed out, but always *played* out, even off the by-line. When, under pressure, the Padova defenders did turf it up the field, they were heartily jeered for this inelegance. Anchored by the sweeper, the defenders were confidently mobile, and comfortable going forward. The first time I noticed the Cagliari keeper kicking the ball upfield, rather than throwing it out to the feet of his back men, was in the eighty-second minute.

Since first I met him, this had been a main strand of Robson's conversation – that on the Continent, 'the defenders can all play'. And where could he get him some defenders like that?

For now, I don't know what he thought of Cagliari's defence. I only know that when he and some of his players went to watch that last home game in a packed, promoted, and partymood Sant'Elia on 27 May (seeking support and PR, sure, but also out of courtesy to his island hosts) he was pleasantly greeted, and he enjoyed himself. He asked wryly, 'Is it like this every Sunday?' – which became a headline in *L'Unione Sarda* the next day. He saw, said the local paper, 'a stadium in delirium'; and while the paper admitted that the 40,000 had other things on their minds, nonetheless the intro-duction of the English players on the pitch did create 'a certain feeling', and Robson himself had 'a serene afternoon'.

And I know, too, that since the party was packed, there was no room for the English press. But a photographer from the *Sun* told a reporter from the Press Association that Robson had been booed and jeered; and in no time at all this falsehood was headed back to London down the wires with all the others.

Meanwhile, back to 3 June and the breaking up of the cavalcade. I went from there with many others to Poetto, where an exceptionally pleasant white sand beach lies along the Gulf of Quartu, looking out to the next rung of coastal hills, tinted now a pastel pink-orange in the slow-falling sunset. Many flags from the procession had become goalposts, and kids played between them on the beach. At the south end of the shore, boats lay moored under the Devil's Saddle, a stony bolster of crag and pinnacle tumbling steeply down into the sea; to the north, the beach splintered up into a tacky strand of resort cafés, and an amusement park.

Cars still paraded on the coast road in their *rossoblu* livery. At some point an ambulance came, which was probably inevitable. The Italians have such an absurdly high danger threshold – boys and girls waving flags on the roofs and bonnets of their cars, bouncing along the rutted and bumpy beach lanes – that sooner or later, someone was bound to come off.

But the bulk of the people had long since gathered on the beach, for a final promotion party and concert. The band played Euro-pop – lyrics in English, predictably – and there was a new Cagliari anthem. In the deepening dusk the growing audience, with their myriad flags and banners – the colours of the club, of the city, and of the island – looked like nothing so much as a medieval army, a mass of people on the shore under a fluttering ocean of heraldic emblems and symbols on a ground of *rossoblu*.

A medieval army – drinking cans of Heineken, and eating the tastiest hot dogs I ever had in my life . . . There are those who say that football, in Italy, is a continuation of war between the medieval city states by other means. And certainly, Sardinia is not like the rest of that country at all.

Sardinia, people told me, was the first piece of Europe to

rise from the waves. True or not, the geology of the place looks weird and fantastical. Great wind-worn lumps of contorted grey rock lie scattered along the edge of the turquoise sea; there's one called 'The Dinosaur', and another – perfect dirty postcard material – shaped exactly like an enormous erect penis.

People have been on Sardinia since the time of the Nuragic civilisation, at least 4,000 years ago. But different invaders have swept one after another across these antique shores, so that Cagliari is not a typical Sard settlement at all. Sardinian towns, more typically, are small places tucked away from danger in the rugged folds of the interior, suspicious and isolated – while all around the coast stands a ring of ninety-nine stone watchtowers, put up by the Spanish when it was their turn to be boss.

The shield of this singular island has four black blindfolded heads, one in each quarter of a white background split by a red cross; but what's doubly singular about it is that it's not actually Sardinian at all. The blindfolds were originally headbands; the heads were an emblem of the King of Aragon, and date back to 1281. The Aragonese occupied Sardinia in 1323, and the emblem was then mistakenly ascribed to the island by a Dutch king compiling an early guide to heraldry. Then later, in the nineteenth century, the headbands began to slip . . . so that even the symbol of Sardinia is not what it seems. Sardinia, in short, is a place very much unto itself – its private soul kept private behind other people's languages, and other people's governments.

It's been occupied by Phoenicians and Romans, Vandals and Goths, Moors and Pisans, Aragonese and Savoyards – so, after all, what kind of difficulty could a couple of weeks' worth of English fans ever present?

Some days later, I hitched a ride back into Cagliari along the forty kilometres of coast road from Is Molas, the England squad's hotel, with an amiable farmer in a disintegrating and manure-smeared old Fiat. 'What,' he asked, 'is all this rumpus in the papers about hooligans? Where are they? What's the problem?' He was one of that growing band of souls who, sadly, feel they must now instinctively distrust every word that they read.

'But,' he said, 'if there are hooligans, you tell them from

me. We are not a tourist trap here, we are not interested in the size of your wallet. You be friendly with us, we be friendly with you. But if you do cause trouble, be sure. If we get to you before the police do, all the policemen will find is a corpse.'

My second Sardinian cavalcade came on 5 June, two days after the promotion parade, and it was a very different business altogether. It was a ride that took us a big distance further into the unreality zone; it was a bewildering vision of what, on Planet Football, the care and management of a national team now involves.

England's last game, before they opened Group F against Ireland on 11 June, was a kick-about friendly with a scratch Sardinian Select XI in Oristano, a hundred kilometres north of Cagliari. (At the end of May they'd beaten Cagliari 6–0 on the training ground at Pula, which, after the FA's PR men took half-page ads in the local papers to congratulate Cagliari on promotion, might be thought a little tactless . . . but then, like they say, there's no sentiment in football.)

This second friendly at Oristano was slated originally for Porto Torres or Sassari at the other end of the island; but the security implications of the squad travelling four or more hours either way – let alone the drain on the players – soon put paid to that. Instead, Stefano Arrica, the son of a big man in the Cagliari club, organised a job lot of local third and fourth division players in forty-eight hours; a job lot graced by local boy Gianfranco Zola, Maradona's understudy at Napoli, who was back at home on holiday.

It was an enjoyable afternoon, made more so by the bleak and baked beauty of the journey, and by the company I had on the outward leg of it. I was driven to the game by the War Correspondent of *Il Giorno* – a charming and drily witty man who, since he'd covered Vietnam, the Congo, the Gulf War, Central America and the Lebanon, got told by his paper, 'You're just the man for Cagliari.' And we talked about a host of things . . .

On Maradona: 'A very stupid human being – a simple-minded slum boy.'

On wars: 'Vietnam was a beautiful war. The Americans provided such splendid facilities . . .' Except he hadn't enjoyed

14

filling in the form to say who'd pay, if he got sent home in a bag.

And on Sardinia, which he loved, and where he often took his holidays: 'This is a bad choice for England. These are a very strange and violent people. In Greece in World War II the Germans and the Italians were marching on Athens, and one Sardinian boy took pity on the people, and gave his bread to a woman with a baby. A German said to him, "You must show no weakness," and punched the boy. So the boy jumped on the German's chest and killed him – with his head. Some of the villages here, you see – the annual festival includes a headbutting party. They run full on into metal doors with their foreheads . . .'

When the Germans and the Austrians defeated the Italians at Caporetto in World War I, the 5,000 men of the Sardinian Brigata Sassari earned undying fame. Entire divisions tried to pass them and failed, until the Sards had lost eighty per cent of their men. 'They are very stubborn. You go see them in the mountains – if you're good friends with a man, you might speak ten words with him in a day.'

Generally in Italy, he said, the great majority of kidnap victims survive. But when Sards are involved, that's not necessarily so. The victims disappear. 'They feed them to their pigs.'

In Cagliari there were, he said, two very hard areas. There was Sant'Elia, 'where everyone's been to jail'. And then there was another district where the working people live, a lot of whom used to be miners, though of course the mines are all shut now. 'These people – they are very good with dynamite.'

I think the War Correspondent enjoyed himself, spinning these tales. After all, I met with nothing but friendliness on Sardinia. But then, he was not like the joke-named 'war correspondents' sent out by the English tabloids to report on fan violence – and, if there wasn't any, to make some up. He was an honest man who, as the tournament unfolded, grew steadily more convinced that for the most part the English, in fact, were behaving just fine . . .

After an hour or so, we came through a vent in the moonscape, and a yellow-brown plain, broiling in heat haze, yawned open before us. We could tell where Oristano was by the helicopter hovering over the arrival of the squad in the

15

distance. The town itself was a dull-looking place of squat square buildings, all breezeblock and dust – but you don't go to Sardinia for the architecture. (The finest things in Cagliari, like the Duomo, were built by the Pisans in the thirteenth century.)

We caught up with the team bus in a flurry of police cars and motorbikes. 'Nothing,' said the War Correspondent, 'will ever have happened in Oristano like this.' The road to the little ground was sealed off.

The ground itself was shabby but homely, with two small stands along either side of the pitch, one of them roofed. There were maybe 3,000 locals there – not, of course, 'strange and violent' at all, but thoroughly relaxed, and pleased about the odd spectacle they were about to enjoy. There were also daft numbers of policemen, keeping a benign eye on the twenty or thirty England lads who'd come up from Cagliari by bus or train for the day.

Some English press grumbled – out of habit, basically – that they were morons and deadheads, when they acted up for the cameras. I made a note, 'You only sing when they're filming' – but why shouldn't they? Why point the bloody cameras at them in the first place? One of the tabloid men (morons, deadheads) called them 'professional hooligans' – a nice way to talk about your readers . . . But I'd met these boys already back in Cagliari, and, if they weren't the brightest in the world, there was no malevolence about them. All they wanted was a fun afternoon – and England sure gave them one.

First, however, players and FA men went around the crowd, giving lollipops to children. They were whoppers, maybe three inches in diameter, and they said 'FIFA World Cup – England – Italy 1990'. Kids slurped on them contentedly; a couple of Red Cross ladies chattered in front of me that it was a nice thing to do.

Then the game kicked off, with a rather more ham-fisted little piece of PR. From the whistle, McMahon took the ball straight back down the pitch, and scored a deliberate own goal. We had an FA press release saying this was a message to fans, that violence was an own goal so please don't score one – but the immediate result was 3,000 exceedingly bewildered Sardinians. Had the heat got to McMahon here, or what?

Still, giving them a 1–0 lead in the first minute didn't mean a whole lot with Steve Bull on the park. He went up the other end and, in the second minute, he made it 1–1. By half-time, it was 5–1.

It was a muggy day, and the overcast sky began to drip the odd speck of unfamiliar rain – otherwise, the second half looked more or less the same as the first. Seaman, taking his turn in goal, missed a twenty-five yard shot that made it 5–2 (though his World Cup was soon to end in more sadness than he'd have felt over that little slip) and then normal business was resumed. The game finished 10–2.

Twenty or twenty-five English pressmen gathered in a circle round Robson on the pitch – Robson turned on one of them stood behind him, whose paper had been laying on some Grade A vitriol lately, and said, 'I don't want *you* where I can't see you.'

I don't see how anyone would have learnt too much. The England lads, mightily amused by their team's afternoon, chanted sporadically from the stand, but found it a bit hard to work out who to sing for. Only one Peter Beardsley? Only one Steve Bull? Only one Sardinia Select?

Outside, small crowds of *ragazzi* gathered to cheer the England bus away. My War Correspondent had vanished, so, seeing Jane Nottage from the Italia '90 Press Office, I hitched a ride in the cavalcade instead. And, rather abruptly, a gentle kick-about in Nowheresville turned back into the fourteenth World Cup.

At first there was the customary swirling mayhem of police cars and bikes, edging their way through the knots of friendly kids; among them, the *scooteristas* weaved back and forth round the throng of our vehicles as the engines grumbled, and the sirens began. Then, slowly, the motorcade fanned out and lined up – and long before we'd left Oristano I'd started thinking, this isn't real life, *this is a movie*.

At the front were two *carabinieri* cars, then a regular police car. Next came the team bus, and the team van for any spare local or FA officials. Then there was a plainclothes car, and after that two Italia '90 cars. Then there followed another *carabinieri* car, a blue bus filled with yet more *carabinieri*, two armoured police vehicles, and two more plainclothes cars. Add to these fourteen vehicles a brace of perpetually siren-blowing outriders (you know the kind of guys, heavy black boots, and seriously dark LA-style gold-rimmed shades) cruising back and forth the whole length of the noisy parade, steering with one hand, waving traffic off our lane with fluorescent red wands in the other, and you have a truly grandiose spectacle.

But still we weren't safe enough. As we came out on to the parched plain, the eerie lunar mountains rising to either side of us, the police helicopter appeared again, and clattered into place up above us. And, describing a circling string of loops to stay in place overhead, it stuck with us the whole length of the journey back home.

So, passing through this strange and savage terrain, past unfenced fields of bleached grain stretched out under jagged, stone-strewn stacks of ridge and rough peak, I thought, just a minute here. Who's in that bus? Bush? Gorby? This month's Italian government? Nah – it's a football team . . .

One of twenty-four such teams who were, for these few weeks, the most important people on the face of the earth – their comings and goings, their passes and tackles, their fouls and their injuries and their goals and their dreams all monitored by thousands of journalists, and eagerly scanned by the billions on TV.

So important, indeed, that absurdly hysterical news had now come from London that Abu Nidal, the devil his very self, was after their hides. Or, as Nottage called him, Abdul Needle. But let's face it – if he was going to do it, he wouldn't tell the tabloids.

And my main personal fear, as we careered through the moonscape, was that if Abdul Needle did opt to have a go, all these zillions of *carabinieri* would as likely as not go terminally doolally and in their panic, shoot *me*.

Ah well. In three days' time it was off to Milan, for Argentina–Cameroon . . .

2   Headlines on Acid

Strange news from Stockholm

FIFA, the International Federation of Football Associations, was founded in Paris on 21 May 1904 by seven countries – Belgium, Denmark, France, Holland, Spain, Sweden and Switzerland.

Eighty-six years later, the governing body of the world game represents 117,000,000 registered players, and has more member countries than the United Nations.

After football's success at the Olympics in 1924 and 1928 – both of which competitions were won by Uruguay – the first World Cup was held in that country in 1930. Thirteen nations took part – seven South American sides plus Mexico, the USA, and four teams from Europe. (The Romanians only managed to get there after their squad was both picked and paid for by King Carol.) Uruguay won, beating Argentina 4–2 before a crowd of ninety thousand. Across the River Plate in Buenos Aires, enraged Argentinians attacked the Uruguayan embassy – welcome to world football.

Sixty years later, the qualifying rounds for Italia '90 involved, initially, 110 countries. Of these, Bahrain, India, and South Yemen pulled out from the Asian groups; and in Africa Lesotho, Rwanda, and Togo withdrew. For Libya, defeat at the hands of the Ivory Coast and Algeria was not, presumably, in line with the thoughts of Colonel Gaddafi's Green Book, and they also withdrew. Meanwhile, in the North and Central American group, Mexico were disqualified – of which more later.

So in the end, 102 countries took part in the fourteenth World Cup. On 17 April 1988 – over two years before Argentina played Cameroon in Milan – Trinidad and Tobago beat Guyana 4–0. It was the first of 312 games, played over twenty months on every continent on earth, to decide who should end up in Italy.

Thirty-two countries in Europe were involved – the definition of Europe extending, for football's purposes, from Iceland to Turkey. In England's group, the opposition were Sweden, Poland and Albania.

England began with a goalless draw against the Swedes at Wembley in October 1988. Not brilliant, but the next spring they put seven past Albania, scoring two in Tirana in March, and five at Wembley in April. This set things up nicely – halfway there, five points out of six.

On 3 June Poland came to Wembley for England's fourth qualifier. It was the weekend of Tiananmen Square, the death of Khomeini, and the Trans-Siberian train disaster . . . there's a little old guy who preaches at Wembley, some games, about the end of the world. On this most appropriate of weekends, he stood on a grassy bank above the Tarmac approaches to the stadium, and told 69,000 sinners that their time was running out.

He looked scared witless, twisting an umbrella round and round in his nervy hands – but his faith sustained him before the armies of the damned. They rollicked past, swigging beer and chanting. He had a cracked, reedy voice, and the oratory was cracked and reedy too. Among the promises of hellfire he spoke of heaven, where those who repented could still find bliss, bliss for eternity with Jesus our Lord who loves you, Jesus who can save you . . .

Does he play for England then?

England ran out an easy 3–0 against inept and dispirited opposition. Gary Lineker scored the first; he helped to make John Barnes's sweet volley for the second, then he stole the ball from the permanent confusion in the Polish defence for Neil Webb to score the third. And the 69,000 knew who Jesus was today:

> *There's only one Gary Lineker*
> *Only one Gary Li-ineker . . .*

They knew where heaven was too:

Que sera sera
Whatever will be will be
We're going to I-ta-lee . . .

So it was ten goals for, none against, seven points out of eight – and nothing left to do but go to Sweden and Poland, and earn two more points to lock it up . . . anybody reckon that's easy?

My *pensione* in Cagliari was tucked quietly away down a sidestreet, one block back from the Via Roma and the docks. It was central, and very convenient – not least because it was opposite the Hotel Italia, which had a bar where you could watch first round games from other cities in relative tranquillity. And staying in the Italia was an odd bloke called Max.

Max was born in Cardiff in 1940, and he worked for the Foreign Office. He spoke Russian and German and worked, he said, on our relations with those countries. 'You're a spy,' said the scaffolder who'd come to Cagliari from Bristol, via Mexico '86 and Australia – on Planet Football, you meet all sorts.

Max – when not relating with Russians and Germans – had followed England to Italy in '80, to Spain in '82, to Mexico in '86, to Germany in '88, and to Stockholm in September '89.

'I was ashamed to speak English. It grieves me to say it, but I was ashamed to speak English. There were people running past people just sitting having a glass in the cafés, and they were slapping them in the face as they went, men, women, children, they didn't care – I've followed England all over, but in Stockholm I was embarrassed to be English. I've seen nothing else like it. It was terrible. Terrible. I was ashamed to speak English.'

My kid brother went on some kind of Euro-rail jaunt into Scandinavia that autumn, up beyond the Arctic Circle – and on the way he met some lads he got on with just fine. Then, on his way back, he wound up in Stockholm on 6 September, and he met them again. 'They were different people,' he said, 'different people altogether.'

But take any England trip, talk to any thousand England fans, and what you'll get is a thousand different stories. I found Alan, who was twenty-five and came from Weymouth, sitting on the floor of Bologna station the day after the Belgium game, waiting to catch a train home. Alan had been in Stockholm, and he'd had a very good time. 'The people were really friendly – especially this bank manager from Gothenburg or somewhere. When we got back to the hotel after the game, he wouldn't let me buy him a drink all night. I did give him my England shirt though.'

And trouble?

Alan didn't see any trouble.

The trouble began on the *Tor Britannia*, a ferry headed from Harwich to Gothenburg. The day before the game the papers (The Daily Loan Ad & Dirty Phone Call Directory, Giving It To You Straight) had a field day:

SOCCER MOB IN FERRY DEATH RIOT

SOCCER'S SHIP OF SHAME

MAGGIE TO BAN WORLD CUP

What, all of it?

In Cagliari I met a Steve Bull fan who had his own business in Wolverhampton, selling fire protection equipment – and he'd been on this VOYAGE OF VIOLENCE. 'Yeah OK,' he said, 'a lot of beers went down, there was a disco, and we were all singing and that – there was a lot of Bradford and Middlesbrough, maybe thirty each, and the Middlesbrough lot were getting funny. About midnight at the disco, there was three of us Wolves, we were with Bradford, and the Middlesbrough come over, they ask who we support. We say Wolves, so they say, "We dicked yer." We say, "What d'yer mean?" "We beat yer." "Yeah, I know. 4–2." "Nah. We *dicked* yer. *After*." Then the Bradford lads come over and say, "Who are yer? Leave it out, there's only three of 'em." So then this Middlesbrough mouth merchant starts giving it the same to Bradford, so this Bradford lad clocks him. Then this bloke in a Man U shirt jumps on the Middlesbrough lad, he hits him a few times, then they're split up, and it's over. I didn't see much more. We said, "We're all England, we should sit together."

22

'Anyway, it was Plymouth lads had the acid, and there was Middlesbrough letting off the fire extinguishers – we heard someone gone nutty over that and jumped off, but we didn't believe it. So we went to bed at two or three, got up at nine, went to breakfast, asked for the arrival time – and then they tell us they've turned round. We docked at Harwich, and everyone following England got put in a bar on the top deck. We were there three or four hours, nothing to eat or drink, then the police took us off, put us in a big room another hour, then told us the captain didn't want us on the ship. And when I got out and saw the papers, I couldn't believe it. None of it was true.'

What is true is that a tripping 24-year-old from Plymouth went overboard and drowned. And what's also true is that the kind of England fans that get mixed up in this stuff will pretty much always tell you, 'We done nothing.'

The problem isn't that they're malevolent, since mostly they're not. They're just stupid – because if you reckon getting totally plastered and throwing things at each other (including punches) is the same as 'doing nothing', then bright you are not.

One man's minor ruck, after all, is another man's terrifying riot – like football, it all depends on where you're sitting. And we all know where the tabloids sit.

LSD DEVILS: ACID-CRAZY SOCCER THUGS 'TALK TO SATAN'

While the acid-crazy soccer thugs were boarding the ship of shame for a chinwag with Lucifer, the England team were on a British Airways flight from Heathrow to Stockholm – along with fifty or so alcohol-crazy journalists, busy guzzling their way through the drink stocks.

That trip was my first for this book. And the first thing Terry Butcher said to me was, 'What paper are you from?'

Mistrust of the press is a standard feature of any English international footballer, but the papers would, on this occasion, be more than good to Butcher after the game to come in Stockholm.

With the regular skipper Bryan Robson injured, Butcher

was captain of England for only the second time. However, given what Bobby Robson thinks of the man, the choice was maybe not so surprising for an important game that England needed badly not to lose.

'We have white hot nights, the tension is white hot, the hysteria, the volatile, hostile atmosphere away from home – you can come up and feel it and you think, fucking hell . . . You have to have players who can walk out of the dressing room and meet that and not crumble. You need players who *love* it, like Butcher, he'll look at it and say, "Just the ticket." He's a player who'll fight the battle right from the tunnel. He'll say, "Right, let's get into this fucking lot." He'll *say* that. Big man, *big man* – he's half won the match before you're out on the pitch.'

Gary Stevens, who plays with Butcher at Rangers, put it a different and rather simpler way. 'Show me a fifty-fifty ball,' he said, 'and I'll lay you money Butch wins it.'

In the tight, compact Rasunda stadium, before a crowd a little less than 40,000, Butcher had a nasty clash of heads with Swedish striker Johnny Ekstrom twenty-five minutes into the game. The wound poured with blood, but he carried on playing. At half-time Doc Crane got seven stitches into it, and wanted him off, but Butcher wasn't having it. (Robson said to the other players, 'Have a look at your skipper. Let none of you let him down.') Butcher said the only way he'd come off was on a stretcher. And Robson said afterwards that if he'd tried to order him off, 'He'd have hit me.'

Butcher said, 'When you skipper England in a World Cup match, you just don't go off.'

So he went back on, hastily stitched and bandaged, in a clean new white shirt – and the stadium filled with applause. Within minutes this new shirt, too, was drenched in red from shoulders to waist. He got cut again, over the eyebrow this time. They put another fourteen stitches in him afterwards.

When Elton Welsby finished interviewing Robson for ITV at the pitchside, he asked if he could go and get some words from Butcher too. He tried a bit of flannel, 'The nation will want to hear from him', that sort of thing, so Robson showed him where Butcher was lying on his back having his head put back together. Gore all over.

'No problem,' said Welsby, backing off. No interview.

24

The result was 0–0, and the game was nothing special, but the point would do, it was eight out of the possible ten. Otherwise Steve McMahon, getting his fifth cap, was an indefatigable replacement for Bryan Robson, which was good news, and Neil Webb ruptured an Achilles tendon, putting him out for the rest of the season, which was terrible. But it was Butcher's courage you remembered.

He said he'd been injured far worse in the past, and it wasn't as bad as it looked, and he'd only been doing his job.

Waiting at the airport for the plane home after the game, he got collared by a journalist who took him aside. Others gathered to latch on and listen in. As he went past he leant my way and said, with a small shrug, 'This is the worst part.'

'Rubbish,' said Hugh McIlvanney of the *Observer*. 'That man'll be feeling good about himself tonight.'

BLOOD SWEAT AND CHEERS

WHAT A BLOODY MARVEL

YOU'RE A BLOODY HERO SKIPPER

But unfortunately, Stockholm the next day was on the front pages too.

We stayed in the Royal Viking Hotel, a bland businessman's bolthole bang in the city centre by the Central Station. It was a pretty town, Stockholm, and I enjoyed walking round it, over the bridges and along the waterways. The Wednesday of the match was crisp and clear, and disturbance in this orderly, expensive, and unexciting place seemed strangely unlikely. A man in a rowboat drifted by with a big net on a crude swivel, cleaning leaves out of the water – very placid, very clean, very Swedish.

There were weary little bunches of England fans sat with their beers here and there in the shade under arches, or on benches looking out over the mesh of channels lacing through the neat urban islands. They'd been told not to come – they'd been told there were no tickets.

All through Tuesday and Wednesday as the game approached, a steady flow of news hacks set off out of the lobby down Vasagatan to the station, keen to be there when rape and pillage arrived off the trains from Copenhagen and Gothenburg. But no show.

And all through Wednesday, small gaggles of fans gathered in the front courtyard of the hotel – but they were a harmless lot, hoping only for a glimpse of players, or a word of news. Talking with two of them, they voiced the universal resentment of the regular fan, fans who, because of the nutters and the Nazis, had been told once again they couldn't go to watch their team. And they didn't see why the hell they couldn't go, what is this, Russia? And they didn't see why the hell they had to pay way over face value (£30 for £10 tickets) at Swedish travel agents who, if the authorities really meant what they were saying, shouldn't have had those tickets in the first place.

And they told me the stories from Germany '88 – with echoes from Mexico '86, stories far too common to be discounted – of reporters and photographers approaching fans, and offering money to get fights started, so news and pictures could be born. They told how one photographer in Stuttgart offered a fan cash to get things goings, so the fan took the cash, then punched the photographer.

Two hours before kick-off, four coaches waited outside the Royal Viking – one for the squad, one for the Under-21s, and two for the press. Alongside the coaches, police bikes waited, and a cordon of police on foot, fanning out round the front of the hotel.

There was also a truck, loading up with the party's baggage for the trip home after the game. I stood on the tailgate as the bags went on, chatting with Brian Scott, who'd soon be moving into the FA to be their full-time travel manager. All about us, the knots of fans were cohering into a larger group, with people added on in twos and threes as the day had gone by. A TV man like Welsby couldn't go outside without the cheers and the chants going up, and people hassling him for tickets – but it was good-natured enough.

Then I heard the noise, and I saw them coming, maybe fifty or more, marching with their flags and their cans down Vasagatan.

Inngg – ger – luh–uhnd
Inngg – ger – luh–uhnd
Inngg – ger – luh–uhnd

No one likes us

No one likes us
No one likes us
We don't care
We are England
Super England . . .

No surrender
No surrender
No surrender to the IRA

And then the national anthem, more barked out than sung, with the whole ugly pack of them raising their arms in the fascist salute. One face in particular won't fade fast from my mind. As bewildered Swedes peered down from the walkway overhead he raised his fist at them, spitting out the chants, piggy eyes screwed up into tiny drunken pink pits, and his mouth frozen in a rictus of undiluted and brainless aggression.

They swilled about a little while, roaring and snarling; a bottle sailed over to smash behind the small rank of police against the hotel's shop window. One of them finished the glass of beer he'd brought with him, and then just threw the glass down. A visibly disgusted policeman waded in to shake him, gesturing absolute incomprehension, and kicking the broken glass back against the wall with a wildly irrelevant Swedish neatness.

Then they were gone. More like one single crowd-creature than a group of individuals – the innocent now, as ever, ensnared in the grim mob-surge of the wicked – they rolled away towards the magnetic attraction of sirens outside the station.

Kill
Kill
Kill the bill

The players came out of a side entrance and made for their bus; the sports writers were mostly on theirs already. As we left, you could hear the sirens gathering.

At the ground, it was only realistic of the police to let in those few hundred English who'd turned up without tickets. And, apart from the nasty few who did the Nazi salute, these ones behaved. They were much taunted by Sweden's own ugly faction, who went in for that awful, jungle-bunny grunting whenever John Barnes or Des Walker had the ball. At the far end from the English, the police went in on one packed section of Swedes who had a few small flare-ups of their own. But nothing really happened. The wicked faction were back in town, hunting for a match of their own – and the irony is that the Swedish police were efficient, and they didn't really get one.

Word hit the press room at half-time that there'd been fifty, eighty, a hundred arrests. A weary gloom settled. But, asked after the game whether the figures didn't make it England's worst night abroad in a long time, the FA's spokesman Glen Kirton said, 'No – it means that the police are learning to deal with it right.'

Because in fact, under Swedish law, there were no actual arrests at all, just preventive detentions. By taking in 102 English, and (a fact less prominently noted) 104 Swedes, the police ensured that what might have turned awful never had the chance to.

The Daily Loan Ad & Dirty Phone Call Directory did not, of course, see it that way:

YOB RIOT

RAMPAGE

THUGGERY

500 FANS LOOT STORES

They made it sound like the centre of Stockholm got stripped bare. But a Channel 4 programme that investigated this gibberish found, by way of an example, one store that the papers said was smashed to smithereens by the scum of Europe – and it hadn't been touched. Not surprisingly, no one from the tabloids would come on camera to defend what they'd printed, but a man from the *Guardian* did. He said the police had told them the store had been looted, so there you have it – the store had been looted.

Why didn't anyone go and check? What's a journalist supposed to do, if not to check these things? A hectic night, maybe – pressure of deadlines, OK – but it doesn't mean you're entitled to file unconfirmed untruths.

But by then it was too late. With Thatcher doing a chronic

wobbly in Downing Street over the headlines (MAGGIE TO BAN WORLD CUP), the Minister for Sport, Colin Moynihan, applied unavoidable political pressure for England's December fixture with the Dutch in Rotterdam to be cancelled – which it was, to Bobby Robson's great chagrin.

Certainly Rotterdam did pose a risk of confrontation between two seriously ugly minorities. But that's not a football issue, that's a law and order issue. And banning the match was nothing less than the people in charge of law and order (i.e. the government) panicking and admitting defeat – all in the cause of 'being seen to do something'.

Meanwhile, Robson asked, how was he supposed to prepare his team to play against the best in the world next summer if he wasn't allowed to test them against the best in the world right now?

No one died in Stockholm; no one was even hurt very badly. But some time later, Robson pointed out to me that in the same week the unfortunate acidhead went overboard off the ferry, and from there to the front pages, another Englishman died after being stabbed at a disco in Greece. And why wasn't he in the headlines? Because he wasn't going to a football game . . .

The following May, on the eve of the World Cup, when the performance of the England fans in Italy would determine whether Moynihan recommended that English clubs could return to European competition, I asked him this question: 'As your support for the return depends upon the behaviour of fans, what criteria will that behaviour be judged by? Because there are people in football who believe that it's headlines.'

He replied, 'No. It isn't. I think it's a naive and ignorant reaction to believe that the way I, or any government minister that I've known, of either political persuasion, are going to respond to headlines . . . the idea that we're going to make policy decisions on headlines is nonsense . . . there is no way we're going to make a decision until after the World Cup, when I've had police reports, when I've had the consular reports, when I've had all my department's reports – and that isn't going to be for a matter of weeks until after English fans are back in this country. I mean, it is naive in the extreme to believe that any government minister of any political complexion is going to respond to headlines.'

'Because the tabloid coverage tends to be extremely exaggerated?'

'Well as I say, I don't read much of it ... there is a disproportionate interest amongst our media in each and every move of each and every football supporter going abroad, certainly during this World Cup, compared to any other country. But I pay no attention to that coverage. I'm concerned about incidents, I'm concerned about factual reports, I'm concerned about police and intelligence and co-operation, and I'm not concerned about headlines.'

So why the instant knee-jerk pressure to cancel the Rotterdam game? Because if Mr Moynihan had really been concerned to wait and see the factual reports of the Swedish police, he (and his boss) might have got a different picture of the 'RAMPAGE' altogether:

The *Sun*: 'More than a thousand drunken England soccer fans terrorised the centre of Stockholm last night.'

Letter to the *Daily Telegraph* from Sven-Ake Hjalmroth, Commissioner of Police, Stockholm: 'In the light of the trouble after last week's England–Sweden soccer match in Stockholm, I would like to say that coverage in the British media has been rather exaggerated. The game itself was played practically without any disturbances at all ...

'There was some tumult in the centre of Stockholm before and after the match. Beforehand, about twenty English supporters ate in a bar and refused to pay; some others in a group of about two hundred broke a few windows and attacked a kiosk; and several beer cans were thrown at police cars ...

'I do not have a total picture of the way in which the British press has handled these events, but it seems that the reports of the size of the problem and the damage caused were greatly exaggerated. There is no doubt that the English fans were provoked by their Swedish counterparts ...'

The Rotterdam fixture was cancelled two days after the game in Stockholm, a week before Mr Hjalmroth's attempt to set the record straight was printed.

But then, in September, football was nothing to the English government but a problem and – let's face it – bad headlines.

*

Nine months later, England played their last game in the World Cup against Italy in Bari, on 7 July. In May Moynihan said he'd not be able to make recommendations on the behaviour of England fans, and the return of English clubs, 'for a matter of weeks'.

So maybe in July he decided to read all his police, consular, and departmental reports in double-quick time – because four days after Bari, Manchester United and Aston Villa were back in the draw for European competition.

And why? I leave you to ask yourself whether it mightn't be, what with interest rates, mad cows, Europe and the poll tax, that the government by July was needing votes wherever it could find them.

3   Terry Butcher

The old tradition

While a small number of Englishmen among the 2,000 in Stockholm succeeded in stirring such a lot of hot air, a different small party of Englishmen who'd headed north to a different country had, by contrast, succeeded over the previous few years in winning many friends and fans. Terry Butcher – whose performance in Stockholm was typical of Bobby Robson's 'big man' – was their captain.

Glasgow Rangers is the richest club in Great Britain, and it has, in all-seater Ibrox, the best stadium too. Most English fans gaped in Italy at stadiums light years ahead of the crumbling urinals where they had, for too long, watched their football at home. But Rangers fans among the Scots who watched their baffling team in the Stadio Luigi Ferraris in Genoa would have felt very much at home, and not just because their side were displaying again that inexplicable Scottish mix of brave grit and daft blunder. The Ferraris and Ibrox are very much alike – four big stands cornered together into a tight box just made for furious, close-to-the-pitch passion.

But the English players didn't cross the border simply because Rangers has money and a good ground. They went because Scotland, unlike England, has fans who all know that violence spoils the party. In Genoa, in the end, the city relaxed its drinks ban because, presumably, they saw that the Scots were even better pissed than they were sober – and not one Scot was arrested throughout. Scottish clubs, for this reason, had played on in Europe while the English were banned.

Rangers manager Graham Souness had brought seven Englishmen north – Nigel Spackman, Mark Walters, Ray

Wilkins, and four members of the squad that Bobby Robson took to Italy: Butcher, Gary Stevens, Trevor Steven, and the goalkeeper Chris Woods. Rangers also provided three members of Scotland's squad – the defender Richard Gough, and the front men Ally McCoist and Mo Johnston.

Signing Johnston in the autumn of 1989 was the most potent sign of Rangers' ambition yet – for the first time in a century, the bastion of Glasgow's Protestant establishment had signed a Catholic. Until that discrimination was ended, how could they be taken seriously in the unfolding new Europe, with a continent-wide Super League for the big boys surely drawing ever closer? But by then, Rangers' ambition was already so plain that in Glasgow, the joke said it wasn't remarkable for Souness to have signed a Catholic – what was remarkable was that the man had signed a Scot.

The signing of a million Mo Johnstons could not, however, diminish for an instant the fierce intensity of the most passion-charged derby in British football – the Old Firm match between monied Protestant Rangers, and poorer Catholic Celtic. It was for this match that I went to Glasgow, to talk to Butcher about being a footballer, about playing football, and about the coming World Cup – three days after England had beaten Brazil.

The morning before the game, Butcher was having treatment for a knock on the knee, and he'd been let off training – a reprieve which he greeted with an exultant, almost childish glee. We sat in the club's entrance hall, and talked while he waited for the physio.

The place felt inordinately grand, with a ton of wood panelling and a wide, rich-carpeted wooden staircase. A club doorman wore a uniform, as he might have done at Harrods, or in some beneficient Victorian Quaker's factory. The place reeked of crusty old money, though the money in it these days is new enough, and there was something almost incongruous about this big and amiable man in his football kit, in this polished and stiff-collared foyer. But then, if at Lever's at Port Sunlight they make soap, and if at Rowntree's they make chocolate, at Rangers they make football.

He was calm enough talking now but the afternoon before the Brazil game the previous Wednesday, he'd been totally coiled up. When the waiter brought us tea, he'd been barely able to contain himself before the man had left, grumbling angrily, 'Did you see that? Did you *see* that? In good hotels – in *good* hotels – (and here he demonstrated) they'll pause just a bit before they put the teapot down, so it goes down nice and quiet. But this bloke, did you see him? Teapot, crash. Cups and saucers, bang. Sugar bowl, wallop. That really gets me.'

He said he knew it was silly, getting bothered by the inexpert setting down of a teapot on a table. But it was little things, little things . . . Other players are quieter, but Butcher, by the time he's in the dressing room he's crazed, he's banging his head on the walls, he's listening to heavy metal on the Walkman – and he shouts his head off.

'I can't help myself. If you see me at home before a game, I'll shout at my children – I never really punish them, but the tone of my voice is enough. I can't help it, I just have to shout.'

Was he that wound up now, with Celtic tomorrow?

'Starting to be, yeah. Last night I was bad, I had to sort out tickets last night, the phone calls get unbelievable, press, friends, people want tickets – it gets a bit of a bother sometimes.

'But it's different for the country than it is for the club, because not everyone supports the club. Especially in Glasgow. You've got half the city supporting the other team, and you get a bit of resentment sometimes, a bit of animosity if you stop at a petrol station, or wherever – nothing sinister, but you just sense someone doesn't quite like you. And you walk away, you get used to that. But with England you can sense everybody's behind you, everybody wants you to do well.'

Butcher was thirty-one years old, and he'd been playing professional football for fourteen years – but still he got worked up over every big game.

'You get worked up even more, if anything, because of the responsibility, and the standards you've set previously. I was fortunate when I came into the England team, I did quite well early on, but that's the standard you've got to maintain if you want to keep in the team. Or at least keep in the squad. As for being captain, that was a bonus – I knew I might be captain when Bryan Robson was injured, and you think to yourself, well, you might be, but there was so much happening with Rangers, and the baby coming, you don't really think about it too much. It's hard to look too far ahead in football, you can't afford to. You look forward to the next game, and that's it – you might get injured in that game. But I've always looked forward to playing, I've always loved playing.'

He had sixty-eight caps and every new one still mattered. He remembered his first – Australia, 1 July 1980, England won 2–1. Now, ten years on, did it ever get too much? On Wednesday Brazil, on Sunday Celtic?

'At the end of the season you can have a good few drinks and just forget about football, forget about getting up in time to train . . . with the World Cup coming up, if we do well in that, we'll probably only get three or four weeks off this year. But we've got a hotel booked in Jersey for the family. (Butcher and his wife Rita have three sons, the youngest born at the start of the year.) Normally we go to America though – we've been there for the last three years.'

They go to Clearwater, Florida. A lot of players go to the States for their holidays, because no one there knows who they are. And it must be good, rediscovering anonymity for a week or two.

Later he said, about his family, 'I've been away so many times, you just get used to it. My first trip with Ipswich was Canada, America, Hawaii, you couldn't ask for a better trip – I was only eighteen, I wasn't really homesick at all. But once you're married, and then you have children . . . when we went to Colorado in '86, my second child Edward was just starting to walk and I missed that, I missed him taking his first steps. But footballers are lucky, you get a lot more time at home than other jobs. You train in the morning and you're back home at half past one, two o'clock – so we're lucky that way. But now with the World Cup you can't say, sorry, I'm not going, I want to spend the summer with my family. You wouldn't have much of a future, would you?

'Anyway it's such a great job, it gives you so much satisfaction, so much pleasure – though it can have the reverse effect as well. Ups and downs, highs and lows . . . the downs? I've broken my leg, had two fractured cheekbones, a broken nose – when you're injured, and you know it's going to be a long job, that's really hard. You've got no build-ups to the games, no peaks, no troughs. When you're injured it's like – it's just a flat line.'

*

Before the Brazil game I drove with Gary Lineker to Wembley from Burnham Beeches, the hotel where England stay before their games at home (scene of the Teapot Hits Tabletop Horror). Lineker is, by some margin, the brightest, the most relaxed, and the most cosmopolitan of England's players, so I asked Butcher whether he thought a defender was a very different sort of man from an attacking player.

'I think so, yes – I've never played up there, I never had that skill. But knowing centre-forwards, they do seem to be on a different wavelength – bound to be, 'cos their job's the hardest to do. They're playing with their back to the goal most of the time, they're getting kicked from behind . . . I've played up front a couple of times when we've been losing, I've been pushed up and it's a horrible feeling, 'cos it's a complete reversal for me, you don't know where people are around you – whereas as a centre-half you know where everybody is, you're coming on to the ball. When the ball's coming to you and you're having to do things instantly, your touch has got to be good.'

Beardsley had described to me how when he was on song, he knew what he'd be doing with the ball before it came to him.

'Yeah, but a good player, he's always got something on – and that saves you from getting kicked and knocked about all the time.'

Beardsley and Lineker both said too – knowing there'd be Brazilians who'd probably kick them – that they knew when to jump. So what does a defender think, when he's got players like those two coming his way?

'When you're playing internationals it's different to club level, the mental agility is so much more than what you're dealing with normal Saturdays – so your level of concentration rises enormously. After an international I'm so physically and mentally drained, it takes a few days to get over it in your brain, let alone your body. You're talking, pushing people about, especially at the back, trying to organise people – you have to organise yourself as well, trying to combat any threats. 'Cos if these players are making their runs, basically you know as a defender what areas can hurt you most – when the ball's played up to a forward in front of you and he can turn and take you on, one on one, that sends shivers down your spine –

it's a situation you want to avoid at all costs. I say at all costs, I mean, if it ends up bringing someone down, I'm afraid that's just the way it is.

'But take Gary, he's got great pace, so he doesn't want you to be in the space where he's going to run to, that nullifies his threat. To me, the danger is if I go too tight on someone like him, and the ball's played over the top, he can spin on me and get past. But if I stand a yard or two off, I can say look, you can have the ball to feet there, forty yards out, you're not going to have room, not unless you knock it past me and do me for pace – but then out there, there's always someone round me to cover that.'

Des Walker.

'Yeah, we're working well. Des is a great player, he'll be a great England player. Very fast. And he's honest, he works hard.'

Honest?

'Honest, yeah, I think he's honest, he's an honest player. If he makes a mistake he'll say, right, my mistake, I'm sorry. See, there's quite a few players who won't do that. Not in the England team, everybody there wants to do well for each other. But in football you get players who'll say, well, you should have got that – I've got my man, why didn't you get that? And you think, hang on . . . but not at this club, and not with England. At England there's honesty right through the team, take Peter Beardsley, he'll run twenty yards back and shut someone down, he'll run his socks off – to me, that's honest work. And if he's going in on goal at a tight angle, he'll not shoot if there's someone to pass to with an empty net – that's good honest play, that's what every coach strives for. And we've got that – if you look at our squad now, I'm excited by it. We get on very well.'

So I dug out a quote from Eamon Dunphy's bitterly eloquent account of a bad season at Millwall, *Only A Game*. 'When you share a job with someone in football, a relationship develops between you. You are communicating as much as if you're making love to somebody.'

Butcher thought that was pretty funny. 'Yeah, when you're playing well . . . apart from a few oohs and ahs. Wouldn't be like my lovemaking, anyway.'

*

England's first game in Cagliari was against the Irish. Did Butcher admire what the Irish had achieved?

'Yeah, very much. It's a bit similar to us, the way the team spirit's so together. But I know for a fact they sing all the Irish rebel songs, which to a club like this, with the religion, it's . . . it's not the done thing. And all the supporters wear Celtic shirts – that's another reason to want to beat them.'

After the Irish, the Dutch, and the small matter of handling Van Basten and Co.

'It's a good challenge, a great challenge. He's a special player, isn't he? But if you've got the chance in a one-off situation to do well against him . . . he must be under enormous pressure all the time, to reproduce that form. And if he does reproduce it, well – you just turn round and say, look, he really is a great player. But me, I want to stop him, that's all. That's my job – get a foot in, disturb 'em, block the runs, challenge, tackle, block 'em physically if needs be – that's the negative side, the essence is to stop people. But if you get that right you can create things too, like a sweeper does on the continent.'

So would England be better with a sweeper, instead of a flat back four?

'I'm very happy with the back four. Most of the players in the League, they'll be playing a back four, and when you've got players that are used to playing that way, if you were to introduce the sweeper system, it would throw everything into confusion. Besides, Sweden play a back four, AC Milan use a back four – it's not like we're the only team to do it. And we've had success with it.'

Eleven weeks later, out of the blue, England introduced a sweeper system against Holland in Cagliari. It was a revolution – and though the result was 0–0, England had two goals disallowed, and looked the better side. Butcher enjoyed himself, too, going forward more than he ever would from a flat four – but then, like Robson says, one of the hallmarks of an international is adaptability . . .

On 31 March the idea that England might so abruptly make this change was pretty outlandish. And from Butcher's point of view at that time, a team that had gone fifteen games unbeaten couldn't have too much wrong in defence, whatever the system. Sure, he'd admitted after the game that they'd been lucky to beat Brazil – they knew Pearce's last-ditch clearance with his hands in front of his chest off the line would have been a penalty ninety-nine nights in a hundred, but that, he said, just helped make sure that they didn't get too cocky. Meantime, for God's sake – we've not been beaten fifteen times, *and still they say we're no good* . . .

'I've had this criticism all my career with England, that I wasn't an England player, and the England defence is bad, it's suspect, there's a problem there at centre-half. But you get blasé about it, you read it so many times, you just think, here we go again . . . Brian Glanville in the *Sunday Times*, he slaughters me. Some games, when England are playing on a Wednesday, I've deliberately got the *Times* the Sunday before, and torn his column out – you don't read it, you know he's going to slaughter you anyway, me and Gary Stevens, he does us both – but then I use it as a bookmark. So whenever I read my book there it is, like a constant reminder: *I'm going to ram this right down your throat.*'

Then the physio called him away for treatment.

We had lunch in the players' lounge – appropriately enough, pasta. The players were watching the midday sports programmes; in the noisy, joshing, boys-together atmosphere, Butcher came up with the quaint information that, if he hadn't been a footballer, he'd probably have become a quantity surveyor. When he left school at seventeen he had a Maths 'A' level, and a place at Trent Poly . . .

'But I always had a secret ambition to be a footballer, I think most boys have – it was just a case of, I didn't want anybody to say to me, I'm sorry son, you're not good enough. I didn't have the confidence in myself, really. That came through my first few years at Ipswich.'

Butcher seemed more together now than some other players. He had a business to fall back on for the time when he'd stop playing, and he had clear ideas of what he wanted to do in the game himself when he did stop. The business was an insurance company, with offices in Ipswich and Felixstowe – the home area that he wants to retire to, where his friends and family are. It was odd, a man the same age as me (but twice the size) sitting there talking about retirement.

He said, 'It's good to have something going – footballers talk about doing things, opening a business, but to actually do it was good. I lived next door to a Lloyds underwriter, he was able to get it going. I would like to stay in the game though, I'd like to give it a go as a coach, or a manager. If I didn't try, I'd always regret it. I'd love to manage Ipswich Town – but you can't be choosy. I'd like to try and pass something back to other people, anyway, 'cos I've been lucky, very lucky – I came into the Ipswich team when I was eighteen, and by twenty I was a regular. That was down to injuries, it was injuries that meant I got into the team. So I was lucky.

'And it still goes on. I mean, six months ago, if you'd have said I'd be captaining England against Brazil and we'd win 1–0, I'd have said, no chance. So many things come along in your life, like, hopefully, going to my third World Cup – I never even expected to go to one. That year, '82, I broke my nose on 23 January at Luton in a cup-tie, and it wouldn't stop bleeding. That was nasty – it took two operations, five weeks in hospital. I came out at the end of February a stone and a half down in weight, I was like a clothes horse when I got out. My wife was seven months' pregnant then, Christopher came on 7 April, so I was on a low, then a high – then I got back in the Ipswich team, another high, and Ipswich were in the running for the championship with Liverpool, neck and neck – we lost that, obviously, but I played against Wales at Cardiff, we won 1–0, played against Scotland at Hampden, we won 1–0 – and then I was in the World Cup squad.

'So from being really at a low point in hospital, to the birth of your child and everything else, it was incredible. When Bryan Robson got that goal against the French in twenty-seven seconds, I was part of that, I flicked it on – dreams are made of that. Then I was the culprit for the French equaliser, when I should have played the man offside but I didn't, and he scored – one thing one end, one thing the other.'

That's football – and this is England. After beating the French and the Czechs in their opening group in '82 to make sure of going through, they could have thrown their third game against Kuwait, and got easier opposition in the second round.

'Right,' said Butcher, 'when you look at what went on with Austria and Germany that year [to the eternal disgrace of both parties, Austria gifted the Germans a 1–0 win so the two of them could squeeze out Algeria on goal difference] – England are above all that. I would hope they'd always be above all that. We play to win every time, and win fairly. There's still the old English thing about gentlemen, you still feel that sense of responsibility towards that … institution, really, isn't it? The old tradition.'

Butcher – and this should surprise no one – is proud to be a Tory.

One of his team-mates span past our table rapping, 'Three buffalo gals go around the outside, around the outside, around the outside …' he looked a bit sniffy at that. He's an Iron Maiden man himself.

Bobby Robson took on Butcher at Ipswich in 1976, for £50 a week. 'It was a fortune then, for a seventeen-year-old, just out of school.'

Confirmation from Gary Stevens – when I told him the figure, he said, 'That's a fucking fortune.'

'So I've been with him all my professional career. I've got a lot to thank him for.' (The Rangers rapper yowled at this point, appropriately, 'He's got the pow-uh!') 'He's funny, he makes mistakes, he gets players' names wrong sometimes, he goes over things two or three times, he's a bit pedantic about things, and little things seem to bug him a lot. But being with him you know his foibles, you know what he's like – and he's England's No. 1 fan, he *desperately* wants England to win. Obviously it's his job, but if it wasn't his job he'd still want them to win, he's that sort of person. There's people in football got auras about them – I think he's one of those people.'

So having seen Robson and now Souness go about their jobs, and seen all that goes with it, what did he think about being a manager himself?

'I wouldn't want to do it their way, I'd want to do it my way. Every manager takes little pieces of the managers they've worked under, you think, that's useful, I'll remember that – but you must do it you own way. If you don't do it your own way, what's the point of doing it?'

*

Butcher's dog had died that week, and, having a raft of supertitions, that bothered him slightly over how it might go against Celtic the next day – though to be fair, telling the kids bothered him rather more.

Chris Woods, Rangers' keeper, has superstitions too. 'I put my left shinpad on first, put my right boot and my right glove on first – I always go through that routine.'

About the game he said, 'We've had six games in a row where we've not won, so we want to win. We've *got* to win. We owe something to ourselves, as well as to the fans ... Celtic, they've got Dziekanowski, he's a classy player, good close control, he's dangerous in the box – but we'll keep him quiet.'

And when I told him I couldn't wait, he laughed. Because an Old Firm game – that's extra-special. Basically, they *hate* each other ... Richard Jobson, ex-Skid, now a TV and radio person, tried out with Celtic when he was a teenager. At one Old Firm game he was stood with the Celtic fans, and some Rangers' kids – can't have been more than twelve or thirteen – recognised him from the TV and waved him over, Jobbo, Jobbo! He figured they wanted autographs, so the police let him through and he went to them – and they gobbed in his face ...

Great city, Glasgow. The accent sounds like you're throwing up in a cement mixer. That Saturday night I roamed from bar to packed bar on Duke Street, and learnt from every conversation I had that the ticket in my wallet was gold dust. I ended up at a disco in the Reidvale Leisure Centre, don't ask me how. The bouncers had baseball bats the size of small trees – one kid got thrown out, yelling and fiercely fighting.

And at Ibrox the next day there were 42,000, three stands of blue against one of green – and the outpost of green was awash with the Irish tricolour. An awesome noise of defiance rose up from among them – and when the players came out the sound in the whole place was volcanic, totally deafening. Who says all-seaters damp down the passion? Not here – you felt the glory and the animal both stirring in your gut. The noise seemed never to stop; and the game kicked off at two hundred miles an hour.

In amongst the mayhem, Rangers looked more coherent; Butcher was solid, he knew where he was sending the ball, and usually it got there. Mark Walters put in some lovely stuff, pelting down the wing, cutting into the box. A few chucked bananas at him when he started, but they don't do that any more. Besides, being black in a blue shirt is no problem, compared to being a Catholic in one. A tiny Rangers hardcore burnt their season tickets when Mo Johnston came – but now it's not the Rangers fans who hate him, after all, the man scores goals. It's Celtic who hate him – the turncoat who came back from France, and signed to the wrong side . . .

On the half-hour Anton Rogan had a brainstorm, and handled Butcher's cross. In three stands the world and his dog rose as one, in a tumult of outrage. Butcher stood with his back turned to the penalty – one of his superstitions, not watching penalties – and Walters fired it at Paddy Bonner, Ireland's keeper. Bonner got to it, but it flew up off his body and into the net. After that, Celtic fell apart. Rangers were pouring forward, and, a few minutes before half-time, Johnston whacked in a second, an electric volley. He celebrated with a sprint all the way back to the half-way line and beyond, arms flying round in windmill circles. The green stand seethed with a grim, silenced revulsion, and the blue all sang:

> Mo, Mo, SuperMo

In the queue for coffee at half-time one boy told me, 'Thass' nae foo'baw owt thair. Thass' war.'

With twenty minutes to go, Rangers got a second penalty. McCoist sent Bonner the wrong way, and became the club's top scorer since World War II. 3–0, and Rangers were taking the piss now. Butcher stood on the ball at the edge of his box, inviting a Celtic player to come get it. What could the man do? He had to run at him, he had to try – Butcher waited, then turned the ball back to Woods. Dziekanowski, who really had been kept quiet, was substituted. Next day my paper said Rangers sang, 'This is so easy' – but actually that's not quite right. They sang:

> So fockin' easy
> This is so fockin' eeeeaa-asy

In the players' lounge, there was a fax pinned to the board from Sheila at Fife Fire Engineers & Consultants Ltd. It said,

'Come on, Rangers, there's thousands of us out here willing you to win. We can't all get tickets so we make do listening to our radios. Lots of luck and best wishes for Sunday.'

Sheila must have had herself one fine afternoon. I know I did. Then afterwards someone told me, 'That was quiet. Kicking off at two on a Sunday instead of three on a Saturday – that halves your drinking time, see?'

God only knows what they're like in that place when they're pissed.

The question of beer also got raised pretty promptly in the lounge after the game. Whether for deep and dark Protestant reasons or not, I don't know, but it was Sunday and the bar was shut. Horror. Players and their wives hung about a bit being polite – but certain among them had just walloped Celtic 3–0, and they wanted a beer. Or several.

So pretty rapidly a loose convoy formed up, Spackman, Stevens, Woods and others and their partners all making tracks for the Holiday Inn where, unbelievably, until he got a house sorted out after his transfer, Stevens had lived for the best part of a year. He said it wasn't too bad ... but footballers are strangely at home in hotels. They are, after all, anonymous places – and you tend to be left alone.

Butcher, meanwhile, with Rita and his father waiting patiently, took a fair while to get to his car – he had to stop every step of the way for kids and adults alike to get his autograph, or to pose with him for snapshots. He did it with a smiling, patient, generous courtesy – but then, they'd won. And inside he was bubbling over, thrilled like it was Christmas morning. Beating Celtic – beating the rebels – that was the best.

Because Celtic had beaten Rangers 1–0 at Parkhead in the Skol Cup, and Rangers owed them this one. The last fifteen minutes of that game, it had been Celtic's turn to take the piss. 'They were smiling,' said Stevens, as if that were peculiarly offensive. 'When it's only 1–0 and there's fifteen minutes left, *you don't go about smiling.*'

Butcher said that when people made a big thing out of beating you, next time you wanted badly to give it them straight back.

Woods said Bonner, after that game, had made sure to sprint to the tunnel as fast as he could, to shake his hand all too pointedly as he went off. So now this afternoon he'd done the same, he'd chucked his gloves to a ball boy and legged it like lightning to where the players go off – so Bonner had to shake his hand, after watching three go past him. 'But he didn't say anything,' said Woods, grinning.

'I don't like U2,' said Butcher, 'that's rebel music, Southern Irish. And Simple Minds – I found out Kerr was a Celtic supporter, so all my Simple Minds tapes, they went out the window. Celtic, you hate 'em so much . . . I was gutted when Dziekanowski went off. He tried to break my leg at Parkhead, full-blooded, six studs. I really wanted to kick him. But he's got a pea-heart anyway. No bottle.'

But after a couple of lager tops he calmed down. 'The kids,' he said, 'it's great, you fall down to earth so quickly. You go home, you say, *we beat Celtic* – and they say, well done, Daddy, can you watch a tape with us now? Can you play this game with us now? Then it's over, history. We'll go out tonight for a curry and a bottle of wine. Or two.'

He said the angriest he'd ever been after a game was at Aberdeen, after a really ugly tackle ripped up Ian Durrant's knee ligaments, and put him out of the game. He kicked in the referee's door after that, and got fined £500. 'Then we went back up there next game, and they'd put a patch over the door – they hadn't got a new door. Typical Aberdonians.

'But I've got to control myself, haven't I? I mean, if I hit somebody it's not going to be a stretcher job, is it? It'll be a brush job. Sweep him off the pitch.'

Later, I went out for a curry and bottle of wine or two myself, with Gary Stevens and his girlfriend (now wife) Sandra. He joked about a different kind of brush job: he said if Rangers won the League they'd go out and get so plastered they'd have to sweep 'em one by one out of the gutter as, smiling contentedly, one by one they floated by. A week later it was reported that, fifteen minutes into another game at Aberdeen, Gary Stevens had broken his leg.

Paddy Bonner, and Celtic's defender Chris Morris, both play for Ireland. Eighteen other members of Jack Charlton's Irish twenty-two play their football in the English League, alongside of English players, with a flat back four, at two hundred miles an hour. There'd be nothing so intense as Rangers–Celtic – but there'd be these same little things every

45

Saturday, little things that run on between players and clubs. There were seventy-two days to go until England played Ireland in Cagliari.

4   The Land of the Last Minute

Rome, Cagliari, Florence, Milan:
Italy gets ready

To get accreditation for the World Cup you filled in a form, stuck on a mugshot, and paid a $500 deposit. In theory, they gave you that back with your press pass come June.

If the official early estimate of 6,000 accredited journalists was correct – they were, they said, 'restricting the numbers' – that's $3,000,000 in deposits. You transferred the money to an account of the Comitato Organizzatore Locale – the Local Organising Committee, known henceforth as the COL – at the Banco Nazionale del Lavoro, an 'official supplier'. And this is the small change of Italia '90.

The COL then sent you an ID card, and an application form for tickets to first round games which you had to send back by fax, by 15 April. That instruction may have been a sensible precaution, taken to avoid the risk of your paperwork meandering away into the dreamy voids and longueurs of the Italian postal service. Or maybe it was just the thorough-going modernity of Italia '90 – a businesslike event in the new world of fast fax.

Either way, when I went to Rome in early April, I thought I better check that my fax had arrived.

You couldn't find a happy taxi driver in the whole city. 'They've known about this thing for years,' growled one seething cabbie in his yellow Fiat, chewing his moustache and grinding his gears through the freeform traffic round the detours and the roadworks (Italy was selected as host by FIFA on 19 May 1984) 'and they barely started really working till six months ago.'

They'd been working on the Olympic Stadium somewhat longer than that, and you couldn't get near it – they were in there around the clock. Rumour spoke darkly of the work being delayed by sabotage bombings, of Byzantine strife among unions and management and architects and government, while the unions (and many others) expressed outrage at the death toll, over twenty men in total, on tournament-related construction projects around the country. At a union meeting, a placard listed the lost names under a headline, 'This squad will not play at Italia '90.'

On this issue I was defensively informed at the COL that, yes, it was very bad news when men died as, for example, at the Stadio Della Favorita in Palermo – portions of the roof going up over the press and VIP sections had fallen in. But it wasn't fair to blame the World Cup for all this.

If, they said, local or national government was doing all manner of things here or there that it should have done five years ago – doing them now in a rush on the back of the World Cup (the World Cup acting as a catalytic drug in the whole of the body politic and economic, stimulating schemes and projects and work in indiscriminate profusion) – if, they said, they were widening roads, laying new gas pipes and new phone lines, and a man fell in one of the holes, then what was that to do with the World Cup, as such?

As we swooped out of Cagliari towards Oristano on the brave new flyovers that had opened mere days before kick-off, the War Correspondent told me that it was remarkable: they'd done in ten months what would normally, in Italy, have taken five years. Then he smiled his little smile and said, 'Of course, it may all fall down later.'

Gripes over cost and time over-runs were, anyway, only a predictable footnote to one of modern Italy's perennial themes – the criticism by successful business of the rambling and obstructive inefficiencies of government. The COL, after all, was a private enterprise body; its General Manager Luca di Montezemolo was a scion of the Agnelli empire, who'd gone from Fiat to Italia '90 via Campari, Ferrari, and an Italian Admiral's Cup bid. So it wasn't surprising, when a thing looked like running late or going wrong, that the blame would be directed mildly (or not so mildly) towards the slow and directionless pace of government bureaucracy.

Meanwhile, monuments disappeared under towers of scaffolding and curtains of green net. Statues and fountains and palaces were washed and polished, dusted and painted. The front of the Pantheon hid behind a wall of corrugated tin and wood planking, swathed in heavy green sheets. The Trevi Fountain was a beehive of drills and hoses, men scrambling over the sculpted chaos of rocks. Tourists slurped their *gelati*, and watched men talk and work.

Such things, of course, are forever being worked on in Italy. Every other fresco or museum you seek to visit so often proves closed, proud signs from the Ministero per Beni Culturali detailing the nature of the restoration in progress – but the World Cup added to these labours of national housekeeping a new intensity of scale and purpose. Every rail station you passed through was being dug up. Every Roman road you drove on led sooner or later to a tangle of red and white plastic mesh, fencing off great dismembered chunks of Via or Corso being remade, resurfaced, rerouted.

And isn't that the way we'd expect things Italian to be?

The British in general are cheerfully ignorant about foreigners, a flaw happily admitted and filed under the 'island race' tag. But Italy's one of those countries – like Ireland, or the USA – about which we are, if anything, doubly ignorant. Not only do we know and understand very little, but we then add insult to injury by thinking, on top of that, that we know and understand everything.

Italy's a holiday destination, right? Been one for centuries – why, the world's first smart hotel was built there by the Duke of Urbino, no less. Peruvians or Chinese may be a mystery to us, but everyone knows what Italians are like . . . a kind of thinking that leads to the most outrageous conclusions.

Since the plays of the Elizabethans and the Jacobeans – in particular the gore and slaughter of the Jacobean tragedies, in which, among many other murders, people are poisoned by paintings, saddles, helmets and skulls – the British have 'known' that the Italians are treacherous double-dealers prone to stab you in the back, hump your wife, sell your daughters, and rub out the rest of your family for good measure while they're at it. With their mayhem and multiple murders, these plays were Scarface on Elm Street for the early seventeenth century. They depend on the popular misreading of what being Machiavellian means, and the popular application of that misreading to the Italians as a whole. In short, a scheming bunch of wops.

In football, the British hold by a modern parallel of that image. The stereotype is that Italians are more clever, more skilful, more technical. Their defences are cynically brutal, and superglue-solid; their strikers are rapier-sharp and lazy, drama queens who score on the break and, otherwise, strut about preening and posturing while the hard men do the work at the back. Their play is slow (hot country, idle people) possession football, intelligent, intricate, and tedious. And their manner is melodramatic, hysterical – they're babies, they roll on the turf in fake agony and anguish, they gesture and protest . . . not British at all. They sit back, poach a goal, then lock up the game at 1–0. And the crowds are nutters, demented, 58,000,000 national team managers. Bring on, at this point, the jokes about how many reverse gears they put in their tanks.

At the other extreme there's Chiantishire. People who think they know Italy think either that it's rotten in every regard (P2 and the Mafia, wormy coalitions and psychopathic driving, Fiat and the Pope, scything fouls and injured innocence), or they think it's just too heavenly-perfect in every conceivable way. These latter read John Mortimer in Tuscany, drink wine with holiday abandon, rave about the food and the art – give them an Umbrian façade and an *insalata mista*, they think they've died and gone to heaven. One little cup of fierce mud disguised as coffee, and that old magic of Italy's made new people of them, undressed their Nordic stolidity to reveal sun and hectic charm – made them, in fact, deliriously and precisely 'not British at all'.

The Palio at Siena, the Kalendimaggio at Assisi, the shoes and the clothes and the furniture and the ice cream, the David and the Pietà, the duomos and the saints . . . you'd have to be congenitally miserable to have a bad time in Italy, right?

And then their football's so good, so much style and flair compared to the thunderous rubbish we Brits churn out . . .

Of course the truth's about halfway (about football, about life). In Italy, like everywhere else, some things work, and some things don't. The trains, for example, are mostly excellent – comfortable to ride, reliably on time, and running often along snaky courses through tunnel after tunnel on tracks that are feats of civil engineering. But just try buying a ticket to get on to the things.

You can walk the platforms at Roma Termini and thrill to that nostalgic, adventure-packed buzz of riding the Euro-train, past carriages for Munich, Vienna, Brussels and Paris. Then you go out on the concourse and the queues for tickets are a whole pocket third world.

You go grey queueing for the window that says you can pay at it with a credit card – then you get to it and learn that the card computer's broken. Anyhow, for this particular train, you need that window down the way. Then, when more worlds have turned and you've attained the next window, you find for this train that you can only buy one part of the ticket you want from this window; the other part, the compulsory seat reservation section, is in the next hall along, with a whole new queue for you to stand in and enjoy. And you can only buy a single, not a return, 'cos you're booking too far in advance; or maybe it's the first Tuesday in an uneven month . . .

Still – once you're through this jumble of begging gypsies and addled computers, once you've escaped the shuffling lines filled with people busy offering each other large quantities of advice, the trains knock British Rail into the nearest cocked hat.

It's a good example of things Italian – a fine system, but with one part of it at least gone wholly awry, unduly complicated for the job in hand. It's like Rome itself – you look at it and think, it'll be great when it's finished. And 'when' is spelt i-f.

Another example: in one corner of the bus terminal in front of the station, there's a little booth that'll print out for you (for a thousand lire, or fifty pence) complete directions by bus and/or tube to wherever you want to go. It's a small neat idea, and a handy way to avoid taxi fares. The only problem in April was that now they'd dug up all the roads, the directions bore little resemblance to the new realities of the bus routes.

To see if my fax had arrived at the COL and, in general, to see what I could see, I needed to go to the Via Della Camilluccia, out north across the Tiber beyond the Olympic Stadium; so I got myself a print-out. When I left the tube at Flaminio, however, it emerged that the 911 bus had moved away into a whole new geography. I roamed the roadworks seeking out its secret path, to no avail, and ended up in a cab anyhow, with another growling driver reduced to taciturn enervation by the traffic, muttering and swerving.

Things Italian: returning into town late one night, I did successfully find the bus I wanted. It juddered forward into a snarl of cars where three lanes squeezed round a tight corner into two, bypassing some tangle of ripped-up tramlines, some overspill of the central reservation across the road. And as we made the corner, we found that the squeeze was bad because even the two lanes, in fact, were only one. Someone had left their car stranded and blocking the other, bang on the crest of the bend. The hazard lights were flashing, and presumably it was broken down. (Though, this being Italy, the driver may well just have stopped there to hop out and see someone, why not?) Cars could cram past but there was no way the bus could round the turn in the space that was left.

No problem. The driver and one or two others got on and off the bus a few times; caps were raised, heads scratched, and suggestions batted back and forth in the hooting, parping night with brief, infinitely expressive gestures of outraged incredulity at this obstacle in particular, and the irrational harshness of life and fate in general. Then a few *ragazzi* were commandeered from a bar, six or seven guys hunkered down round the abandoned car, and, with swift and organised economy of effort, they hoiked the thing bodily aside on to the kerb.

The COL employed about one hundred and fifty in Rome, and another hundred round the eleven other cities that would play host to the football. The main offices in Rome were housed in an unprepossessing, unobtrusive five- or six-storey box, set back behind a small walled parking lot. The Via Della Camilluccia on which it stood was a narrow road, sloping up the hill past the trees of the other walled properties in a smart but not extravagant neighbourhood. At the gate a policeman and a policewoman, lounging by their car, pointed me the way.

A larger than lifesized model of the Italia '90 mascot, Ciao, stood at the bottom of the steps down to the entrance. Ciao was a figure cast in athletic pose, as if striking a ball; his stick-man body was constructed of square kiddies' building blocks in red, white, and green, the colours of the Italian flag. Perched on a white stump of a neck his head was (of course) a football.

The COL was set up in Zurich on 3 December 1984: the competition for Italia '90's mascot and logotype was announced a little over a year later, in January 1986. Winners were selected by a panel of Italian worthies – an industrialist, an adman, two architects and the COL President – from over 60,000 submissions. Then the marketing boys in Lucerne and Milan and Monte Carlo went to work, flogging the logo, raising the sponsorships.

The name Ciao was selected later, in an extraordinarily convoluted 'election' run through Totocalcio, Italy's football pools, over a period of eleven weeks in spring 1989. (Millions of votes were cast in this process – fully fifteen months before the tournament eighty-five per cent of Italians recognised the mascot.) Other names on the shortlist had been Amico, Beniamino, and, gloriously, Bimbo, or Dribbly. How I'd *yearned* for Dribbly, which, surely, would have been the PR gaffe of the decade . . . still, an earlier possibility had been the gapingly tactless Bomber, so I guess we should be grateful.

By then, anyhow, the name didn't matter, only the image mattered – a strutting little stickman, with the world's ultimate mass-culture icon where his brain ought to be.

Ciao was derided by some to begin with, but his success must have had the sponsor folk creaming their jeans. He spread like a virus of enthusiasm from the arrival halls of airports out to the petrol pumps at garages, and on to the crowded shelves of bars. He cropped up on rolls of film and bars of chocolate, on key rings and postcards, on bags and Coke cans and beer bottles and cars and planes and buses, on T-shirts and posters, and on the pages of every paper. At the absurd fiasco of the televised draw for the finals in Rome in December 1989, the backing dancers wore Ciao leotards . . . thus did Italy become a logo.

You wrote home not with postcards of the place, but of the mascot that stood for it. Ciao, poised forever in the art of striking – another little masterpiece, it must be admitted, of Italian commercial design. Except occasionally, you wondered how on earth he'd ever score that phantom goal – *he didn't have any feet.*

From the COL's reception I was passed a few floors up to the poky workspace of one part of the press office, and into the hands of Jane Nottage. Nottage, it became clear, had little space, less time, and too many phone calls. She was talking just then with the man seconded from Alitalia (another official supplier) to run the World Cup tour operator, '90 Tour – they were trying to sort out some accommodation issue for a VIP party from Egypt. She said she'd send a note of the details by fax.

Out in the corridor two fax machines sat on a table; Nottage tried several times to get the first of these to send her message across Rome to '90 Tour. But the machine wasn't having it. It blipped and buzzed and hummed and shook; it went silent mysteriously, looked back at us balefully, kept us in long and breathless suspense – and then each time, eventually, delivered up a statement, in the brief but oracular language of hi-tech, that it had failed to function again.

Lines busy. Transmission not effected. Transmission not received. Systems overload. It must, I thought, be the first Tuesday of an uneven month again.

I imagined the message going AWOL, going walkabout in the telecom catacombs of Rome, then cropping up in unexpected places. In an accounts department or a sales office or a showroom, the fax suddenly chatters; a small knot of people gather to scratch their heads over obscure information about the travel plans of Egyptians. How many ways can the World Cup touch your life?

Nottage grew more fiercely dismayed. She tore the failure reports off the paper roll as they printed out; the paper didn't tear easily, and she began wrenching it in crumpled gobbets from the growling machine. She pressed buttons and flicked switches, and the fax winked its little lights, clicking and farting like some malevolent mechanical Star Trek reject. In terminal exasperation she ripped the wires out of the back of the thing and turned to the second machine.

The second machine wasn't having it either. We stared at it. It took in the message and sat sullenly, obdurately inactive. She tried feeding it the message again; no dice. She retreated a step or two, with the exhausted resignation of one who knows that the opponent has the victory. Then the fax belched and clattered and started printing. It sent Nottage her own message right back to her.

And I thought, if they can't get a fax across Rome, what chance have 6,000 journalists around the world all got?

I never found out whether my own fax arrived or not, and it didn't seem to matter. Somehow when Italians say, 'no problem', the way they say it makes you feel like believing them.

Some of the English sports press were not so relaxed. You were supposed to have the reservation forms in by 15 April; but ten days later than that, at Wembley for England's friendly with Czechoslovakia, there were journalists who, they said, still hadn't got back their accreditation IDs in the first place.

Then on 22 May, there was word in the press pack – at Wembley again, for the last home game against Uruguay – that some twenty of their deposits hadn't appeared yet in Italy. There was a fear, maybe, that the accreditations of those involved might be revoked. Imagine going to Italy to report the World Cup – then finding you can't get into any games.

Still, this particular glitch, if it existed, would just as likely have been the journalists' fault as the COL's. You soon learnt to take complaints from some journalists with a sack or two of salt – because those boys, give them an empty space, they'll fill it with a grumble in no time.

And sometimes, as the frenzies of preparation grew louder in the last weeks, you got the feeling certain members of the press had long since determined, with a kind of exultantly resigned certainty that brooked no dispute, that things would go wrong. England would get beat, hooligans would riot, and the whole bloody opera would be a nightmare of crumbling sets and disintegrating choreography.

Patrick Barclay of the *Independent* said it was always the same, worries and consternation, it was a World Cup ritual. People said there'd be nowhere to sleep – but then you got there, and every town you passed through had rooms. People said the stadiums would never be finished – but then you got there, and every one of them turned out to be just great.

At the COL, the accreditation department was another small room in which the clean, simple lines of the Italian office furniture had all been interred long ago, under mountains of brochures and micros and files. Nottage took me to see a confidently friendly woman there who said about my ticket reservations (the way they do), 'No problem.' It was true, she said, when Argentina played Cameroon in the opening game in Milan, for that I might have a problem. There were 1,700 seats for the press, and 3,000 applications – but otherwise, no problem.

I remembered meeting this lady before, at the draw back in December. She was handing out passes and freebies and info-sheets to the mêlée of the world's press at FIFA's base in the Hotel Jolly Midas where meetings were over-running, conferences were late, news was uncertain, and stories abounded. Hacks pressed their way from room to room, bar to bar. The famous, Bobby Charlton, Karl-Heinz Rummenigge, passed from one conversation to another in the foyer, followed by a swirling eddy of lights and microphones and cameras.

And I remembered this lady saying, yes, it looked like chaos now, but don't worry, no problem. 'Fifteen minutes before kick-off we'll be ready.'

Italy, people told me – in Cagliari and Rome, in Florence and Milan – it was the land of the last minute.

I went in mid-April from Rome to Cagliari and found, around the stadium, a wasteland of rough bare earth and drainage work. Pipes and cable drums and rubble and dirt lay all about in alarming confusion. Roberto Pappalardo at the local COL said that everything you changed, even moving a painting from one wall to another, had to go through the *comune*, the local administration. Sometimes it took half a year to get approval for things . . . in Cagliari they were lucky, because the stadium was only twenty years old. But there'd been little maintenance done since then, and it was right by the water. If you dug two metres, you hit seaweed.

Still, he said, they'd be ready. Inside the stadium there was little left to do – just a lick of paint here, a spot of wiring there. The seats were all in, and their biggest thing, the new and more powerful lighting for TV, was pretty much sorted. There'd be parking space for 4,500 cars – and the refurbishment costs, at £16,000,000, were a snip compared to the sums spent elsewhere.

Come the big day, there'd be a thousand people working – ticket people, catering people, stewards, drivers, press assistants, attendants and attachés for the teams and the officials and FIFA, people at the COL desks at the airport and the hotels . . . and security? Seven thousand police and *carabinieri*. They would, he said, be ready. Because the World Cup was, for Sardinia as a whole, a major promotional investment.

I asked how he expected the two weeks of Cagliari's tournament to be. He said, 'Sometimes I don't like to think of it. Of course we get more excited as it approaches – I've been working more than two years on this, so I want it to come good, but the actual two weeks . . . I prefer not to think about it. But what has been good,' he said, 'is the relationship with the English FA, Glen Kirton, Mr Robson – Robson's a very nice man. And he's checked everything, really *everything*. He even asked the hotel to get longer beds for the players.'

Marius, too, said Robson was *molto gentile*. He even paid him the ultimate Italian compliment – he said he was chic . . .

The FA invited a party of Sardinian COL people to the Brazil game at Wembley at the end of March, and chauffeured them about in a Rolls. Robson, ever the diplomat, ever minding every detail, went to Cagliari half a dozen times before the tournament.

The Irish, said Pappalardo, didn't even have a hotel booked yet. 'Please,' he said, 'don't tell me any Irish jokes.' Jack Charlton was the only manager who didn't go to the draw in December, and he hadn't been to Sardinia yet either. Pappalardo went to Rotterdam, got on fine with the Dutch – then, he said, Charlton turns up with his copy of the *Angling Times*, and says fishing's all he's interested in . . . the first telex they'd had from the Irish FA was three days ago. No wonder they'd not got a hotel yet.

Pappalardo was annoyed at Jeff Powell from the *Daily Mail*, who'd written a piece that quoted him saying rude things about the Irish that (he said) he'd never said. He wanted everyone to be happy, that was his job – but why couldn't the Irish get their act together?

The problem was that the Irish wanted a hotel right down the road from where the English were staying, and the police didn't want them in that kind of proximity. 'And we have,' said Pappalardo, 'to live with the police here for the rest of our lives.' Charlton being Charlton, in the end the Irish did get their hotel.

A few days later at the Cagliari–Padova game, I met an Irish TV crew who were just a bit piqued at these manoeuvrings. It was a bitch of a draw, Pappalardo was a double-dealer, and the English would be playing 'at home'. So, I asked, had the Irish FA asked anyone from Sardinia over to Dublin? The crew laughed, 'Have they hell.'

Compared to the Favorita in Palermo, they said, at least the Sant'Elia here was finished. And indeed, in the four days since I'd first gone there, vast tracts of the parking lots had miraculously been tarmacked. 'Look,' said the Irishmen, 'see those trees (lines of six-foot saplings, marching in ranks across the lots) none of those were here yesterday. They've all sprung up overnight. A wondrous Italian spring.'

So Cagliari would be ready. And one thing's for sure, whatever the finaglings, whatever the truth about careful English diplomacy, and obstinate Irish disorganisation – with 7,000 police and *carabinieri* about, there'd not be many English fans who'd feel for a minute like they were playing at home.

I went home to watch England stuff the Czechs 4–2 on 25 April – Paul Gascoigne booked his ticket to Italy by making three and scoring the fourth. Gary Stevens didn't play, but he was fit and in the squad – the reported broken fibula wasn't broken after all. The previous Saturday he'd played in the Rangers' side that beat Dundee, and won the League, but they didn't float away belly-up in any gutters. The club took them out for a meal with their partners, and the next Sunday he was getting married. Then on Monday the club was taking the players away for a week's break – so, he said, 'I'll be spending my honeymoon on my own.'

Strange business, football. It takes you over, and it never ends.

On 1 May I was back in Rome. It was Labour Day, a public holiday – but at the COL there were no holidays any more, there weren't even weekends. The World Cup was thirty-nine days away.

Jane Nottage took the day off anyhow. She told them she was 'having lunch with a journalist' – then we went to the beach at Fregeno. It was a broiling day, and most of Rome seemed to have decided to spend it on the Via Aurelia; by the time we got out to the coast, the small lanes through bright patches of trees to the shore were littered with endless ranks of cars.

On the beach, knots of bronze boys kicked their footballs about. No one swam, the water's a pollutant stew – even cheery old Fodor's got pollution reports these days on the state of Italy's seaside waters. Remember Slime '89 on the Adriatic coast, when hundreds of miles of sea off the beaches of Rimini and Ancona turned into algae soup? Above us, the jets whined down into Fiumicino.

Nottage was worried about the technology. There would, in theory, be monitors in every press box – for every two journalists, a screen so they could catch all the replays. Then there was the Databank, a monster information resource for the world's press, a system that would bring to your fingertips every fact and every figure you might care to dredge up, right the way back to Uruguay 1930. There'd be the results of every World Cup match ever. Whatever you needed to know, just ask the Databank.

Nottage's worry was that by the time these systems were in, there'd be no time to rehearse them. Kick-off would come, and they'd either work, or they wouldn't. Italia '90 would switch on, and pray . . .

Back in town, we had to slow up and work carefully with the other cars round a nutter in the middle of the street. He was performing an extravagant slow-motion dance, with an Italian flag for a cummerbund, a baroque, silver-tipped cane, and an entirely bizarre Heath Robinson tin hat, all shiny turrets and nodules. He pranced about among the cars, an absolute loon.

'And that,' said Nottage, 'is the poor bugger who organised it all last time.'

*

I got back to my *pensione*, went upstairs – and recoiled in appalled amazement from the astounding aroma in the toilet. It smelt like someone had been shitting pure mozzarella.

Vanishing bus routes, recalcitrant fax machines, dodgy data bases, madmen in the street and awful pongs in the loo . . . I thought, *What the fuck am I doing here?*

On the beach I'd got sunstroke. I got up three times in the night to throw up in the mozzarella room, then got up at six anyway to catch a train to Florence at seven. When I got there, feeling terrible, I drank too many cups of fierce mud coffee – the legal equivalent of a serious cocaine binge – then damn near got myself arrested for a major sense of humour failure in the telephone office, gibbering in a caffeine rage at the remarkable ability of Italian telephones to run you up huge bills, when all they've done is connect you to a crackling void.

One of the great things about Italy is that there's always a church to hand. At times like these – when you've been travelling back and forth too long, and there's a whole lot more travelling left to do – talking to God has the straightforward advantage that, since he doesn't exist, he doesn't talk back. So I got myself a piece of that cool and dim duomo silence which (unlike the silence of an Italian telephone) doesn't hiss in your ear and cost you money, then, refreshed, I went to check out the stadium.

It was a dusty chaos of blocked roads, fences and scaffolding. Piles of paving stones wrapped in polythene waited to be laid, but someone must have reckoned they'd be there for a while – they had local election flysheets pasted all over them. Under a blistering sun, showers of sparks flew down from the upper rim of the stands as the railings went in; chunks of stone, tossed casually off the top, flew down through the bright sparks and the burnished air. There was a constant bash and hammer and drone of drills and mixers and JCBs, and a stink of fresh-laid Tarmac; sand and grit sat in great piles before massed ranks of portacabins. Men painted and plastered; RAI TV people jabbered in trucks festooned with cabling, and packed with banks of winking hi-tech. It was 2 May and in Florence they had until 10 June, when the Americans went out against the Czechs.

They had, in Florence, to engineer their way round one

particular difficulty. The stadium was built in 1932 and was a national monument not far from the heart of the city – and whatever the alterations they were obliged to make inside to meet the new safety standards, they were also obliged to leave it unmessed with on the outside. So for the capacity to remain at a decent figure after the reduction imposed by making it all-seater, what they'd done was to lower the pitch by four metres, and then slip into the space thus created a new inner tier of seating. Brilliant. Cost: £40,000,000.

At the Florentine COL they said they'd had many, many problems. They'd meant originally to finish by the beginning of November, and then by March. 'It is,' one man told me, 'a typical Italian story.'

As with eleven other typical Italian stories, from Milan to Palermo, at the last minute it was finished, and people who watched the games there said the stadium was splendid.

The losers in this were the city's club Fiorentina. They had a good side, with Brazil's Dunga to anchor the midfield, and the Czech Lubos Kubik alongside him. But above all, they had the sporadically very brilliant Roberto Baggio, Italy's version of Paul Gascoigne. Nonetheless, they hadn't gone great guns in the League – and maybe it didn't help that for a season they couldn't play at home, because home had turned into a building site.

Still, they made it to the all-Italian final of the UEFA Cup against Juventus; and I watched the first leg of this contest from Turin, on a videoscreen in a snug at the back of the Bar Ribolta. In the second leg of the semi-final, I'd seen Fiorentina go past Werder Bremen on TV back in Cagliari, a game in which Marco Nappi, running at full speed, brought the ball out for Fiorentina *on his head* . . . I had high hopes, and I wasn't disappointed. But it might have been better to watch it in Turin.

Juventus won 3–1 – and who says Italian football's not exciting? This was fast, adroit, end to end stuff, and the tackling was ferocious. Juventus went one up after only a couple of minutes, after this little guy they had went streaking down the flank, beat two men, and lashed in a cross for Galia to put away.

The little guy's name was Schillaci. Who he?

Then, in the tenth minute, Baggio danced clean through three men into the left side of the box, knocked the ball in, and Buso made it 1–1.

The boys I was watching with hit the ecstasy button, leaping and whirling and yelling in every space of the little room. My table at the back became the repository for everybody's beers, because in the event of another Fiorentina goal, on any other table they'd all have hit the floor. And Fiorentina were on top, too, with Baggio always creating, always bright. In the first half Juve had to make eight saves to Fiorentina's one.

Then, against the play, Casiraghi got a second for Juve on fifty-nine minutes. The fury in the bar was alarming. The goal was scored with the aid of a push on a defender. I said, 'In England people sing, "Where's your father, referee?"'

'Here we sing,' they told me, '"Where's your mother?"'

There was some sort of crowd trouble beginning in the stands. And just as I was thinking, how could you *ever* have trouble at a Juve game again – this the club, after all, that lost thirty-nine people when the wall collapsed in the trouble at Heysel – the boys in the bar began singing:

> *Liverpool, Liverpool, Liverpool . . .*

I felt it was only justice in the face of these boys, when De Agostini got Juve's third. The game had got manic, awash with dives and frantic scrambles and stoppages for injury. At one point in the first half there'd been a ridiculous scene when a Fiorentina defender headed the ball behind, took a whack in the head off an elbow in the process, and went down pole-axed, rolling in histrionic agony over the by-line. After a bit a Juve man, pissed off with the guy delaying the corner and taking the heat out of the moment, went over and gave him a little kick. The guy was up in an instant, right as rain and fit as fury, heading for the man who'd tapped him – until he remembered he was hurt, and buckled melodramatically to his knees once more . . . who needs this? Towards the end, the game was full of it.

The boys stood depressed, and swore at the screen. One of them told me, 'Juve are shit. Agnelli's got too much money, all Italy thinks so.' And, true – even down in Cagliari a graffito said, 'Thank you, Liverpool'. He said, 'I want to kill Juve supporters. Italy? Fuck Italy. I'm not interested in Italy, I'm only interested in Fiorentina.'

When three Juve players turned up four days later at the national side's training camp near Florence, they needed big police protection from the enraged local fans. Imagine attacking your own national side . . .

UEFA forced the second leg to be played away from Florence. The two sides drew 0–0 on 16 May at Avellino, so Juventus took the trophy. Then, two days later, they rubbed salt about as deep into the wound as it would go. Gianni Agnelli brought out his fat Fiat wallet, and paid a world record £7,700,000 to take Baggio to Turin. Fiorentina had long resisted – but they'd lost a pile of receipts in a year without a stadium, and that kind of money was unanswerable. In Florence, police had to break up a demo outside the club's offices.

Not that they're all angels in Turin.

An intelligent man, an intelligent woman, Father Christmas and the tooth fairy are all together in a room. The lights go out, and when they come back on, Father Christmas is dead. Whodunit?

Answer: the intelligent woman. Neither of the other two exist.

A joke told me by John Williams from the University of Leicester, where some of Britain's livelier football research gets done. In Florence I went to a conference called 'Football And Europe', a beanfeast for the sociological cottage industry that mines the rich vein of football to produce a bewildering profusion of academic papers and books. Some of it made sense, a fair bit of it didn't, and Williams made rather more than most. I was particularly struck by the notion of Happy Mondays fans setting off to, say, Paris, for a 'Manchester Music Night' – where the idea, basically, is to get pissed, do drugs, dance, and nick stuff. Who says it's football's problem?

For example: any half-sound analysis of Liverpool shows a city about as poor as they come in the whole of Western Europe – a place of which it's been said (by an economist) that if it didn't exist, no one would now invent it. Many people there don't think the city even fits into England, let alone into the EC, and it has, of necessity, a burgeoning hidden economy, involving a considerable moral flexibility about the handling of stolen goods, and the management and circumvention of the measly benefit system. After all, for too many people if you don't live by your wits, you don't live much at all.

But if getting by means conjuring all manner of scally capers round the edge of the crumbling economy, there is still – always – the saving pride and grace of Liverpool Football Club. And the permanent presence of Liverpool in Europe – before Heysel – did make of some scousers a most unlikely kind of Euro-folk. They were the first to sing a Euro-chant, '*Allez les rouges*,' learnt at St Etienne. And they were the first to go in, in a big way, for the adoption of casual Italian style.

They'd come back from their adventures with designer leisurewear, costly and interesting items nicked and then worn to demonstrate that you'd been – that you were a loyal supporter. Thus you resisted the idea that there was nothing to your city but worklessness and poverty – that there was no opportunity to consume, as the ads were all screaming at you to do. You refused to go without the dominant images of the good life on the simple basis that if you couldn't buy them, that didn't mean you couldn't *have* them . . .

A fair few Liverpool fans – like my Fiorentina boys – probably wouldn't bother following England. But when the sociological wisdom extended to the England following as a whole, excluding the racist/nationalist hardcore fanatics, the picture develops of a predominantly young, white, urban, male section of England's following whose home environment, like too much of Liverpool, is, culturally, economically, politically, morally, all played out.

So that there's little civil restraint left.

So that they *will* descend, they *will* steal, they *will* be offensive and difficult. And is this football's problem?

When I got to Milan after the conference was over, I saw a *Sunday Express* headline:

3,000 RIOTERS SHAME SOCCER

Doubtless it was less than 3,000, but whatever the numbers, Leeds had torn through Bournemouth. And all I'd like to ask is, why exactly does that shame soccer? Do those people only exist on a Saturday?

What it shames is *the society that produces them.*

So it's not merely football's problem. And more to the point, as Italy made ready, it's not merely England's problem either.

On the same weekend that eighty-five were arrested in Bournemouth, incidents on the Continent involved seventy-five arrests in Germany, forty-two in Belgium, twenty-four in Holland, and the assault on Juventus members of the Italian squad by the furious boys of Fiorentina . . .

The conference had kicked off on the basis that 'football is one of the most tangible of today's European realities'. We were told how it provided the continent with an alternative geography and an alternative history, whose capitals were the clubs, and whose past time was recorded in the dates of matches. We were, in fact, told many fine theories.

It's no theory, however, that for some people left behind in today's wondrous, new, uniting, post-industrial Europe, the tangible reality is that football's about the only remaining thing they can identify with. And can football help that?

There are other things football can't help.

'Look at Rome – incredible confusion, the traffic, the state of the roads. Or Naples, that's an unbelievable town, the infrastructure, the politics, the economics . . . those towns have so many troubles and problems, you can't ever expect to solve them just by holding the World Cup. But Milan is better, because it's accustomed to working hard – you know the saying here, "In Milan we work, in Rome they eat"? So apart from the stadium, as a city we're in good shape, we were pretty much ready from the beginning. Of course it's not perfect, you try calling a cab here – three nights ago I had to wait forty minutes.'

Milan: rich, smug, efficient, and powerfully attractive in a solid, unembellished, un-Italian sort of way. At the local COL, appropriately in this most cosmopolitan of cities, two of the people who fielded my questions weren't actually Italian – one was Swiss, and the other was a black girl from Ohio, who'd joined recently from an import-export company in Genoa.

Argentina–Cameroon, as a match *per se*, was not so interesting to them. It was more exciting as a spectacle, the city seizing the chance of the opening ceremony to put on a good show. For the football, West Germany was more of a draw. With Matthäus, Klinsmann and Brehme all playing at Inter, there was good local interest – with a month and a day to go, Germany–Yugoslavia was (unlike the opener) sold out. But Colombia was also interesting – AC Milan beat Medellin 1–0 to win the World Club Cup in Tokyo in '89, so the city knew a bit about them too.

Milan's big problem had been the pitch at the San Siro (renamed the Giuseppe Meazza, not that many paid much mind to that), a pitch that had been, all season, a steadily worsening bare expanse of tenuous grass and patchy dirt.

'The pitch? It's *beautiful*. They worked five days and nights around the clock, after the Milan–Juventus Italian Cup Final – they laid eight and a half thousand square metres of entirely new grass, and now it's green like your Pentel. We did worry a lot about this – but you come and see.'

So I did. We had a daft ride in a Mini out to the stadium, it was like *The Italian Job*, spinning down prohibited bus and taxi lanes at dizzying speed – and then, when we got to the stadium and found that the entry road was taped off, the driver just said, What the hell, and whipped the little car through a narrow gap to the side, went in and out of a ditch, over a ramp of bare stony dirt . . . and there before us opened up a scene that made the travails of Florence look like the building of a garden shed.

Cost: £90,000,000 . . .

We careered across a vast expanse of bone-dry brown dust. Dumper trucks and lorries and steamrollers snarled and growled and bounced over the ribbed and battered earth. Beneath the huge grey bulk of the stadium, packs of ant-sized men drilled and welded, talked and pointed; we pulled up and parked among them, before the white semi-cylinder-shaped tent on its airy frames of steel that would, in a month, be the press centre that welcomed the world to Italia '90.

Inside, you stepped through an enormous litter of flat-pack desks in various stages of assembly – mostly early stages – trying hard not to trip over serpentine lengths and coils of cable and wire spilt in all directions on polythene sheets over

66

the half-carpeted floor. Men were bolting shiny chunks of duct and piping into the roof; in the whole place there were, so far, two working telephones.

Absolute chaos. People pored over blueprints, shambled past clutching unassembled pieces of furniture, or watched the local election results on a TV the size of a matchbox. The Swiss girl said, 'It's an adventure to work here.' Then she saw me wiping my forehead – it was another fiercely hot day – and said, 'You're in the World Cup, don't worry. We will have conditioning air.'

She took me out over unsteady piles of rubble and debris towards the stadium. Before I knew it, I was out of the dust zone, through a tunnel, and the noise was all gone. In a cool, shadowed, glorious silence, I walked on the new grass at the San Siro.

It's an unbelievable stadium. At first there were two tiers, but for the Mondiale, they bolted another tier on top, then put a roof on top of that. It's not pretty, it's a great fierce box of a place – four vast steep walls of seats sweep down towards you, it's intimidating – and it's electric.

To hold up the new top tier, all around the outside they built thick spiralled columns, which also serve as walkways to get you up to the higher seats. Strapped across these to support the roof run massive matt red girders – the lengthwise ones must be well over a hundred metres long, and these were set into place in a morning each, *in one piece*.

A crowd came to watch them do it. In all, the work took two years, and, this being efficient old Milan, Inter and AC carried on playing uninterrupted every Sunday throughout.

The San Siro was the greatest stadium I'd ever seen in my life. Like I say, it's not pretty – on the contrary, it's positively threatening, a grey brute bulk of a place, and the great mass of the squat spiral pillars outside makes it look like some terrifying kind of alien machine-beast, coiled to spring. It's by Spielberg out of Orwell. It seats 80,000, and it's the closest encounter you'll get to the future of football.

I walked on the new grass at the San Siro, under the tall sweep of the empty seats, and I thought – the World Cup starts here?

No problem.

5   One Inch of Woodwork

Frayed nerves in Silesia

When you go in there's a sign in five languages that says, 'There were four million'.

I broke down about halfway round Auschwitz, walking away from the wall against which 20,000 people were shot. There's a shrine there now; schoolgirls were laying flowers and lighting candles.

But it wasn't that particular detail that got to me. And it wasn't the stark physical evidence in earlier blocks of the conditions in which people had lived, sleeping seven or nine together on straw in three-high tiers the size of double beds.

It wasn't the enormous glass-fronted displays in which, on angled boards sometimes dozens of feet long, lay great piles of wretchedly battered old boots, or children's shoes. It wasn't the bank of suitcases, their owners' names clumsily written on them in faded paint, or the heaps of broken spectacles, of shaving brushes and hairbrushes.

It wasn't the case the length of a barrack room in the block whose subject was the 'Exploitation of Corpses', the case filled with a bank of human hair, or the small case to one side of that, showing the tailor's lining that was made from it.

It wasn't the relentless documentary evidence, the methodical, systematic, compulsive bureaucracy of mass murder.

And it wasn't the block beside the yard in which the shrine now stands, in whose basement are the 'standing cells' used to punish prisoners, measuring ninety by ninety centimetres. People were wedged together into these bare brick cubicles, and left to starve or suffocate pinned helplessly upright. In other cells in the same basement, the first experiments with Zyklon B as a means of mass extermination were conducted.

It was all these things cumulatively crushing you, a seeping of evil from every wall and corner of the place, from every brick of every block, until you reach your limit and it overwhelms you. For a short while I found myself crying, leaning against the wire. Like they tell you – the birds don't sing.

In paintings and drawings by Auschwitz inmates, the guards are shown leering and jeering at the suffering of their victims – enjoying themselves.

On the morning of the October day that England qualified for Italia '90, a small group of Englishmen were seen by some of the sports press at Auschwitz, laughing and posing as they took pictures of each other – doing the Nazi salute.

A few of them in Katowice had also been in Stockholm. Later, when we left the hotel for the stadium, they were on the grass bank outside taking pictures, and doing that salute again. Two of them wore Thatcher masks – and there was something especially hideous about that, something that struck an awful chord, these paunch-bellied slobs slouching about hidden behind caricatures of that woman's strident face.

It isn't a game that produces people like these. Because whatever they are, they are not England fans.

But they carry the Union Jack, and it's England that produces them.

Imagine the outcry if the German team, say, or the Italian, were left twiddling their thumbs for a delayed two hours in a dreary dump like Luton airport. The steps on the chartered aircraft wouldn't retract. The aircraft wasn't even at the airport yet, it was still someplace else – and this, mind you, for a fixture we'd known about for *two years*.

At the press conference after training the next day, asked whether that kind of cock-up wasn't exactly what the players could do without, Bobby Robson said, 'We're uncomplaining.'

People felt tense. No one would visit Katowice for choice – the place was grey, it smelt, and the phones didn't work. Outside the front of the hotel, tower blocks rose out of debris-specked rough ground, patches of mud and weed crossed by broken paths. Over the road two tall chimneys belched ugly smoke, and the big wheels turned above the minehead at the coal pit. There's a lot of coal in Silesia, and a lot of bile-brown coal smoke, fugging up the streets, drifting up your nose and in your throat, mingling with the acrid wafts of diesel, and with an aftertaste of sewage off an oily, grey-black stream, running in a litter-laden channel between the hotel and the centre. It looked like the town hadn't seen paint in fifty years. And that, of course, is why Poland bring you there for the big games – it's tough country. Robson called it, 'the belly of Poland'.

To make sure of going to Italy, England needed a draw – one more point. And people felt tense because the last time England went to Katowice, in 1973, the Poles won 2–0. It was a qualifier for West Germany '74 and it meant that when the two teams met later at Wembley, England needed to win. In a long-remembered game, their keeper Tomaszewski worked miracles to keep us out; it ended 1–1, and England stayed at home. The Poles went on to Germany, and finished third.

Surely, this time, they couldn't knock us out again – they were nothing on the team they'd had sixteen years ago. But since their 3–0 drubbing in June they'd got a new manager, and a lot of new blood – only three of the eleven they sent out in Katowice had played at Wembley. And they couldn't play that badly again, new faces or not, not at home in bleak Silesia.

While we waited for the plane, the players sat about playing cards, signing the odd autograph – someone found a globe, and the *Star* and the *Express* got pictures of Butcher pointing helpfully at Italy. Do their readers not know where it is?

I talked with Bobby Robson. He was confident about the game, and fed up with the papers. One of the Sunday tabloids had run critical extracts from a book by Terry Fenwick, a defender Robson had taken to Mexico.

Robson said Fenwick was an arsehole. He could put him on the front page of every Sunday paper, the things he knew about him. In fact he might just ring him up now and tell him, 'I'm going to put you on the front page of every Sunday paper. How d'you like that, my son?'

Then he said, 'But you don't do that, do you?'

Besides, he had bigger problems by far than Terry Fenwick.

English football, he said, was losing out immeasurably for as long as the clubs were forbidden European competition. Robson took Ipswich into Europe for ten years in succession. His players (Butcher among them) had known what it was like to go to Cologne, to Bruges or Barcelona, needing a result. We'd had seventy or eighty players going into Europe every season – how many now? The national team a few times a year, and who else?

The side Robson announced the next day included Lineker back at Spurs from Barcelona, Waddle at Marseilles, and Stevens and Butcher at Rangers, who'd just recently been beaten by Bayern Munich. So outside of an England shirt, only four had any regular recent contact with the way other people play football, and the kind of places they play it in.

He also criticised more generally the way football's run in England. That the FA and the League were different bodies was ungainly – and there were far too many games. He wanted eighteen sides in the first division, not twenty; and he wanted shot of what he called 'Mickey Mouse competitions', when there were the Littlewoods and the FA Cups already.

He said he got his players for only twenty-four days a year, and he wanted twice that. He knew he'd not get it – but he said we did have to decide how much of a priority we really meant the national side to be, and then act accordingly. In the meantime, how much could he do with players he only had for a few days at a time? He could only work with what the game in the country provided him. People criticised the English defence, but take Stuart Pearce, for example – all heart, sure, but Robson couldn't turn him by magic into a fluid, silky, continental-type defender – and the boy came from Nottingham Forest. Where better could he look?

Forty-eight hours later, the Poles ran the likes of Stuart Pearce right off the park.

We also talked politics. Robson and Kirton said Moynihan was just the messenger, and his boss that sent the messages knew nothing. Stockholm was more proof of how trouble was persistently exaggerated, and Thatcher wasn't briefed, when she reacted to those headlines. To suggest withdrawal from Italy showed a lack of any idea of what was happening in football. More generally, it showed a major failure of political understanding. She had, they said, a complete inability to register the nature and status of football as the national game, and all that it means to millions of people.

Of the withdrawal threat Robson said, 'I'd like to think they wouldn't dare.'

What is it about airports, that they have to have those disgusting soap dispensers – you want water on your face, you need freshening up, there's another journey in store, so you press the lever, and it looks like someone just came in your hand . . . I had a nervy premonition of all the stations and airports stretching away before me, of going to Italy and running out of clean clothes, of waking unshaven in railway waiting rooms – but these are not the worst fears of a journalist. If you stink, if you're so hungover you want to puke, it doesn't matter – nothing matters, just so long as the telephones work.

In Poland, quite a lot of things don't work. At Cracow airport we stumbled and jammed our way off the Tarmac into a tiny arrival hall with all the creature comforts of a medieval woodshed. Customs involved passing one by one through a tatty pair of blankets hung in a doorway. Outside was a nation of brave, unruly, and long-struggling people who'd just become the first in Eastern Europe to offload their Communist government, and now the place was turning into Latin America with lousy weather. There's a rule of thumb for foreign parts, that the prettier the currency, the less it's worth. Poland's zloty are very pretty indeed.

We had an entrepreneurial sort of a guide called Thomas who smoked, he said casually, sixty Bensons a day. On the way to the hotel in the bus he sold beers from a cool-box to the thirsting pressmen for a dollar a can. When they ran out, he stopped the bus and got more from the luggage hold. And he gave us a detailed low-down on matters Polish.

'The situation is changing every day.' Who knew how many zloty you might get for your dollars? Or when the exchange desk might be open for you to get any at all. If you took a taxi ride, whatever the meter showed at the end of it, you multiplied that by thirty-five . . . but of course, you paid the driver in dollars anyhow. Thomas's brief was extensive, covering even handy hints and tips should we require what he quaintly called hookers. He didn't tell us that the phones didn't work.

The driver who took me and two others to Auschwitz the next day said his wife earned 109,000 zloty a month. That was about £10 – or, the way he put it, a couple of pounds of meat.

At the end of the first evening, one drunk bargirl threw a punch at another whom she thought – as far as I could gather – wasn't dressed with a sufficient degree of flash, and was lowering the tone. In heels and black stockings and a mini and a dry mask of make-up, the puncher was blonde and hard-voiced and coarse. The comment passed among those who'd not been wise long ago and gone to bed, that the girl had a good right hook.

In that kind of weary moment, most football writers will sooner or later tell you theirs isn't really a job for grown men.

On the second night, maybe six or eight of us sat talking and drinking in the hotel foyer; a girl or two passed by now and then among the cabbies, wanting dollars for their thick wads of zloty. Looking at them, one guy described the kind of physique most preferred by another of those present, and the atmosphere came close to going nasty. The guy whose preferences had just been described grew defensively angry, pointing at me. 'He's writing a book, how do I know what he's putting in it? Just fucking watch what you're saying.'

This is what I'm putting in it: that he was with the girl whose physique had provoked the discussion the next morning and that I won't go into the detail of his preferences. Because while Poland's one of those places that seems abundantly blessed with beautiful young women, that's not what you'd say of the girls who make a living in the bar of the Hotel Warsawa, Katowice.

At two in the morning when they were shutting up, the puncher from the night before came out drunk to lurch about in front of us, holding herself round the waist, stroking herself up and down and saying, 'I am sexy,' with a desperate sort of smile.

No one took her up on it – I'm not sure if any of us that were left really could have. The sports press get pilloried in some quarters for being a whoring bunch of sots, but that's not quite fair. Some of them neither drink to excess, nor sleep around – and most of those who do drink drink so much, there's not much chance they could get it up afterwards if they tried.

Still, going home from Fiumicino after the draw in December, one of them did suggest to me that the boys were a bit worried about what I might write. 'Some of them have families,' he said.

Ironic, that.

Gary Stevens: 'When you get people writing about your private life, that's the thing that bugs me. When I left my first wife ... Richard Gough left his wife, and he put out a statement saying he had, so nobody's interested. But unfortunately I wasn't cute enough to do that. So they had a go at my family, they upset my family, and Sandra ... it's just character assassination, it's just so sad, so difficult to come through. It took me a long time to get over it. And they've done it to Bryan Robson, Bobby Robson ... why? I don't understand it.

'Thing is, we go away with the press – and it's not the football guys who come away with us who write the stories about who's having affairs with who – but if only we could put the shoe on the other foot. Obviously we see it, we see what they're doing coming away, we know they've got families back home – but there's no way I'd ever go round talking about what they do. I mean, women, Jesus – what's that one who fancies himself called? That was the lowest thing – after we were beaten by Holland in Germany, we were out of the championships, we're down, so we've had a few drinks, I've gone out with a friend of mine who works for *Shoot*, we're good friends so I'm at ease with him, and I'm paralytic – and that guy was at the bar – and thank God when I get drunk I still know what I'm doing because he started asking me questions, what did I think about Bobby Robson, what did I think about Peter Shilton ... that was so low, when he knows I'm drunk. He's sitting there and he's got a bird, *he's got a bird* – he's married, he's got family, and he's got a darling by him, and I'm paralytic and he starts asking me questions ... at a time like that. Of course we're all bitter about the press.'

Trying to book a call, one of them asked how long it might take to come through, and was answered, 'How long are you here?'

74

Katowice was an abyss of broken contacts and silence. They stood for hours in little gangs at the reception desk, fraying at the edges. There were no direct lines to London, you had to go via Warsaw. People got through, and then were cut off a few paras into their stories, never to be heard of again. Drinks were left untended as men sprinted for a connection – they'd get to the phone and hang there, calling uncertainly down the mouthpiece into the hissing void of Polish Telecom.

As the game approached, the paranoia level rose – would the phones at the stadium work? How would they file their coverage of the match? They feared the hideous excommunication of the stories in Thursday's papers being written by people back in the office who'd watched the game on TV.

And then there are the photographers. They bring with them all-singing, all-dancing laboratories-in-a-box. 'Go see 'em,' said one writer. 'They come with bloody pick-axes.' They unbolt panels off the wall, jack into the system, rig up their super-tech photo-faxes, all winking lights and a mini-screen – then they scan and transmit their negatives down the wire in a few minutes per image.

But asking for a few ungarbled minutes on a Katowice phone line, that's like asking horses to sing. I watched one of them hunched over the equipment on his bed, trying to get a picture through – he'd been trying all day. What little had appeared in London so far came out looking like smudged piles of coal. Like Katowice, in fact.

Still, most of the nationals had pictures from the game the next morning. The *Independent* had the most appropriate image – a wall of English defenders flinching as another long-range Polish fireball came hurtling their way.

We came close to a mutiny. Word started round that with the phones so bad, it'd take the press an age and a half after the game to get their stories and pictures through. And they couldn't have the squad and the FA types parked in a plane on the Tarmac just waiting for the press while the wires failed to hum.

So the idea was to let them go and, once the copy got through, to bus the rest of us overnight up to Warsaw. They'd pack us in hotels, and fly us home from there – somehow.

But how long does it take to buy fifty plane tickets in Warsaw? Anyhow, it's 200 miles away – and with a Polish bus driver, for Christ's sake . . .

Someone fiercely proclaimed how he'd courageously lost his rag with Brian Scott. There was whispered outrage, and expressions of solidarity. If one is left behind, we all stay behind . . . Poor things. If this had been a holiday, they'd never have bought it.

Me, I quite fancied a visit to Warsaw. But there you go, I'm not a working man.

Thomas, the bus driver, cabbies, barmen – anyone Polish figured Poland would lose. The day before the game, we learnt that only 6,000 tickets had been sold, when the Slaski holds 72,000 – that had a promising ring to it. But no one English could say confidently how we'd do – only that it wouldn't be easy. In the *Mail* Powell predicted that if we got safely through the first half-hour, then we might just win it.

The Slaski's a barren grey bowl of a place, wide open to the sullen Silesian sky. And I strongly suspect that if it had been full, England might have lost there. Even less than half-full, the Poles generated an atmosphere of piercing, whistling hostility, roaring their team on – and their team ran us ragged.

All across the park they showed an invention, a pace, a desire pouring forward that had us stumbling back like felled trees. Pearce and Stevens had a miserable time; the shots rained in. Powell beside me revised his forecast upwards – we had to survive the whole first half. And after the break, he revised it upwards again – if we get through the first hour . . . it was utterly absorbing. And the fierce cold steadily deepened as the night came down.

But in the second half, it became slowly more possible to believe that England could nick it. They buckled and they creaked, but they held. This was the defence that had gone five games in the group without conceding a goal, that had been persistently picked on and moaned at, but still they'd not let any goals in when it mattered. And they weren't letting one in now.

Pearce and Stevens may not have enjoyed it much, but they

ran and ran, and Butcher and Walker were sound in between them. With McMahon and Bryan Robson falling back in the middle, the Poles only once got a chance at close range. Of all people it fell to Dziekanowski, Celtic's new man, who had a clear header a few yards out. He muffed it, and Shilton pushed it away; Shilton said afterwards the guy should have scored.

There were other times enough when Poland might have scored. When they found they couldn't get in the box, they queued up instead to pepper the target with shots from long range – and if sometimes they let loose from absurdly ambitious distances, a lot of other shots seared in murderously well struck and true. But Shilton saved them all – and saved England in the process.

PETER THE GREAT

PETER THE POLE CAT

SHILTS MY INCREDIBLE HULK

Peter Shilton, forty years old and playing like he'd learnt a thing or two since the Poles put two past him in that other qualifier all of sixteen years ago . . . it's an unbelievable thing, that the man had been in England's goal for over half my whole lifetime.

In the first half especially, he made four or five outstanding saves. And as a swerving ball comes rocketing in, the dive of a great keeper across what seems an impossible space to touch it away is as breathtaking, as gravity-defying as a Carl Lewis long jump – and a great deal more dramatic.

This is football.

For the great part of the game you're under siege, but frantically you defend, your keeper works miracles, and you survive. As the final whistle draws ever closer, the failure of your opponents' efforts, the growing weariness those efforts have incurred, and the steady quietening of the crowd as it seems a goal will never come, all combine to give you heart. You've stuck it this far, you can see it on through. As they tire, you begin to get up in their half – you even start making a chance or two . . .

Then, in the ninetieth minute, Tarasiewicz let fly from maybe twenty-five yards. It was a beauty, dipping down towards goal as it came. Shilton went up for it – it hammered against the crossbar and flew back into play. Shilton said afterwards it was always going over; he didn't put a hand to it, because he didn't want to give away a corner. I think he was joking.

But just those few seconds of action, a few seconds away from the end of the game – one shot, and one inch of woodwork – that's the difference between going to Italy, and watching it at home on TV.

That's drama. That's your heart in your mouth, and your guts in your trousers.

That's football.

England earned their point. It wasn't elegant, and the Poles weren't lucky – but they could never have kept it up for ninety minutes, and we wore them away. If they didn't score, that's because, one way or another, we didn't let them. And you might also say, there's a harsh and unforgiving cycle of justice in football – what Tomaszewski did to us at Wembley in '73, Shilton had now done to them in Katowice.

Bobby Robson said afterwards that the Polish that night were the best team we'd played since the Dutch in Germany '88 – they'd been ferociously fast. Asked whether he thought the changes in Poland (the new management in Warsaw, as well as in the football) had upped the spirits of the Polish side, he referred the question politely to his opposite number. 'I'll let him answer that – I have enough problems right now with Mrs Thatcher.'

But there was another reason, tactfully not raised at the conference, why the Poles had played so well – and why they might still play with all that fire and skill against Sweden in their next game, though there was no chance now that they could make it to Italy.

With governments tottering and restrictions easing, Polish players who shone in such displays might find that, like Dziekanowski in Glasgow or Tarasiewicz in Switzerland, they'd booked themselves a transfer to dollars and the West.

The morning of the game, Jon Smith flew in. He was the

agent who'd taken Dziekanowski to Celtic. He has offices in Warsaw, Buenos Aires, and London. And – when not digging up talent in Eastern Europe – he also represents the England World Cup squad. Now we were qualified, the wheels of business would begin to turn.

When the managers quit the press room, the security boys came on instead, two big, mild-mannered guys buttoned up in tight grey.

A bloke in a purple jumpsuit from a fanzine wanted to know if the hooligan problem was exacerbated by the mass media. Hostile groans all around, 'We *are* the mass media.'

But fair enough: there was a guy from the *Express*, for example, who really wanted to be told that there'd been trouble. I mean, he was *eager* for bad news: 'I saw twenty-five people arrested outside the Hotel Silesia. Have you had problems, what were they doing, what have you done with them?'

The police were patient and polite. There had been no arrests. The people they were talking about were detained because they were drunk – or, as the interpreter put it, 'absolutely stoned'. They were released when they were sober, except for seven who'd been so far gone they couldn't stand. These were taken to a doctor, and then (an ominous sort of phrase in Katowice) to 'a place where drunk people are kept'.

The only trouble had been some Polish fans wrecking a train on the way here from the north. There were courteous words to the effect that the English had not misbehaved, and were always welcome – the Poles, though disorganised, were always more than hospitable. Or most of them were . . .

There had been no trouble at the game. The English fans were still in the stadium, waiting to leave. 'We have controlled the situation.'

Precisely as these words were spoken, an English fan came into the press room. His face was splashed and streaked with blood, and he held a cloth to an ugly, glistening wound on his scalp. He and other English leaving the stadium had been ambushed by Polish fans, and had retaliated, and there'd been stones and bricks and bottles flying every which way, and chaos was too good a word for it.

End of press conference.

The press were round the injured man like flies, pushing past each other to get a look and a word, standing over him and the gaggle all around him on chairs to get photographs. Some of the sports men looked on in dismay, and turned away. I heard one guy asking, 'Are you married?'

'That's my business.'

Pushing through the room on his way out, Glen Kirton, ascertaining what had happened, was succinct. 'Shouldn't fucking come, should he?' But why not? The guy was half-Polish . . .

The FA, again, hadn't wanted fans to travel – but the Poles needed hard currency, and had happily sold tours and tickets in London to get it. A couple of days after Stockholm – just in case the bad boys couldn't work it out for themselves – *Today* let them know where to go:

TICKETS TO INVADE POLAND GO ON SALE

Other fans who made their own way there, ticketless, had no trouble getting hold of them – here's the state of the pretty zloty for you – for the sterling equivalent of twenty-five pence.

In the Hotel Italia in Cagliari I met a 23-year-old from Essex; he worked in a travel agency, which may or may not have helped, but he'd been all over Europe with England, starting in Denmark when he was sixteen.

He said, 'One of the reasons you go – obviously it's first and foremost the football – but you get to see countries you'd never normally think of. Poland was great – I mean there we are, weeks before the wall comes down, and we're travelling through West and East Berlin – it was magic, to see the difference. But actually there, at the stadium, that wasn't so brilliant – they keep you in after, they lay on coaches, they get so much right – then they won't let you get on the coaches unless you're with them on an organised tour.

'So you're stuck miles from the centre, and there's all these Poles screaming down the street, you can hear them. And you think, fuck this, this is frightening. We bribed a police car to take us back, otherwise it was fighting, there wasn't any choice – we went down the road and it was like a war, people going down, getting bricked, stretchers, the lot. I mean, places like that, now I'm old enough you think you'll pick and choose where you go. Something like Poland, that's not worth it . . . but you still go, don't you?'

I was, of course, on an organised tour myself – the English press tour, see the world and grumble.

And slowly the bus filled up, as all the copy finally lurched home down the wobbly Polish wires; Thomas sold us cold beers while we waited. Eventually there was only one guy left working, a smudger who'd got two pictures through already, but who was (greedily) trying to get through a third.

'Let's go.'

'Yeah, come on, let's go, let's get out of here.'

'There's still the minibus.'

'Yeah, let's leave him behind, let's fucking go.'

There's solidarity for you. I mean, these guys really did want to leave Poland.

People griped as we lumbered along through the empty dark, Thomas, Thomas, get this guy to go faster. Thomas tried to explain Polish speed limits. Then he tried telling a joke. Then he gave up and went to sleep. We spent ninety minutes going forty miles.

When we boarded the plane, Bob Harris, a loud individual then with *Today*, went past me in the aisle and said, 'You should put all *this* in your fucking book, if anyone thinks it's such a glamorous job.'

There you go, Bob.

Thomas's joke: A Polish priest and a Polish bus driver die, and they meet at the ticket booth by the pearly gates. St Peter says the driver can come in, but the priest, forget it.

'Hey,' says the priest, 'what is this? All my life I been saving souls for you people – and this guy, all he did was drive a bus.'

'When people listened to your sermons,' says St Peter, 'they went to sleep. But when this guy drove his bus, boy, *did those passengers pray*.'

*

Stuck waiting in the plane for the happy gang of pressmen, Bryan Robson, Terry Butcher, and Gary Stevens drank a bottle of champagne each. They had qualified, after all, for Italia '90. Then we took off, and they drank some more.

At Luton airport Butcher stood knackered and glowing with champagne, but also upright, and still adrenalin-high. He handled an interview with considerable courtesy – though one of the questions was, in effect, now we're there, what happens if summer comes round and you don't get picked (i.e., if you're too old and crocked by the end of the season)?

When he came away and I asked him how it felt, he had an uncontrollable big smile, and a wide-eyed shaking of the head at the things to come, the greatest possible things – playing with the best in the world, in front of the world.

'Unbelievable. I'm blotto.'

6   Bobby Robson

*On players young and old, and the
way we play*

What had Terry Fenwick said that made Robson think he was
an arsehole? He'd said that being with England was boring.

'I just think,' Robson told me later, 'what he did was
disgraceful. I tell you what though, he's on about being bored
– I bet he's bored now with a broken leg. I bet he's sitting at
home thinking, fuckin' hell . . . 'cos life is a bore, isn't it? The
guy who works in a factory, who does that every day, or the
feller who's mixing the cement, or lugging the bricks – it's a
bore, isn't it? And he's saying it was a bore playing for
England, 'cos sometimes there was nothing to do?

'I was amazed at him, putting that out the Sunday before an
international match – tarnishing the game, tarnishing your
reputation, tarnishing the England team. For money. At the
most damaging time, at the time of most impact, *for money*.
He was a limited player, but he was tough, we took him to
the World Cup – he should have gone on his bended knees
and been grateful for what came his way internationally under
me.

'But I tell you what – if you're bored with England, you
shouldn't be there.'

Robson loves England, and Robson loves football, and when
we talked at the FA in Lancaster Gate in November after
England and Italy had drawn 0–0 at Wembley, the two things
fused in the way he talked as if they were one, indivisible.

'Pele called it the beautiful game, didn't he? It's a perfect
game. It's a game of athleticism, a game of power and competiton and strength – anybody who thinks football is just a

game of deftness of touch without those other things *wouldn't win*. You need courage, you need steel in your make-up. But it's the deftness too, the control – Waddle, Barnes, Pele, Di Stefano, Puskas, Denis Law, George Best – the spontaneous things players like that can do, that's what beautiful.

'And then it's the national game. Every weekend two million people in this country play it – not watch it, play it.' In England there are forty-two thousand clubs, and two and a half thousand leagues . . .

'The national team is the flagship of that – but it's more than that, the dimensions of it are frightening. When you become the national manager, you realise how important it is to the country, because people are patriotic about it, And winning does mean such a lot. People say it's life or death, it isn't, if we win people don't die, if we lose people don't die – but if we win what it means is happiness, elation, a good feeling for millions. The morning after a match I walk from that tube station and if we've won, people stop in the street, they tell me, "That was great last night, keep it going" – that's what winning means.

'I remember when I was picked to play for my country, how proud I felt – it means at that time in that position, you're the best in the nation. So whoever I pick, he's the best. And I pick him, not the papers, not the fans, and that's a tremendous honour – it means that boy's No. 1, he's No. 1.

'When I was picked I felt ten feet tall, nothing could stop me. Sometimes people say the players aren't trying, it's not true – they try *very* hard. They know what they've striven for, they've been on a long road – but they love it, cherish it, there's nothing they wouldn't do to be at their best. Look at Shilton, he's forty, and he's still training like a maniac. He's arguably the best keeper in the world – I like Dasaev, and the Italian keeper's good, Zenga – but Shilton's got such stature, presence, he commands the first thirty yards, he talks, he nails people to positions – and why? It's love of the game, it's desire, it's enthusiasm . . .'

Things that Robson is also possessed of in abundance – and a good thing too. 'It's an extremely demanding job, and you deserve every penny you get. You earn your money. And I might tell you, the job doesn't pay what you think it pays. I've been quoted £100,000 a year for years by the *Sun*, people like

84

that. It doesn't pay that. I earn less than half of what some of the First Division managers in this country earn. And they couldn't handle my job.

'Take losing 2–1 to Argentina in Mexico. That was the worst moment in my career, worse than the European Championships, because we'd just about pulled that game off the fire. It was 0–0 at half-time and we hadn't played that well, but we knew we could play better second half. And I knew we had John Barnes and Chrissie Waddle to come on. Maradona wasn't such a threat – we just knew we had to play better ourselves. Then within a few minutes of going back out we're a goal down, with the handball. It sets him alight, deflates us, he comes in with a marvellous second goal, we're 2–0 down – but we came back very well. In the last twenty minutes we were fitter than they were – and Barnes and Waddle frightened them, Barnes particularly. When the referee blew the whistle and we were out ... it was unlucky. In the last twenty minutes we were better against them than at any time they'd been against us. We had them on the rack. And you felt it in your gut, that we were out, we were finished, that was it. That was it for four more years.

'I took this job to win the World Cup and the disappointments can be horrific. If you're in charge of England, don't lose at Wembley – to walk those seventy yards from the touchline to the dressing room with eighty thousand people behind you, and you've lost the match for your country ... it's happened to me a couple of times at Wembley, only a couple – we haven't lost for five and a half years there – but I remember the last time.

'So it would be Utopia, to win the World Cup ... but every time England wins, it's the most marvellous feeling, every time. Because you know you're representing the whole nation. When we did well at Ipswich, we did well for that community – but when Ipswich win, nobody in Plymouth gives a monkey's, do they? Nobody in Carlisle gives a monkey's. But when England win, the postman in Carlisle, and the girl who sells papers in Plymouth, they care. Because it's the nation.'

England got to Italy by winning three, and drawing three. They scored ten goals, and they conceded none – the only country in the world to pass through the qualifying rounds with a clean sheet. Then, after the game in Poland:

Jeff Powell, *Daily Mail*: 'Bobby Robson's England stumbled blindly on to Italy last night . . . it has to be wondered if there is any more point turning up next summer than there was in going to West Germany for the European Championships last year.'

Bryan Cooney, *Daily Star*: DONKEYS!

'There are so many donkeys in his side that Robson should open an animal sanctuary and dispense carrot juice . . . they have got about as much chance of winning the World Cup as Salman Rushdie has of emigrating to Iran . . . I predict catastrophe.'

Brian Glanville, *Sunday Times*: 'Could England conceivably be as bad as they looked, slow-witted and slow of movement . . . it is perhaps a pity that Poland will not be going to the World Cup rather than England.'

Bobby Robson: 'We qualified for the World Cup, and I couldn't believe the papers afterwards. But it's five years now, they've forgot what it's like to play in Europe – well, I haven't. I'll tell you what, we beat Poland 3–0, *our* pitch, *our* ball, *our* shirts, *our* crowd (here he punched a fist into his palm) – we smashed 'em 3–0. Great – two points, they get nothing. Then we've the second leg to play in Poland – different match, you were there. We fought it, we *fought*. I know we were under the cosh, but you can't take one thing away from the players in terms of a hundred per cent commitment. So what I'm saying is – we played a tough away match, and we got the point.

'If that had been a European club match, we'd have been in the next round, we'd have knocked out that team 3–0. If Liverpool did that, the papers next day would have said it was a great fighting performance, English pride, weathered the storm, Liverpool at its best – but the national team doesn't get that, we get nothing.

'There are people who are completely destructive and irresponsible. The more abusive and scandalous and sensational they can be, the more it sells – so they're not prepared to write good stuff. I'll tell you, when you come into this job, don't listen to the press, don't do what the press tell you to do. To appease the people writing about me, I'd have to play twenty-three players against Yugoslavia next month. And I don't think the regulations allow that.'

Robson's attitude to the press is hardly surprising. Apart from the way the news pages tore into his private life, he had in his eight years to endure some astonishing abuse.

PLONKER!

IN THE NAME OF GOD GO!

Or, after a 1–1 draw with Saudi Arabia in Riyadh, when he said he was made to feel about as welcome back in the country as Hitler,

IN THE NAME OF ALLAH GO!

What happens under these waves of vitriol is, not surprisingly, that you develop an instinctive perception of the press as one beast, one co-ordinated and perpetual onslaught of wild and slavering voices, always eager to do you over one more time. And once it's got to that point, one note of criticism sounds louder every time than any ten peals of praise.

There were, in fact, a good few plaudits for England when they qualified – Colin Gibson in the *Telegraph* was particularly upstanding – and where the praise was tempered by doubts, some of those doubts were more than reasonable. Robson himself was happy to admit, in calmer moments, that some people wrote good, thoughtful, constructive material – he cited Patrick Barclay, and David Lacey in the *Guardian*. So what did those two say?

Lacey wondered whether, in Italy, England's players would 'achieve anything more than a suntan ... Robson's format looked tired and dated'.

And Barclay wanted wholesale revolution. 'Far from resting happily on this team, Robson ought immediately to disrupt it, to set aside his obsession with results, to experiment with players and tactics ... England's 4–4–2 system remains too rigid. The Poles played 3–4–3, with a sweeper, and looked by far the more flexible. Robson tires of pointing out that England always have a spare man, but unfortunately this often turns out to be Gary Stevens, an orthodox full back, perhaps incorrigibly so.'

Barclay, for some time, had been pushing the sweeper system.

The doubts and criticisms, in sum, focused on three related issues – on scoring, on defending, and on selection.

Firstly, Sweden 0–0, Poland 0–0, and then Italy 0–0 – 270 minutes of goalless football. How and when were we going to start scoring again?

Secondly, the defence. They may have conceded no goals, but in Poland, at times, it did look a desperate business. So when it came to the big time, mightn't it cave in altogether? Because against our 4–4–2 – against a flat back four and two wingers – the more flexible, sweeper-based formations (3–4–3, 3–5–2) had a numerical advantage in the middle of the field. Overrun, the two-man centre was forced back to shore up the defence against attacking midfielders flowing in from all over.

For example: England beat Denmark 1–0 in May, when by rights the Danes should have had several – on occasions they were spilling through from midfield seemingly at will. (Afterwards I asked Butcher how it had been. He said, 'What? Being done for pace? I was shitting myself.') In that situation, the wingers too have to back-pedal and muck in. So then the service from midfield to the front men dries up – with the result, as noted, that you have trouble getting goals.

You might compare the systems thus: the defence, English style, was a brittle wall that, if you punched it enough, would sooner or later implode. But continental defences were more like tough rubber sheets. When you punched them, they absorbed the shock – and before you knew it they'd bounced back and were heading at speed towards the other end of the field.

Then thirdly, selection. The spine of the England team – Shilton, Butcher, and Bryan Robson – was deemed irreplaceable. It was also hard to see who might be better than Lineker. But we had us some new boys – Paul Parker at the back, Paul Gascoigne and David Platt in the middle, Steve Bull up the front – so would Robson try them? If so, when, how, and in place of whom?

*

On the issue of selection – the stalwarts, and the younger men coming up who might play with them in Italy – Robson's answers were couched in the kind of bulldog language, so natural to him, that speaks volumes for how he thinks.

'Robson's outstanding, the captain – you could put him in any trench and know he'd be first over the top. He'll go into the unknown, wouldn't think about it – he wouldn't think, well, Christ, if I put my head up there it might get shot off. He'd say, c'mon, over the top. There's very little to choose between Shilton, Butcher and Robson in that light. All absolutely hundred per cent – you can put your hat on their peg – totally reliable.

'And you need men like that – because you bring your wives out for the first week, OK. But then when you're near the competiton it's bye-bye, we're off to war. It *is* war – well, OK, it's not a war, but it's the biggest sporting prize you can have. You have to be accomplished, like a platoon going out on a mission. We've got eleven, they've got eleven – and you've got to get out there and steal the goodies and get back before they know.'

When England played football, for Robson it sounded sometimes like it was El Alamein all over again – pound the shit out of them and march forward, brave men and true. Losing was inconceivable, especially at Wembley. 'Like Butcher says, this is our empire here, nobody beats us at Wembley, let's get out there and make it our pitch.' (In another tellingly appropriate metaphor, Butcher once said that telling Rita he'd have to go away on a club trip would go down 'like a burning Spitfire.') So it was all about character – the kind of character Bryan Robson displayed, when he scored twice against the Yugoslavians the following month.

And the big question was – did Paul Gascoigne have that character?

Robson said he had six games left for experiments – Yugoslavia, Brazil, Czechoslovakia, Denmark, Uruguay, and Tunisia. So just how much experimenting could he do?

Paul Parker got his fourth cap against Yugoslavia, Steve Bull his third. David Platt had won his first as a substitute in the last ten minutes against Italy; he came on for thirty-five minutes against Yugoslavia, then started for the first time against Brazil. These players might, or might not, prove important in Italy.

Over none of them, however, did there hang the great freight of expectation that came with Paul Gascoigne. Twenty-two years of age, bought by Tottenham from Newcastle for £2,000,000, Gascoigne had six caps to his name, five of them as a substitute. But as time passed, and the clamour for him grew, so also there grew the fear that – obsessed with workrate, with character – England once again might fail to find a place for an outstanding but difficult individual.

In the game against Albania at Wembley, Gascoigne came on with twenty minutes left. He scored a good goal from a tight angle, danced and pranced all round the pitch, and the crowd loved every minute. But a few weeks later against Scotland Gascoigne tried, though pressed by defenders, to repeat the Albanian angle. He missed when he could have passed to a teammate unmarked before an empty net.

Robson said after the Albanian game that Gascoigne played everywhere on the pitch but where he told him to. He said when Gascoigne played, the team needed two balls – one for Gascoigne, one for the rest.

Against Poland at Wembley, when for a while England were looking stuck at 1–0, the restive 69,000 began to cry:

We want Gazza!
We want Gazza!

But he stayed on the subs' bench, as he did in Katowice. In Stockholm, he played for eighteen minutes after Webb's injury. And for Italy, Robson played him in the B team, as he'd also do when Yugoslavia came to town.

In between those two games Robson said, 'My question mark about him is not in talent or precociousness, it's in his reading of the game at the highest level. I don't think he understands the game, not yet, not at world level. And he's daft in his attitude. He doesn't know about releasing the ball at the right time, he doesn't know about being secure with the ball in dangerous positions – he still does irresponsible things. He's got to learn about the game, how to play it properly – he's still a kid playing backstreet football. Lot of talent, lot of freshness, there's unbelievable things he'll do – but I'm talking about playing Argentina or Brazil, about being in the last eight in the world. You have to be utterly reliable.'

When we got back to Heathrow from Stockholm, I went to

use a phone and Gascoigne, by chance, was on the next phone along. He was calling someone who'd had the temerity to go out while he'd been away – he'd called, but no answer, where'd she been? – and the torrent of foul-mouthed abuse that ensued was just staggering. It was an ugly display of really noisy immaturity and, remembering it, I figured maybe Robson had a point.

But when I asked him later which players he looked forward to seeing in Italy, the answer was equally revealing.

'It'll be interesting to see whether the boy Baggio comes to fruition. I think Donadoni will be good, I like Donadoni. And I wonder how good Hagi will be, the Romanian, he's got enormous talent – one of the finest players in Europe. He came to light when we played Romania, when we qualified for the last World Cup – he was only young, about twenty years of ago, but he's a great little player, a magic player. And then, obviously, Gascoigne. He's got to get picked first – but you just know, with his genius, he's capable of doing things that make you think, *bloody hell* . . . his free kicks, his dribbling. He's something special.'

On the subject of whether we should ditch the 4–4–2 and play a sweeper, Robson was contemptuously abrupt.

'First of all you have to look at the way we play football in this country. Do you have to change it, or is that the best way for the present crop of players? We play a system which is familiar to the players, they're comfortable with it, they understand it. You look at a good team, Holland in the European Championship, there was technical excellence right through that team – they've got a sweeper, but they push one forward, so if there's only two up against them, they play with three back – and *we do that too*.

'So look, it is *trash*, it is *absolute rubbish* . . . I keep getting told, we must play a sweeper. Why? Why must we play a sweeper? Why? We've played thirteen matches, and conceded three goals, home and away, at international level. So why do we need to play *more* defensive?'

So I asked Robson about his front men, and his wingers – the people who were supposed to be making and scoring the goals we'd not seen in three games. The answer developed into something just a little bit surprising.

'Waddle is now very accomplished, probably now you can rely on Chrissie Waddle. It takes a while. I can remember three years ago the kid got booed, and he can hear that. And if you don't have the character you can just disappear. But he's worked his way through that, I've kept faith. I've said, Chrissie, forget about the crowd, I'm picking you, you get out there, son – they don't pick the team, I pick the team, and I picked you – get out there. 'Cos there's only one way to do it, you perform, it's performance changes the crowd – and he's changed them.

'Now in a sense we're still waiting for Barnes, but we all just know, *I know* – there's no better player in the wide position in England than John Barnes. Tell me, if he broke his leg tomorrow, who would play? There's nobody equal to Barnes, nobody else in the country can play like him.

'But if the Beardsley–Lineker thing doesn't work, what do we have? What's our alternative? I need to look at Bull, and Platt. We haven't seen much of Bull yet, but we will, eventually. And we're waiting for Lineker to come back to the form he had before the hepatitis, we're looking for Peter to be the player we all think he could and should be. But I can't wait too long . . .

'You know who could play up front for us? Waddle, and Barnes. That would be very interesting. I only wish I had more games to try things. Rocastle and Hodge on the outside, Robson and McMahon in the middle, or Robson and Gascoigne – that'd change the scene, wouldn't it? Put your creative players in front positions . . . I saw Waddle play at the beginning of last season as a front player in a couple of games, he was sensational. We tried it in Albania, he was poor – but that's one match. If you were a club manager you could say, Chrissie, you were fuckin' awful, but we'll have a go at it again next week. Me, I had to wait six weeks before we could try it again, and then it was a big World Cup match – and you can't take the chance.'

But talk about taking chances . . . Drop Lineker? The highest scorer in Mexico '86? Twenty-nine goals for England? Play Waddle and Barnes up the front? Nah . . . Robson had a paranoia attack. 'This is confidential, isn't it? This is for the book? This isn't for any paper? The *Sun*'d pay £50,000 for this.'

ROBSON TO DROP LINEKER SHOCK. ROBSON BLASTS STRIKER IN GOAL DROUGHT HORROR. You can imagine the damage it'd do, to confidence, to morale – the *Sun*, or its yob brothers, would have no compunction about that.

I couldn't see Robson doing it. But three months later, when we were driving through South London to Selhurst Park, I asked him again – was he still thinking of playing Barnes and Waddle up front? Neither Lineker nor Bull, after all, had scored against Yugoslavia.

'Sure. It's at the back of my mind.'

And Lineker?

'Well, if he's not scoring goals . . . Gary Lineker's got to score goals. If we're making chances and he's missing them, y'know – you have to make a decision.'

We had, in February, only five matches left in which to try such a thing.

'Yes – but they're both such good players, Barnes and Waddle are such good players that quite frankly I doubt it needs a practice, I'll just do it, one day I'll say, right, I'm changing the team – you two play through the middle.'

So maybe it's a good job for Lineker that he scored the next month against Brazil . . .

Gascoigne, meanwhile, had lost his head in a game at Coventry and taken a swing at someone – he cracked a bone in his forearm. The match he came back, at Chelsea, Robson went to watch him – and he did it again.

'I was really annoyed with him. I thought, will you not learn? He's just broke his arm swinging a punch – and then he does it again.' Robson said he'd be having a word with him about what was expected of an England player – and that Shilton, Butcher, Bryan Robson, they all wanted it putting right too. 'He hasn't been around them long enough yet, but they'll sort him out. They'll do it on the field, where I can't.'

In late February I went to Sheffield. At Bramall Lane I saw United play Newcastle – a dreary and directionless exercise in hoofing the ball through buckets of rain, in a difficult wind – and I interviewed Dick Wragg, the Chairman of the FA's International Committee. The interview was dreary and directionless too, most memorable not for what Wragg said, but for the warning beforehand, from someone who really ought to have known better, that Wragg was 'a cantankerous old cunt'.

In fact, he was an amiable old cove, but the operative word here was old. Inside the FA, I'd had it morbidly suggested to me that they were waiting for him to die in his job, because taking it away from him would kill him . . .

At seventy-eight he has, I suppose, every right to be as time-warped and complacent as he likes. Whether, at seventy-eight, he has the right to be (theoretically) in charge of England's international football team is a different matter altogether.

For example: when I asked about the racist chanting, of which there'd been sporadic outbursts at the game, he said, 'They're so used to seeing all-white football teams, that they don't like to see darkies introduced . . . I'll tell you this, a lot of my friends don't like to see a lot of black people in the teams. But as far as I'm concerned, I tell everybody this, knowing the English players, and our own dark players, they are normally better dressed and better spoken than seventy-five per cent of the white people. The dark fellows who come into the England team, they're tremendously well-behaved, they really are.'

Three cheers for the dark fellows.

Robson, he said, was 'a good bloke'. But what made him the right man for the job? 'Because he's an honest bloke. You know from the papers, people try to get me to knock him all the time. But the committee support him a hundred per cent.'

Robson, when I told him next day that I'd been to Sheffield and seen Wragg, didn't seem much impressed to hear of that support.

He had a year of his contract still to run after Italy. But at a FIFA gathering in Zurich a month later, FA Chairman Bert Millichip was reported to have said, in effect, that it was win the World Cup, or quit.

It was the time of the gales and the floods. Gloucester became the lost city of Atlantis. Cornwall was blown flat and drenched, powerless for weeks. An hour north from where I live, the town of Towyn was reclaimed by the furious sea. Roofs departed from buildings. Water spilt down culverts, and sheeted across the roads; mud slipped, trees fell, and British Rail became a museum of torn signals and shredded track. There was an eclipse of the moon. Ah-ah-owh-wwhh-hooooooo . . . we's a-howlin' in the Greenhouse.

Games were off all round the country. If we had fewer clubs in the principal divisions, we could have a winter break like they do in much of Europe . . . and pigs might fly.

At Selhurst Park, where Charlton were playing Arsenal, they'd thought about cancelling the game – they were worried about the floodlight pylons in the wind – but they went ahead. The spice of danger this suggested at least gave the match a frisson of excitement. The football certainly didn't.

I went with Robson from Lancaster Gate, where I found him enthusing about the imminent victory of England's cricketers in the first test in Jamaica. Robson's from a mining village in Country Durham, where you get fed cricket with your milk – it's the summer game, isn't it? When you're not playing football, you play cricket – a fact of nature, in the same way that when it's not raining, the sun shines. Besides, he liked seeing England win at anything.

Robson's secretary Michelle Rogers and her father, a Charlton supporter, were going to guide us into the wilds of South London – Robson and I were to follow in his Jaguar. Robson said from Bayswater he might get to Victoria, but no further – he said maybe Michelle's dad should start a business, steering lost football managers from ground to ground around the city. Robson himself came to London in the early fifties, to Fulham, beginning life as a professional when he was seventeen – 'very frightening, very lonely'.

The notion of the manager-moving business started a vein of banter that continued through the evening – maybe Michelle could go into it with her dad. 'No,' said Robson, 'she's all right. She'll still have a job next year.'

After the game a tanned, dapper man who'd played with Robson at Fulham came to talk with his old teammate. He had a business now, something to do with welding gear, and he was doing OK with it. Work had just taken him to Nairobi and Johannesburg – and the tan was from a skiing trip he'd enjoyed so much, he was going again. So they talked about skiing, and golf; Robson said he'd not had a break since August. He'd been here, there, everyplace, Egypt, Italy – he was going to Switzerland soon, but he wouldn't see much snow, he had a FIFA coaching course to do. Then he said how next year, he'd have plenty of time, wouldn't he? He'd ski and play golf to his heart's content.

The committee are a hundred per cent committed . . . they'd stood by him through bad times after the defeats in Germany, and when the tabloids made merry with his mistresses. But now the papers were on all the time about who would be next – about Graham Taylor in particular, as Aston Villa challenged Liverpool at the top of the table. And Robson talked like a man who knew the hundred per cent commitment would evaporate in seconds given bad results in the summer – or, maybe, like a man who had thoughts in his heart to quit anyhow.

Still, he liked going to the games. He liked having so many people recognise him among the stewards and the fans and the car park attendants – he signed programme after programme, uncomplaining. He said, 'I suppose one day I'll come, and no one will know me any more. I'll be *praying* to be recognised then.'

About United and Newcastle, there was lurking disdain in the way he asked of United, 'They play a lot of long balls, don't they? I see so many games . . .' He trailed off, and thought about it.

'They say all English football's like that. But my team don't play that way.'

We talked about Brian Clough. Many people, for many years, wanted Clough for England manager. Robson said he didn't know the man – he wondered if anyone really did. But he said, answering a question about League managers in general, that, yes, Clough was helpful – if you could get hold of him. 'He's never there, I wonder how he gets away with it. I always have to leave a message, everyone does. He gets away with it because he gets results – but he has to be helpful, doesn't he? He made such a fuss about wanting the England job, he has to be.'

And we talked about England's defence again. He said of Des Walker, who plays for Clough at Forest, that he was fast and secure, always there when there was danger. But he couldn't go forward – Clough didn't like him to cross the half-way line.

There was a period when Clough was banned from the touchline, for hitting spectators who'd come on to the pitch (an incident that throws ironic light on Clough's comment, 'Football hooligans? There's ninety-two club chairmen for a start'). Robson saw a game at Forest with Clough up in the box during that time, and he was still yelling at his players from there. 'And what he shouted most,' Robson said, 'was, "Des! STAY!"'

He'd just seen Italy and Holland stroll to an indifferent o–o draw in Rotterdam, and though he hadn't much liked the game, what he said about the players was telling. 'The three centre-backs there for Holland, Van Tiggelen, Koeman and Rijkaard – *completely different* centre-halves to the centre-halves we produce in this country, who are just defending players. Now those three players are all defenders – y'know, their job is to cover each other and head the ball away, intercept and tackle, keep it formidable, not be leaky and all that, but in possession . . .'

Rijkaard, I said, had been all over the pitch.

'*They're all footballers.* They can all bring the ball out, run it out, pass it. We produce centre-halves who can defend – but in possession they're limited.'

Did that apply to Terry Butcher?

'No, not so much . . . Terry Butcher won't run it out of defence, but he gets a lot of the ball, our back players are happy to turn the ball back into him – because they know he'll deliver it. He can drop it in and he can hit the long ball, he can go from left to right, he's a great server of the ball – he's a good footballer coming out of defence. Not in terms of bringing it out, but playing it out. He's our best.'

We'd talked earlier of how our players played Saturday, Tuesday, Monday, Wednesday, so many games – did that inhibit them? Did that hinder their chances of learning to do that bit more, like a Rijkaard can?

'Of course. Because they don't train, they don't practise, they don't develop techniques. We don't train in this country. We train at the beginning of the season to get fit – once the season starts, we're a nation of match-play footballers.'

*

We talked about the racist taunts I'd heard at Bramall Lane the Saturday before. Robson's on record as saying, 'If the best eleven players in the country were black, that would be my England team' – to which he said simply, when I recalled the quote, 'Yes. The best team plays. The best man plays.' And he described with evident disgust and disbelief the incidents, on a South American tour in '84, when NF thugs had barracked John Barnes.

'But how can you educate thousands of people into not being . . . racist, as you say. I don't know how you can do it. You see – I'll be careful here, but they may have been a little, ah . . . anti-colour, up at Liverpool at one stage. Barnes has turned that. Barnes has changed the mood up there. By going up there as a Liverpool player, living in the community, playing to such a marvellous degree of technical ability – they love him. And then suddenly they're not throwing banana skins on the pitch any more.'

About the hooligan thing in general, he said, 'We abhor it. The players hate it. It just creates around us a feeling of . . . oh bloody hell, they don't belong to us, do they? Do they really? It just creates a feeling around us of being unclean – because we know that they are England, and they're our supporters, and it's something we don't represent – yet we do, because they follow us. And we hate them. We just hate them.'

I said that the ninety minutes of a game for the manager must be unbelievably frustrating. Against Yugoslavia I'd sat on the bench and watched him hunched there, shoulders knotted, leaping up and shouting, pacing back resigned – face working with all the thoughts you can't get out on the pitch because it's all gone from your grasp, there's no more you can do.

'Yes. You see every little flaw – you're right in the cauldron of the thing, and you see every little mistake.'

Didn't it make him want, sometimes, just to put his head in his hands?

'No. Fortunately I experienced the beauty of being a player, and the frustrations of being a player. And I hope I never ever forget that.'

So I asked what was it like in Sweden, in 1958.

'Well ... I was a young player. But it was a marvellous experience, I loved every minute. And I realised how hard it was. It's another ... I don't know what the step up is, but league football to international football ... it's a prodigious step, honestly. I mean, I was a good, accomplished footballer when I played for West Bromwich, for England – but it was way above what I'd ever, ever imagined.'

Robson also played in Chile in 1962 – so which meant more to him?

'The first one. Pele was seventeen then ... I was twenty-five, I was young. I thought the game was so difficult, so demanding, playing against bright players, quick players – quick, not just physically, you take that as accepted, but *quick up here* [he tapped his temple] – people saw things, did things in a second.'

He talked with affectionate memory of men he'd come up against who'd been difficult – one was Luis Suarez, now managing Spain. 'He was a very talented player, you had to be careful with him, otherwise ... I've met Luis several times since, it's very nice. I just wish I could speak Spanish, because he can't speak English.

'And Denis Law, I've just done an advert with him for television. He kicked me nineteen feet in the air one day ... I've still got the bruise to prove it.'

Robson had gone to watch the Arsenal players – Adams, Dixon, Rocastle, Thomas, Smith, Winterburn – and to have a look, also, at Charlton's fast little striker Paul Williams. As the game started, he pointed out with pleasure how Adams was reading the play, holding the line, offering a yard of security, always alive to the dangerous ball. 'He's a high-profile player, always talking. He'll make a good captain of England.'

The next Terry Butcher? Would he take him to Italy? But in that position there was also Mark Wright, or Gary Pallister. In the car he'd said that Adams was still learning to be 'a bit of a footballer'. Now, he was the best thing going for a leaden-looking Arsenal.

And Robson looked like he'd seen it all before. At half-time and afterwards, with the Charlton people, he was polite and politic, saying it was difficult for the players out there, with a lot of swirling wind. But during the game he was blunt. Both teams were 4–4–2, like most of our teams, the same predictable formation (ironic, that). 'Everybody's comfortable, no tactical surprises. Both back fours are condensing the play, it's one-on-one all the time. The game will be won by the team which, in the midst of the play, has the individual who shows through.' And no one did, except – and this is the joy of football, even at so ordinary a match – an eighteen-year-old called Scott Minto, playing left back for Charlton.

Robson grew wearily exasperated with Rocastle – by the second half, he and Don Howe were wondering about his fitness. 'He should dominate Minto, he's twenty-three, he's played for England – he's got to look for the ball and then roast him. And I'm looking to see if he does – because if he can't do it to Minto, how will he do it in the World Cup?' But when he might have pushed up, Rocastle was pulling up instead.

The second half bumbled bargingly onward, fast and incoherent. Robson said, 'They're playing for the break – but there's not a lot of craft on the pitch to make one. Everybody's cancelling out everybody else. It's stalemate, sterile – I see it so often . . .'

But still you couldn't, as with Holland–Italy, say categorically that it'd end 0–0 – because this was the English League, and points mattered; and it began to open up in the last fifteen minutes, as the wind and fatigue made things looser. Rocastle began, at last, to get to the by-line.

To the partisan, there's your English excitement – hectic stuff, and the hope of a goal as things get crumbly before it ends. But to the unattached observer, there's little joy to be taken from a game where, if there's to be a result, it'll come because one man's knackered, rather than because another is skilful.

In this ragged-edged deadlock, what you needed was for players to start 'going for a stroll, taking a wander, so they don't have you under lock and key all the time – so you pull things out of shape for their back four. I have,' said Robson, 'to say this to Barnes a lot.' But no one had said it to anyone tonight.

So we enjoyed Scott Minto instead – he had the audacity,

once, to nutmeg David Rocastle. On another occasion, the ball came high into a crowded box – and cool as you please, as it came down, the kid sidefooted it into his keeper's hands, barely a yard in front of the goal line. The Charlton directors' box collectively wet itself.

On the field, Minto looked eighteen – frail, scrawny. But he had pace, skill, good positioning and covering – he wasn't afraid to try things. He was balanced, moving nicely, swimming in his element, transformed by football, not at all like the gawky, uncertain kid we saw later in the clubroom, trying to look mannish with slicked curly hair, a hint of acne, and wearing clothes that, somehow, looked misplaced on him. He was too young to try cutting a dash yet; and you could see him glow inside when the England manager made a point of going over to praise him for his game. Robson made sure a picture got taken, his arm placed with that easy sportsman's matiness round the boy's thin shoulders.

We drove back through the empty, ill-lit streets of South London. When I said I'd get a cab to Tooting, where I was staying, Robson told me, 'Not at all – I'm the best cab you'll get.' At a set of lights his window hissed down, and he leant out to call to the guy in the next car, asking directions – and the guy, recognising him, looked surprised and energised. He said he was headed our way, and hared off in front of us as if suddenly appointed on a magic mission – another guide for a lost manager. I imagined him getting home to his wife, boosted, saying who he'd helped to get home . . .

Before we got to Tooting, I asked what effect he thought he'd had, congratulating Minto the way he had that night, and he simply said, 'I'd never thought of that.' When he had thought about it, he said, 'I suppose it must give the boy confidence, lift his spirits. You want him to play better, don't you? To do well.'

He feared Minto would prove too old, by a matter of a few short days, to play in the U-19 side. England's U-19 team had qualified for the UEFA Finals in Hungary in July, and Robson said, 'We beat France and Czechoslovakia to get there. And who ever writes or hears about that? But they're the future, those boys.'

Saying a few words to Scott Minto – one of a host of things the England manager does in his job that no one ever notices. Us, we're busy lathering on in our pubs and in our papers about whether Lineker, say, will get the goals we all want – and we forget how the next Lineker's got to be brought on from somewhere.

Michelle Rogers has worked at the FA for five years, the last two and a half of those for Robson; so I asked what he was like to work for.

She said, 'It's an absolute ... well, I wouldn't say an absolute dream, but he's a lovely man. He's a bit scatter-brained, but he doesn't mind if I boss him about, and I do ... 'cos he has a hell of a lot on his mind, all the requests people bombard him with, the media attention's just huge, and he doesn't ever stop – he's too generous with his time. But deep down I know he loves it, he loves being busy.

'But they love to tear him apart, and I think that's wicked, 'cos he's such a nice man. I was so ... he rang me, the night before it came out [the *News of the World* mistress splash]. He rang about twelve o'clock at night, my dad came and got me, and he told me about it. And I was so upset. Because at the time I thought that was it, he was going to go. He said, we were a good team, weren't we ... I really didn't know what was going to happen. But it shouldn't matter – he's so committed to his job, no one could ever accuse him of not putting in the time. That's all that should matter.'

Brian Clough had said he'd not got the job because he had left-wing opinions – she laughed out loud over that. 'I don't think that's the reason why ... to be the manager of England, you've got to be an ambassador. Mr Robson, when he goes abroad, he's a charming man, he's always got time for people. He gets queues and queues of kids waiting for his autograph, and he always does it.

'See, there's a lot of people who criticise him, people who've never met him. But anyone who met him – they wouldn't have a bad word to say about him.'

7   World Cup Fever

The agent, the beachwear,
and the rise of Paul Gascoigne

On 28 March England played Brazil before a full house at Wembley. For the first time, the 80,000 were all seated. The fixture had been arranged by Jon Smith.

In the press bar Brian Glanville told anyone who'd listen that Bob Harris, who'd just left *Today* to become sports editor at the *Sunday Mirror*, was, 'A moron, a baboon.'

In the tunnel, there were bigger issues to be settled. England were unbeaten in fourteen games – and so were the Brazilians. I'd been down there before but the buzz, this time, was in a whole new league.

It's a shabby, cavernous concrete vault. The banging doors, the studs clacking on the floor, the calls of officials and the TV men waiting at the top all echo dimly about. In the middle of the dull noise, and the last arrangements being made, players trot lightly on the spot, shaking their arms, rolling their heads; others stand, shifting their weight slowly from foot to foot, quiet, or just saying the odd few words – two close lines of men not looking at each other much, maybe just stealing a glance now and then, glances speaking a whole complex of emotions, pride and fear, curiosity and aggression . . . they face up the tunnel, towards the muffled pulse of the beast outside.

As you go forward, the great bowl looms wider and wider through the opening ahead. Under the bruised colours of dusk, the green brilliance of the floodlit pitch, and the dark and stupendous mass of the people all about it, take on the trappings of a vast and brutal stage.

You walk into the heartbeat of the people's great drama.

Leading the way, Butcher looked down as he walked, his

face a mask of ill-restrained intensity. The legs had the dents of fourteen seasons, battered and scarred. During the anthems he stood rigidly, awkwardly to attention – and he must have been concentrating pretty hard to stay upright like that through the Brazilian anthem. No disrespect, but it's a whole five-act comic opera, it goes on for ever.

The game kicked off, and Brazil immediately put together fifteen passes on the trot; they started stroking it about and you thought, Uh-oh . . . but they rarely stroked it anywhere purposeful. England began slowly to get a hold on things. The substitutes sat chewing their gum, jaws working like metronomes. Among them, Gascoigne was busy barking his little comments, admiring this, mocking that. David Bloomfield, the FA's press officer, said, 'We can beat this lot.'

In the thirty-sixth minute Beardsley took a corner and Barnes flicked it on from the near post. Lineker dropped to his knees, and headed it in. Cue the roar.

England 1, Brazil 0.

After eleven minutes, Shilton took a cut on the head from a clash with Des Walker – it needed eight stitches – and Chris Woods went on.

He said later, 'I've always wanted to play Brazil – but you just have to concentrate so much. They mix their game up so well, they were so good touch-wise, playing the little short balls – but when it needed to be spread out, it was just one look up, and they've pinged it across. Then the free kicks, they're hitting balls from ten, fifteen yards further out then we would. The one he hit in the first half, it must have swerved a good yard and a half.'

Branco was taking run-ups so long on those kicks, if he'd started any further back, he have been starting in his goalmouth.

Woods was a forced substitution, though Robson most likely would have given him the second half anyway. Meanwhile, all around where we sat on the bench, the fans let us know what they wanted. 'Put Gazza on! He's a fuckin' Newcastle man.' When he started warming up, the cheers were uproarious. With eleven minutes left (symmetry, that) Robson took off Beardsley for Gascoigne.

Afterwards he said of Beardsley, 'He ran his little socks off. I'm not here to exhaust him.'

And how many points would he give England out of ten?

'I don't have to answer that. I'm not a schoolteacher, I'm a football manager.'

At a press conference next morning, he got annoyed with a Dutch photographer. 'Haven't you got enough of me, feller? You've been around me three days.'

The photographer smiled, but he didn't move.

'I'm serious. I'm asking you to leave. I'm not here to get snapped all the time.' And then, to another, 'Who are you?'

Norwegian press . . .

The conference began. 'You must be a happy man this morning, Bobby.'

'I am – until you lads start getting into me. No, it's OK, we're friends. I don't bear grudges.'

When it was over, and people were gathering round, there was talk about the cricketers in the West Indies, and whether Gower might be called up to replace the injured Gooch. Robson said he'd told the team last night, 'Let's get a double tonight. We'll beat Brazil, and they can beat Barnesy's lot.'

His disappointment at England missing out on a second test win was palpable.

On 25 April England played Czechoslovakia.

The afternoon of the day before, on the lawn in front of the Burnham Beeches Hotel, the players modelled suits and, more spectacularly, what the marketing boy from Top Man called 'resort wear'.

Shilton went past muttering, 'Just what I want to do right now. Put on a suit.'

McMahon, a tough and terse man anyway, said, 'This is ridiculous.'

Gazza loved it.

But I think most of them did really, fooling about in naff hooded T-shirts, and ultra-lurid, multi-coloured, baggy day-glo shorts. They were given hideous anti-glare specs, with sickly yellow lenses. Photographers and wardrobe girls fluttered about, fussing and primping.

On another patch of lawn, a video crew recorded interviews

with players, one by one – they were making, said Bloomfield, a history of the England team.

A commercial job?

'What isn't? Just 'cos it's commercial doesn't mean it's tacky.' He gestured behind him to the hotel, a gleaming white, squeaky-clean country pile. He said, 'This isn't Wembley, is it?'

McMahon and Bryan Robson kicked a beachball back and forth; cameras clacked and whirred.

Lineker did an anti-drug slot for Malaysian TV, reading phonetic Malaysian phrases off cue boards, like Bob Dylan in the 'Subterranean Homesick Blues' film.

'Apa kabar sire Gary Lineker. World Cup fever's on right now, and as a pro footballer I've got to keep in shape. That means physical training, good diet, and certainly – No Drugs. So if you want to keep in shape like I do, jaw he dari da-da.'

Aside: 'Dunno about the physical training bit.' Lineker's not a big man for training – he prefers to read, or lie about in bed. Or both. He looked benevolently bemused.

'To all my Malaysian fans out there, salamat menonton. See you at the World Cup on RTM Malaysia. Teri ma khazi.'

Got a lot of Malaysian fans, Gary?

'You should see my mail.'

Then, on request, he turned out an exceptionally fluent anti-drug message, off the cuff. The camera doesn't phase Gary Lineker.

I had a cup of tea with Terry Butcher. While we watched the weird palaver going on all over the lawn, he said, 'The boss gets accused of being pernickety, but all the preparation pays dividends. The Scottish are like that too – but Roxburgh's a ned. Good on preparation, crap on football.' (When I'd asked Robson about the other home nations, he said anyone who underestimated the Irish would get slapped. And the Scottish? 'No chance.')

'Y'know,' said Butcher, 'Scottish players can't report sick. The club can't say they're sick. They have to go all the way to Glasgow from Liverpool or wherever, see the Scottish doctor, he says OK, you're unfit, then go back. Ridiculous. Players,' he grumbled, 'are just pawns.'

Whether he'll see it quite like that when he's a manager remains to be seen. Meantime, if they were pawns, with World

Cup fever on the boil they'd most certainly not be poor ones.

The Top Man thing was one of Jon Smith's deals: 'Official Fashion Suppliers To The England World Cup Squad'. A PR handout (with a photo, among others, of Gazza in an 'Ozone Friendly' sweatshirt) claimed breathlessly, 'The England players believe that in their striking new Top Man wardrobe they will be dressed to thrill and will come back as World Champions.'

So who is Jon Smith?

He's one of only six agents in the world licensed by FIFA to arrange international tours and matches.

He's small, fast, permed, immaculate – shinily shod, and lightly tanned. He looks ten years younger than he probably is; he looks like the kind of guy whose idea of growing up is to stop going to nightclubs, and to start owning them instead – he looks like an over-age Wham! fan. He looks, in short, like eighties money, charming and smooth – a wide boy transmuted into shimmering essence of wallet. The boy done well.

At the Royal Viking in Stockholm I was talking with Elton Welsby and Smith arrived hotfoot from Warsaw. How, asked Welsby, did he manage comfortably to arrange his many travels?

'No problem,' said Smith. 'I bought a travel agency last year.'

Smith is chairman of the First Artist Corporation plc. A couple of weeks before the Czechoslovakia game he told me, 'First Artist was actually a company owned by Barbra Streisand and Dustin Hoffman. And I was sitting in my little house in California – I was in the record business before I sold out, and I spent a lot of time in the States, I did a bit of property dealing – and one night I was watching the news, and Hoffman and Streisand had decided they didn't want to be in this company any more; the First Artist Corporation wasn't going to exist any more. And I thought, What a great name, I like that. So I phoned the registrar of companies in Sacramento the next day. They said, well, if they don't use the company, you can have the name a year and a day later. So I made a little note, and thirteen months later I got it.

'I didn't know what to do with it, except I kept coming back to England, I spent a lot of time watching football, and I thought, I wonder if I can apply some of the things I learnt in America to football. Paul Mariner and I were old mates, we got together one day over a cup of tea and said, right, let's take the football world by storm, I think we can do it. By the way, I got a great company, great name . . . and that was it.'

Fourteen weeks later, Smith was representing – according to the way he tells it – both the England squad and Diego Maradona.

Smith earned the England players something in the region of £1,000,000 from Italia '90. The money was shared in a pool between the squad, and a handful of the principal staff – Robson, the coach Don Howe, the physios.

The main source of money was commercial. There was £80,000 from a carphone company; there was £100,000 from Top Man. A sponsorship with Mars also netted an initial £100,000, with more to come, and the players didn't have to do much for it – just make a few ads, and wear the logo on their gear.

Smith earned Mars their investment back in no time. On the morning of the match in Katowice, the inside back pages of the *Mirror* ran a '*Mirror* Sport Exclusive' headlined '£1M: ENGLAND'S SWEET TASTE OF SUCCESS'. The story was about the commercial incentives awaiting the players if they qualified that night – how they'd signed up to become 'The Men From Mars'.

It featured such gems of the sportswriter's art as, 'Mars are one of the most successful snack food firms in the country. They estimate that ninety-seven per cent of the population have tried a Mars bar at one stage of their life . . . the England plane will be laden with Mars bars on the road to Rome . . . the England medical experts recommend the players eat chocolate on the night before their big games. Now they will turn to Mars to help them work, rest and play!'

The Mars PR department must have creamed themselves. Smith described the story as 'headline-driven' – it was, in effect, written in First Artist's dinky little offices on Wembley Hill Road. I asked Smith, how come? He said, he'd done the

Mirror sports desk a few favours in the past – what he called, 'free stories'.

Smith quantified the payback for those favours as £103,000 of free publicity.

And what logo do Maradona and his teammates sport on their Napoli shirts? Who is one of FIFA's official World Cup sponsors? Mars.

Apart from corporate sponsorships, Smith also screws down revenue for the pool from the press and TV. In theory, there'd be strictly stipulated 'open' times in Italy – at training grounds, at the hotels – when the press could get in and ask questions. Anything else, you had to pay for it. When this book was getting under way, and we were discussing access during the tournament, Smith – doing his job – airily mooted a payment to the pool of perhaps £10,000.

Then he said it didn't matter what I paid; if Dick Wragg didn't want me in the hotels, that was it, I wouldn't get in.

In Sheffield Wragg had said, 'I'm in charge. Completely in charge.' And he also said, 'I would prefer the agents to be out of the game. I'll be realistic, in the modern world we've got to have them. If they're decent agents I don't mind, but there are one or two . . . you get the bad apple everywhere.'

Jon Smith, I said (piously), was by all accounts a reputable man.

Wragg took on the look of a man discussing creatures crawled out from under stones. 'Let me put it this way. I've never really found him out doing things wrong. But he takes more advantage than he ought to do. If you can switch that off a bit . . .'

There followed an unclear tale about clothing contracts.

'He's done himself no good. Because whilst I'm chairman there's no way I will agree to him coming and eating with the players, and we used to let him do that . . . there's *no way* he's coming in for a meal with us.'

Like he said, he's in charge. Or, as Glen Kirton put it, 'So long as you give him the impression he's in charge, you'll get along fine.'

'With respect to him,' said Smith, 'I find his attitude outdated.'

At Burnham Beeches, Wragg drifted through the drawing

rooms like a ghost, a pale presence in the background. But outside on the lawn, while the players posed in their beach-wear, Smith paced energetically back and forth, forever murmuring quietly and urgently on his portable phone.

So who *is* in charge?

I never paid any money. Robson said I didn't have to, and Smith never pressed it. He said, 'They did a research on you, you know that? I've had phone calls.' He laughed and said, 'Of course I told them I thought you were a prat.'

The World Cup's awash with strange and feverish money.

At the draw in Rome in December, in the teeming TV glare of FIFA's hotel foyer, I found myself talking to the manager of Bobby Charlton Sports. In between hale handshakes with an amiably bewildered gent from the Lebanese FA – Charlton's soccer school was, laudably, proposing to take one Christian kid, and one Muslim, which goes to show that football can and will survive anything – this man told me I should get a sponsor for my book.

A sponsored book? I looked fuddled – how would that work?

Simple. Gas, Telecom, some corporation like that, we can find you a few of their thousands to top up your budget – and all you got to do is make sure their pitchside hoardings are prominent in your pictures . . .

There aren't, I said, going to be many pictures.

But to the money men, the pictures are everything – because where football is the medium, logos are the language.

For example: Mastercard – the 'Official Card' of Italia '90 – gave a lunch on the day of the draw. Two hundred of us swilled round groaning tables of salmon and pasta, drawn there for one reason only – they'd laid on buses to the Palazzo dello Sport afterwards. And what do Mastercard get from this? Simple . . .

The key 'guests' were Bobby Charlton, and Socrates of Brazil. The great men were 'available to talk to you' on the back left and right-hand sides of the dining room respectively. Now Socrates is a foot taller than Charlton, so the Mastercard logo was hung a foot higher on the wall behind him. The TV cameras turned as they talked to all-comers, glued to their marks – and the logo sat neatly in the frame.

Thus, on football programmes round the world, the thoughts of the great men came to the screens of millions decorated with the red and yellow circles of the card. And why buy ad time, if you can get your logo on worldwide TV for the price of two footballers? The PR man – a short, shoulder-padded, double-breasted little creep from Brooklyn, with greased-back hair and a pencil-thin moustache – roamed the room like an oil slick. For all the two hundred journalists cared, the lunch could have been hosted by the KGB, but that didn't matter to him. The journalists were just background noise for the interviews and the logo – the pictures, the TV, the turning wheel of money.

When I asked Smith what he was doing at the draw, he said, 'Touching base. Shopping.'

For what?

'We've been accused of raising the profile, raising the stakes, making it more of a commercial exploitation – but all we've done is make footballers commensurate with other sportsmen, like boxers. And it's been successful – this World Cup pool will be the richest ever.

'Our role is basically twofold. Firstly, we have to protect the players against wrongful exploitation. In other words, if a company wants to use them in a manner not appropriate to the image they should be projecting, or that, financially, is not rewarding them as it should be – because don't forget, they've got a very short time, one World Cup might be the highpoint of a career . . . so we protect their commercial interests.

'Then at the same time, we exploit and promote whatever they do off the field. So there's Mars, Top Man, Tonka Toys, Thorn EMI, Esso, Wilson Golf Clubs, Panini Stickers, MCA Records, Wembley merchandising, Umbro, Grand Slam computer games . . . there'll be an England team book, and England phone lines, the 0898 numbers – which, incidentally, are doing brilliantly, they took two thousand calls in one day last week – those are the main ones. A good few of them are six figures.

'But let me tell you about something else, very much part of what we do. We've nurtured and cultured a very strong relationship with the media. So when the England team are asked to do a photo, or an interview, or perform for TV, it'll normally come through this office. Like ITV, for instance, who I'm seeing this afternoon . . . so, as opposed to just being the commercial agent, we've now put ourselves in a role of off-the-field management – always under the direction of the team boss. Bobby, fortunately, is very co-operative, and we handle a lot of his affairs off the field anyway, so everything goes through him – and we clear everything through Glen Kirton's office as well. Now Glen's a smashing chap, and acutely aware of how valuable this perk is to the players – so much so that the bonus structure the players are offered is reflected in it. So when the FA sit down and work out how much the players are going to earn, they take the pool into consideration, which they never used to.

'So what you'll see, over the next few weeks, is a lot of shots of the England team walking around wearing certain things, like a Mars T-shirt with an Umbro diamond on it. And that is maximisation for the sponser. It's part of our duty to deliver that.

'The key is to use as little time as possible. So if they're walking around wearing Umbro diamonds, because Umbro have paid for the right to have leisurewear put on the players, we clear it with Umbro that they don't mind a Mars thing on it – then we're delivering to the sponsor millions of people every day through papers and TV, without the team even having to think about it.'

I asked where the balance lay between the exploitation of the players' market value, and the need to protect them, not from unlicensed exploitation, but from hassle.

'That's a good question. I think we've done that, by putting ourselves in the middle of things – but it's taken us three or four years to be trusted by all parties . . . because agents have got a terrible reputation. And it's not fair on the ones that are good.

'Everybody thinks if you're a football agent, you're automatically making a lot of money. But let me tell you, the average agent will only make his money from one item a footballer works with – his boots. Because there's nothing else visible that's a tangible asset. The agent can't get money from the kit, because that's a club deal. Suits? How often do you see a footballer wearing a suit in a newspaper? How often do you see a footballer promoting a product in a newspaper? With the exception of Bryan Robson, Maradona, a few others – you can count them on the fingers of one hand. There's only a handful of agents that are going to make any money from the exploitation of a player.

'So it's transfers where the agent gets a bad name. The bad agent will put his player into the club, get a percentage of the signing-on fee – some even take a percentage of his salary – get paid by the club for doing that deal – leave him in there for a year – then agitate to get him out, and put him in somewhere else. That's where they get a bad name.'

'Us, we take twenty per cent over and above what a player would have had anyway. We don't touch his wages. So supposing – hypothetical figures – a player gets offered £50,000 for signing on. And we get it up to £75,000. We'll take twenty per cent of £25,000 – we don't think it's fair to take twenty per cent of the whole lot, 'cos he'd have had that without us anyway. Now that doesn't amount to a great deal of money. But when the club says to us, as a thank you for setting the whole thing up, we'll pay you . . . then it's worthwhile.

'We've done £7,500,000 in transfers in the UK this year. That includes the Polish guys coming over. And then we've been asked by Poland to act for the government, to sell the football team to raise money, then take the money back to Poland in the form of British goods . . . I mean, it's a really strange contract. They actually want goods, because they haven't got any, and the hard currency that we can raise – we've sold footballers for them to Greece, Scotland, Norway, Switzerland, Australia, the States, we've raised something like $8,000,000 for them – that doesn't go very far. They need hundreds of millions. So what we do is buy, at specially discounted rates, $8,000,000 of tangible goods that they need.

'Because their football clubs can't afford to buy kit. The big ones are obviously sponsored, Legia Warsaw, they're always in the European Cup, they'll get their kit from Adidas, or Puma – but the rest, it's a real problem, because the supply line from the Soviet Union's stopped. So we come back here, we go to Hi-tec, Nike, Umbro – we say, best rates please . . .'

Later he said, 'I particularly enjoy working with the Poles – taking them out of a lifestyle which has been very hard, taking them into a more affluent Western Europe. Just seeing their eyes light up when they walk past Woolworths, you know, all those things they can buy – that's been a particular delight. We're now talking with the Soviet Union . . .'

*

I don't know if he talked to any Czechs – they weren't a bad side, after all, quarter-finalists in the end – but on 25 April Paul Gascoigne made them look like damaged goods.

At the back, Robson gave Arsenal's Lee Dixon his début. With Barnes and Waddle unavailable, he gave Trevor Steven and Steve Hodge a run-out down the flanks. Up front, he had another look at Bull and Lineker. At half-time, he put Seaman in goal for Shilton – he would have tried Woods again, but, fiddling with his tracksuit waistband, he'd cut a finger open with a penknife the day before. In the defence, he took off Walker and Pearce for Wright and Dorigo; and, after seventy-five minutes, he let McMahon take over from Bryan Robson in the middle. But by then, Gascoigne was running the show anyway. He was, quite simply, breathtaking.

This wasn't Italy or Brazil, and only a little over 20,000 came. So if you stayed at home, let me tell you – you missed out.

The Czechoslovakian anthem's stirring, film score material – the kind of music where the lone pilot walks back to his girl through the heat haze on the desert runway from his burning plane . . . but my enjoyment of it was abruptly stomped on by an unbelievably rude little pillock from Wembley security – tinted specs and walkie talkie, a right Joe 90. I was standing by the bench where I usually did when games were about to kick off, talking to BSB folk and others – and he came barking and snapping at me like a dachsund. Apparently, standing just there was a major league offence, not that it had been at the last two matches – and who did I think I was?

So I told him.

A book? Don't get lippy with me, mate . . . funny, isn't it? Some people, you give them a badge and a two-way radio, next thing you know they're Genghis Khan.

Robson had told me I should sit on the bench because 'you see a different game down there. When you're close to the pitch you'll be amazed at the pace of the game and the power, the physical contact. Up there (in the press box) you don't see it all, you can think, oh, it's a game of poetry and space – but down there, it's frenetic. It's frightening.'

I saw what he meant when Pearce took an ugly, full-speed, clattering lunge into Dragan Stojkovic's legs in the Yugoslavia game, on the touchline right under our noses – you could hear the bones crash and jolt, you could hear the breath punched out, the body wrenched and thudding on the turf . . . Robson called the tackle 'reckless'.

In three previous visits, the Czechs had never scored at Wembley – after eleven minutes, they put that right. Tomas Skuhravy, one of six Sparta Prague players who went to Italy (and who scored five times there), put a header past Shilton. They'd started well – unlike Gascoigne who, after two unduly fierce tackles, had to be told by the referee to calm down. But then, he was so coiled up over this game – in the tunnel beforehand, he nearly decapitated me, bouncing a ball off the wall bare inches from my head with a really manic aggression. Because he knew – this was his ticket to Italy tonight.

In the seventeenth minute, he played a pass fully forty yards, bang on the nail. It was one of those lovely things you watch this game for – the kind of pass you can't learn but that's born of pure instinct, that speaks vision and precision, and the most immaculate control. Steve Bull was roaring clear of his marker on the edge of the area, and the ball fell like it was guided by computer, just exactly where he needed it. Barely breaking stride, he chested it down in front of him, waited for the bounce, and then battered it in the net like he wanted it coming out the other side and setting off into orbit.

It was the kind of goal where you know, the man had no complication in his mind, no doubt in his soul – that ball was going in.

Seven minutes later, Gascoigne dropped a corner into the heart of the Czech goalmouth, Butcher headed on, and Stuart Pearce bundled through to thump it in. The flipside of reckless, after all, is fearless. Bloomfield looked thoroughly pleased with himself – he'd written in the programme notes, 'It cannot be long before Stuart scores for England.'

England had it by the neck now. At half-time I picked another run-in with Joe 90 – on the grounds that security folk ought to learn a thing or two about customer relations like everyone else – then I went up to the press box to get an overview on things. After all, with Gascoigne on song, the game really does have space and poetry. He was picking up where he'd left off, spraying inch-perfect passes about as easy as walking the dog. And the more he did, the better he got. In the fifty-sixth minute he set off with the ball at his feet, left two men standing stock-still behind him like he was a ghost and they'd never seen him, then landed a cross on Bull's head like a dart in the triple twenty. 3–1.

After that, it was all England. Gazza was trying it on all over the park; the Czechs were losing interest. Bull missed a couple of chances – but it was surely sewn up. So towards the end, I set off back towards pitchside, through the labyrinth of bare and echoing stairways – and emerged from the tunnel just in time to see Fiorentina's Lubos Kubik make it 3–2 with a curling free-kick. Ay-ay . . . I stood transfixed for the last ten minutes in the mouth of the tunnel as England poured forward, and the Czechs, revived, tried hard to pour back.

Lineker, tackled on the edge of the box, dived and fell, hands out and sliding over the turf. The steward beside me grumbled, 'He learnt *that* in Spain.'

Bloomfield said, 'If he was fouled as often as it looks like he's fouled, he wouldn't be about. He'd be knackered.' Gary Lineker, Euro-man – there was some banter about the boy picking up dirty suspect foreign habits . . . until they were silenced abruptly by Gascoigne. In the last minute, he decided that since he'd made three for the others, it was time he got one for himself before the whistle went. In a wide position, Dorigo gave him the ball, and he set off – like, this is mine, and I know where I'm going. He cut in, danced round a defender on the edge of the area, left him for dead, then wellied it in the roof of the net. The keeper never had a chance. It was fast, it was bold – it was inimitable.

Robson said afterwards that the boy's socks were down, he had cramp, he'd been thinking of taking him off. Good job he didn't.

England 4, Czechoslovakia 2.

Sixteen games unbeaten.

That morning – presumably with the aid of Jon Smith, and the wallet of Robert Maxwell – Gazza'd appeared in full colour on the back of the *Mirror* in a clown suit.

Now, as he came off the pitch, the camera crews waiting for Robson asked if he'd do an interview, if he'd say something for the viewers. But he ducked and shoved past, saying only one thing.

He said, 'I hate the press.'

Why? Because they'd done a picture of him in a clown suit? Then don't put on the clown suit in the first place ... the cameramen tapped their heads and turned away.

But really, why? The press had been screaming to see him in an England shirt for a year.

And in the press conference they were asking Robson why, after a performance like tonight's, he'd not played the boy more often, and earlier. In other words, admit you were wrong.

Kirton stood at the back muttering, as the questions flew in, 'You don't have to answer that. You don't have to answer that.'

Robson said, 'I'm saying to you, you were clamouring for him a year ago, and he wasn't ready a year ago. I'm a football manager, I managed a club for fourteen years on the development of young players, I couldn't go out and buy people, not at Ipswich – so don't talk to me about developing young players. And all right, tonight he's passed the test – and they've done well at Tottenham, he's slimmer, fitter, he's matured, far better discipline ... but you're still not a player after one match.'

I asked Kirton what the press from other countries might think, about the way our boys hunt issues like this in a pack, taking turns to phrase and then rephrase the same question, round and round and over and over. He said it might look a bit hairy to the Czechs. 'But the Italians would think he gets off light. The way the press try to angle a story is probably the same all over the world – but I suppose for intensity, we're near the top. The Germans are worse. Maybe the Spanish.'

Robson was talking about how England hadn't been given a penalty in four years or more – because tonight, Bryan Robson had been denied a certain penalty, an unanswerable penalty. 'The guy's ripping half his arm off. But he's honest, isn't he? He knows he's being impeded, and he still goes on and tries to score. What d'you think Vialli would have done?'

He banged his palm down flat on the tabletop.

'He'd have fallen over, right?'

I got back from Rome on 14 May and interviewed Bert

Millichip the next morning. England were playing Denmark that night.

Millichip – known among the fans as Bert the Inert – is Chairman of the FA. And he knew, that morning when we talked, that PSV Eindhoven had already approached Bobby Robson with a job offer – he knew the discussions were under way. With hindsight, that lends the conversation a good gallon of poignant spice.

I started by asking him how old he was. He said, 'I will tell you, but I don't want it advertised. I'm seventy-five years of age.'

Later, I raised Wragg's remark that Robson had the FA's absolute support.

'Obviously. Otherwise he wouldn't be there now. Especially after certain things . . .'

And his contract runs to 1991.

'I'm not going to talk to you about Bobby Robson's contract. And I'd hope you'd not raise that question with anybody else at the Football Association.'

We talked about the nature of the job.

'One needs to be brought into the job very gradually. Certainly it is something that would exercise my mind, if I am personally involved, at any time when we're thinking about changing the managership. I would like to think that we could give someone a good time to let him learn what the job was all about, before he was actually pitched in.'

Then he talked about the difficulties of player availability, about injuries, about the time between matches, and about discipline.

Was Graham Taylor pitched in, or what?

To be fair, he also talked about the delicate problems that would be posed for the incumbent, if you did have a successor appointed to play himself in under the existing man's eye. Either way, he said, it wasn't easy.

But they'd not made it any easier, had they? – when their absolute support for Robson included indicating to him that his contract was most unlikely to be extended.

I said I'd ask one more question on the issue. If we were to be successful in Italy . . .

He said, 'I'm not making any comment about Bobby Robson, and the managership of the England team. It's dynamite at the moment.'

I said the book wouldn't be out until October, minimum.

'Put your question again.'

If we were to be successful in Italy – semi-finals, say – would the FA consider extending the contract beyond 1991?

'Bobby Robson's got a contract which extends for twelve months beyond the World Cup. It was done for a specific purpose, by me. I did not want Bobby Robson – or whoever it might be – going into the World Cup knowing that his contract was finished, and that we'd not be talking about a new contract before we saw how they got on. It would have been an invidious situation. So he knows he's safe.'

When Robson told them of the PSV approach, he was allowed to understand that he was going into the World Cup with a contract that would not be renewed. Safe?

Millichip talked about circumstances in which Robson himself might decide to go – be that winning in Rome, or losing in Sardinia. Naturally, he did not suggest the circumstance of being offered a job in Holland.

But then Millichip was, here, in an invidious situation himself. Everything he'd just said, knowing what he knew, was piss in the wind.

It's no way to run a railroad, is it?

I wondered idly, at this point, how old Robson now was – fifty-seven, wasn't that right?

'Just under sixty, yes . . . I do believe that probably sixty is a very good retiring age for a man in that situation, I would say sixty is right. And indeed, sixty is an age that we place upon our coaches. So it's unlike a person in an administrative job, going on to the age of sixty-five.' At which point, presumably remembering his own age, he became a little discomposed. He said Bobby Robson was a young man yet.

Ah well. Guy Thys, the newly recalled Belgian manager, was sixty-seven – and he did all right.

That morning I had a meeting booked in with Graham Kelly as well, the FA's Chief Executive. But he and Millichip had to go off somewhere so we agreed to re-arrange it.

Denmark was the game in which, Butcher told me, he'd been 'shitting himself'. Robson played what then looked to be his first choice defence – Stevens, Walker, Butcher, Pearce – with

Barnes up front beside Lineker, and Hodge and Waddle on the wings. McMahon and Gascoigne were in the middle – and they were overrun.

As the Danes spilt forward – playing 3–5–2 – and the English fell back, leaving Barnes and Lineker often stranded and impotent, a group of Wolverhampton fans a couple of yards away through the wire left the bench in no doubt of what they reckoned would solve this dire situation.

> *We love you, Bully, we do*
> *We love you, Bully, we do*
>
> *Stevie Bull – must go to I-taly*
> *Stevie Bull – must go to I-taly*
>
> *Woolly Bully – ooh*
> *Woolly Bully – ooh*

Bull sat on the bench looking down, snatching a glance at them now and then – he looked hideously embarrassed. When Robson came down from the VIP box for the second half, the meanest-looking bloke among these fans came to press his face against the fence, and loudly announced, 'You'll never win the World Cup with this lot.'

But the second half was, mercifully, more even-handed – and after fifty-five minutes, Lineker scored his thirty-first goal for England. On the bench, Robson talked close into his substitutes' faces, sending them on with fierce, urging exhortations. To Platt he said, 'Work, work, cover, cover,' like a man consumed – but with five English and two Danish substitutions, the game was crumbling into a bit of a practice session. The edge was off it – though Woods, who'd gone on for Shilton at half-time, made an outstanding save in the dying minutes to preserve England's lead.

England 1, Denmark 0 – and the run was now seventeen games unbeaten.

England's record run of unbeaten matches stood at nineteen – a record achieved by the side that won the World Cup in '66. And now, as each of these last friendlies at Wembley went by, that looming record was, very definitely, beginning to weigh on people's minds.

So also, raised again by the fast and fluent Danes, were all the old doubts.

Barclay wrote in The *Independent*: 'One tires of saying it, but to play with a back four like England is to leave the midfield hopelessly outnumbered against sides like Denmark who play 3–5–2 . . . Robson, asked if in the World Cup England could cope with such a formation, which is bound to be prevalent, admitted that the Danes "tended to have an awful lot of players to spare".'

In the bar afterwards, Butcher said the Danes had been brilliant. 'They were such good runners, so fast – the two forwards pulled us wide, the midfielders came through . . . some game.'

Then Gazza went by, and whacked him in the back as he passed – one of the boy's little habits. I asked, didn't he ever get on your nerves?

'Nah,' said Butcher, 'he's a good laugh, you get used to him. Mind you, Woodsy's gonna twat him one of these days.'

Butcher hadn't gone on Rangers' championship-winning celebration jaunt to Marbella – one Spitfire that didn't have to go down in flames after all – but Gary Stevens had. It was, he said, 'A bit heavy. It rained for three days. We had to take shelter.' He looked significantly at his beer, grinning.

Trevor Steven said he had six days to wait, before finding out if he was going to Italy or not. 'I'll be heartbroken if it's no. You could say, it's agony waiting – but I'd rather be here in contention and have the agony, than not be here at all.'

At the bar, Gazza was raving about how he'd 'never talk to the press again in my whole career, not TV, not radio – the slaughter I've had in the last two years, me, my family . . .'

Actually, this is bollocks – firstly because it just is, the 'slaughter' being next to nothing compared to what others have endured in longer careers. And secondly, because when Jon Smith came along bearing cheques – Gazza talked all right.

It was, I think, just a kind of learnt behaviour – he'd seen the older players' wariness, and simplified it Gazza-style into an extreme and excitable statement. He was, after all, only twenty-two – and he is, also, in Robson's half-affectionate phrase, 'daft as a brush'.

He said, when the President of the Danish FA was presented to him in the line before the game, he said hello. 'So the

Danish bloke says, hullooo, Danish-like. So I say, how's your family?' He cackled.

I think proving the big occasion doesn't phase him is a bit important to Paul Gascoigne.

I told how I'd been at a press conference with Maradona six days earlier, in Rome, and I said how short the man was – I gestured with my hand, chest high.

'Nah,' said Gazza, 'that'd be his wallet you're measuring, right?'

Then he asked, 'Is it true he won't play for his country if he doesn't get paid? That's unbelievable, that is.'

At some point amid all this I'd seen Graham Kelly drifting by – a cross between a blancmange and a container ship. I went over to re-arrange our meeting, but he said he'd decided he didn't want to talk to me because I'd been going round just 'picking off council members'.

The FA's unwieldy governing body may well have ninety-two members – some so ancient that the front row's called 'death row' – but, as I pointed out, seeing the Chairman (Millichip), and the Chairman of the International Committee (Wragg), hardly amounted to just picking them off at random.

He was miffed, I think, that I'd not come to him first, the Chief Executive. And now he was unwilling to talk because, he said, he might contradict something that Millichip had said. It's a pretty sorry excuse – if politics worked that way, after all, we'd live in a house of silence.

He also said – as loftily as his squidgily hesitant manner would allow – that since I'd not started with him, I obviously didn't understand the workings of the FA.

On that, he's right. Who does?

Bloomfield once said that, handling some issue or other, the FA had 'glided into action'. Then he smiled and said, 'Well, no – the FA doesn't glide. We sort of . . . clunk.'

There was, of course, no reason on earth why Graham Kelly should talk to me – other than that he'd agreed to. Still, when he not only had the World Cup imminent – the squad were leaving in ten days' time – but also his manager talking (with his and Millichips' permission) to PSV into the bargain.

And he'd have known, from Millichip, that I'd be asking him questions that would touch on that.

But he's not paid to have an easy life, is he?

And his decision not to talk to me, and the feeble reasons for it, leave me, I'm afraid, unable to report anything about the man other than that – unlike Paul Gascoigne – he appears to be a complete charisma bypass.

It wasn't only journalists who had doubts and fears about the way England played their football.

Chris Waddle had a terrible game against the Danish – he was virtually invisible – and he knew it. 'I played crap tonight, OK – but I'm tired. We just won the French League, we won it Saturday – I don't know how many games I've played, but I'm tired. It takes three or four days to get over a game – give me a few more, I'll be fresh as a lamb. For Uruguay I'll be fine.

'But also, see, the game here's so different. In France I'm an attacker, they know that. Here I'm running up and down, up and down, defend, attack, defend, attack – I'm shattered. And the papers, three games they've been saying I'm world class – I know tomorrow they'll slaughter me. [McIlvanney next Sunday said he was 'so catatonic that practically every touch produced an error']. They're so *fickle*. And what do they know? Have you ever seen journalists playing football? It's embarrassing. To say they've got two left feet is being kind. What do they know? What do they know about the problems players have?'

He then came up briefly with the notion that players should write the match reports – until he remembered Emlyn Hughes, who's now a one-man slag-it-off-if-it-moves industry – and he backed off from what is, let's face it, a ridiculous idea.

Because writing those reports really isn't too easy. They say, when you've been doing it twenty years, it's like riding a bike – but it's still impressive, seeing the ranks of bleary men tap-tapping away on their lap-tops as the stadium empties, filing the stipulated x hundred words within ten or twenty minutes of the whistle – because I know, I tried it myself a few times. I tried to write accurate accounts of a game or two that quickly – and most of what I came up with was dogshit.

123

Whether Waddle could write about it or not I don't know –
but when he talks about it, he generally makes good sense. He
said, in France, every player in every position was, in effect, a
'converted midfielder'. He said they all learn technique first,
that finding their position comes later – so everyone's got
skill, from the back to the front.

'But you can't change English football, you'll never change
it. You'd have to start right back in the schools, right back at
youth level – how would you do it? It'd be like throwing a
sponge at a wall.'

After a rocky beginning he was loving it in Marseilles – and
not just because the League title there was the first medal he'd
won since promotion with Newcastle. He talked about the
way the game was played there like a man who'd passed
through a magic door into a land of bright light. He said, with
a smile and a little faraway look, 'I hardly ever have to head
the ball any more.'

At Marseilles, Waddle was playing alongside the Uruguayan,
Francescoli. And he said he'd be warning his England team-
mates about this man when it came to the game next week.
'He's brilliant when it's tight. You should always stay a bit off
him – or he'll roll you and be gone.'

On 21 May Robson named his squad. At Burnham Beeches
there were more press than ever; packed in the foyer, crunching
on the gravel drive and milling round the lawn. There must
have been a hundred of them. Walking in from the coach after
training, Lineker made his private, eyes-rolled-to-heaven face.
He mock-stumbled through the cameras and dictaphones.

Robson asked them to leave the skipper alone; he had a
sore heel after the Cup Final. 'Don't go chasing him. I'm
telling you – that's sufficient.' He was keen to play against
Uruguay, 'Mustard keen – but if it isn't better we won't play
him.'

Then the photocopied sheets were handed out, with the
twenty-two names. Of the twenty-six players he had there
in Berkshire, Robson had left out the Chelsea keeper Dave
Beasant, and the three Arsenal players Adams, Smith and
Rocastle. They were, he said, 'Very disappointed – but they
took it like men, and wished us good luck.'

Mark Wright was picked over Adams – but there was doubt about a bruised thigh that had kept him out of training for two weeks. He'd left the hotel at 6.45 that morning ('a nice surprise for him') to go into London for an X-ray and a scan – the results were promising. 'I've explained this to Tony Adams – the decision is made in terms of the player.'

So how did he separate them?

'I have to make a decision. I don't have to say why.'

Was it the strongest squad in his career?

'On paper. We had a strong squad going to Germany in '88, I think we'd lost one in sixteen – but we didn't have Butcher, and Waddle and Lineker weren't really fit. So yes, arguably, it's the strongest squad we've had. We've not had to leave anybody behind for injuries – only on selection. It was either or, either or – Wright or Adams, Bull or Smith . . . the mix is good. And the nucleus has always been there, it's strong, it's mature – it's getting older, but it's quality.'

He felt, he said, particularly sorry for David Rocastle – he'd played in all but one of the qualifiers. 'Poor old Rocky – six months ago he was a certainty. Then he has an injury, his form goes off – and Trevor Steven's a campaigner, he's had a good season. Rocky's time will come, it'll be America for Rocky . . . but they're all unfortunate. Adams came into the side four years ago, played in Spain when we won, what, 4–2? He looked like he'd be a real nugget for us. And he is, he *is* – so it's a tough pill to swallow. But time's on their side, and him and Rocky, four years from now, they'll be leading England players. Not that that's much consolation.'

And the journalists pored over the twenty-two names. Which eleven would go out against Ireland? Desperate for some chink of light into Robson's thinking, they scoured the photocopied runes – like witches with tea leaves, they swilled round the numbers ascribed to each player, and tried to see into the future. The first eleven on the list looked a plausible side, all senior names. Why was Gascoigne at nineteen? Did that mean he wouldn't play?

'It's a number on a list. Gascoigne's nineteen. He'll play at nineteen. If he plays. I'm not prepared to talk about one, and make another look less good. They've all been terrific boys for us. There are no moaners. I'm not taking anyone who'll moan if they're left out.'

Steve Curry from the *Express* asked how important it was that they all got on.

'Crucial. Crucial. They're away for six weeks . . .'

A guy from the *Sun* said, 'Bit like us, Steve.'

Quick as a whip Robson shot back, 'You don't have to get results. You don't have to rely on each other. My lads do.'

In the afternoon the players did more modelling – it was Savile Row sunglasses this time, and they each got a monogrammed pair. Butcher said, 'All this is alien to a footballer really. You just want to train, eat, sleep, play.'

On the lawn there were kids running round – little teeny kids, not more than eight or ten years old. They were 'Soccer Stars', part of the FA's youth development programme – sponsored (like the World Cup) by Coca-Cola. They wore a red Coca-Cola strip; they turned and slalomed nippily back and forth between plastic markers on the grass, holding the ball at their feet with obvious talent, and obvious pleasure. Butcher laughed, 'I couldn't do any of that. I was happy if I could just kick it fifty yards.'

Egypt – England's third and last opponent in the first round in Cagliari – had just gone to Aberdeen, played beautifully, and thrashed Scotland 3–1. McIlvanney said of his country's team that they were 'worse than pathetic . . . there hangs around their football the dank, depressing odour of basic inadequacy'. Afterwards, one of the Egyptian strikers had promised he'd roast Terry Butcher.

'We'll see about that.'

He had trouble controlling his excitement – he was like a big kid again. 'I can't believe it. It's my third, but I still can't believe it. Just feel like I want to go out . . . ooh. Just great. And for the lads picked first time – I know how that feels.' He remembered the Nou Camp in Spain, the Azteca in Mexico. 'They're both something. You come out and there's just . . . *walls of people.*'

On the gravel drive a minute later, I was talking with Chris Waddle; Peter Beardsley backed his Mercedes slow past us, taking it to Wembley so he could get away after the game. With a look on his face like a little kid acting innocent, Gazza opened the car door as it passed. Just a few inches. Beardsley noticed, stopped, and told him quietly, 'You're a fucking wanker, aren't you?'

In reception, Waddle went to talk with Michelle Rogers – she was arranging all the players' insurance, all the bits and bobs of paperwork that go with shipping twenty-two expensive properties to Italy for six weeks. Gazza was still with us. He tends to stick around Waddle, they're both Newcastle boys, and they room together – one of the reasons Gazza went to Spurs was because Waddle was there. Other players said he was really cut up when Marseilles took Waddle away.

The phone rang at the desk and the girl there called over, 'Michelle, can I talk to Paul, please?'

'Sure,' she laughed. 'I don't want to talk to him.'

Waddle said with Gazza it was non-stop, non-stop. 'Now he wants to go down in the basement and play headers in the pool. I don't know where he gets the energy. But then you put him in front of a paper or the telly, five minutes, and he's out like a light. Then he's awake, boom, and off he goes again. I dunno what he'll be like when he's older – he won't be able to keep it up. Except he'll probably think he can – in his head he won't change. Maybe then he might have problems ... I suppose I better go see what he's up to.'

Michelle said Waddle was Gazza's babysitter.

They can be a lordly lot, the English sports press. There were men among them that I liked – Colin Malam from the *Telegraph* springs to mind as a pleasant, moderate, and intelligent man – but with few exceptions, I don't recall any of them ever being wrong about anything.

In the stand at Wembley, Bob Harris magnanimously informed me that I was 'all right'.

It was a shame, he said, that I'd 'got off on the wrong foot'. My crime had been to ask a question at a press conference. It was when Robson announced his squad before the Italy game in November – they were taking turns to press him on who he'd picked and who he hadn't, and whether this man or that man would be playing. To be fair, for their sins, that's their job – but Robson really dislikes explaining or justifying his team selections, above all beforehand.

There'd been, someone said, a lot of hype about Kerry Dixon.

'Where? By whom?' (On another occasion, when someone mentioned public opinion, Robson tartly told them not to confuse public opinion with press opinion.)

'Well . . . was Dixon considered?'

'I considered everyone.'

After a while, bored of this, I asked Robson if he'd enjoyed the Italy–Brazil game he'd gone to see.

'Nice change of subject.'

Later, Bloomfield said they'd complained to him about me. I'd 'interrupted their flow'.

I kept quiet after that, and let them get on with it. And now, said Harris, I was 'all right'.

He's a loud Brummie who wears luminous and amazing blazers, and owns some lunatic quantity of pairs of glasses, sixty or seventy – one pair in particular I remember, the frames every colour of the rainbow and then some, and sort of spangly with it, with BH monogrammed in silver on one tinted lens . . .

On the pitch the band marched about, limbering up for the Uruguayan anthem – another magnificent-men-in-their-flying-machines affair. Gazza went out with the fizzy tooth-rot marketing men to make a pre-match presentation to a Soccer Star kid, and, fooling about, tried to trip a TV cameraman – setting an example to the nation's youth there, Paul.

In the stand, Harris nobly presented me with a plastic freebie case from some journalists' lunchtime bunfight. 'They're magnificent pens,' he said.

It was a bottom-of-the-range Parker biro, with a Barclays Bank logo on it.

So nice to be accepted.

Harris said Gazza'd asked him after the Denmark game how he reckoned he'd done. Ay-ay, thinks Harris, he's not spoken to me in ages. 'You did all right,' says Harris, 'just keep it going.'

'You're a fucking cunt,' says Gazza, 'and I'm not talking to you ever again.'

But you love to watch him. You never know what he'll do next. He takes the ball and surges forward on those dancing runs for goal . . . and a Uruguayan brings him down. Will he clout the guy? Or will he get up and shake his hand, pat his face and ruffle his hair, then embrace the referee?

We started out looking good against Uruguay. Parker was playing for Gary Stevens's place, and setting off down the right with pace and purpose. Pearce was doing the same down the left; Hodge was busy, Gazza was everywhere. Pearce forced a spectacular save from a searing free kick ... then, in the twenty-seventh minute, Francescoli broke through the middle, and set Alzamendi free on the left. As his cross came in Shilton advanced uncertainly, neither coming out for the ball, nor staying on his line. Ostolaza, unmarked, met it sweetly with his head, and looped it over the stranded keeper into the net.

They were all over us for a while after that, awash with skill. Their defenders brought the ball out at their feet past Barnes and Lineker, back-heeling, turning people – at one point one of them just put his foot on the ball and waited, then rolled it out of the way as the tackle flew in, and the tackler found nothing but air, and then, while the Englishman slithered away behind him headed nowhere, he looked up and, click: the sudden killing pass over the heads of the defence again.

A lot of games had felt like this, England always surging, surging, while the other lot looked lackadaisical, just strolling about – until suddenly they'd break and be haring forward all over the place, and what you thought was a sturdy castle was just a house of cards, pierced by stilettos every which way, torn and holed and tumbling down. There was a lovely moment where one of their men, running forward, found the ball arriving fast at his ankles behind him, so, still running, he flicked it up and over his head and on to another man off the back of his feet – and, it seemed, he barely broke stride in the whole smooth and sweet movement.

But England went back out and took the second half by the throat. They immediately won three corners, one of which, flicked on, was only barely tipped over – then Bryan Robson thundered through three men and was denied another penalty when they brought him down.

> *The ref-uh-ree's a wanker*
> *The ref-uh-ree's a wanker*

And Gascoigne did it again. Six minutes into the half he

played a perfectly weighted ball forty yards out to Pearce on the left. Pearce's cross came in on the button – Barnes at full speed brought it down off his chest, and struck it first time from the edge of the area. It was, like Bull's first goal against the Czechs, both beautiful and ferocious – it had power, it had grace, it took only a few seconds, pass, cross, strike and you're out of your seat and screaming.

England now were everywhere, Barnes slipping past them at will, Pearce and Parker racing forward, Walker and Butcher mopping up behind them when we lost it, setting things off into motion again . . . then, in the sixty-second minute, Perdomo took a free-kick thirty yards out. It dipped and swerved round the wall – Shilton, diving, watched the ball fly in off his hands.

England 1, Uruguay 2. The end of the unbeaten run. And the first defeat at Wembley in six years.

The journos tap-tapped on their portables in the press box; the keys rustled and clacked, a sound like the scurry and whisper of mice. The man from *The Times* sipped liquor from a hip flask, and passed it along. The sound system played some dreary pulp muzak, violins and guitars, a horrid, sad sort of slop that sounded like it was far, far away in the vast and hollow spaces of the empty stadium. The last few stray fans drifted away, dots in the great red and blue banks of seating. A crocodile of disabled spectators in wheelchairs rolled round the sandtrack past the pitchside hoardings – Ladbrokes, Superglue, Smirnoff, Mornflake Oats, Barclaycard, Alcan Bacofoil. Stewards and police in yellow jackets stood in knots by the featureless bleak gleam of the pitch, under the harsh brilliance of the floodlights. And the electronic scoreboards ran travel information for people who were, already, long gone and travelled; it said, 'Congratulations Uruguay. Well Played England'. It was the first time I'd seen England lose.

Well – the Uruguayan keeper made a couple of fine and brave saves. We were better than we'd been against Denmark.

But what about Shilton? He should never have stranded himself between Ostolaza and goal. And he should surely have seen Perdomo's free-kick – it should never have left him groping that way. Seven months on from Katowice, had Peter Shilton lost it?

And all the doubts and fears remained – even if Gascoigne had been as good again as ever. 'After a performance like that,' said Robson, 'how can I leave him out?'

Lineker said afterwards that Uruguay were 'all very nicey-nicey, but no punch'. Meeting them again come the real thing wouldn't worry him – and, he said, it was no bad thing, to have the business of chasing the record run off their backs. They hadn't got it, and that was that. It would have been a whole lot worse, after all, to see the sequence get broken by the Irish in three weeks' time.

He said, 'We didn't play badly tonight. We gave away two soft goals – Shilts doesn't normally let 'em in from thirty yards.' He wasn't sure that the Bryan Robson thing was really a penalty – but he said Barnes should certainly have had one, first half. He got shoved in the back at the near post on a corner . . . but there you go. 'We don't get penalties, do we?'

Then he asked if I'd seen the *Sun* that morning. They'd run a story about Rocastle:

I'M * * * * * * OFF!

The story was trash – Rocastle had never spoken to anyone, he'd just packed and quietly left. 'Arsenal Star Storms Out Of England HQ'.

'Scandalous,' said Lineker, with a small weary smile, and a shake of the head. 'Scandalous.'

There was far worse to come.

At the European Cup Final between AC Milan and Benfica the next night, English journalists learnt from Dutch journalists about Robson going to PSV Eindhoven.

The tabloids started, groundlessly, to connect the resignation to the threat of a book in the offing from one of Robson's alleged mistresses. (What on earth would she write about?) A press conference was hastily called, came close to being turned into a riot by photographers crowding cameras in Robson's face, and then proceeded shambolically and angrily to its sorry conclusion. And how they loved it.

I QUIT! RAGING ROBSON BLASTS SMEARS

I'M OFF BEFORE I GET SACKED

ROBSON SELLS OUT FOR A POT OF GOLD

PSV OFF BUNGLER BOBBY

The full-time football writers, by and large, gave him fair and decent tribute. The hatchet work went to others.

John Sadler, the *Sun*: 'Robson should not have been appointed in the first place ... whatever happens he'll come out of it all smelling of guilders.'

James Lawton, the *Express*: 'He has taken his thirty pieces of silver before a ball is even kicked ... what is really monstrous is the level of FA loyalty Robson has spurned ... English football has rarely been sold so short.'

And on, and on ...

What was really monstrous was the level of incompetence on display from the poor puddinghead Kelly and his septuagenarian sidekicks. Everyone knew Beckenbauer was leaving the German job – no problem. Everyone knew Lazaroni was quitting Brazil for Fiorentina – no problem. So how come we got in such a pig-awful mess?

And what was even more monstrous was the scurrilous bile and innuendo poured out in loutish newspapers by men some of whose fidelity to their own marriage contracts is, at best, questionable – and who would, if a better-paid job came their way, jump into it without a second thought.

Robson had been offered a job. When he told his employers, they gave him no assurance that the job he had with them would stay his. They gave him permission, instead, to pursue the Dutch offer – so where's the treachery in that?

His crime in all this was, characteristically, just terrible naivety – did he really think he could keep the thing quiet so many days? The trouble is, outside of football, he's simply not that astute or well-organised a man. And so what? No one's paying him to be Einstein, are they?

The whole business, in sum, was dismally modern-English – mismanaged and sloppy, noisy and oafish. Like everything about us – our schools, our hospitals, our railways, our government – it reeked of the people in charge being bereft of common sense or ideas, possessed only of the most complacent irresponsibility.

It reeked of a way of doing things that's tired and stupid – a whole way of thinking that's all played out.

Whether this would apply to the way we played football remained to be seen.

Glen Kirton said in Cagliari that Robson had told him, 'He felt the remarks the Chairman made to the press at the Zurich meeting in March had effectively put him on offer. PSV noted what the Chairman had said, and approached Bob. He then asked the Chairman for permission to talk to them, and the Chairman said yes, so he'd clearly got the message that there wasn't a job for him after the World Cup.'

Some of the coverage of the announcement of his departure had been, I said, iniquitous.

'Yes. But we dealt with it probably not as expertly as we might have done. Bob had made his mind up, and Graham Kelly wanted to make the announcement as quickly as possible, because he knew it would leak, as these things always do. On the other hand, the team were gathering on the Thursday night with their wives and travelling on the Friday. So you're going to be exposed to the media on the Thursday night, you're going to be exposed at Luton airport on the Friday morning, you're going to be exposed at Cagliari when you land – so we agreed that we'd try and keep it under wraps until after the weekend, until the first serious training session on the Monday. Bob would tell the players then . . . but we didn't get the chance. It broke on the Wednesday night.

'So we hurriedly called the press conference on the Thursday. And it was a shambles, because of the behaviour of the photographers – they wouldn't allow the people from the written press to see. They forced them out to the edge; Graham Kelly gave them five minutes, then asked them to stop, and they refused. With hindsight, I think he and Bob will agree, they did the wrong thing – they got up and walked away, which only gives them the photograph they want . . . but it was dealt with eventually. All the questions were answered – and the next day, there was some incredible vitriol . . . our day to day press contacts weren't involved, the sports writers, they were down here, it was the casuals, the news men – and I think Bob understood that. He's professional, he goes on.

'But it certainly affected . . . I wouldn't say it's changed his attitude to newspapers in general, because we've conceived our opinions of certain areas of the press over a period of time. But one or two papers, I think, have really hurt him deeply. The *Sun*, *Today* – the usual ones. And all that garbage about his personal life. The *Express* just did a regurgitation of the stories from a year ago, didn't it? The *News of the World* ran that story, full of innuendo, 'He has been associated with a blonde, a businesswoman, and a Dutchwoman'. I suppose if it was a blonde Dutch businesswoman there'd be one third as much to it . . . but he's ridden it. He's got his lawyers working on four or five different stories.'

On the eve of the Ireland game I said to Robson, some of the papers were grumbling that the players wouldn't talk to them.

'Don't blame them. They want everything, the papers. Give nothing back. Don't blame them.'

Because of the way the papers had been behaving?

'Is this for the book? Well – I think they moan about nothing. I mean, they're so demanding, they're insatiable. We're here to play football – but they think the World Cup's for them. They actually think the World Cup is for the papers – they put their job before the game. Fuck 'em. I do a press conference every day, and they come sidling up to you, and the next day they turn you over.'

So I asked how he felt about what happened when his resignation was announced.

'They torpedoed the whole thing. I did that honestly and above board, with the approval of the Chairman and the Chief Executive. They gave me permission. So then we planned to do it properly, and tell the players first – and through their digging and scraping like they always do, they've run incorrect stories with no foundation, no truth. I didn't announce my resignation – they announced it. They wouldn't let me do it properly. They scuppered it. They weren't thinking about the effect on the team. Just selling papers.'

When had PSV approached him?

'Well, I'm not here . . . is this for the book? Not very long ago. After the papers printed a story where the Chairman said, win the World Cup or go. And I had a slight approach. I said, look, I'm under contract – we're qualified for the World Cup, I don't want to be talking about another job. Then I went to see Mr Millichip before the Denmark match, to try and clarify my position – and he couldn't guarantee anything. So I said, well, look, obviously, I need to know about my future, everybody does – and there was no guarantee. So I said, can I pursue that enquiry? And he said, yes, find out if you really want to go, find out what they're offering you – and if it's attractive, come back and tell me. So I did. In between the Denmark and the Uruguay match.'

And the shit hit the fan.

Back in March, Peter Beardsley had told me how he'd like to go into coaching – 'I love the game too much just to walk away from it.' But when I asked if he might become a manager, he said, 'No, I don't think I'd be strong enough. I'd have to be a coach – I'd have to be a yes-man, I think. I don't think I could take the pressures, dealing with the directors and all that – I couldn't do what this feller does, anyway.'

By 'this feller,' he meant Robson. He said, 'I'm surprised he's not in a box. With gold handles. Feller's just took so much stick it's unbelievable – but he comes back for more. And that's why we love him. Because he's never slagged us off, he always tries to defend us as much as he can. Sometimes he's defending us and he's cut his own throat. But that's the sort of man he is – he tries to be so fair to the players, when in the end it's down to us. He can't be out there kicking the ball for us, can he? If you've had a bad game, you look at yourself first, don't you?'

What other country in the world would send its players to the World Cup with a headline, WORLD CUP WALLIES?

There was one last extra stir to the stinking pot.

GAZZA BAR BRAWL

Three weeks later I was talking with Gazza and John Barnes at Is Molas, the hotel on Sardinia. Barnes said he'd just sued for ten grand from the *Mirror* for a story that had him signed, sealed and delivered to a club in Europe, when he was no such thing. Then he asked Gazza, was he going to do the papers for the story about him busting some guy's nose outside that Newcastle wine bar?

'Nah,' he laughed, chirpy Mr Puck. 'I whacked the cunt, didn't I?'

8   The Minnow Turns Pike

Argentina–Cameroon

'It may be that I am marking Maradona in the opening
match. We know all about him – but he doesn't know
anything about me.'

– Charles Ntamark, Cameroon

They knew about Maradona in Argentina when he was eleven.
He played in a side called *Los Cebollitas*, the Little Onions –
they were so good that Argentinos Juniors signed them up, *en
bloc*, to be one of their youth sides.

He was playing in the First Division by the time he was
fifteen; he first played for Argentina a year later, in 1977, as a
substitute against Hungary. Word that he'd be on the bench
filled the River Plate stadium.

Three times he broke the world record transfer fee. In 1979,
Boca Juniors in Buenos Aires bought him from Argentinos for
£1,000,000. In 1982, after the World Cup in Spain, Barcelona's
price was £3,000,000 – and after two seasons there, he went to
Napoli for £5,000,000. They've since won the Italian championship twice, when no side from the south had previously won it
for seventy-five years.

When he won the World Cup for his country before 115,000
people in the Azteca Stadium in Mexico City, the press in
Argentina said he was:

the omnipresent,
strong as a bull,
fast as a missile,
the star of the century,

passing like the air through narrow spaces –
in his veins doctors will not find blood, but rocket fuel.

You can talk about the others – Cruyff, Beckenbauer, Puskas, Garrincha, Bobby Charlton – and perhaps it's a meaningless debate. But most rational reckonings would set two great players above and beyond all others in this, the football century: Pele, and Maradona.

But what different men.

At the draw in December, one of the celebrities playing 'come on down' to the tacky extravagance of the television stage was Pele – now fifty years old, but still looking nearer thirty.

It was an extraordinary moment. Throughout the thousands of people in the Palazzo dello Sport – the musicians, the technicians, the TV people at their massed ranks of desks and monitors, the world's press and the politicians and the organisers, and in the gallery the hundreds of schoolkids wearing green, white, and red in three stadium-style blocks of colour, all whipped up in a gruesome cocktail of ersatz adrenalin and noise – throughout all these people, a quite different feeling very suddenly took hold.

Just for the moment, there was no element of calculation in the excitement; it was no longer manufactured, but, instantly, spontaneous and genuine. The new feeling – more overwhelming by far than all the riot of applause and pappy pop music that had gone before – was *love*.

Pele said, 'This makes me very happy, because this is the history of football. People love you, and I love you too.'

It is impossible to imagine Maradona drawing from any audience an equivalent surge of such heartfelt, yearning affection and respect. For pretty much everyone outside Argentina and Naples – and maybe, after Italia '90, for a fair few people in Naples as well – a grudging acknowledgement that the man can play football is about as far as it'd go.

Maradona's season kicked off in petulant farce. He said he'd not report back to Napoli for training from his holiday in Argentina because, 'I am convinced there is a plot against me, my wife, daughters, brothers and parents, which places us in real danger.' In a transatlantic communiqué he raved about threatening phone calls, about mysterious intruders in his and his family's houses, about his Mercedes being vandalised. 'As a man and a father I bear the responsibility of defending the greatest treasure I possess: my family.'

The police in Naples said sceptically that they'd started an inquiry. 'But frankly we don't think there's much to the idea of the Camorra getting at Maradona.'

Maradona was four hundred miles up the Rio Parana, in the little town of Esquina – fishing.

He was supposed to be in Naples by 16 August. Reports began to suggest that the 'tubby truant' (*Daily Telegraph*) had a weight problem akin to Marlon Brando's. Before he finally arrived on 4 September, he'd cancelled thirty-four flight bookings.

On 1 November Napoli's general manager sent Maradona home one hour before a second round UEFA Cup tie – he'd not been turning up for training sessions. He said, 'There's something behind this, there's no point hiding it. As I see it, this is the final rift.'

It wasn't – and by Christmas Napoli were four points clear at the top of the Italian League. But that wasn't really down to Maradona – looking overweight and slow, he had only six goals from sixteen games, three of them penalties.

Meanwhile, in December, he was rash enough to say in public what the rest of the world was wondering in private – that the draw was fixed. Of course he didn't see it the way other people did – while others wondered how Italy had got the easiest group, Maradona groused that with Russia, Romania, and Cameroon, the Argentinians had the hardest. Try telling that to Uruguay, Belgium, Spain, and South Korea in Group E . . . there were implausible rumbles from FIFA, not for the first time, about banning him from the World Cup. General secretary Sepp Blatter said, 'What he said was an idiocy beyond description. I don't know what to think – either he is stupid, or bad.'

Maradona said, 'All I did was say something a lot of people were thinking. I'm not repentant, but I'm ready to clarify my position if need be. If I have to say sorry, I will.'

And so it went on – gripes and grumbles and injuries.

He has, of course, been kicked from pillar to post all round the world by pretty much everyone. When he was younger and less experienced, he kicked back too. In Spain in '82, the Brazilians tormented him – journalists present said that when they sent on Batista as a substitute, the man had a blatant gleam in his eye, like, now it's my turn.

So, sure enough, he kicks Maradona. Maradona gets up, turns round, and boots him in the groin. When he comes out of his red mist, the ref's waving the red card . . .

Jon Smith was, he told me, 'very close to Diego'. He'd been at Ossie Ardiles's house in Hertfordshire a few years back, when Maradona had rung and asked Ardiles to take over as his agent. Ardiles said he'd love to, only he was still playing, and he couldn't be that man – but, he said, he knew a man who could. So Smith – by being, like Lineker, in the right place at the right time – scored what he called 'agency rights' in Diego Maradona.

In April Smith told me, 'He has a problem, no doubt. He's physically suffering, because of his back problems – he has large amounts of cortisone injected into him by his personal physicians, and as such . . . it's wrong to say he's not healthy, he's extremely healthy – but it's not a healthy situation, to have that amount of cortisone pumped into you. Makes you a bit of an irascible person.'

Cortisone is 'a glucocorticoid hormone, the synthetic form of which has been used in treating rheumatoid arthritis, allergic and skin diseases, leukaemia, etc'.

A doctor writes: with cortisone in big quantities, you're talking a seriously heavy drug. Cancer patients puff up, they get moon faces and, on their backs, a thing called 'buffalo hump'. While the short-term purpose of it for orthopaedic injuries is anti-inflammatory, in the long term it prevents the normal processes of healing – your joints fuse, your bones thin out. It also stunts your growth – and, used to excess, it can induce psychosis.

In other words, to keep the poor bastard playing, there's a doctor out there somewhere whose treatment risked turning Maradona into a fat, mad, immobilised dwarf. If it hadn't done so already . . .

In April Smith said, 'He has too many people around him, giving too much advice . . . Diego is under enormous pressure, as is any megastar. But if Paul McCartney throws a tantrum people say, oh well, he's a big rock star, that's the way they are. They don't say that with Diego Maradona. They say, little Argentinian twit's at it again ... mind you, he's playing very well again now – but he's expected to be one down from Jesus Christ, week in, week out. And that's a tough order.'

In Cagliari in June, Smith told me Maradona'd come off the cortisone in the spring. At Napoli, he played better and better – and they won the championship again.

Some muttered that he'd been getting himself in shape for the World Cup all along – that he only came good for his club *en route*, as it were, to defending his trophy. But I find that hard to believe. A man who needs thirty-five attempts to get on an aeroplane sounds too stupid to plan a wheeze that Machiavellian to me.

Months before the tournament, the Argentine manager Carlos Bilardo announced that he knew what his side would be: 'Maradona and ten others.'

On the afternoon of 9 May, after playing two uninspired 1–1 draws in Austria and Switzerland, the world champions arrived in Rome to go to their training base at Trigoria. They were not the first – Costa Rica had arrived the day before – but no one much turned out, said an Italia '90 girl sympathetically, to say hi to Costa Rica. (Of his squad's meagre ambitions, their crafty Yugoslavian coach said, 'One point minimum.')

To pass the arriving squads and their retinues smoothly and securely through the airport formalities, a piece of Fiumicino had been sealed off, turned for the duration into a kind of football Vatican – a small slice of territory belonging no longer to the state procedures of an international transit point, but occupying instead the alternative geography, the myth-zone of Planet Football. Squads arrived not in Italy, but in Italia '90 – logoland.

Surrounded by clusters of gun-toting *carabinieri* in the fenced-off parking area, a gleaming white Iveco bus (officially supplied) stood waiting; the classy graphic ident of the tournament, a stylised football broken out into a few clean curves of primary colour, was splashed discreetly along its side.

I got through the first knot of ID checkers at the gate, and was led by a steward round the unfinished back of a new plastic-box building, a kind of hi-tech portakabin. The steward apologised for the incomplete state of things – planks and drums lying about; bits of meshing strung round unsurfaced patches of rough concrete. In the land of the last minute, there was still a month to go.

In front of the airport, each time I'd come through since September, I'd seen taking shape the futuristic new metro line, lancing away towards the city. The last stretch of the bus ride out to the terminals runs parallel to the new track; it climbs elegantly in a sinuous curve up on to pillars, and sweeps over farmland and the approach roads into the raised airport station. The power lines suspend from an even-spaced chain of bright yellow hoops arched overhead, a ribcage of electricity hung along the spine of the track, shining against the hazy and featureless glare of the flat coastal horizon.

The station itself is a sci-fi hangar, an elliptical cylinder – it looks like a B-movie ray-gun cannon laid down flat on its stilts, to fire trains like projectiles towards the mother of cities. Glossy white new walkways reach out from it to the different airport buildings, striding the sky past the building work beneath and the jostling cars.

I asked the steward when they figured the new line would be running.

'It'll be finished,' he said happily, 'at the end of the month.'

Italian journalists flashed press cards at the door of the lunar-style conference cabin, flicking open their wallets like Hollywood detectives. They were a younger, better-dressed lot than the crumple-suited English crew I was used to – but no one from the English press was there.

The holders of the World Cup arrived in Italy, captained by one of the greatest players of the century – and no one from the English press was there.

For sure, you'd not expect them to fly specially to Rome just to hear Maradona and Bilardo say polite nothings at an airport – except the day before a number of them were in Rome already.

They were following Moynihan on a round of meetings with the Italian authorities – and hoolie news, of course, chills more blood and sells more papers than Diego Maradona. Outside the COL HQ after one meeting – at which Montezemolo was exceedingly polite about how welcome the English were – Jeff Powell told an Italian TV station to expect 'a co-ordinated army of villainous and violent men'.

Going just a bit far there, Jeff? Helping to create the very problem we all hoped to avoid?

Powell said it was no good the foreigner being polite all the time. They should be getting the guns and dogs out.

And who wants to know about the cheating dago anyhow?

You'd have thought *someone* might have shown ... an Italia '90 press officer said it was always the same. He said, 'Always the superiority complex, right? The rest of the world is rubbish.' He didn't say it impolitely – but he wasn't joking either.

A clutch of uniformed Italia '90 girls moved around the room as the media gathered. They looked like airline hostesses. When I asked one where I could get a soft drink, she was upset to realise that there was as yet no fridge, no Coke, no mineral water – she was profuse with apology. 'We're not ready,' she said, 'until 21 May.'

Never mind, they were ready enough. Six low black chairs sat facing fifty-six seats for the press over a broad and low black table; an eighteen-inch Ciao stood on either end of it. People stood about gabbing, under a 3-D ceiling of black metal struts arranged in an interlinking molecular design, a stellar structure laced through with shiny air-conditioning ducts. The grey plastic partition walls had a dull, textured sheen; and the obligatory World Cup house plants lurked in the corners.

Every Italia '90 place I went to had these mini-jungles of office plants. At the COL in Milan the day before, an eight-foot tall monster of a house plant (a house tree) actually keeled over and died on us, going down with a great thud halfway through a meeting. And this Pisa-inclined greenery played its part, everywhere, in the Italia '90 house style.

Every branch in every city had its designer-grey office carpets, and its designer-black office furniture; they all had their keyboards and their monitors, and their glossy prints on the walls of construction work at stadiums, or of the official Italia '90 poster, a green pitch set down into the Colosseum.

In short, Italia '90 (when it was at home) looked like nothing more nor less than an advertising agency ... welcome to logoland. Welcome to the land of King Sponsor.

Navratilova played tennis on TV – the Argentinians were due to land at 3.45. At 3.50, Montezemolo bundled briefly in and out of the room, saying hullo scattergun-style to whoever happened to be in front of him; a small, slight man looking careworn, with bags under reddened and watery eyes.

It had been said of him by Franco Carraro, the Socialist Party's minister for sport and tourism who appointed him, 'He's bound to have a nervous breakdown. After all, his predecessors in Spain and Mexico both did.'

And a woman who quit Italia '90 in '88 said, 'The pressure is insane ... he has three choices: slow down, take drugs, or crack up.'

The press officer was scuttling in and out too, not looking any more relaxed than his boss. He seemed permanently wide-eyed, darting glances every which way; he had a tic, an appealingly random way of blinking. He roamed through short spurts of conversation, waiting.

At 4.09 a line of photographers took some secret signal to hunker down at a matt grey side door. Four TV crews banked in beside them, mikes bobbing in the jostle and shove.

At 4.13, Maradona came through the door with Montezemolo and Bilardo, followed by a brace of goons from the Argentine FA. He was wearing, as the UPI man's report later fetchingly described it, 'a powder-blue warm-up suit'. He said Ciao, chewing gum; and disappeared behind the lensmen all fanning around him, as he moved behind the table to sit down.

Montezemolo gave a brief and careful speech of excruciating politeness. I sat there thinking that Carlos Bilardo must have the biggest nose in the known universe. I wondered if it came from having to explain the gibberish his captain came up with all the time.

And Maradona? He speaks of himself in the third person. About Mexico he said, 'Maradona was on great form, but Maradona alone cannot win.' Modesty, Maradona-style.

On 7 June I got up in Cagliari, like an idiot, at 5.20 in the morning for a 9.20 flight. Better, I suppose, than the other way around . . . first signs of confusion out in fantasy land. In the real world, Russia was disintegrating – but where the hell was the real world any more? Where I was, all that mattered about Russia was whether Protasov & Co. could get goals past the Romanians come Saturday afternoon.

Flying to Milan I found myself sat next to Roy Collins, the chief sports writer on *Today*. The English press pack were forty kilometres out of Cagliari in the Forte Village, a ghastly holiday complex like a vast version of *The Prisoner* – but Collins was in the Italia, across the road from my *pensione*. He liked, he said, to actually *be* in a country – not to get marooned in some luxury barrack. And he liked to try and learn a little bit of the language – as at the Seoul Olympics, where he'd learnt the Korean for the journalists' most import-ant phrase of all, one beer. 'Or, as they say in Korea, Beer one.'

We got to the press centre at the San Siro – and the transformation was remarkable. Where a month ago there'd been dust and tangled wiring, and unassembled furniture on polythene sheets, there were now counters for car hire, for train, plane, and hotel reservations; there were information, banking, and insurance services; there were post, telecom, and 'teleinformatic' desks, and a side-room with forty-odd phone booths; there was a conference centre; there was a bar, a cigarette kiosk, and – of course – there was a merchandise shop, selling T-shirts and caps and key rings, Ciao in all his myriad incarnations. And then there was a working area, throbbing with the low hum of many voices in many languages, and the clatter of fingertips at terminals and type-writers.

The place was finished – and it was heaving, just heaving. The queue for tickets and accreditation was as thick as the spiral pillars propping up the top tier of the stadium outside – and about as immobile as well.

One of the girls I'd met at the local COL a month earlier (echoes of Nottage's fears for the technology) said, 'We have so many problems with the software. The connections to Rome centre keep going down. Me, I didn't tell you anything, but I tell you this – I will never buy an Olivetti.'

Then she asked how things went in Cagliari, and I said fine,

fine, it was quiet enough. She said it was the Italian fans that worried her. 'I've seen the Fiorentina fans here at an Inter game, they are *so* violent – but also Juventus, Atalanta ... I think there'll be a tragedy. And you know how our police are ...'

Meanwhile, anyone who felt like it could have walked right in with a bomb in his bag. With your press pass you got a blank grey plastic card in a transparent sachet to hang round your neck; there were little security gates you were meant to walk through, and if the card was good and you were clean, the machine just went *blip*. But if the card was a dud, or you had detectable items in your bag or on your person, the machine went batshit and started frantically *blip-blip-blipping* like it was the four minute warning at Ground Zero.

Every other man or woman in the shovelling mêlée through the gates was setting them off; the press centre doorway was a constant noise overlaid of high-pitched and highly strung electronic gee-whizzery – and not one soul was stopped or searched.

The girl at the ticket desk was, she said, going crazy. She'd been there since 14 May – and only yesterday had Rome told them they could start issuing press tickets.

A German journalist next to me had seen his ticket coming off the printer at ten that morning – it was now 2.50 p.m. – and it had torn. For mysterious reasons, they were unable to give him a reprint.

'I will send a fax to Rome,' said the girl, trying hard to reassure him. I hadn't the heart to tell him that in my experience, an offer to send a fax at Italia '90 was a promise of certain death to your cause – an absolute assurance that you and your problem were to be dumped for good into the tournament's memory hole.

A bearded Italian sat feeding plastic sheets to Fuji machines at the accreditation desk next to me, singing quietly to himself, 'Still crazy after all of these years.'

The German was having a public blood pressure problem.

The girl told him, 'I'm really, really, really, really, really sorry.'

The German went into an orbit of apoplexy.

When it got to be my turn, I handed over the pass I'd collected from the Cagliari computers – and there was, on the Milan computers, no record of it. I'd ceased to exist.

I told her that was OK – I'd ceased to exist in Cagliari yesterday too. You get used to it, not existing.

I have, in my life, woken up to mortar fire in Central America, and been charged by an enraged black rhino in East Africa. Is waiting three hours for a ticket to a football game really so bad?

'No,' the girl said, issuing a new pass, 'if I were you I'd be really, really, really, really, really angry.'

I felt quite the opposite – my heart was filled with an enormous, a most wondrous sense of joy. I had in my hand, hot off the printer, a ticket to the opening game of the fourteenth World Cup. I was *a privileged being*.

I asked how we'd be getting tickets for the second round. 'You'll be given,' she said, 'a form like this – and when the groups are all finished on the 22nd, you'll fax it to Rome.'

What? All 6,000 of us? In fact, we were nearer 7,000 by then ... 7,000 faxes crashing in a simultaneous heap from twelve cities into the oblivion zone of Italian telecom. I must have given her the biggest grin she'd seen since she started back on 14 May.

I went to ring the friend I was staying with in the centre of town; I'd forgotten my diary, so I rang directory enquiries at the dreaded SIP, the rage factory that masquerades as a national telephone operation. 'SIP!' chirruped an unjustifiably cheerful recorded message; it told me I was in a queue, and would be answered in turn. I listened to this message for fifteen minutes, 'SIP! You are in a queue! SIP! You are in a queue! SIP! . . .' until my mental and spiritual health was in danger; then moseyed off to look into the freebie pack they'd given me.

At the draw back in December, the freebies had been so numerous and weighty – most notably, sixty quids' worth of lavish art book about Botticelli that was bigger than most respectable atlases – that the freebie bag they came in had fallen apart under the strain. Never mind – now I had another one. In it there was some weird literature from the Italian pharmacists' association, a FIFA map of the world – in the alternative geography of football, England came fifth in the all-time rankings after Brazil, West Germany, Italy and Argentina – and two media guides, one about the twenty-four participants, and another about hotels, restaurants, shops, museums and monuments in the twelve cities. As if I had time or money for any of that . . . I bet Cagliari will have been thrilled with the copywriting, too.

'The decay of the city is patent: plunder of the artistic patrimony, churches still closed after ten years for restoration work, an approximate management of what is left. For instance, the Museo del Duomo has been closed indefinitely after thieves emptied its Treasure two years ago; similarly bolted is the church of saints Cosma and Damiano . . .'

Makes you want to speed there post haste, doesn't it? I mean, hang on guys: I *liked* Cagliari . . . still, what else did we have? A pair of JVC headphones; Gillette shaving kit and playing cards; a hideous yellow FIFA 'Fair Play Please!' T-shirt and matching pen; a naff white sports shirt with a baby Ciao on the right tit; an ISL Marketing pen that started leaking in all directions within minutes of being used; two Mars bars and two packs of M&Ms, yum yum.

I realised, as I rootled in my goodie bag, that a TV briefing had started up around me. On the vexed question of car parking, an official dramatically announced, 'I only have fifty tickets for the whole world!' A team of scrambled-looking Hungarians meandered past. There were Koreans, Africans, Americans . . . I saw a bloke I knew from Capital Radio; he'd just been at the bank. I asked if he'd got his $500 deposit back yet.

He said, 'I haven't got my deposit back from Germany '88 yet.'

At six that evening Carlos Menem, the President of Argentina, was due to do a conference. In the conference area, stewards waged a constant and unseemly losing battle against photographers, trying to get them out of the 250 seats, and away to the aisles at the side. There were eleven TV crews on camera positions round the back; there was translation in five languages. Up on the dais there were five microphones on a long desk; above them, five monitors silently and inexplicably showed us the French Open Tennis, water polo, and bowls. At 6.35, Menem arrived in a small ruck of heavies and jowlies and adviser types – another small man with big problems.

Maradona kept him waiting fifteen minutes. But when

you're running a mess like Argentina, let's face it, you need Maradona plenty more than he needs you . . . Menem looked, in the famous phrase about Dukakis, like a baby shark that just burped. Or, with his weird hair and his nervy, wall-to-wall grin, like a chipmunk that got dipped in an oilspill.

Pop videos flick-flacked silently across the screens on the gantry overhead . . . I remembered the War Correspondent telling me *en route* to Oristano that Argentina was fine until the fifties – then the hard-working half of the population that was Italian looked at the other half that did fuck all and said, why should we bother? 'At that moment they became Argentinian.' And now they all want to come home; the queues at the Italian embassy in Buenos Aires are mighty, mighty . . . Maradona arrived.

Menem had come in to give him a new passport. He said he was proud to create for him, the son of our motherland, this new post as consultant ambassador for sport throughout the world. 'We here inaugurate a new form of accreditation, a new type of diplomatic image . . . Plato said sport makes wise and careful men – the type of men the world needs now.'

'The world needs,' inquired Gary Lineker idly when I told him all this 'wise and careful men like Diego?'

The guy next to me muttered, 'Does this mean he'll stop cheating?'

Applause. Handshakes. Bilardo kisses Maradona; Maradona looks like a kid in a candy store. 'I'd like to thank the President not so much personally, but on behalf of my parents, who'll most certainly be proud of their son today. We shall now start defending Argentina in the World Cup.'

Not, you'll note, defending the World Cup for Argentina . . . and even with the vagaries of simultaneous translation, that struck me as a most telling inversion.

There were questions from Egypt, Mexico, Haiti, Italy, Austria, England, and the USA. A man from *The Times* asked Maradona if, after ten years at the top being persistently kicked and abused, he still had the same appetite?

'Yes, most certainly – Maradona still has the same appetite for triumphant victory.'

A bearded American in a seed cap with a Milan badge asked if the World Cup was a challenge.

Do they sell shares on Wall Street?

Now Menem at this time – as if the Argentinian economy wasn't enough – had been having serious public tiffs with his wife, ejecting her from the presidential palace with police and lawyers and all sorts. So the last question, from an Argentinian, was a blatant plant. Would he say something about his wife?

'You tell me how things are with your wife, I'll tell you how things are with mine.'

Exit President Chipmunk, still hectically grinning under his petroleum toupee.

From Buenos Aires to Milan, that's an awful long way to go for a sound bite ... an awful long way to go, in the desperate scrape for brownie points with your suffering electorate. I sat there feeling sorry for Argentina.

But for Maradona, never. He's got more cash in the bank than the whole of Cameroon.

When people say, I don't like football, I say, you haven't been. When you've been you can say, if you must, I *hate* football – fair enough – but once you've been and you've seen, it can't ever again be a matter of merely like, or dislike.

Because at a football game you don't just watch, *you take part* – and the emotions involved are not soggy or middle-ground material.

The daughter of the friend I was staying with said she hated football. When AC Milan beat Benfica in Vienna, she said, in Milan it was like the end of a war. So Bobby Robson's not alone with that image ...

And now a new campaign was beginning – the biggest of them all.

On 7 June Milan woke up to find that hundreds of new signs, yellow metal placards, had sprung up overnight all round the city, naming every park and every palace, every garden and grand house. Me, I was in the Casa Rossi, by the architect G. Pestagalli in the 1860s ... spruce yourself up, here comes the World Cup.

In one shop they even had, of all things, World Cup *torches*.

On the morning of 8 June I felt like my stomach had turned over. I rang a friend in London – she said later I sounded like a man on helium, talking too fast and too high.

It was Friday, but it felt like Sunday; the city held its breath. Outside the multi-spired, fairy castle Duomo, under heavy slate-grey skies and in dense humidity, small groups of Argentinians and Africans waved flags among the pigeons. There were Germans in large numbers, waiting to take over once Argentina moved to Naples; and there were Dutch with orange-painted faces, heading south to Sicily. On strangely empty roads, sirens sporadically howled and wailed here and there, near and far.

Fans were spilling from trams towards the brute bulk of the San Siro four hours before kick-off, past hundreds of police with tin hats and truncheons. Cars streaked past with men standing up from all the windows bar the driver's, waving the blue and white of Argentina, and sounding off on their monstrously noisy foghorn hooters, the *trombe nautiche*. But there were few of them, really, compared to the great mass of the Milanese – because it was a long way to come (unless you were the President) for a people as poor as they are now in Argentina.

And this was not, after all, to be any kind of love-fest for the champions – this was to be a hate-fest for Diego, the fat brat from the barbarian south. In the wealthy north, sick of paying for Naples, a separatist Lombard party had just got near twenty per cent in the local elections . . .

A bunch of English boys went by with their Union Jacks, singing, to the tune of 'Here We Go',

Cameroon, Cameroon, Cameroon

And who were these guys Argentina were playing? Who were these African underdogs, these Indomitable Lions whose equally thin contingent of fans strode the vast parking lots in their flowing robes, their red, yellow, and green? Do not, I kept thinking, underestimate Cameroon . . . Maradona didn't. He said, 'Watch out for Cameroon.'

In Spain in '82 they'd drawn with Poland, Peru and Italy, and gone home on goal difference amid dark mutterings about Italian corruption – then, in both '84 and '88, they'd won the African Nations Cup. Their 35-year-old keeper Thomas N'Kono had been African Footballer of the Year in '79 and '82, and was still playing in Spain, at Español; while the 38-year-old Roger Milla on the subs' bench, who'd come out of retirement to come to Italy – at the request of President Paul Biya – had won the same award all of fourteen years ago. Nine of their younger players were professionals in Europe, most in France – and all of these men, like their Russian manager Valeri Nepomniachi (though doubting voices feared he'd organised them to death) would surely know what they were about.

So do not, I kept thinking, underestimate Cameroon.

They were, after all, the squad with the biggest number of birthdays to celebrate in the course of the World Cup . . . in the press centre, the Databank was working. I went trawling for other Fascinating Facts.

The commonest player's surname in the history of the World Cup was Gonzales: there'd been fifteen of them. There'd been thirteen guys called Rodrigues, twelve called Lopes . . .

Actually, I had a personal databank of my own: World Cup matchboxes. According to this invaluable info-source, Cameroon had 200 clubs, and less than 10,000 registered players – whereas Argentina had over 3,000 clubs, and over 300,000 players. The Argentine FA had been founded in 1893 by Englishmen among the 45,000 expats then living there – the first club was formed by members of the Buenos Aires Cricket Club in 1867. Cameroon's FA, on the other hand, was only one year older than Diego Armando Maradona . . .

On CNN, on the monitors all round the room, grave American senators discussed an anti-crime bill. What you gonna do, guys, make it illegal?

Experienced pressmen told me how all the interest and attention at the start of the World Cups went to the minnows, the Costa Ricas, the Cameroons, because they'd all be going home soon . . . ha!

James Mossop from the *Sunday Express* was with Ken Jones of the *Independent* in the TV lounge. Mossop was just in from Malta where, he said, the Irish had been thoroughly relaxed. But in Cagliari, he'd heard, it wasn't that way – the English press and players were barely talking to each other . . .

Jones: 'I've no patience with it any more. Like a bunch of fucking kids. And Robson's no better.'

Blyeagh. I went back outside into the breathless sun, and gazed up at the vast and surreal murals erected round the parking lot. One showed a smiling woman with a black eye, hero-of-labour style, doing a balletic header; a fashion model strutted across another over symbols of Lombardy in a suit and shades, with a beachball-sized football balanced on her hairstyle. They were surrounded by Dali-esque squiggles of trains and buses, goddesses and globes. The unreality zone . . . Argentina–Cameroon. You must, I thought, be dead, if you weren't excited now.

I rode the lift up the outside of the stark grey walls to the press box. Inside, the massive steep stands were packed. Three helicopters rolled around overhead. The video screens and speakers pumped out the Italia '90 anthem, a dreary slice of Euro-bland from the Giorgio Moroder pap factory:

> *To be No. 1, running like the wind*
> *Playing hard but always playing fair, oh yeah*
> *To be No. 1, running like the wind*
> *Reaching high in the blue Italian sky*

Aside from the boy-girl duo earnestly belting out these noble sentiments, the video had lots of film of Maradona running about in Mexico '86 with a kind of golden-glow surround, like the Readybrek kid . . .

But the fact that it's dreck doesn't matter once you're there. The music's calculated and anthemic; play it loud enough to 73,000 people boxed into this fierce and lusting spaceship of a stadium under what was now, in the late afternoon, a gleaming, gorgeous, and very blue Italian sky – and you're talking a manipulation of these people, through the potent fact of their own willed gathering in such a mass, in such a place, into a state of expectation and desire so strong that it makes your chest ache.

Every city had its promo video, and the opening ceremony began with Milan's. To acoustic guitar music, kids played with a football among the pigeons in front of the Duomo; then there was some synthy choral stuff, sweeping up in a surging wash around aerial images of the San Siro, with its glistening roof and its monster alien walls – and I thought, my God, I'm really here: this is me, in this emotion machine . . .

Two hundred gymnasts bearing flags pranced out on to the pitch; armies of models set off around the touchlines wearing red for the Americas, capes and gaucho hats and Indian headgear, wearing black for Africa, black gowns and djellabehs veined with many colours, wearing yellow for Asia, diaphonous saris and veils, and wearing green for Europe, ballgowns and bathing cozzies . . . the music was a medley of salsa and Morricone, oriental twangs and African drums and 'All You Need Is Love': the whole thing was utterly daft, sensibly brief, and extremely beautiful. A fashion parade at a football game? Only in Milan – only in Italy . . .

CRAK-CRAK-CRAK, smoke bombs went off one by one above us all round the rim of the roof. The gymnasts made flowing patterns of dance and colour across the green turf. Twenty-four balls in the centre circle in the colours of the twenty-four participants opened into flowers and released balloons into the sky, sparkling against the bright, 'copter-buzzing blue. Flashbulbs popped like fireflies all round the sea of people in their four walls of sound, in their steep massed banks of delirium – and the applause went on and on, as now they brought us Verdi live from La Scala, and great soft waves of chord and choir rose up over the chants and the hooters, the roars and the songs:

Cameroon, Cameroon, Cameroon

In this mad and lovely tumult, football pushed its first tear of the summer down my cheek. Pele: people love you, and I love you too.

And there'd be more tears a-plenty before the end, for Brazil, for Italy, for England . . . the tears of millions.

Because you are in the heart, now, of the greatest drama on earth.

Courage and danger, speed and skill, strength and violence, grief and desire, grace and beauty . . .

The fourteenth World Cup.

The teams came on at 5.50.

The Argentine anthem's a dirgey business, and was roundly and universally jeered and whistled. And of course it's disgraceful – but the people's drama requires villains, and the people like to let the villains know what they think of them. And then, if he didn't strut and cheat and whine . . .

When his name came round as the players were introduced, the booing and the shrieking redoubled in ferocity.

The Cameroon anthem, by contrast, was an altogether jollier affair, a parade ground colonial hangover; and each of their players was mightily applauded.

Maradona shook hands with his opposite number. He then flicked a standing ball up from between his feet into the air, caught it on a raised foot, knocked it up on to his shoulder, juggled it with four neat shrugs four times up and down off that shoulder, and let it fall to his knee – then he stroked it away to a team-mate, the whole thing done as easy as opening a door and walking through it. Opening a magic door, and walking out on to Planet Football . . .

And so we begin.

The Argentinians played 3–5–2 – Nepomniachi, on the other hand, went in mega-cautious: 5–4–1. And it did at first look like avoiding disgrace was an honest limit to their ambition. Argentina were quickly into the Cameroon half, forcing N'Kono into action in the third minute; Massing was booked for stomping Maradona's ankle after ten minutes. Now and then, when Argentina saw the pass and broke upfield, they looked like they might find real speed and incision – but instead, after that initial surge, it settled down into nervy stuff, and threatened to be dull. The most common score in World Cup opening matches was 0–0 . . .

Then Mfede tripped lightly through three Argentines, and passed into the box for Omam Biyik; under pressure, his shot limped wide. They linked again, both looking sharp and fast; Cameroon had a third, a fourth, a fifth move forward. They'd played themselves in, found that Argentina were pretty ordinary – and, plainly, they'd decided to go for it. They were coming right from the back, chasing up through the alarmed Argentinians with a limitless energy – Cyrille Makanaky, hard to miss with his orange dreadlocks, looked like he could run for ever.

In the twenty-second minute, seriously flustered by Makanaky charging through the middle, Basualdo nearly gave away an own goal; Omam Biyik forced a good save out of Pumpido.

Ndip got booked for kicking Maradona in the shoulder, though the challenge was more clumsy than malevolent. Maradona sat down and looked aggrieved for a minute; the crowd gave him the bird. When one of his own men got booked for a blatant handball, he protested (ambassadorially) with that little-boy look on his face, spreading wide his hands in injured innocence . . . the man *invites* opprobrium.

Just now and then his touches were deft, his vision immediate – once or twice he'd suddenly set off, and bundled through people like they simply weren't there. But these were brief and rare flickers of his talent. Often enough, Cameroon defenders had no trouble relieving him of the ball. Then he'd stop and stand there, looking like sombody'd gobbed in his Bovril – he really didn't look like he fancied it much. After Burruchaga kicked out at someone who tackled him, the referee called Maradona, and told him to calm it down – and he walked away looking like this intervention was a personal insult. What sort of captain is that?

And between the two sides, there was this clear and basic difference: when a Cameroon man went down, *he got up*.

The Argentine midfield was jammed and directionless – and after twenty minutes or so, no question, Cameroon looked better. A band of Argentinian drummers and cymbalists, with blue and white Argentinian umbrellas, went on a noisy march round the upper tier – but it seemed, in the circumstances, a faintly desperate and solitary sort of sound. All the attacking came from the guys in red, yellow, and green. They were passing people, finding space, pushing up – and their every move was cheered to the glossy rafters.

Bilardo put on Caniggia at half-time – and the man is fast, really fast. If he spent more time playing football, and less time coming on like Greg Louganis going for gold at the Olympic pool, he'd be very good to watch. He got Cameroon a third booking – and they weren't ashamed to wallop people – but you only had to show Caniggia the laces on your boot, and he was into a triple somersault with multiple tuck and twist before you can say, And the Oscar for the best actor goes to . . .

Early in the half, Omam's brother Kana Biyik looped a header inches over the roof of the Argentine net. Then, in the sixty-second minute, he went after Caniggia – Caniggia tripped over himself, not deliberately, he was just running at full pelt, and his left toe caught the back of his right calf – but he fell flat with a solid thunk, and Kana Biyik got sent off. Seventy-three thousand people erupted in outrage, and cheered him all the way to the bench.

Forza Cameroon!

A few minutes later an Argentine hacked down an African and was barely spoken to. I sat there growling, my brain shrivelling up – I had awful visions of myself turning into a *Sun* reader.

Cameroon took the free-kick. Makanaky deflected it up into a ballooning arc across the Argentine box, and Omam Biyik rose from the ground like he planned to put his head into geostationary orbit. The Argentine defence just stood there and gawped. At the moment of contact, the tops of Biyik's socks looked about level with the top of his marker's head.

Two out of five people on the face of the earth – and Nery Pumpido, amazed and floundering – watched the header bounce down off Pumpido's knee, and into the net. An absolute shambles.

The stadium was on its feet and yelling so loud, they could have turned down their tellies in Buenos Aires and listened to it live. And the Cameroon players were off their feet too, stacking up in a pile of exultant bodies by the corner flag.

Argentina 0, Cameroon 1.

In 1962 Walter Winterbottom, England's first manager, said that an African side would win the World Cup.

In 1978 Tunisia beat Mexico and drew with the Germans, to come a respectable third in their group. In 1982 while Cameroon got three draws, Algeria beat West Germany 2–1, and were only diddled out of further progress by that shameful footballing replay of the *Anschluss*.

And in 1986 Morocco drew with Poland and England, beat Portugal 3–1, and came top of the group. In the second round, the Germans struggled to beat them by one goal.

Minnows?

But – unless you read *World Soccer* – what do you ever hear about African football?

You hear that senior Swaziland referee Sport Diamini has decided to retire, after being stabbed six times in the back by enraged fans at the big game between Mbabane Highlanders and Denver Sundowns. 'I am getting out of the sport,' said Sport, 'while I am still alive.'

Or you hear that in the Zimbabwean League, Tongwara have been banned for life. On the advice of their witch doctor, they'd attempted to ensure victory by urinating simultaneously on the pitch before a game. They lost 2–0 . . .

And sure, we can laugh. When Zaïre reached the finals in 1974, that appalling crook President Mobuto gave each player a car, two weeks' holiday for two anywhere in the world, and a house 'built of durable material' . . . in the qualifiers, one Zaïrian ju-ju man claimed he'd put a jinx on Zambia's goal, and another that he'd ruined the opposition by conjuring up a vision of a naked girl in their dressing room. The Yugoslavian coach Blagoyev Vidinic retorted, 'I'm the witch doctor here. I touch them on one leg and say, "You score with him".'

Nor were Cameroon free of the wackier kind of stories about African football intrigue. N'Kono wasn't their first-choice keeper – that would have been Joseph-Antoine Bell of Bordeaux. But not surprisingly, Nepomniachi dropped him after he told the press that Cameroon had 'no chance of coping with either Argentina, or any other team. We will go out in the first round without much glory.' Bell, who never played, later said he dare not go back home; that he feared for his life if he did so. President Paul Biya was, meanwhile, offering the team $50,000 and a villa each for a place in the quarter-finals – he seemed pretty keen on picking the team himself.

By chance, at this time, I was reading a magnificent novel about Africa called *Interior* by Justin Cartwright. There's a marvellous moment when, after a coup, the new foreign minister announces that the new government must go out and negotiate immediately with three vital world bodies. They are: the World Bank, the United Nations – and FIFA.

But do we not bumble and intrigue ourselves? And now, Argentina 0, Cameroon 1 – the sniggering stopped here. And that was long overdue.

FIFA have since announced that there will be three African nations at the next World Cup, not two. And when you look at the performances of Scotland, Sweden, and Austria, you have to reckon that the loss of a European side in place of a third African one can only be the World Cup's gain.

The goal was scored in the sixty-seventh minute. Twenty-three minutes to go, and Cameroon had ten men. And yet it was them, not Argentina, who went on looking the more likely to score. Roger Milla came on with eight minutes left, and twice he took aim – while any high balls that came in at the other end, N'Kono just punched them all away, rock steady. Even their back passes were cheered.

In the last few minutes, Caniggia set off like Carl Lewis. One man had a go at breaking his legs, but thought better of it at the last minute. A second man then tried, and didn't bother pulling out; but Caniggia somehow hurdled the assault, kept his footing, and kept on going. Then Massing, his third assailant, showed the other two how to do it. He executed a kind of full-pelt, waist-high, horizontal flying bodycheck. The general intention seemed to be not so much to break Caniggia's legs, as actually to separate them from the rest of his body.

It was a dreadful foul, and unlike Kana Biyik he fully deserved his expulsion. They still cheered him off though – it was so heavy in there, the hatred was so deep, and the love for Cameroon so strong, you wondered if they'd have minded if Massing had just pulled a gun on Caniggia and shot him. It would certainly have been more elegant . . .

And with nine men left, the Africans still carried on attacking. At the final whistle, while the 73,000 went spare, poor old Menem stood smiling in awful solitude in the VIP box, like the nerd who doesn't know anyone at a party.

The Cameroon radio commentators rushed over to the English positions and jubilantly cried, 'We have avenged the hand of God!'

Nepomniachi said modestly and studiously, 'Perhaps we were slightly lucky. I repeat, we were lucky. We had no game plan – Maradona is Maradona, you can't do much about that. We scored, and that's about it. There aren't any tactics to deal with Maradona.'

And he said, 'An African team's never won. Maybe we can change that.'

Bilardo stood in a corner looking about as glum as you'd

expect, and then some. When he came on the American with the Milan seed cap asked, in a tone so pompously self-assured that it was obvious he knew the answer to his question, 'Were Cameroon guilty of dirty tactics? Did they set out to beat up on Maradona?'

Bilardo said, 'No, I never think this of my adversaries. Once the game's over, there's nothing to say on that head.'

Maradona – appearing an hour and a dope-test later – was equally decent. 'I don't think the referee was right to send off the first player. I don't think Cameroon intentionally thought of beating us up.' And he said, 'I cannot argue, nor can I make excuses. If Cameroon won, it was because they were the best side.'

With a somewhat bitter irony, given his own treatment by Italian fans outside of Naples, he also remarked, 'I am happy because I participated in making Italy non-racist. All the support was for Cameroon. I think that was very nice.'

And – asked by an Egyptian whether Egypt could pull a similar result over Holland in Palermo – he smiled and said, 'If Holland play like we did, maybe.'

Remarkable. Maybe he's not so bad after all.

Back at the Casa Rossi, my friends had taped the game. In the first half I counted four fouls on Maradona. Massing's stomp on his ankle was naughty, and Ndip's boot to the bicep was plain dumb – while the other two were a silly trip and an innocuous bodycheck, to both of which Maradona reacted like he'd been pole-axed by Mike Tyson.

I didn't bother after that. Because if the foul count was three to one against Cameroon, I'd lay money that for every foul they made contact, there was another where they made none, and where the referee was just had – by players who ought to know they're too good to waste their time, and ours, diving about like children.

So three things came out of this game. Firstly, the refereeing was diabolical – an ominous portent.

Secondly, Argentina were crap. They didn't look like they'd be staying in Italy long, and they didn't look like their stay would have much in the way of grace about it – a prediction of which the second part, at least, came horribly true.

And thirdly, Cameroon were indeed Indomitable Lions – except that they had one big problem.

They knew what to do with the ball going forward – but getting it back when they'd lost it revealed a reckless naïvety. Apart from Massing's attempt to turn Caniggia into hamburger, they weren't malevolent – but they could be very, very clumsy.

It was a clumsiness that would be meat and drink to the rapacious appetite of Gary Lineker.

9   Gary Lineker

Being lucky, scoring goals

'Every time I go through a lean spell I've lost a yard; every time I score a goal, it means I'm over the hepatitis.'

– on scoring his first hat-trick at Spurs

I asked Jon Smith, at the end of a long interview, whether there was anything else he'd like to tell me. In PR terms, you could say the answer scored a goal at both ends.

'I'll tell you what might be fun for you. Why don't you come in and watch us if we get one of the FA Cup Final pools. It's a bit of an obscene procedure, really. Well, not obscene – but it's a money-grabbing exercise. Unlike the England players' pool, which I can justify from here to kingdom come – but the Cup Final pools, the players get to Wembley and they say, right, we've got three weeks. We're hot property. So it's wham bam, thank you ma'am, earn as much as you can. Then go out and spend it . . . that's good fun.

'And the only other thing I'd like to say is that a lot – not a lot, a percentage – a percentage of what we do with the England team, it goes back to good causes, like leukaemia research. A reasonable percentage. And then the players outside of that, they do an awful lot more themselves. It's never recognised, no one asks it to be – but look at Steve McMahon, after Hillsborough. He talked a kid out of a coma; he sat with him for four hours, and talked him out of a coma. And it's hard . . . McMahon's a tough nut, but he just broke down. And no one ever writes about that.'

At Anfield a few days later, McMahon said, yes, he'd done

that. He said. 'We still go out with the families. They come up to my house, we go to theirs, we go out of an evening for a meal together – so I've kept in touch with them. Because I think it's important – and they're nice people. It's not as if . . . I'm not doing it because I feel as though I have to. I'm doing it because I want to – and because they're nice people.'

I liked Steve McMahon – he didn't have an ounce of bullshit about him. When I asked him where confidence came from, he looked at me like I was a complete idiot.

'From winning games.'

And he said about his job, 'Obviously we're lucky people. Since I was a kid, the only thing I ever wanted to do was play football. For me to play football, and make a good living at it – it's a bit special. And now, to be considered for a place at the World Cup . . . it's more than I ever thought of.'

Gary Lineker and Peter Beardsley drove down the M4 to Wembley – one in a Jaguar, the other in a Mercedes – a little like the way they played football together. They went extremely fast, jockeying smoothly back and forth – and everyone else on the road just seemed to melt out of the way.

Footballers have a sense of balance about them, an ease of movement that can make you feel helplessly clumsy. Now it seemed they even drove that way. But when you drive a Jaguar, that probably helps.

It was the eve of the Brazil game; I asked Lineker about all the media fuss and the sponsorship palaver.

He said, 'This is a bit of an exception, to be honest, it's not usually this busy. And anyway it's part and parcel; you tend to get used to it.'

I said they seemed sometimes to answer questions on automatic.

'Yeah, but you get asked the same things, time and time again. So you get to the stage where you don't repeat basically the same answer, but exactly the same answer. I've definitely thought, I've said this before – particularly about the World Cup. People ask, who d'you fancy? So you say you fancy everybody, you try to be polite about everybody – and that must have been asked me by forty different people, from forty different countries. So it becomes a routine. But it's the TV

163

you have to get right – because invariably if it's press, they'll put it in their own words anyway.'

So did it bother him?

'Gets a bit boring sometimes. We had training yesterday, medical tests, signed two hundred balls, did fourteen different interviews . . . without being rude, you do try and cut them down a little bit. Because you've got other things to do. Yesterday afternoon, say, I had to see a girl I'd written to a couple of times, she's got leukaemia, and I had tea with her – she's very ill, the bone marrow transplant didn't take . . . that's the other side of things. Hopefully, in this particular case, she'll be OK, she'll get through it.

'A few weeks ago I went to see a little kid in hospital, he'd had a couple of heart operations, and he was going in for another one – and they said he was a big fan, it might cheer him up. So I went to see him before the operation. He seemed a really nice little kid – he was only about seven and he was dead enthusiastic, good-looking kid as well. I said I'd come back after the operation, so I did – and things hadn't gone too well, he was on a life support thing, and he was . . . he came round a little bit, sort of saw me, squeezed my hand. I said I'd come back later, when he came out of that. I went back a week later, and he was still in there. Then a couple of days later I got a call to say he'd died. Things like that, it's upsetting. You feel for the parents.

'But a lot of players do their fair share. Because if you can't be bothered to do that sort of thing for people, when you're so lucky yourself . . .'

Earlier in the season, Trevor Francis at QPR had fined one of his players £1,200 for going to his wife's bedside for the delivery of their child, rather than turning up for a match.

Bobby Robson didn't think too much of that – what use was the player to you anyhow, if his mind wasn't on it? Four years earlier, Francis had complained in the papers that Robson had betrayed him when he took Beardsley to Mexico instead of Francis.

Robson said, with some satisfaction, 'He's learning about management now, isn't he? He just got the sack.'

And the player – Martin Allen – said, 'The manager told

me football is my life. Go and tell that to my cousin Paul, whose son had a brain tumour. That is life – not ninety minutes on a Saturday afternoon.'

'I am lucky,' said Lineker, 'I know I'm lucky. Touch wood, everything I've done in my life has been what I wanted to do, workwise . . . and my health's been good. Health's the main thing. If you've got that, then you're OK. But I've had everything I could want out of life.'

Did he always want to be a footballer?

'I did really, yeah. Sounds a bit corny, but I think a lot of kids do. It was football or cricket, really – in the summer I used to go mad on cricket, then the winter would come again and it was all football, playing in the garden every night with my brother . . . every spare moment was football. So, yes, I did – but I never really thought I would. Because you always know how difficult it is to get to the top.

'And everything I've done has surprised me. When I joined Leicester as an apprentice, I always wanted to do that, but I didn't really think I would – then I signed as a professional and I thought, well, I didn't think they'd take me on. Then I played in the first team . . . and everything that came was more than I'd ever hoped for. Then it went to being top scorer in the World Cup, and playing for Barcelona, I mean – all those things, if I'd been told even a year before they happened, I just wouldn't have believed it. I wouldn't have dared dream it.

'It's difficult to explain how you actually feel, it's a bit of self-doubt in a way – I think I know a bit more what I'm at now, what I can do, after doing it so many years, but there's a lot of luck involved. Before the last World Cup, and the first two games there, I went six games without a goal. And then six in the next three made me top scorer. If they'd come in the games beforehand and I hadn't scored in Mexico, I wouldn't be the name I am now. So there's a great deal of luck involved, and I appreciate that – but then, having said that, I think there's something inside me . . . the big games, I don't know why, I've always done reasonably well. Sometimes I really need the adrenalin to be going – I feel at my sharpest when it's a big one.'

I asked – as I'd asked Butcher – whether a striker was a particular breed.

'I can only speak for myself, I don't know other strikers well enough, but I think you've just got to want to be the best, to score the most goals. I always want to win the top goal-scorer award, every season – I've got four Golden Boots, three for the League, one for Mexico – and I'd like to win another this season for the League (he did) and, who knows, the World Cup ... you've always got to want to do it. If you've not got that absolute desire, you won't – you've got to really get in there and believe. And it does get stronger ... I don't know where it comes from, I think it's inborn. I mean, as a character, I think I'm pretty laid-back, but ... I just have a burning desire to score the maximum amount of goals possible. If I've got two in a game before half-time, and I don't score another, I won't be too pleased. Once I get one, I desperately want another.'

Ian Rush said – in the stupendously naff *My Italian Diary* – that he had an instinctive idea where the goal was, and just hit it in the general direction.

'With all due respect, I think perhaps he's not thought about it enough. Maybe that's what he does, I don't know – he's been very fortunate to play in great sides at Liverpool, where you get a lot of chances ... but I can only explain how I feel.

'I'm a sprinter, really. I haven't got stamina, I'm not one of these players who can run up and down all day – but I know where to run, where to get space, and how. I think that's why I score more than other people – even when the team's struggled a bit this season, I've still managed to score.

'I score goals by losing defenders, first and foremost by making dummy runs, by taking a chance and running into space – and then if the ball comes to where you are, invariably you've got in front of your defender, and you've got an easy tap-in. That might sound pretty obvious, but what a lot of players do is follow the ball – and that's basically what the defender does as well. So then it ends up fifty-fifty, and it's practically impossible to get any sort of shot.

'The big thing is, everybody says it's being in the right place at the right time. But it's more than that, it's being in the right place all the time. Because if I make twenty runs to the near post and each time I lose my defender, and nineteen times the ball goes over my head or behind me – then one time I'm three yards out, the ball comes to the right place, and I tap it in – then people say, right place, right time. And I was there *all the time* ... but obviously if the team's playing well it's easier, because they'll get more service in – if you get no service, you can't score goals. Unless you're Maradona and you can beat four players, which I'll never be.'

Later he said how, just recently, he'd scored against Manchester United. 'I think it hit the top corner from twenty-five yards – that was a bit different for me. One of my ambitions, that was, to score a screamer – I really did give it a whack. And it was a big buzz, it was so unusual for me. It probably wouldn't have been that extra-special if I was Chris Waddle, someone who scores them all the time – or, certainly not as seldom as I do.'

I asked what it was like to score in a big game.

'Now that's *very* difficult to explain ... it's the ultimate in joy, really. I can't think of anything that could possibly make you higher ... you can use all the exclamation marks in the world, but it wouldn't describe it. It's everything you work towards, then it happens, and it's a split-second of sheer joy. And sometimes, relief ... when it's really important, like the first one against Poland in Mexico, that was joy and relief all in one. People talk about players jumping for joy and cuddling each other, but it's just ... you tend to go a little bit uncontrollable after you've scored. I know I do, I love scoring so much – it's that desire thing again. You go, *yes*, you really scream it out – then you become a bit aware, you realise what you've done, where you are ... it's the most difficult thing in the world to explain. You've got to live it. The roar – you're totally oblivious for the first few seconds, and then ... there's not words written.'

He said it'd be good to have a go at writing it down sometime, to try and put across what he thought, and what he'd learnt. When I asked, had he not done a book yet, he laughed.

'Must be one of the few who hasn't. But I think I'll wait until I've got something to say.'

The public image of Gary Lineker is as a mild-mannered and

intelligent individual. I saw no evidence to suggest that the public image had it wrong.

'I suppose I am pretty mild-mannered – I certainly haven't got a temper. I've never been booked in my life, or sent off, not just in professional football, but ever – that should say something about being mild-mannered. And intelligent? I'm not over-intelligent. But I'm not stupid either. At least I hope not.'

Well, he'd gone to Barcelona, learnt Spanish, fitted in and enjoyed himself when other players have a terrible time because the food's funny, the people speak strange . . .

'Yeah, but . . . like I'm saying, I'm not stupid. I looked at British players who went abroad and were successful, and they were the ones who learnt the language, and adapted to the culture – look at Liam Brady, Tony Woodcock, Ray Wilkins – they all learnt the language. The ones that didn't tended to be home pretty quick – Ian Rush, Luther Blissett . . . I knew Tony Woodcock, I talked with Ray Wilkins.

'But it wasn't easy for me, I didn't pick it up in five minutes. Me and Michelle, we went to school three times a week for two years while we were in Spain – I'm no natural linguist, it was bloody hard work really. But I was doing interviews, pretty badly, after three months. It helped with the people, and the press tended to be a bit kinder to you. And I loved it there, I didn't find it difficult. It's just down to the way you are, I went out there looking to enjoy it, not just do two or three years to get a few quid and get home. You've got to go out there wanting to adapt, to live the experience – and I loved every minute.

'It was a great place to live. It's got everything, the weather's brilliant, the food's great, the people are good – and it's a busy, interesting city, culturally. Then there's the beach – and in winter, there's skiing only two hours away. Fabulous place. And the people took to me, which was nice.'

Lineker himself couldn't go skiing – that, along with such other entertainments as rollerskating or motorbikes is contractually right out. But if he was away playing, Michelle would go and ski – he said having no kids made it easier.

Did you ever wonder why so many footballers play golf? Because you can't break your leg at it. 'Also, we mostly only train in the mornings. Me, I used to play snooker – something to occupy the mornings. Now, with publicity things, I'm generally too busy. I find golf a bit tiring, really – I'd rather rest than walk round a golf course. It's a bit of a slog.'

He was, he said, getting three journalists a week from abroad, wanting long interviews after training. 'It's a pain in the backside sometimes, but you get it done – you've got to look after everyone the same. It doesn't do you any harm, and it's no great hardship. So you make the effort, and you know they appreciate it because some players, they don't want to know.'

Did he think we'd suffered by being out of Europe?

'Financially we have, that's for sure. Football-wise, yes, but not as much as people say. The team's pretty regular at international level, so we get the experience that way – but it's a shame, because they're great competitions to play in. Obviously, the young ones suffer more than anyone else. Though having said that, when I broke into the English team and played in Mexico, I'd never played any European competitions in my life – so it can't have hurt too much. I think if the players are good enough . . .'

Were England good enough? Was our game all thunder and no skill?

'We've got skilful players. But if you look overall, yes – we are technically inferior, and our game's played at a much greater pace. It's a generalisation, but it's pretty true.'

Earlier, talking about the attributes a great player needed, he'd said, 'You'll never do anything without ability. You can have as much character as you like, if you can't play you'll never win anything.' Then he said, with a faintly dismissive distaste, 'Well, there's Wimbledon . . . it can happen, I suppose. But not the League. Not the League.'

I saw Liverpool beat Wimbledon 2–1 at Anfield a week later; it wasn't a great experience. Wimbledon had a travelling support of about eight; it snowed. Liverpool played football – they weren't really buzzing that night, but Barnes, sporadically, was brilliant. Wimbledon, on the other hand, put the ball three times on the roof of the stand. For long periods they never saw it at all; when they did, the limit of their ambition was to hoof it, barge about causing chaos, and hope. When they kicked Barnes, the fury of the crowd was immediate, and touchingly possessive. The weary comment of the man beside me summed it up: 'C'mon, c'mon – they're *crap*.'

The Kop sang,

> *You're so shit it's unbelievable*

But Liverpool were going through an oddly unsettled phase back then – five days later, I watched Crystal Palace mug them 4–3 in the FA Cup semi-final – and the Wimbledon game, which had been all theirs, 2–0 up at half-time, got nervously jammed at 2–1. By the end, even back passes would do. The man beside me said as the ball went back, 'That's the way. Anything'll do against these buggers.'

Wimbledon – the very essence, distilled to an oafish purity, of all that's dim in English football. Whack it up the front, stick it in the mixer. Did we really have to carry on like that in 1990?

Lineker said, 'The problem is, it comes through from kids watching how it's played, that's how they pick it up – so it's difficult to say, hey, let's change. But there are a lot of skilful players, and I think, I hope, they'd be the players the kids follow – people like John Barnes, Chris Waddle, Peter Beardsley. Hopefully, they'll be the ones they follow.

'I do think there's a lot of skill in the English game; I think the basic difference is that the continental *defenders* are skilful, rather than just the forwards. In general our defenders just defend – they can't play.'

It was, of course, precisely what Robson had said in February.

He said, 'They can all play abroad. You never see them just hoofing it into the stand – even in the corner, when maybe there's a time that you *have* to whack it away – that's like a point against their ego. For a start, the crowd'll give them stick; and secondly, it's like losing a mark. Like, that's not me, *I can do a little bit . . .*'

The Italian manager Vicini described his formidably able sweeper Franco Baresi as being 'on first-name terms with the ball'. Who did we have like that?

In Spain, said Lineker, 'They've all got such good technique, they're all confident on the ball. Of course there's things that annoy you as well, the rolling around and diving, stupid things, pretending to be injured – and also, sometimes, they weren't really positive enough. They need, sometimes, to play a bit quicker, like we do – the perfect game would be a cross between the two. Real skill, at high speed.'

Milan, 10 June: West Germany 4, Yugoslavia 1.

The way, I asked, that AC Milan had been playing? You could, in Milan, buy a T-shirt that said, 'I Love Italian Pressing'.

'Pressing, well – the way Milan play is the way Liverpool have played for years. Basically the coach, Sacchi, he's an English football nut, and he's copied the best style of it – Liverpool. But he's done it with some of the world's greatest players. It's one hell of a side.'

Gullit, Van Basten, Rijkaard, Baresi, Maldini, Ancelotti, Donadoni – when people defend 4–4–2 by saying that AC Milan play it, it's worth remembering that with players like that on your side every week, you could play 1–1–8 and turn it into a fashion.

And then what English manager would say, as Sacchi once said, 'I believe that football should be considered like an opera. You must assign a role to a player, and it's up to him to interpret it. My players must have physical, technical, artistic and cultural qualities in order to carry it out.'

Lineker laughed. 'That's one way of putting it. There's not too many who'd understand it . . . it's all right if you can get hold of that kind of player, if you've got the kind of money Milan have got – because there's not too many of them about. So he's got a nice job . . . probably not a job I'd want.'

I then quoted Enzo Bearzot, who led Italy to victory in '82 – and who also liked to watch English football. He said of our game, 'British players have great assets – application, bravery, physical strength. But they lack direction, organisation – they need traffic wardens to show them the way. It isn't always best to go forward. Getting the ball into the opposing penalty area is not the first principle of modern football.'

Lineker said, 'I don't think all our teams play like that. Liverpool don't play like that. I don't think Nottingham Forest played like that when they won the European Cup. And I don't think England play like that – we play, basically, a continental game. We don't hoof the ball forward.'

I'd seen Charlton–Arsenal . . .

'Oh, well – they might play like that. There's a lot that do ... but it's always easy to make these comments, looking at the thing as a whole. We do play a faster game, a more positive game if you like, looking to get the ball forward quicker overall – and sometimes with teams that try and stop you playing football, you have to revert to that a bit. But I think the sides that have been consistently successful in this country aren't the ones that have played that way.'

So I asked what it was like to play with Barnes, with Waddle, with Beardsley.

'We all love to watch them. They've got the gift, being able to run with the ball, and do things other people can't do – I'll never be able to do that.' Then he laughed and said, 'It certainly makes life easier. It's a lot easier playing with players like them, than with players who can't play.

'Because a striker, he relies on the rest of the team. If I go a few games without a goal, and then I get the stick strikers do – well, maybe the team wasn't playing well for those few games. But it's not looked at like that – he's not scored, he can't have played well. And equally, I'm the first to realise that when the team's going well, it's the striker who gets practically all the credit – when maybe it's been down to just a tap-in off the team's play. But they say, he must have done well, he scored. We get all the publicity, for one reason or the other – and it's unfair either way.'

He then predicted, with another of his easy little laughs, what the headlines would be, if he scored the next night: 'LINEKER BASHES BRAZIL IN THE NUTS'. He wasn't far wrong.

LINEKER NUTS BRAZIL

He'd like to go into television, when his playing time's done. It's easy to see him making a good job of it. He reads the *Independent*, and, to keep up with Barcelona, *El Pais*.

So it was no big surprise, when it turned out he wasn't a fan of 4–4–2.

10 We Are England

The boys come to town

I flew into Cagliari on 1 June on a near-empty charter from Luton. At the back were a dozen or so England fans, among them Robert Neill, Andrew Buckley, and Lee Forster from Wolverhampton, Northampton, and Telford respectively. And a fine holiday these boys had.

The dogs at customs got Forster's dope in no time. At the Bar Svizzera in town he showed me, with a kind of stunned indifference, a tatty, hand-typed police document. It said they'd confiscated his five grammes, and left it at that.

The three boys looked about them like they'd landed on Mars; they grumbled about the price of the beer. 'Where's the life in this place?'

On the plane they'd talked about taking the ferry to Tunisia, for England's game there tomorrow. Now, having discovered that it was a fourteen-hour trip, they'd decided against it. Besides, Tunisia – 'that's Libya, innit?'

Two days later I went to the same bar, and there they were again – in the back of a police car. They had, they said, been collared for stealing the sheets from their *pensione* – they'd wanted them so they could sleep on the beach. Court reports in *L'Unione Sarda* later added that, before making off with the bedding, they'd 'devastated' their room.

But *L'Unione Sarda* was a notable victim of what the War Correspondent called 'hooligan psychosis'. Five beery boys singing 'God Save the Queen' was, in this paper, a major outbreak of mob violence – so 'devastated' might be stretching it a point. These lads were not such terrifying outlaws, after all, that they hadn't paid their bill.

They sat in the back of the police car, their faces vacant

with that same stunned indifference. They were dim, they'd got drunk, and they'd got nicked for twenty days.

I came across another of the boys off the plane at ten the first evening, swaying and malcontent in the arcade on the Via Roma.

He said, 'They're taking the piss.'

How?

'They're fuckin' starin' at us, aren't they?'

With a bulldog on your chest, shorts from another galaxy, and no socks – what d'you expect?

'They think they're brave 'cos we're outnumbered. But we won't be next week. See him, he's calling me hooligan.' 'Him' was a wasted local tramp-youth cuddling an empty litre of wine. 'But we're not hooligans . . . not till next week we're not, anyway.'

Brave boy.

I pressed him – in what way, exactly, were they taking the piss?

'They stare at us, y'know . . . fuckin' stare. We're in a bar, right, and they come in the fuckin' bar and . . . they only talk fuckin' Italian, don't they? Fuckin' windin' us up.'

This boy was not so much all played out, as never played in. But his talk was just the paranoid and beer-fuelled bravado of a kid who'd landed in an alien place, and not yet even begun to work it out. I saw him several times in the next few weeks, and he wasn't mean – just thick.

Just English.

He was the typical fan that gets in trouble, a typical member of the visible minority – too straight to start a fight, too stupid to avoid one.

The same couldn't be said for the bullet-necked crophead they called Chelsea – this one was better-dressed, and better-muscled. As I tried saying to the drunk boy that, in Italy, they do things different – that they do tend, on the whole, to speak Italian – Chelsea looked at me with a vicious and absolute contempt. He looked at me as if any knowledge or toleration of things Italian was an offence against the natural order.

He said, 'This isn't the fuckin' flower show. This is the fuckin' World Cup.'

*

And at the fuckin' World Cup, the fuckin' phones didn't work.

The pressmen who'd gone to Tunis with the team had found, on arrival, that their bags hadn't gone with them. This was a bit mysterious, because all the team bags had got on the plane OK – and it had been the only plane at the airport.

Sant'Elmas can only handle five planes, full capacity. So with the Irish and the Dutch threatening to come in and out from Palermo on thirty-odd charters each, it looked as if the Sant'Elmas baggage handlers were making a subtle point, wages wise, about their imminent great travails.

Someone had got the bags on to the next flight to Rome; but then Alitalia's Tunis connection had left them behind there as well. At the COL, Nottage tried to salvage this – but the phones didn't work . . . SIP!

There were 140 English press accredited, and they were getting more care and attention than journalists from any other country. They had their very own COL person running round pampering them (Nottage) – because if they were rude about Italia '90 in Belgium or Costa Rica, that was a shame; but if they were rude about it in *The Times*, that went world-wide.

So it was good, she said, having them out of town for two days. We went out west to Chia Laguna, £16,000,000's worth of holiday complex with a gym, a conference centre, a shopping mall, three restaurants, and the kind of pool where you expect Blofeld to open the gates and let the hungry sharks in any minute. The coastline was ravishing – cypress, wild olive, cactus and eucalyptus.

'So it's all right if you've got a cold.'

'Or a koala.'

Jagged hills fell parched into a turquoise sea; we passed a couple of the watchtowers from the Spanish occupation, pale ochre beacons on the rim of the land. On the twisting road, cyclists from a club in Milan poured sweat along the hair-pins.

En route we collected David Gambier from Sportsworld, the agency that was handling flights and hotels round the tournament for a good portion of the English press. Just getting the scribblers back and forth in the comfort to which they're accustomed was, I calculated, a piece of World Cup business at the high end of six figures, minimum.

Gambier said trade for the first round was lousy. Regular punters couldn't afford the package prices that '90 Tour had put together – and the corporates, buying freebie jaunts for their staff and their clients, weren't interested in Cagliari. Who wants to buy a valued customer a holiday then find they've dumped him in the middle of a riot? The business boys were off watching Italy or Brazil instead.

As for handling the press, he sighed, they are so *hierarchical* – you've got your No.1's, your No.2's . . . Harry Harris from the *Mirror* or Alex Montgomery from the *Sun*, they had to have top grade rooms; then Nigel Clarke and Brian Woolnough from those papers, they had to have second grade . . . while photographers got the lowest grade going.

You began to get the impression – though Gambier never actually said so – that handling the English press required the kind of constant attention normally reserved for small children; that it was very wearing indeed.

The England squad got back from Tunis at 8.30 on the evening of the 2nd. We barrelled out on to the Tarmac under a blood-orange sunset, into a throng of maybe fifty cops and COL folk; the Tunis Air 727 banked in over the town behind us. While we waited, we learnt the latest Italia '90 Fascinating Fact: the tournament was employing 677 stretcher bearers.

So who was the poor bugger who'd have to carry someone off on his own?

The plane taxied to a stop before the waiting chain of team bus, team van, and multi-vehicle escort – and a seriously disgruntled set of people began to disembark.

'I don't think,' said one Italian journalist, 'England want to play friendlies any more.'

Paul Parker muttered as he passed, 'Worst country in the world, that is.'

Scraping out of the place with a 1–1 draw can't exactly have endeared it to them. African minnows? Cameroon had got past Tunisia 3–0 on aggregate in their qualifying play-off; against England, Tunisia went in front on the half-hour, and it had taken Steve Bull, going on with only ten minutes left, to pull the draw off a very embarrassing fire.

The Italian sports boys were mightily unimpressed. 'They're

so predictable. They can only score from crosses, corners, free-kicks. They were abysmal – they have no chance.'

Butcher had been substituted for the first time in his career; he'd left one of the Tunisians clutching his face on the floor. Did he butt him? And why did he take his shirt off and throw it to the ground? There were juicy headlines bubbling under there. Mark Wright had gone on for him, and played well; was this the end of the old tradition?

And to cap this fine English show, the journalists had been treated, in the bar of their hotel the night before, to an incursion by half a dozen of the brightest and best. 'It was,' said one Italian, with colloquial precision, 'effing this, effing that, bastard this, bastard that.'

They had one beer, then left cursing at the price of it. From the doorway as they went, one of them loudly told the belly-dancer, 'You're a fuckin' ugly cunt, aren't you?'

The Italian journo said, with satisfaction, 'Never mind. They'll get a truncheon between the eyes over here.'

The fans, the team – on the evidence of Tunis, we were all played out – and we hadn't even started.

Sad news, meanwhile, from Is Molas: Dick Wragg, who was not only a septuagenarian, but also a diabetic, had started getting hypos – he had a fluttery heart; he'd started losing his balance, and keeling over. They'd got him into hospital, and stabilised him; they'd be flying him home.

And there was something hideously apt about this, something symbolically appropriate in the saddest and most tired sort of way. The man who'd said that when England went abroad he was 'in charge, completely in charge', was too old and too ill even to be left in charge of himself.

He should never have been there in the first place. And there were plenty who thought the same about England.

The Butcher business grew exponentially in the headline hot-house. What else was there to write about, with eight days still to go before Ireland in the Sant'Elia? The BBC ran film 'proving' he'd butted the Tunisian – BUTT-CHER.

So they worked themselves up into a lather of self-righteousness. He should, they said, be sent home. How could the FA seek discipline in the domestic game, if they were to tolerate a leading member of its flagship side going round butting poor unsuspecting Africans? And – as if this were a worse crime – the shirt, the shirt . . . he'd torn off and thrown down the England shirt. They made out like he'd gobbed at the Queen – which, knowing Butcher's archaic politics, is ironic, to say the least.

You could take the noble morality of this press censure a bit more seriously if you didn't know, firstly, that most of them had been wanting Butcher dropped for years and years anyway – and secondly, that a fair few of these people now raging against his treatment of the shirt were themselves so thoroughly a-patriotic, that they seriously wanted England to lose. I remember calling one of them a day or two before the Brazil game, and saying I looked forward to it – and he said, 'I hope they get stuffed. I hope they get absolutely stuffed.' Now this particular writer was Scottish, so fair enough, to a point – but enough of his English colleagues felt the same. And what price the shirt, when you go to matches thinking like that? When you go to matches – I quote the chief sports writer of *Today* – thinking, 'Robson's a cunt. I hope they don't fucking qualify. Terrible team.'

I too could get weary and depressed at the way England, sometimes, played an unimaginative and medieval kind of football. But whether they played well or badly, I didn't go into it actually wanting them to lose.

They raised the supercilious red herring, that an Italian or a German player would never have thrown down his shirt. But the Germans and the Italians haven't been without their heat-of-the-moment blemishes in the history of football. Who was worrying about shirts, when Schumacher broke Battiston's jaw in '82? And Claudio Gentile – he didn't need the moment to have heat in it, when he decided sometimes to turn men's knees into mince.

Butcher later said, 'First their No.18's grabbing and holding, all the way through the first half. Then the sub comes on, and he's doing the same. It was ridiculous. So after he's been at it a few times, I give him a warning.'

In fluent Arabic?

'I swung an elbow. I mean, I didn't hit him, but I let him know. But he didn't take the warning. So the next time, he's coming across me – and I just dropped my head on him. See, the wound I got's round the side, behind the back of the ear here. If I was going to butt someone, I wouldn't do it with my ear, would I?'

You got the general impression that if he'd really meant to give the man a full frontal Glasgow kiss, he'd not have got up quite so quickly afterwards. They'd have been calling for the 677 stretcher bearers . . .

Butcher knew he'd done wrong. He'd been getting badly frustrated on a dog of a pitch against crafty opposition, knowing England were playing poorly, and at risk of losing for the first time ever to an African team. And he knew throwing the shirt down was dumb – but like his boss of fourteen years, he's not Einstein, is he?

He's just a very large footballer – straightforward, courteous, and good company off the pitch – and straightforward, in a rather different way, on it.

To suggest he should be sent home for these Tunisian indiscretions was ridiculous – this was football here, not a hand of bridge over a glass of sherry. And like Glen Kirton said, with a small wry smile: 'We're not in the business of undermining the team just now.'

Unlike certain sections of the press.

In the news update on the Databank, it said Maradona'd bought a running machine for £8,500. It was the phoney war, and serious news was scarce. The Pope blessed the Olympic Stadium in Rome.

I got accredited on the 3rd. The accreditation was P1, press; it gave access to the press centre, the conference room, the training field, and the press box. For the latter you also needed a ticket – but Rome wasn't releasing any yet.

There were forty-one different types of accreditation. There were two for FIFA, four for Italia '90, one for teams, one for team officials, seven for RAI TV, and seven for radio and TV from abroad. Then there were one each for referees, security, medical, 'hospitality', photographers, and press, plus two for sponsors, and two for two other unspecified kinds of media. Finally, there were nine different types of service staff – the catering and bar people, the newspaper salesgirls, the local COL volunteers, the stewards and stewardesses.

So we wandered around labelled and tagged like museum exhibits, every genus of the fauna of Planet Football minutely classified and *blipping* through the security gates like it was Cape Canaveral, mission countdown under way . . .

In the back room, an unfortunate little Fuji man toiled in an agony of diligence on the ID machines. He'd had three hours' sleep between Japan and Rome, got off the plane, then done twenty-three hours straight at the press centre there. Now, he was pelting round eleven other cities, looking worried sick in his running shoes.

Around the work area and the service counters, meanwhile, the press centre filled more full by the day with armies of alarmingly beautiful girls in blue COL uniforms, in red Coca Cola outfits, or, occasionally, in green Carlsberg suits. The Coke girls loitered by big fridges from which you could avail yourself freely of Coke, Diet, Fanta, Sprite . . . a counter-productive sort of marketing effort, really. After five weeks, I never want to see another can of that fizzy crap again. The dentists on Planet Football must have done a roaring trade.

The touts on the Via Roma certainly did. The Ireland and Holland games were, theoretically, sold out – sold out, like I eat metal and shit cars.

The FA had been allocated less than 3,000 tickets for each of the first round games – of which only 140 per game were the cheap £9 tickets in Category 4. Locals, who'd got Category 4 tickets months earlier from the Banco Nazionale De Lavoro, were now selling sets of three for the first round at £50 to £70 a go.

Interestingly, fans accepted this, or were at least resigned to it – touting was a fact of football life.

What they were less inclined to accept was the ubiquitous presence of the media. Why, they asked, will they not leave us alone? And why must they keep asking, are we hooligans?

Barmen and waiters in the different places they were drinking all confirmed, they were quiet, they behaved, and they paid. And the barmen and the waiters also said, all these press people are persistent and irritating, and they make the fans unhappy . . .

I spoke with a bunch of boys at the Caffe Roma. There was an electrician from Mitcham, and a mechanical engineer and a machine operator, both from Bideford. There was a painter from Brixton, a postman from Plymouth, a stonemason from Jersey, a labourer from Harrogate, and a bloke from a cotton mill in Manchester. There was a bank clerk, and an assistant manager of a branch of Horne Bros, both from Taunton – there was a chef from Redhill, an Irish labourer called Hank from Kilburn, and there was one girl, a hotel receptionist from Wallasey.

Of these fourteen, seven had thrown in their jobs to come to the World Cup. And all bar one – the electrician – had come without tickets or accommodation. Why?

A mate of mine looked into flying to Cagliari, just for the Holland match – one game, two nights. But the ticket-and-package price was near £500 – and that's outrageous. You can fly there for £200, or less – and my *pensione* was costing me only £8.50 a night.

Patrick Barclay later told me, when I asked about the supporters' regular and disgusted complaint against the journalists that they had the posh hotels and the best seats free, and what did they know about anything? – 'I don't think my service to readers at home would be improved by my living on a campsite, and not having any tickets to the matches.

'But I will say that supporters' discomforts at this World Cup have been much increased by the over-pricing of tickets, as sold in the form of packages. On the record: if I'd come to this as a fan, I'd have come without tickets – I wouldn't have been able to justify the cost to my family. And I probably earn twice the average industrial wage.'

So why had these boys come? Because, of course, they knew they'd get tickets – even at tout prices, it'd cost them less than the packages ever would. And – of course – 'because we're the real fans.'

Or, as another boy put it more tellingly, 'We are England.'

And you can say that they're stupid – a fair few of them are. But it's not a crime to be stupid – the crime lies with the people who run an education system in Great Britain in Western Europe in 1990 that produces such stupid people.

And maybe you could say of some of these boys, when they say 'they are England', that things in their lives must be pretty well played out, if the only way left to assert their identity (and their masculinity) is to follow the football team like dogs after a meat truck.

But you might also say that, given their lack of what John Williams called 'cultural capital' – given their inability or disinclination to pick up much if any Italian, or to fathom too much about Italy beyond how to order a beer there – that setting off broke and surviving for weeks did, in fact, take no mean reserve of both balls, and initiative. After all, I'd say not one of those fourteen outside the Caffe Roma was yet twenty-five years old.

So consider – next time you or the papers want to trash the England animal abroad – the example of one Robert Didd, twenty years old, and a qualified electrician as of two months before the start of Italia '90. At the age of sixteen, earning £30 a week as a YTS trainee – 'but that doesn't mean anything, I did a lot of overtime' – he began to follow England. And he'd been to more countries than there were years in his life.

He hadn't made *every* game, he said, as if this were only reasonable – he hadn't seen the B side in Switzerland, for example, because he'd had to see Eddy Niedzwiecki's testimonial at Stamford Bridge instead.

He had two passports – one of them for Israel, so he could go to Arab games on the other. He hadn't made it to Riyadh, because the Saudis didn't give him a visa – but he'd still put down £630 at the travel agent, just in case they did.

And he was, he said, one of a hundred and thirty-seven who'd got visas for Albania – though three of those, he added, with a slightly sniffy precision, didn't turn up.

So why did he do it?

'For the football. And then, to see all these places – because why else would I go?'

For Didd, in other words, the international fixture list was a constantly eye-opening itinerary through the alternative geography of Planet Football . . . and just how alternative that geography is, may be gauged from the revelation that his favourite trip had been, of all places, to Iceland.

His pleasure over Iceland was partly the exclusivity of being one of only eleven souls in Reykjavik for a B international.

The flight had cost him £208, and he'd stayed for three nights. And he'd got his principal pleasure not from the game, but from hiring a Landrover with his mates the day afterwards, and setting off into the heart of the island. He had, he said, never seen any place on earth like it – utterly wild and fantastical. His eyes were bright with the memory.

Then he told a gruesome story about a mate who'd been in a bus crash *en route* to Mexico City for the Argentina game – in the middle of the night the bus had turned over, the driver had died, and his mate had cracked his pelvis. So he went to the game and then hobbled about for a week before he finally got home and found out what the problem was . . .

Didd had been in Tunis; now he was going home to his sister's wedding. It was a bit of a shame, he said, he couldn't have a good drink-up really – he had to be at Luton early the next morning, to get back to Planet Football . . .

Every day, one last little bit more got done. Beds were dug and planted along the road to the stadium; flagposts went up, and I'90 arrows telling you where to go; a plastic case materialised over the sandwiches in the press centre, and stopped their edges curling up. Overhead, hovering helicopters became a regular presence. Was that for Abdul Needle? Or was it for us?

The weather was acting weird. It hadn't rained properly all those years – 'We are like Africa,' cried Marius – and now the seasons were spinning mutant and awry. They'd had, people said, spring in November, and then summer in February – high twenties, shirtsleeves weather. They'd had a procession praying for rain; they'd petitioned the Pope to pray ditto. Back in April, and now at Oristano, sporadic speckly showers suggested it might be working. If it did, I figured England would find they'd come out good and early to acclimatise – and any day now it'd start snowing.

On the Via Roma, thirty-two tractors went past in an angry, horn-parping protest parade. The farmers said the banks were screwing them; no water, they said, meant no crops – and no crops meant hunger.

Unlike most of the others, the labourer from Harrogate was a mean, squinty-eyed little shit. When I said he didn't sound

Yorkshire, he said no, he'd moved from down south. I said my wife was from Huddersfield; he said that was a crapheap, 'full of Pakis'. He sat grousing about the bloody noisy Italians in their tractors. Cagliari, he said, was 'a disgusting fleapit'.

I sat groaning with Rogan Taylor at the narrowness of his spirit.

Rogan Taylor left school at fifteen; his mum had run off with a major in the Territorial Army, and he'd done a year in the Army himself, most of it in jail. Getting out at seventeen, he hit the road; he worked in Sweden and Denmark – another time, hitching in the general direction of the Mediterranean, he got a trucker headed for Iraq, and ended up teaching English in Baghdad for a year. Back home, he was a bus conductor, and he had a job in a glue factory for a while 'but I couldn't stick it'.

He went to the Far East, to India, and Malaysia – he worked fourteen months in an Australian state mental asylum. In India, he bought two horses, and walked over a thousand miles through Bengal, in and out of Bhutan, and into northern Burma – one horse died, he sold the other, and ended up back in Liverpool. He got a job as a gardener with the council, and got interested in reading – Freud, Reich, Jung. 'I'd be sitting in the corporation hut on rainy days doing Archetypes and the Collective Unconscious.' Thirty-three years old, he went to Lancaster University, did a twenty-minute interview on Nietzsche, Bo Diddley, and George Best, and got a place on a psychology degree.

Shamanism was Taylor's big thing, so he wrote a book about shamanism and rock'n'roll – 'it starts at 35,000 BC, and ends up with Jimi Hendrix'. It got published in March '85 – and then, a few weeks later, he saw Heysel on TV.

'After a few very painful weeks, I decided to try and write something about how supporters were presented, and represented – you're paying two-thirds of everyone's wages, and no one's ever asked you the time of day. In the middle of doing that I rang a fellow Kop-ite, Peter Garrett, to ask for the name of the ref in the Liverpool–Inter game in Milan in '65 – the second leg of the European Cup semi-final, when the ref was bribed, the thing Glanville's always banging on about.

Because why had no one ever connected the fact that the first incidents of Liverpool hooliganism abroad were in '66, after we were robbed in '65?

'Peter said he was sitting watching the cricket, thinking he'd never go to another football game again. But we talked about having some sort of trade union, or our own consumer body, for fans – and so we did. There were two women, three men, Liverpool and Everton people – it started from there.'

The Football Supporters' Association was born in 1985, out of the frustration of regular fans who'd been treated like dirt for too long. Then, in '88, the government came up with its cock-eyed and dangerous ID card scheme. Taylor put together an anti-ID programme, and gave it to the FA, the League, and Wembley Stadium Ltd. They split the cost in three, and covered the budget in a week. Then Hillsborough happened . . .

After Heysel and Bradford, a tragedy too far.

Out of it came Lord Justice Taylor's report, which finally pointed a way forward. The government dropped the ID folly; and in the next budget, it dropped two and a half per cent off the pools levy, so the money – £100,000,000 over five years – could be redirected into ground improvements. One man at the FA confessed himself gob-smacked at this sudden and wholly unexpected largesse – but, remember, the government was getting vote-hungry by then. And who cares what the reasons were, if at last they'd seen sense?

Rogan Taylor, meanwhile, had emerged after Hillsborough as a fluent and persuasive man in front of a camera. The FA mightn't like him – the FSA, they said, was 'political' – but the TV did, and the FSA was getting hard to ignore. So the first faint and nervy steps to an accommodation began to be taken.

Obviously, not everyone likes Rogan Taylor. Jeff Powell said he was a cunt.

Taylor shrugged. When a man's got the bottle to tell a racist oaf three times his size, 'Listen, pal, I haven't got time to be bullied by the likes of you', he's not likely to be worried too much what Jeff Powell thinks. He said, 'They have a saying at the FSA – "as thick as two short Jeff Powells".'

By the time Cagliari came round, Taylor'd gone to work with John Williams at Leicester University; the *News of the world*, ludicrously, now called him an 'egg-head boffin'. New people took charge at the FSA – among others in Cagliari, there was Craig Brewin, the new chairman, who works in local government in London; Steve Beauchampe, unemployed, from Birmingham; and John Tummin, a community relations worker from Manchester.

These people, in Cagliari, attempted something that had never been done before – a football embassy, run for fans, by fans. And it was a sign, like the Taylor Report after Hillsborough – that maybe things weren't played out beyond hope after all.

Meanwhile, there were signs from the FA that they too, at last, were beginning to touch base with reality.

Glen Kirton is a pleasant, able, and intelligent administrator who has, at the FA, to present policies laid down by the septuagenarians with which – I personally suspect – he may not always entirely agree.

At 'Arrivano Gli Inglese' in Cagliari in April, he was the last to speak. He said afterwards he'd been uncertain about coming, even reluctant – he wasn't sure it'd do any good; and he said, when you've been sniped at for so many years, you get wary about putting yourself on the line to get sniped at again. But he shouldn't have worried – what he said, potted as follows, seemed sensible, coherent, and honest.

He, like Rogan Taylor and John Williams, had been at Hillsborough – and they would never forget. It was the FA's job now to learn the lessons, and implement them. They couldn't say that fans must behave differently, or clubs, or the League – the FA was the governing body, and it was they who must act.

Lord Justice Taylor's report was the lifeline – friendly, compassionate, and understanding. Football was a force for good – if the necessary action was taken.

The problem was that people had learnt over the years to think of fans not as customers, but as a problem. In doing so, they had maligned 99.9 per cent of the people who go to football because of every 10,000 who go, three are arrested. Yet for the sake of those three, an aura of criminality had been imposed on the other 9,997.

They had, he said, carried out any number of policing and

punitive measures, to the point that the FA was actually discouraging people from going to watch their own country playing football.

As he'd said of the man with the bloodied head in Katowice in October: 'Shouldn't fucking come, should he?'

Now he said, 'What a corner to have got in. So how do we get out?'

Firstly, by obeying the Taylor Report all the way, no matter what it cost. A reasonable estimate for the necessary work at ninety-two clubs was £500,000,000 – half a billion. But so be it – even if it meant ground-sharing, so be it. Better to share a ground, than cease to exist altogether.

Secondly, the Taylor Report contained a criticism that hurt very much – a criticism that the leadership of the game over the last twenty years had been poor.

But that criticism was correct.

It was a problem that sprang from history, and the different origins of the FA and the League as separate bodies. Today, he said, we see the result – a League with too many clubs, subject to takeover by people whose motives were sometimes thoroughly questionable.

So what would the FA do?

In a few days' time at a council meeting, it was proposing to streamline the organisation, by creating an executive board of ten or twelve, with League representation. Through this body, the FA would take firmer and more decisive charge of the game – to put the bricks, the mortar, and the all-seat standards of the Taylor Report into place.

Then they must, he said, care more about their market. At present they not only didn't care – they didn't even know what it was. But an industry can't prosper, if it doesn't do its research. He wasn't necessarily agreeing with Rogan about fans getting seats on boards – but at present, there were about five million people in England going at least once a year to watch football, of whom only 15 per cent were female.

Who were they? What could be done for them?

And what about the other forty-five million?

Afterwards, Rogan said he'd never heard anything like it from the FA in his life.

The idea of the new board was Kelly's, and was supported by Millichip, and was patently a good one.

But the problem with having ninety-two buffers of varying vintage with a vote apiece was, when you asked them to vote themselves out of executive control, you needed a bit more oomph than Graham Kelly's got to get them to do it . . . and they didn't.

So, memo to ninety-two buffers: Recognising the problem's one thing, boys. And doing sweet FA about it's another thing entirely.

The FSA, meanwhile, made mistakes to begin with themselves. Turning up in Cagliari with no money, no tickets, and no accommodation, their demeanour inclined the authorities to ask whether they were any different to the hooligans they appeared – to the authorities – to represent.

Mouthing off about the unpreparedness of the place in the media back home compounded the insensitivity of their approach. Being short, maybe, of a little cultural capital themselves, they looked at the land of the last minute a few minutes too early – and they didn't believe that as much would be ready as, eventually, was. One of them was quoted as calling the place 'underdeveloped' – not wise at all. A friend in Cagliari kindly suggested that, perhaps, they'd meant 'unspoilt' . . .

But they did make suggestions – for example, a fan camp – that people in the Cagliari *comune* said they'd take up, and then didn't. And they really didn't have any money – they ran their whole operation on a budget of barely £10,000.

The FA chipped in £2,000 of that. The biggest contribution was from a well-disposed ex-referee who'd made good in the States; other donors included the Professional Footballers' Association, and four fanzines – the *Leyton Orientear*, *Tired And Weary* from Birmingham, and *Rodney Rodney* and *King Of The Kippax* from Manchester.

They got an office on the Via Malta, close to the Via Roma in the centre of town. You could go there and find out about tickets and accommodation, about transport and entertainment. They'd put you in touch with the FA's office by the consulate, if you wanted tickets – or with the consulate itself if you had a problem. They tried to organise football games with Cagliari supporters – though the authorities weren't too helpful about providing a place to play – and, because Sardinia has a problem with thalassaemia, a red cell blood disease, they organised England fans to give blood.

And last but not least, they produced a booklet – so even if you never went near them, they might still get a word of help near you. There was a pocket history of the island and the city, together with information about the Sant'Elia, about hotels and campsites, about how to handle the media, how to get around, 'how to cross Italian roads without getting flattened' – and about how to get away to the mainland, once the first round games were done. They also gave a skeletal list of Italian words for basic foodstuffs – and an invaluable translation of 'Stevie Bull is better than Vialli', so you could make lots of close personal friends.

There were mistakes in this document, as there were in the way they handled themselves overall. But the FSA were, crucially, fan-friendly – and it was an achievement that they didn't make more mistakes, on a shoestring budget, when no similar exercise had ever been tried before.

They helped a lot of people out. And sometimes, in Cagliari, helping people out would involve a considerable measure of courage.

While the boys were getting organised on £10,000 in town, twenty-two footballers were getting organised at the Is Molas Golf Hotel. The FA's bill for full board, extras not included – for three weeks at Is Molas, and a week before that with the wives at Is Morus on the beach – was £250,000. (And FIFA paid a subvention that covered some of that.)

Along with the players were Bobby Robson, the coach Don Howe, Doc Crane, the physios Fred Street and Norman Medhurst, Mike Kelly the keepers' coach, and Adrian Titcombe the equipment manager. There was Kirton, Bloomfield, Brian Scott, and Giacomo Malvermi, the FA's Italian attaché and link-man. There was Kelly, Millichip, and Jack Wiseman, a senior member of the International Committee – there was Les Walker, the security man – and there was the BBC, who'd cut deals with the FA and the pool, and were paying their own bills. Moynihan would also be staying there. 'But I think,' said Kirton, 'we might forget about charging Mr Moynihan. Though he has offered.'

This party had taken over the whole of the main body of the hotel; only a small group of self-catering villas down the road were still doing normal holiday trade. They had two kit rooms, five rooms for the local police, and a couple for British Aerospace . . . for who?

British Aerospace put direct sponsorship into the FA's youth programme of about £25,000 a year. But there is, more nebulously, more to it than that. British Aerospace strikes deals with its customers – Saudi Arabia, or Malaysia – whereby a percentage of their profit goes back into development work. To meet those commitments, they'd tied in to the FA's missionary role as a promoter of football in foreign parts, by chipping a piece of that recycled profit into Middle and Far Eastern football development . . . so when England kick the round ball about in Riyadh or Kuala Lumpur these days, they're helping sell a bit more than just the beautiful game.

British Aerospace also have a construction company, with whom the FA are hoping to build a new national stadium. Will that happen? Speaking, as ever, with one voice, Millichip said it would, and Wragg said he couldn't see it – but they had their two rooms anyhow.

Kirton said they'd pay their own bill – if they came. He said, 'British Aerospace are potentially a very big partner of the Football Association – and we're looking to cement that relationship. But then, Umbro are already a big partner, and they're here – they've got a room, if they want to come. All our sponsors were offered accommodation – Mitel, Coca-Cola, Tennants.'

So the FA took over Is Molas; it became a strange place, with the military drivers loitering out the front by the Italia '90 cars, the satellite dish humming by the reed-roofed car slots and, hanging over everything, an air of arrested expectation.

Eleven of the players had been in Mexico together; they knew what it was like. They sloped about in their Umbro gear, keeping out of the heat; they got matey with the staff, and signed autographs. They'd had Daddy's Sauce and tomato ketchup brought over; but the food was so good, the bottles weren't emptying that quickly. There were cornflakes specially supplied, and new colour televisions in the rooms – in the games room, they'd put in a pool table. Kirton and Bloomfield had direct phone lines installed, and fax machines. At first, also, they had the papers couriered in every day – but then they decided, at £400 a time, it was too expensive. 'It's not worth it,' said Kirton, 'not for the shit you read, is it?'

Everybody, he said, affects not to read the papers – but of course when they did come in, the players descended on them 'like a plague of locusts. 'Cos everyone likes to know what's going on. They can't falsify the cricket scores, can they?'

Is Molas was tucked two or three kilometres off the main road, thirty-five kilometres west of Cagliari. It was quiet, it was beautiful; and it had police at the gate and along the driveways day and night.

The main attraction was the golf course, with the dry hills rising up sharply behind, and a wide view down to the sea in front of you as you played – and Bobby Robson likes to play a whole lot. As he set off to the first hole with his sponsored and monogrammed golf bag, Bloomfield, watching him, said, 'We've had letters, you know, about his resignation. Hundreds. I'd say . . . six to one in his favour.'

Bloomfield had been organising interviews with the players for Italian TV. Des Walker said he'd do it, but he was nervous – 'I've never done this sort of thing before.'

'Clough won't let him,' said Kirton.

The Italians asked Walker if he and Barnes were so fast and skilful (putting it tactfully) because they were Jamaican.

'I wouldn't know,' says Des. 'I was born in Hackney.'

The players watched the Derby – Grundig had given them a big screen for the games room, and the BBC set up a direct feed. Meanwhile, in the spartan and airy comfort of the bar, Kirton and I talked about the ticketless boys in town.

Corporate folks, I said were happily giving the agencies five and six figures' worth of travel trade, to ship, say, fifty salesmen on an incentive programme to watch Italy or Brazil. But they weren't coming here. Regular punters weren't buying the packages. And the streets were lined with touts.

'What d'you expect me to say?'

Shouldn't be happening, should it?

'You can't stop it. There is absolutely no way we can stop tickets going on to an open market. Absolutely no way.

We've done our best to make sure that tickets are available for those people who want to be officially identified as non-troublemakers through our Travel Club. But we've told FIFA, and we've been telling FIFA for the last six months, that any spare tickets should be offered to the national associations concerned on a sale or return basis. FIFA say it's not our problem, it's '90 Tour – and '90 Tour say they're not going to do it sale or return.

'So if people come and buy tickets on the black market, it's outside our control. But I don't think it's really a major cause of concern, for the simple reason that it's very difficult to get here. In Germany, where exactly the same situation pertained, there were about five hundred who came without tickets – and that was far easier to get to. So we really don't anticipate thousands . . .'

I doubted if there were a hundred in Cagliari so far – it was five days before kick-off. But barely any had tickets.

'We're prepared to enrol people in the Travel Club right here. With luck we'll get hold of more tickets, and we'll enrol people, and we'll sell to them. But we're not prepared to get into what might be a million pound's worth of ticket debt, simply to do the security job that FIFA and '90 Tour should have been doing.'

Getting tickets for people was one thing. What about looking after them? The FSA, I said, were up and running in town.

Kirton said, 'Craig Brewin's their most political . . . he's stood as a Labour candidate in local elections.'

Rogan Taylor's since told me that the National Federation of Football Supporters' Clubs, with whom the FA feel somewhat more comfortable, is run by a Conservative councillor – so just what's political and what isn't? Ironically, Dick Wragg had said that the best ever Minister of Sport – 'and I'm not of a Labour persuasion myself' – was Labour's Dennis Howell . . .

Kirton said Brewin was, 'the one who does least for relations with the FA'. And in Cagliari, he said, 'They've turned up and told the police that if the police don't deal with them, they can't guarantee there won't be any hooliganism. But they can't guarantee there won't be any hooliganism no matter what they do. The police have got them labelled as hooligans themselves.'

But like he'd said earlier, 'Hooligan equals English person at the moment. They don't know, do they?'

And he did feel – tentatively – that the FSA had a role, as an advice centre. He asked, grinning, had Rogan joined the Travel Club?

Besides, he said, things were changing. Hadn't I felt it at Wembley, since it went all-seater, how the visitors' national anthems didn't get booed any more?

And the government had stopped saying, put your house in order – the FA had stopped saying, it's not our problem.

Slowly, people were coming together.

'We've not had any negative feedback yet, not here. People will look for the anti stories – Bob Driscoll and Alex Montgomery have run this thing about the Italian press being disgruntled over surly English players, and how they're going to lodge a complaint with FIFA – it's not true. There's always problems ... but we've not had any negative feedback. Not locally.'

Back in town, Signora Franca Orru who ran my *pensione*, La Perla, was furious with *L'Unione Sarda*. In the wake of the sentencing of Forster, Buckley, and Neill, the paper had gone round the town's cheap hotels, then run a story headlined:

HOOLIGAN? WE'RE FULL

'Hotels shut their doors,' said the story; it quoted Signora Orru worrying about 'turbulent persons'. 'But look,' she cried, 'everyone here is English!' She waved a fistful of British passports; she threw open the register to show how she, for one, wasn't shutting her door.

She was a delightful woman, constantly flustered, always working; she went out of her way to be helpful to all the people that stayed with her, letting them know about places to eat, about the launderette, about day-trips to see Nuragic archaeological sites, or about *Aida* being performed in the Roman amphitheatre.

And yes – England football fans went and poked about at the mysterious remains of an antique culture. Yes, England football fans went to see *Aida* – one of them complaining when he got back that the intervals were too long.

And would he ever in his life have seen an opera if he *hadn't* been an England fan, mucking in and making friends in Sardinia?

One bloke did come back horrendously pissed after the midnight lock-up; she asked him to leave the next morning. Then a few nights later, another did the same, and she wanted him to leave too. But the next morning he stood there looking so dreadfully dim and meek and sorry – which, given the likely state of his head, probably wasn't too difficult – that she relented.

Neither of these boys was rude or violent – all they did was get falling-down incapable. And they were the only problem she had in the whole time of England's presence on Sardinia.

She gave people knick-knacks of unglazed local pottery when they were leaving – ashtrays, or little jam-pots – with La Perla painted on them, to remind you to come again.

Because people behaved, people paid, and they were welcome to come back. But this, of course, is one headline you'll never read.

ENGLAND FANS BEHAVE

11 All Played Out

England–Ireland

On the 9th I got an early flight back from Milan, and ran into some lively work from *L'Unione Sarda*:

BATTLE IN CAGLIARI

The story talked about 'moments of authentic urban war-fare' –and there did appear to have been, in the glorious Italian phrase, a bit of *fuggi fuggi* on the streets downtown.

Hank, the Irish labourer from Kilburn, had moved into La Perla; he told me what he'd seen. He'd been sitting in the Via Roma arcade, him and other Irishmen among perhaps eighty or a hundred English. (So they can't have been the nasty mob – or the unmistakably Irish Hank wouldn't have been telling the tale the next morning.) He said some of the English were drunk – a few dead drunk and crashed out in their chairs, others dancing and singing. And some of it was noisy when it came to 'God Save the Queen' – but there were Italians stopping to watch as they passed, and they didn't seem spooked. Hank said they seemed to be enjoying it.

From about 9.00 onwards, police in riot gear started gathering across the way on the central reservation.

Hank stressed, the Sards seemed to be enjoying it. 'They must have been five deep between us and the police. They'd watch for ten or fifteen minutes, then move on, and someone else'd take their place. They were men, women, all different ages – some came in to talk with us, it was really no problem.'

But police in vans still pulled up across the road from the cafés. They put on their helmets as they got out, and thwacked their truncheons on their thighs.

'It was very threatening. And there was really no need – we

were sitting about minding our own business. At least, on the tables around me we all were. I think, if they hadn't come on like they did, nothing would have happened.'

The bars had run out of draught, but they were carrying on selling cans – and everyone was paying – they were queuing to pay. Then, as if pre-planned, the tables were cleared away; the police moved in to send people on their way.

I heard later that five minutes before they did so, an Italian TV crew turned up. Funny, that.

Hank said people went more or less peaceably – some weren't too happy about the manner of it, but there were no unduly aggressive objections. People were backed up an alley – Via Baylle – and then some idiot threw a glass.

Others told me later that the idiot in question was the mean-eyed gobshite from Harrogate.

In Stockholm when they'd chucked a glass, the Swedish police looked disgusted, and tidied it up.

In Cagliari, they charged.

Hank was at the top of Via Baylle with six or seven others. He didn't hang around to find out what happened next.

Hank said the drinks ban wouldn't mean much. People would find drink if they wanted to – or else they'd buy dope, you could get it easy anywhere. 'But they're asking daft prices, £10 for a few joints' worth. Do they think we're stupid, or what?'

After he'd got away, he went to a disco. Three Sard boys tried having a go at him – but other locals intervened, and stopped them. He left there at four, and walked the streets till six; then he sat down in the Via Roma for a couple of hours before coming back to bed when La Perla opened. Where he'd sat down – where the BATTLE IN CAGLIARI took place – the streets were 'pure clean like nothing happened'.

He said it was a pity. The Irish fans like himself would drink and have fun, then clear off to Sicily on Tuesday. But the English had to be there another two weeks – 'and they're getting trouble just for being themselves'. He said some were saying, after last night, they'd go up north. They'd bought tickets on the street, but they'd end up watching the game on TV in Alghero, or Sassari – for the sake of one jerk who threw a glass and gave the police their cue to wade in. After which, of course, other missiles would have been thrown, and everyone English became guilty.

English boys told me later they'd been lined up against a wall, and given an exemplary taste of truncheon. The police told them, 'You're in Italy now.' Fourteen were arrested; a bar was reported 'devastated'.

Hank said the Sards were great. 'I'd love to stay here for six or twelve months, that's honest. If you just try and speak a little they'll help you, and they'll love you for it. And there's English trying too. And none of the English have gone after me – sure, one or two give it the IRA and that, but they're not NF, they're friendly – I turn a blind eye, I'm not here for the fight. And these English, they mix with the Irish, there's Irish here, English there, all around the tables – there were even two fellers from Norway supporting England, dressed in England gear and all. There was never any problem.'

I walked down Via Baylle, where the BATTLE IN CAGLIARI began. There were two lines of baby palm trees in pots; the alley was top-to-bottom with little clothes stores, and a jeweller's shop – and all the clothes stores had outside them on the walls the shallow, wooden, glass-fronted cases in which back-street Italian stores display their wares.

There was no broken glass in any of the cases; no sign of damage or hooliganism of any kind whatsoever.

'We will sit here. Write that down. The pitch is not quite perfect. Write that down.'

A Teuton from FIFA came down to Cagliari to inspect things. He went to Is Morus, to ask Jack Charlton for the Irish team's programme.

The answer came back, in effect, what programme? If they felt like training they trained, and if they didn't, they didn't. Ditto talking to the press – which the players all happily did anyway.

Nottage said the Irish were unbelievable. Ten of their journalists had turned up without accreditation. But they had no complaints, and no problems – they operated with a happy conviction that everything would work out OK.

They were, in fact, rather like the Italians . . . except for the way they played football.

*

In Bologna, Colombia put two goals past the United Arab Emirates. The English referee, George Courtney, appropriately, a school headmaster, was much admired for his sangfroid. When players put on the histrionic rolls of agony, he told them to get up and get on with it – so eventually they all did. John Williams said it was a splendid and colourful afternoon, sheiks and salsa and skill – and he reported a delicious World Cup image.

There is, in Bologna, the longest covered walkway in the world, winding up the hill above the Stadio Renato Dall'Ara. And as a little old Italian lady in black went slowly up it, a Colombian kid raced past her coming down the other way, slaloming in and out of the arches with a vast flag fluttering, red, blue, and gold . . . the football festivities were under way.

In Bari, the Romanians beat the Russians 2–0 – Marius Lacatus scoring a beauty late in the first half, then putting home a dodgy penalty in the second. The ball must have been handled a good yard outside the area – but the Uruguayan referee Juan Cardellino (a salesman when he's at home) didn't see it that way.

The football was fluid, fast, athletic, and intelligent. An Italian hotelier, mindful of gruesome doings in Romania, bought tickets for a thousand of the Romanian fans.

I watched Russia–Romania in the Bar Svizzera with a printer called Radio Mitch. He'd gone to the States twelve years ago, to Philadelphia – but he hated it there, the change from summer to winter was 'thermal shock' – so he moved to Oakland, in the Bay. He loved America – but he was English to his boots.

He said, 'I hate Maradona. He's a fuckin' girl.' And when they replayed Omam Biyik's goal for Cameroon, he said of Pumpido, 'My mum could have saved that. What a fuckin' woman.'

Mitch had spent $500 on a short-wave radio, so he could listen to the League on the World Service. With California eight hours ahead, he'd get up at six on Saturday mornings; the three-hour broadcasts started at six-thirty his time, with the games kicking off at seven. He'd cook himself his once-a-week treat, a full-on English breakfast – bacon, egg, tomato, sausage, beans and mushrooms, the works – then he'd listen to England going about its Saturday business.

In the first half, he said, they tell you all the goals as they come in – 'so I'm sitting having breakfast in Oakland, listening to Carlisle go one up over Hartlepool. Lovely. Then in the second half, they go live to one particular game. So when they say, "Welcome to World Service listeners" – that's me out there. I love it. I was eleven,' he said, 'when we won in '66. I went out in the back garden, and I cried.'

Mitch was with three friends. One worked in a marina in Florida; the others, one of whom was Florida's brother (an engineer), were both from Storrington, near Worthing.

Florida told me, 'We're all frustrated footballers at the end of the day.' He'd tried out with Chelsea when he was fifteen, when he'd been captain of Sussex Schoolboys; he said, with a smile that had the disappointment still tucked inside it, 'I'm still waiting for the phone call'. Later, in 1972, he'd had a trial for England Under-18s, in Skegness – and until only recently, he'd carried on playing in Florida. He'd played there, he said, alongside Johan Neeskens, from Cruyff's 'total football' side.

The four of them had met in Monterrey during Mexico '86, and they'd kept in touch. And when they'd arrived there, they said – a year after Heysel – the local papers had been full of HOOLIGANS, ANIMALS, MURDERERS.

'But individually,' said the engineer, 'the people were charming – they'd pick you up and give you lifts to wherever you were going – they'd take you in their cars with their families. There was bonhomie everywhere, the Mexicanos were magic. I felt embarrassed, because I knew they'd never get treated that way in England – one gentleman did remind me of that, he'd been at Everton in '66, and said it was a right shambles – but they wanted to impress, they wanted to be welcoming, and we really *felt* welcomed.'

And I only wish I could say I felt equally welcome while I heard these stories. But I wasn't – because at seven o'clock after Russia–Romania, we went off together to my favourite food haunt, the Trattoria La Taverna, to get a meal before Italy played Austria at nine. And as we arrived there, it came out that I had a press pass. They already knew I was writing a book – but the press pass made them instantly disbelieve that.

Not seeing English tabloids every day, Florida and Radio

Mitch were less hostile. But the other two were deeply, aggressively suspicious. They clammed up; they wanted me out of their company right away. And they weren't stupid men – at thirty-five, Radio Mitch was the youngest of them, and they were straight and articulate. In vain I told them, the press pass just came with the job I was doing – I really was writing a book. It didn't matter – the loathing and mistrust was potent and absolute. I'll condense what they said as follows, and I hope they'll agree that the précis is fair:

'You listen, pal – England fans have been libelled and maligned *en bloc* for so long, by so many lying scumbags who wouldn't know the truth if it bit them on the leg, that if you think some bullshit about a book's going to make us say *one word* to you, then either you're not living in the real world, or your just *right out of order*.'

There was a story that in Monterrey, there was a man from the *Sun* going round with a brick tied up in a note that said the brick was from England. And he'd go into bars offering fans a couple of hundred quids' worth of pesos to put it through a shop window.

I'd heard that story – or variants of it – enough times to reckon there might be something in it. Now, from these men, it seemed unanswerable.

It was about the most depressing and hard-fought conversation I've ever had over a meal in my life. They did, in the end, tell me their stories – but the two from England were grudging to the last.

When we parted company one of them said, 'I hope your conscience is clear.'

And when a press pass has become the mark of Cain like that, what hope can there be for the press to tell the truth *even if it wants to*?

Italy were magnificent – but so was the Austrian keeper Klaus Lindenberger, resplendent in an outfit like a day-glo zebra crossing in a swimming pool.

So although Italy's play had such a flow and a pace to it, such grace and skill and invention, they still had this big problem – they couldn't score. In seven previous internationals they'd only got two goals – against Algeria, and Switzerland.

And you don't win the World Cup, if you don't score goals
. . . ten times they missed, or hit the post, or hit Lindenberger.
Carnevale forced two saves, and scooped a sitter over the top
from a couple of yards; Ancelotti and Vialli both missed
twice; Giannini, De Agostini, and Donadoni all saw chances
go astray – and Donadoni was denied a clear penalty by the
Brazilian referee.

With sixteen minutes left, Vicini sent on Salvatore Schillaci,
the little Sicilian who plays his football at Juventus. It was his
fourth cap. Four minutes later, Donadoni passed, Vialli crossed
– and with his first touch of the game, Schillaci rose high to
head it home.

Comes the hour, comes the man . . . Italy 1, Austria 0.

It was fine football – but I've have enjoyed it more if I
hadn't been with men scared to open their mouths in case I
stitched them up, in a bar perpetually circled by film crews
and photographers.

And if the *carabinieri* hadn't been gathered and watching
outside the place all evening, tooled up in big groups by their
vans, blue lights flashing in the dark.

Next morning, the day before England played Ireland, I took
the bus out to Pula; a kind man in a bar drove me the last few
kilometres from there to the guarded gates of Is Molas. When
I said I'd seen Argentina in Milan, he said of Maradona, 'He
thinks he is king, so he opens his mouth too much. A great
player, yes – but also a complete idiot.'

The England players had a row of eleven rooms to themselves,
along the lower tier of one wing of Is Molas. They looked out
across a dry lawn towards the pool, and the sea beyond. They
sat on their little terraces, waiting to go to training.

Bryan Robson was doing a crossword, and was phased by
the last clue. 'Six letters,' he said, 'a shrill violent woman.'

'Missus,' said Shilton.

'It's a shite crossword anyway.'

I told him, 'virago'. A helicopter roamed overhead.

Butcher watched it pass. 'Dollarville, isn't it – fucking
Dollarville.' He'd just read my book – they sit and read book
after book, Ludlum, Martin Cruz Smith, Sidney Sheldon,
anything that'll pass away the days.

Butcher said, 'This is the worst time. Been waiting so long now – you just want it to start.' He was unshaven, and he said he'd stay that way, 'until we win or go out'.

Millichip wandered about in an Umbro shirt, shorts and sneakers; Kelly lay beached by the pool. In the foyer, Brian Scott showed his arms and said unhappily, 'I'm still white.' No poolside time for him.

Des Walker said he'd talk with me – but he wasn't too happy. 'I know you're not press – but when the book comes out, the press'll still pick it up.' Brian Clough's strictures hung round him and Stuart Pearce like a ring-fence.

But I'd already spent my time that morning with Bobby Robson, and now they had to leave for training – so Des stayed safe from the press anyhow.

Exclusive: Bobby Robson eats prunes and peaches for breakfast . . .

Robson said he'd told Don Howe the team that'd start against Ireland on Wednesday 6th, the day after the kickabout in Oristano. He said, 'You have to clear your head. You can't go around saying, is it this, or is it that?'

Was Oristano helpful?

'A bit. A fraction.'

Was Tunis helpful?

'You take a risk. You take a gamble wherever you play. Prior to the World Cup you know, if you have a sub-standard performance, you'll get done – papers'll go mad. And they don't worry about players, they rip you to pieces – then they want to come and smile, and talk to you. Would you do it? Honestly, would you do it? I'm not saying they're all bad, they're not, some write good stuff – David Lacey, I'd share a glass with him, I'd go anywhere with him. But the tabloids, the muck, the derogatory stuff . . .

'Look, it was hot in Tunisia, it was eighty-two degrees. We got off to a decent start, we made some chances – could have had two before they scored. Then we make the most unbelievable error, and we're severely punished for it. Quite extraordinary, 'cos the feller hit about a forty-yard shot – and you're now in a different game.

'And are you going to tell me Tunisia are nothing? Look at

Cameroon – I thought Argentina might win 1–0. But when they go ahead they become elevated, these fellers – like Egypt, if they score first, they can do you. They'll get confident, they'll get aggressive – it was only through bloody persevering that we nicked a draw. Well, we didn't nick it, if you look at our possession – Peter Shilton did nothing second half, saved one free-kick – but you can't get through. They know how to defend.'

And the Butcher incident?

'I didn't see it. All I know is we got a lot of free-kicks, and they hang into you, they grab you – and the referee won't give penalties. So you're waiting for a free kick, you know the run you're going to make, and they're baulking you, they're dragging you, they're holding you – so Butcher's just gone, "Geddaht the way" . . . and he's caught the feller. He hasn't butted him, have you seen where he's cut – he's just shook the feller off 'cos he's grabbing him. And then I took him off, 'cos he's booked for it – knowing Butcher, he could make one injudicious tackle, one long-legged tackle, and we're down to ten men. And then, I needed to look at Wright anyway.'

I asked if he was over-loyal to a player like Butcher. He said he didn't play him because he was loyal to him, he played him because he was the best. Look at Shilton . . . then, recalling how Shilton had been criticised over Uruguay's two goals, he went off against the papers again. 'They fuckin' murdered him. SHILTS WILTS, all that – and then they expect him to talk to them? We are human people. Take Butcher, you look at what he's done for us. In September, I thought he had a red shirt on when he came off that pitch – thought he was playing for Wales. So now it's eighty-two degrees, he looks a bit slow, he's got his name taken, he's took his shirt off – and they go WHACK. No fuckin' loyalty.'

I asked how he answered the criticism that England were predictable.

'By results. We play the same way as Liverpool – we play the same way as Jackie Charlton. Jackie Charlton plays 4–4–2, he kicks the ball long – I don't see any criticism there. He's got results. Me, I've lost one in nineteen. Before the European Championships we lost one in sixteen, played everywhere – and I tell you what, when you're England, people want to beat you more than anybody else.'

So how did he feel, with thirty-six hours to go?

'Fine. I'm looking forward to it. I know the pressure I'm under, I've been through it before. I won't crack. Christ, if I couldn't cope I'd have cracked weeks and weeks ago, wouldn't I? Years ago. I just find it all sordid and bloody wicked, I really do . . . never mind.'

I wondered then, as we finished, having watched him work for nine months, whether there was ever any time when he wasn't thinking about football – about the next match, the next opponent, and the best team to tackle them.

'On the golf course. Or listening to music. I like the old evergreens, the old ballads – Ella Fitzgerald, Dionne Warwick, Shirley Bassey, Neil Diamond . . . love it. Or reading. I like James Michener, or Wilbur Smith. Robert Ludlum, James Higgins, stuff like that – I don't like the heavy highbrow stuff, can't take that. I like action. Who's that American guy . . . d'you ever see that picture with Humphrey Bogart where he's Captain Queeg, he's got the ball bearings in his hand – Herman Wouk. Brilliant . . . but otherwise – people think I'm drifting sometimes, but I'm just absorbed with it all really. I'm consumed with football, I have been for twenty years. Picking the team, training . . . people say I won't be able to retire. But,' he laughed, 'I think I will.'

I thought we were done then – but as we were about to get up and go back across the lawn he said, as if it was worrying him, 'I don't feel as though I've come out of this very well, talking about this press thing – but I just find it's a bit unfair, that's all . . . the players have conducted themselves ever so well. They're here to play the World Cup, and sometimes they want to keep out of it, keep out of the papers – I'm like that. I'm trying to keep out of the bloody papers, not get in 'em. But they want to see you all the time . . . the week with our wives, I thought it was a holiday – I never got a holiday.'

I asked in what way he thought he mightn't have come out of it well.

'Oh . . . by being a bit aggressive about it. But when I think what I've done over the last eight years . . . you should have seen them the other day. There's the English and the Italians together, and some Italian guy says, "Mr Robson, can you explain to me why it is, with your record, and the success of the England team, that your press are so critical of you?"

'I said, "You're asking the right question, but to the wrong person. You'll have to ask them."

'Silence. So I said, "They obviously didn't hear. Perhaps you'd like to ask it again."

'So the guy asks the same question. I said, "Good. Good question. You've asked the right question, but again, sir, to the wrong person. You have to ask them."

'*Not one replied*. They all sit there, heads down – not one stood up. Not one had any integrity to say anything to that question. And it just shows you what some of them are made of. I said, "There is your answer. We don't need to say any more."'

Then Millichip and Wiseman rolled past with a fat sheaf of newspapers. Wiseman said that Doug Ellis, the Aston Villa Chairman and Graham Taylor's boss, had written 'a lovely little article about the Chairman, that he's going to meet him on his yacht. "I'm going to invite Bert to settle the deal."' The deal was, of course, compensation to Villa for Taylor moving into Robson's job.

'Forty bottles of champagne,' mumbled Millichip mysteriously in the background.

'So he's got about as much chance of us going on there as flying,' said Wiseman.

'Strike the deal before you go,' said Robson, 'then you can pop the champagne.'

Wiseman asked, 'Can you imagine what the council would say?' They descended into conspiratorial whispers, and bumbled away – happy old boys in their shorts in the sun.

Then Robson turned back to me, and to the story of how no English journalist had stood up that question. He said, 'I saw Bob Harris a bit later, and I said, "Your industry came out very well this morning." He didn't say anything.'

Harris was writing a book with Robson, a World Cup diary. They'd done the same together in Mexico – when I tried to get a copy from my library, they said there were two copies in the county. One in a prison, one in a youth custody centre . . .

Robson said, 'I still haven't answered that correctly, you know, about how I felt when we left. I felt dreadful.'

He was worried about being aggressive? He said, 'If this was a war, you'd shoot them.'

*

There's a story where it's raining, so Robson's with the press in one of the dressing rooms at the training field; and he's wanting to give Peter Went from the PA a real public bollocking for the rubbish story about his being booed when he watched Cagliari. But there's this woman at the back ... Robson's got his temper restrained, while he tries uneasily and impatiently to find out who she is – and it turns out she's one of the journalists' wives. He wants her to leave, so he can get on and roast Went – but he doesn't quite know how to ask for this politely. Then anyhow someone tells him, it's raining outside. Robson snaps, 'Get her an umbrella.'

Typical of the man: he didn't want a woman in the room while he was swearing ...

England trained on a little ground in Pula with one low stand, and a bare concrete wall all around. Opposite the locked gateway was a grubby dirt car park; milling about waiting in the sun and the dust were maybe a hundred press, photographers and TV, plus a fistful of fans, tanned and tattooed.

Barclay wondered aloud, 'What fiendish schemes are they hatching in there? England's legendary free-kicks ... give it to Stuart Pearce, and close your eyes.'

I told the *Daily Mirror*'s Harry Harris how I'd had such a gruesome time with Radio Mitch's mates. He said, 'All right, but who's being stitched up? The fans? Or the guy who's getting his head sewn back together in the hospital? You ask England fans – they never start it, do they? Who does start a fight? At school, when it's one on one in the playground, who starts it? The kid who calls someone a four-eyed tosspot? Or the kid who punches him? That's hard enough – so how do you tell when there's a thousand of them?'

Fans always innocent, papers always guilty ... the world isn't that simple.

Inside, Mike Kelly was firing shots at the three goalkeepers. Bull and Bryan Robson passed a ball idly back and forth in the middle, watched by Lineker – he'd said earlier, 'I'm doing nothing this morning. Noth-ing.' Gazza joined in with them, singing,

> *Every day, things are getting better*
> *Going faster, like a rollercoaster*

The others played a game in a tight area marked out with

little yellow plastic cones, different players taking turns in goal; they were limited to a couple of touches each, then pass, pass – the ball thudded off their boots as they called out to each other, Widdly, Widdly, Webby, Webby, Macca, Macca, – Webb belted a shot in, and Platt saved it in his gut, *ooooph*. Webb grinned. 'Platty, you daft bastard.'

When they were done, they headed for the white bus with its splatter of logos. On their way, some talked a bit with pressmen here and there; others didn't, and walked straight past. Butcher talked to TV and radio, because 'tape can't lie'.

And he talked to the man from the *Star* – because he's got a contract that means he has to.

And a large hole gapes open in this I-hate-the-press scene.

Because whatever they said, they could never impose any press black-out *en bloc* – not when player after player was taking money from paper after paper, to talk 'exclusively'.

Bobby Robson does his diary with Bob Harris; and he's long been signed up for a few pieces a year in the *Mail on Sunday*. Then Waddle talks to the *Sun*, Lineker to the *News of the World* . . . and so it goes on.

In *The Glory Game*, his account of a season with Spurs in '71–'72, Hunter Davies tells a story of how he and four football writers are mistaken for Spurs players when they get off the plane in Nantes for a UEFA Cup game.

All four of the journalists in that story, nineteen years later, were still on the case in Sardinia.

Love 'em or hate 'em, these boys have been around. They have relationships with people in football, so that every player has a writer or two that he trusts – not necessarily from the paper he's taking money from, either. Bobby Robson, for example, said Steve Curry of the *Express* was a friend of his.

So the England fans proclaim that they're all innocent; and the England squad strike that aggrieved and harried tone of men perpetually misused . . . the world isn't that simple.

On the eve of England's first game, the fans, the players, the press – together we were tipping over into the broiling and fevered air of Planet Football, where the antagonism's veined through with unseen friendships and deals . . . back in

Florence, Gordon Taylor, the intelligent and likeable Chairman of the Professional Footballers' Association, would laugh with me or John Williams or Rogan Taylor about what an amazingly difficult man Brian Glanville could be.

Then he'd have dinner with him for three hours.

'Because,' said John Williams, 'they're all in the club together, aren't they?'

Wherever football goes, they all go too – the players, the writers, the administrators. They jockey and they bicker, like politicians or businessmen in any other large but essentially enclosed corporate entity.

And the flipside of their fraction and friction is, always, an unsplittable symbiosis.

They need each other.

'It's bollocks, this getting wiser as you get older thing. You might maybe get better at pulling birds but otherwise, you know – if you're not mature when you're fifteen, when will you be?'

'Who was it said life's a bowl of cherries? Wittgenstein?'

'Nah – it was Terry Downes. He goes up to the pianist and he says, "Can you play life's a bowl of cherries in 5/4 time?" And the pianist says, "Surely you mean 4/4?" "Nah," says Terry. "Life's – a bowl – of fuck – in' cherries . . ."'

We were headed back up the road to Stalag Forte, the luxury beachside press cage – me, Barclay, two others. 'In Argentina in '78,' says Barclay, 'there was this mangy cur that used to drag round the dustbins looking for scraps, out by the training field Scotland were using. And as Scotland's fortunes lurched from disaster to apocalypse (defeated by Peru, drawn with Iran, Willie Johnston sent home after failing a dope test) Ally MacLeod came over to do his conference one day, and he's pale and drawn – and he pats the mongrel and he says, "Ah well, least this little feller loves me." And the dog bites him.'

They recalled an article about MacLeod that began with the famous four-word para: 'Is the man mad?'

'Sitting on the fence a bit, that was.'

Barclay said it was his fourth World Cup, and he still loved it – the only problem was having to write about it . . . and also that, being a Scot, he was no England fan. 'I think they're the most unattractive team in the tournament. Don't get me wrong, I like the English – when they've lost. Winning doesn't suit them. They're like the Germans – they don't wear prosperity well.'

His favourite tournament had been the European Championship in '84 – no British sides. The football was fantastic – and all the paper ever wanted was just a few hundred words.

Over lunch by the gleaming sea, amid throngs of fat Germans and windsurfers, we talked about Milan Seed Cap, and the amazing banality of other American questions they'd heard. A gridiron player was once asked before a Superbowl, 'If you were a tree, what sort of tree would you be?'

'Bobby Robson,' said David Lacey, 'would be a weeping willow. And Bryan Robson . . . Dutch elm.'

Michelle Lineker was there, slight and pretty and, like her husband, fluent and intelligent – the only player's wife to spend the tournament in Italy. She was friends with the violinist Nigel Kennedy's Californian girlfriend – she, and Kennedy, were with ITV in some unspecified capacity. The Linekers have no kids, so it wasn't a problem – and then, as one journalist said, they weren't short of a bob or two.

In Harry Harris's room, I watched the Czechs slaughter the USA 5–1 in Florence. The TV had thirty-six channels, including the BBC, and a German station; the 'room' was a small apartment. It had two double beds – one of them had been commandeered by Marcel, a Dutch journalist whose luggage had all gone astray in the bowels of the Italian airline system. He was now living off Harris's fruit bowl and canapé tray.

Up in Florence, the Czechs got lazy – they should have scored eight. An American journalist later told me, 'It was like watching a train wreck.'

I had a ticket for Italy–USA in four days' time. Jeff Powell wandered in from his room next door, and said after a while, 'Fuck me, they'll get twenty in Rome. They should play it in the Colosseum.' When an American got sent off he said, 'He's lucky, he's just missed out on the Italians. What sport does he play anyway?'

Harris dictated the back page lead for the next morning's *Mirror* down the phone, off the top of his head. He'd spent two hours doing a fifty-five para preview for the inside spread – a 'fly the flag' piece, asking for a restoration of English pride after the traumas of '88. In the office, he said, they'd added a few paras – and one said that in Germany, England were 'outfought, outmanouevred, outclassed'. That, said Harris, was too heavy – he'd changed it. We'd been outfought by the Irish, outmanouevred by the Dutch, outclassed by the Russions, but not all three all at once . . . they could be naughty, he said. On his Argentina–Cameroon byline, they'd put 'Harry Harris in Milan' when he was in Cagliari. 'It'll be caught out and end up in a column somewhere. Why couldn't they just put, "Harry Harris in Italy"?'

Now they needed a think piece for the back page. While he watched the game he casually intoned, 'Paul Gascoigne faces a World Cup baptism of fire tonight . . .'

Harris speculated in fluent tabloid-speak on how Charlton would send out the Irish to wind up Gascoigne. Some guy back in the office would whack a headline on it.

'How many paras is that? Another couple, OK – "There will be more familiar battles . . ."'

When the game was done – and the drinks drunk, and the valet persuaded to bring the *right* hired BMW to reception – I got a lift with Harris and Steve Curry back into Cagliari. And this is how they defended their trade.

Curry said, 'The difference between the sports press and the rotters (the news men) is that we're on semi-holiday – we enjoy ourselves, we like the football, and we like the people in it. And it's very sad that they don't like us any more. But over the last five years in particular, with the intensity of the circulation war . . . the trouble is, there's just too many men here. Each paper's had two men out here from two weeks before it's even started – and there's not enough material for them. So the No. 2's are exaggerating little things, just to get something in the paper. The No. 2's are top-spinners, their game's putting spin on to quotes – but it's only really in the eighties that the papers ever made this a two-man job at all.

'Then in the last five years, you've got the new breed of sports editor [as Barclay succinctly put it, 'Yobs']. They're more interested in the headline than the content – the *Sun* took a tiny Shilton injury and ran a huge scare that it could wreck England's chances. And it was bollocks – we all knew he'd be training the next day. But then Harry's editor rings up and says, why didn't you get that story? And Harry can say, because it's not true – but which one will the punter buy?'

When Robson's move to PSV came out, the *Sun* – the same paper that was telling the guilder-stained traitor to PSV OFF – stuck notes under his hotel door, offering money for his story. The first offer, Curry and Harris were sure, was six figures – and they went back with new notes, two or three times . . .

'The *Sun* are liars,' said Harris, 'proven, unashamed liars – making out Peter Shilton's at death's door when all he's done is knock a knee, that's nothing to them. And they invest an awful lot of money in trying to dig out the dirt – but that's their game.'

From the man whose own paper was about to run the Hostess Isabella story (however much he himself may have disliked it) calling the *Sun* liars was just a touch disingenous . . .

Curry, while he thought Robson had behaved with great dignity, said, 'I have to say that the FA has no decent kind of PR, they're totally amateur – Glen and David, they're very nice men, but they've no grasp of our needs. If the FA were in any kind of competitive industry, they'd have been out of business years ago.'

As to how the players felt, he said that with the No. 2's all scuffling about trying to find something (as if the No. 1's were above all that) each stretch, each exaggeration, each lie – naturally, it got the players more and more antagonised. 'I personally haven't found it that bad. But they have been turned over, so they're very, very careful – and you really can't blame them. And the situation's deteriorated, just recently – though I'd say it's not as bad as '82, with Keegan. Players were hissing and spitting when they came into press conferences then.

'The thing is, you can't all the time be praising people, can you? People criticised Butcher in Tunis – but why? Because he did something unbefitting to an international player, is why. Now someone like Gary Stevens, I can understand it, he's taken a pounding, including from me – I've given him unrelenting stick. But our players are more sensitive than others – when things are going badly, the Italian press can be far more vicious than we'll ever be. They crucify their players.

'Also, when players are criticised, they moan about it – but they sing like budgies when they're being paid.'

Then he said that actually, players fifteen years ago used to behave far worse than they do now, getting pissed, getting laid – 'There was a certain international goalkeeper, after a big night in Europe, we all got on the coach for the airport the morning after, and unbeknown to us, he's only just arrived back in the hotel and gone to bed. So we called from the airport and they put him in a taxi, and he's totally slaughtered. There's some car up on a dais on the concourse, and he's sitting in it, singing away at the top of his voice – an absolute embarrassment.

'But back then we misbehaved with them, they misbehaved with us, and there was an area of trust – it didn't get written. Those were the days, when we used to stay over Wednesday nights . . . and with the rotters now, that's all gone.'

Those were the days . . . when merry bands of Brits bonked and boozed their way round Europe, and not a soul ever to chide them.

Ever since Poland, I'd thought two things about the press. Firstly it wasn't, in the end, that they were bad people – it was, simply, that they were boys.

The players had got the best job, the job every boy dreams of, the job that lets you stay a boy for ever and be a hero too – but there's nothing heroic about writing. The writers couldn't play, so they got the second best job – and sure, it was a job any bright, cocky boy back at school would have been eager to get – but then they found it meant cursing your way down the aisle of a plane in the arse-end of Silesia at midnight, while the heroes drank champagne on the other side of the curtain ... and it was all just harder and nastier than anyone ever told you. You went from city to city, stadium to stadium, bar to bar, season after season, with the yobs in the office on your back every day, demanding you write shit you knew was shit even as the words hit the screens of your lap-tops – and like any other teenage boy you got confused, you lashed out, you had great unreasonable drinking jags ...

So football may well be, like politics or business, a great and amorphous transnational corporate entity, with its many different workers bitching and jockeying for kudos and position.

But with this big difference: it's an entity *populated by boys*.

And there's the tragedy of sport: that the boys have their dream – but the boys get older. And for every boy who doesn't get to the heart of it, playing on the field – for every boy not graced with the luck and the legs to live out the dream for real – for every boy bar those, the dream becomes a snare.

Football's a woman you can't leave (they say in Argentina, you can change your wife – but your club and your mother, never). So you may well fall out of love with it – but you've still got the mortgage round your neck, and another bloody game come Saturday to write about.

> *The burly striker soared above the heads of the despairing defence to head home unerringly.*

> *The silky skills of the subtle Latins left the Saxon yeomen lumbering.*

Hell – *I'd* drink ...

Then there was this second thing I'd thought about the press, more and more since Poland – and it was a question not just about them, but a question that goes wider, to all of us: namely, in what way were they different to the hooligans? Looking back, as they do, to their youthful golden age of Euro-wide liquor and nookie . . . because for sure, they drink in better bars, and they don't smash them up afterwards. But they still drink – they drink, some of them, enough booze to float a battleship. And then, a lot more rarely, they fuck – just like English fans, or English tourists, or English businessmen, on packages on Corfu or the Costa Brava, at trade fairs in Hamburg or Houston, on sex safaris in Mombasa or Bangkok . . . just like Englishmen in general.

The hooligan is not some animal apart. He is our own logical conclusion.

He is us, all played out.

This is how RAMPAGE begins . . .

I went to the Bar Svizzera to watch Brazil play Sweden – and as a man in Kansas once asked me, did you ever see sardines in a can?

The place was packed with English, Irish, and Sard, all having a party time drinking together, and enjoying the game. It was noisy, it was cheerful – and it got photographers and TV crews like shit gets flies. People drank bottles of wine – way cheaper than beer – and they drank bottle after bottle, singing happily *Que sera sera*, England England, Cameroon Cameroon, You'll never walk alone, Cockles and mussels alive, alive-oh – and in honour of their hosts, they also chanted,

> *CA-LYAH-REE! CA-LYAH-REE!*
> *EE-TAL-YAH! EE-TAL-YAH!*

Best of all they sang, in unison,

> *We – all – agree*
> *England and Ireland are magic*
> *Are magic*
> *Are magic*

The hostility level was zero; the Brazil–Sweden game was wonderful. At half-time, Brazil were a goal up . . . but it was becoming impossible to see or hear any of it – and the little old lady who ran the place was getting scared.

I don't know if she called them, or if they came of their own accord – but outside, the baton merchants were gathering by the vanload.

And the trouble with the fans is, they can't see the end of a good thing. Several of us – one or two Irish, me, Radio Mitch – tried to tell people the *carabinieri* were with us and looking mean, and cooling the noise down would be a seriously wise move. But (with justice, after all) several replied that they were doing no wrong – while others were simply too boister-ously drunk, too high on being together in a sing-song gang and, basically, too dumb, to know how or when to calm it down. The smarter and the more sober – the likes of Mitch and his mates – saw the danger, and began to leave. It only takes one glass . . .

Then the scum arrived – with a whole train of press in tow who'd been following them from bar to bar, just waiting for them to get things started – and giving them, of course, the global audience they crave. There were only four or five of them; they got up on to tables with their crewcuts and their piggy little eyes, and they barked out their poison, and their 'No Surrender to the IRA.'

It was wholly out of character with a loud but harmless evening, and it soured it utterly. They turned on the ice cream machine – brave boys – and green and white slop started spreading over the marble floor.

The regular fans, even the drunk ones, wanted none of this crap – more people began to leave. Others were still singing – though interestingly, when someone told the venom-heads that the police were on the brink of coming in, they hopped off their tables and – so courageous – fell silent immediately.

And, this time, it didn't go off. There was no RAMPAGE. But it had been only an inch away . . . and if it had gone off, a lot of people who did no wrong would have had their heads whacked hard, and their pictures in the papers.

There was, however, this great encouragement. You couldn't get the fans to pack it in because the police were there – but a good number of them packed it in for themselves anyway, when the ugly crew came, and walked away.

Out on the pavement among the swarming media, I found Colin Moynihan's press secretary. I believe – I hope – that he would have seen it that way too; and the next morning he did stress, at a conference for the rotters, that any trouble so far had been exceedingly minor, compared to the numbers of English in town.

Disappointed, the scum moved on with their eager retinue, and went looking for someone else to wind up. The old lady and her friendly waiters started mopping up the aftermath. With relief, no doubt, but also with genuine kindness, she said goodbye and goodnight to all the boys as they left. Several among them gave her little presents, English and Irish favours, green wool bracelets and a three lions pennant; while others charmed and flustered her, by giving her great boozy bear-hugs to say thank you – a strange and pleasant cross-cultural sight, these large and plastered boys in their ragged shorts and torn T-shirts, picking up and embracing this amazed, embarrassed, and rather delighted old Sardinian sweetie. And others shook her and the waiters by the hand – friends were made here, and it was *grazie* all round.

So I didn't see too much of it – but while we were narrowly avoiding RAMPAGE, Brazil beat Sweden 2–1; Maradona's Napoli team-mate Careca scored both the goals.

More ominously, the Germans stuffed the skilled and fancied Yugoslavs 4–1 in Milan. Captain Lothar Matthäus scored two screamers, and played Dragan Stojkovic off the park; while his Inter Milan colleague Jürgen Klinsmann put away a spectacular diving header. Together that night, Careca, Klinsmann, Matthäus and Rudi Völler all served notice that – though the Italians might have trouble scoring – there were Italian-based Germans and Brazilians who knew very well where the net was.

Meanwhile, German fans had a bit of a rampage of their own, smashing windows and looting for four hours through the city centre . . . two were jailed for a year, for attacking a policeman; forty-three were deported. And word came in of a new phenomenon: *East* German hooligans.

It's a common European home, boys.

I went back across Largo Carlo Felice to La Perla, got up to my room – and then the sirens went off, and a roaring of engines, and a screeching of brakes. Beneath my balcony a ragged group of English and Irish fled the flashing lights and the racing police vans out on Carlo Felice – then they span and hared back the other way, as a knot of Italian boys came pelting towards them, and spilling out across the main road. I legged it down the stairs and got outside, and found a pair of Irish, breathless and alarmed at the end of the sidestreet. One said, 'I'll tell you two things. I'm glad as hell I'm out of here to Palermo come Tuesday. And you wear an Irish shirt these next two weeks, feller – 'cos they're picking up anybody English out there just for nothing. For nothing.'

Hank appeared round the corner then with Duncan, an English boy who was also at La Perla – they were sweating and breathing fast, and absolutely scared shitless.

They said they'd been coming off a sidestreet at the top of the Largo to come down to the *pensione*, and they saw three English boys walking across a zebra crossing – doing nothing at all, just crossing the road – and suddenly an unmarked white Fiat with its lights off comes streaking up the hill; narrowly it misses these three boys, as it screeches spinning to a halt. Then out jump three plainclothes men; two of them grab one English guy, the other two run.

'And the third police guy,' says Hank, 'he goes down in a crouch like it's fucking Los Angeles – and he's got a fucking gun. He's waving a fucking gun about. And he's shouting in Italian to the other two to stop – but what use is that?'

Meantime, the other two agents are pistol-whipping the one they've grabbed on to the back seat of the car.

So now being English on a zebra crossing is an offence to be dealt with by handgun?

Out on the Via Roma, Italians and English were making little runs at each other – *fuggi fuggi*, nothing serious. And the police were even whacking the photographers . . . Duncan said he saw one English lad on the floor with a bloodied face.

Then he said that since four in the afternoon (and this was confirmed by fans all over Cagliari the next day) there'd been press and TV from every country in Europe buying drinks for the boys all round town.

No arrests; one boy hospitalised for the night.

And like Harry Harris said – just who *does* start all this?

The BBC's Rob Bonnet filed material suggesting that the police were being insensitive and provocative.

Even the *News of the World* talked about 'bloodthirsty Italian police' – but then, the tabloid agenda had an interesting spin on it.

Moynihan's press secretary said one radio report about the *fuggi fuggi* had been so over the top, it had been brought up at a Downing Street briefing – where people were told that this exaggeration didn't help. This was not, of course, what they'd been told after Stockholm – but now it was be-nice-to-football time, and the government was saying we don't want RAMPAGE any more . . . so the tabloids started laying into the Italians instead.

PASTA JOKE

The Italians had 7,000 police and *carabinieri* on Sardinia – more police than there were England fans . . . '90 Tour had sold less than half of their 3,000 packages; with the FA selling most of their allocation of 2,816 tickets, and then a few hundred buying in the street, I'd say the Irish outnumbered the English in the Sant'Elia by two to one at the very least.

A pathetic cretin called Chris Wright – 'the man in the top hat' – went about in his ghastly crimson and sky-blue Crystal Palace gear, telling people there'd be a march on the stadium from the rail station at six. With abominable irresponsibility, he told people if they turned up that way without tickets, they'd get in . . . fat chance.

The stadium was an armed camp. Hundreds and hundreds of police and military were ranged all around it, with rifles and handguns; there were mounted police, and police with dogs, and a pair of helicopters circling above. Round the back of the ground, dozens and dozens of dark blue police buses and vans stood empty in rank after rank in the parking lot, and spilled over in a long line along the sealed-off overpass where the main road went by. I thought, who's worried about Abdul Needle? The force was so heavy, Saddam Hussein would have thought twice.

By the quickest way, the stadium was a half-hour walk from the centre of town – but you couldn't go the quickest way. You had instead to go north-east along Viale Armando Diaz, beyond the stadium, and then cut back and come down to it from the far side. I really don't know what the point of that was, especially as it took you through shops and houses –

whereas the quickest way went under the main road by the south side of the industrial estate, well away from any breakable property. But then, like the Light Brigade, it's not the football fan's lot to reason why . . .

Along the way, locals sold wine out of car boots. Drinks ban? Ha – some of the boys who'd been on my plane turned up from their campsite that morning, in a van loaded with crates of beer they'd bought the day before . . . but it did work overall. Along the Via Roma all day, fans sat subdued in front of mineral water and Coke – a sorry and rather comical sight.

When they got to the stadium, they were searched and searched again. All their coins were taken off them, and you can understand why – but you can't call it fair that they didn't get them back. And people lost all kinds of other stuff, in this draconian shake-down – shaving foam, toothpaste, even plastic mineral water bottles were confiscated when, arriving three hours before the game, it was hot in there. But that was too bad – get out your notes, and buy the franchise man's sponsor-fizz instead. I saw one Irishman staring in disbelief, as a policeman frisked his green teddy bear.

Arriving in big bands, the Irish sang,

Oooo – laaaay . . . o-lay, o-lay, o-lay

And the English march arrived from the station, singing 'God Save the Queen'.

I got into the press centre at 5.25, twenty-five minutes into Scotland's game in Genoa against the perky Costa Ricans. Hugh McIlvanney sat in torment before the TV by the bar; he said, 'They're fucking hopeless – just like we thought.' Then he pointed at Jeff Powell and said, 'Him and his lot'll be getting the sneers ready.'

Sure enough, the English journalists were grinning fit to burst. When I asked how it was going, one said, creased up, 'Oh, they're holding out. Costa Rica have only had three or four chances.' And at half-time they said, 'Only forty-five minutes away from a point.'

In the fiftieth minute, one Juan Cayasso performed the four-yearly ritual of breaking Scottish hearts – a colleague's deft backheel set him free, and he scored from close range. At the other end, Luis Conejo acrobatically kept out what little the Scots could throw at him. McIlvanney jerked and jumped at each lost chance in his chair, his face a kaleidoscope of rage and despair over the wretched fate of having to follow his unbelievable team.

Costa Rica 1, Scotland 0. Or, as the *Guardian* splendidly put it:

SCOTLAND PLUNGED INTO CAYASSO

In Glasgow, the *Daily Record*'s headline said sadly:

STOP THE WORLD CUP, WE WANT TO GET OFF

The Costa Rican President moderately announced, 'This is driving us crazy with satisfaction.'

But there was worse to come yet from British football tonight.

The England team arrived two hours before kick-off with four outriders, and seven or eight cop cars all flashing their lights. The chopper that had attended on their passage joined the other two over the stadium; they buzzed and clattered close above our heads, drowning out the shuffle and whisper of fans' feet across the Tarmac. They walked in lines past the railings, and weaved through the staring gangs of weaponed and uniformed men. The green of Ireland was everywhere; they'd come in whole families, men and women and children, and they looked a happier lot altogether.

But then, if they lost they'd not cry over it; whereas if England lost again as they'd done in '88, with the Dutch still to come . . . that was *unthinkable*.

Clouds sat along the ridge-tops of the far hills across the bay; the hills stood in a gorgeous hazy rank of grey-blue silhouettes against the last, soft-edged evening light. I turned and went up into the wide bowl of the Sant'Elia.

With half an hour to go, the Curva Nord was all tricolours; the Curva Sud was Union Jacks, and the Cross of St George. The message that appears at sports events the world over was here too: 'John 3:16'.

The verse reads, 'For God so loved the world that he gave his only Son, that whoever believes in him should not perish but have eternal life.'

The Irish had put their own private twist on it: 'Jack 3:16'.

The Union Jacks, meanwhile, announced Gravesend and Aston Villa, Poole Town and Hull City, Oldham and Wood Green ... we are England. On poles opposite the press box flew the flags of the four nations in Group F, along with flags for Cagliari, Italy, and FIFA – the two spheres of the world on two footballs.

There were *carabinieri* with dogs and rifles all round the running track; others stood in big bunches round the upper rim of the top tier.

The new floodlights were bright under the darkening sky – it was now a rich indigo sheet, laced round the horizon with tufts of mauve and pink cloud. It was very breezy, too, and a little bit chill – a lot of the journalists were shivering in shirt sleeves. But not me – the excellent Signora Orru gave me weather reports every match day, for my £8.50 a night ...

The teams came out, and the stands popped and crackled with flashlights. Oddly, the Irish turned to face away from the cameras across the pitch, when their anthem was played. A man from the *Sun* said, 'Not many of them know the words.' This is a side, after all, whose Irishness is determined for the most part only by the odd grandparent here or there – there's a story of a new Anglo draftee joining the team on some foray into Europe, and the anthems get going, and he turns to the player beside him and says, 'Blimey, this one goes on a bit.'

And the other guy says, 'Shush – it's ours.'

Where do they come from, after all? Apart from the scouser John Aldridge playing at Real Sociedad in the Pays Basque, the Irish side starting in Cagliari had two Celtic players, two Liverpool, and two Aston Villa, with the rest coming from Millwall, Blackburn, Norwich, and Everton – so you want English football? Go watch Ireland.

When the sides were named, Stevie Bull – as a substitute – got the biggest English cheer; but the Irish names garnered far greater and more noisy support, and Jack Charlton the biggest roar of all. Can a crowd have an accent? Sure can:

OIRE-LAND! OIRE-LAND!

The Irish looked dangerous immediately, a long throw on the strong wind going right into the heart of the box; Shilton got crunched in a sandwich of green shirts. And sure enough, they were off and at it at 200 mph; Gascoigne got warned, as the tackles started flying. It was hassle, hassle – two men on Barnes every time he saw the ball, forcing error, shutting down space – not football, just mayhem, with the ball in the blowy air all the time, and no end of argy-bargy in the box.

Surely England had the class to overcome this dreck ... Bryan Robson headed a Gascoigne free-kick wide – Moran tumbled Lineker after a neat touch had him turned and left standing – then, on eight minutes, Waddle released an immaculate ball from the flank into the teeth of the wind, and into Lineker's sprinting path. He chested it past Bonner; Bonner tried to bring him down with a leg swung at his knees – but Lineker hurdled him and just kept to his feet, stabbing both himself and the ball all together into the net as two desperate Irishmen fell crashing on his back.

It was a brave and typical goal, wolfishly taken with electric pace – his thirty-second for England, in fifty-two games. And that's no mean record.

> *You're not singing*
> *You're not singing*
> *You're not singing any more*

But the Irish shovelled back into it. Gascoigne was showing nice touches, playing smart passes round the middle; but Ireland defended in dense numbers, and pressed and pressed without cease – they kept on sticking two men to Barnes to cancel him out, and they bundled Lineker and Beardsley around without compunction.

In the wind it was awkward; the German referee kept interfering – and the brutish hullaballoo didn't give him much choice. The wind grew stronger; a shivering journalist joked, 'I always knew it'd be a difficult contest for the Irish in this heat.' Getting bored, the English sang,

> *We won't pay no poll tax*
> *We won't pay no poll tax*
> *La la la la*
> *La la la la*

After twenty-five minutes, an alarming incident: chasing yet another long ball, Aldridge and Des Walker tussled and fell together over the goal line, and Walker crashed into the advertising hoardings. He played on, but for the rest of the game he was limping – and Des Walker with an ankle sprain was bad news indeed, with the likes of Van Basten lurking down the road.

Meantime, every Irishman who got the ball, you could tell what he was thinking like he was shouting it through a megaphone: 'How high and far can I kick the thing this time?' Floodlight height ... things got scrappier and scrappier, England sinking with their opponents to the Wimbledon level. And always there was the vague and unlikely fear that they'd lose a goal, as the Irish kept hoofing it at random into the box. They didn't make chances, they just caused confusion – but that kept Shilton more busy than Bonner ever was. Butcher, I noticed, yawning, as he headed away another moonshot, had shaved after all.

The thing degenerated into abject chaos. Either the ball ricocheted about like it was pinball, not football; or some rare and brief interruption that threatened English quality was abruptly terminated by another train crash of a tackle. Barnes was invisible – his first look of something like a real run wasn't until nearly forty minutes had gone by. He was, of course, sent arse-over-tip, and the free-kick led to a chance; but it was the first clear thing that had happened in ages. At half-time we watched our monitors, wondering grimly what RAI TV might do for highlights – because the goal apart, there hadn't been any.

I went out the back of the stand to go down to the press centre for a coffee – and there, rushing towards us across the Gulf of Angels, was a vast and spectacular electrical storm. Huge streaks and ructions of lightning flew from fierce black clouds all round the bay.

It hit us just as the second half began, and the rain came sheeting down ... so much for acclimatisation. We might as well have been on Merseyside, or Tyneside.

The postage stamp roof over the press box didn't cover all the out-lying positions; we scuttled for shelter, as monitors fused and died all around us, and sat grousing in a huddle at this continuing worthless jungle of a game. It picked up where it had left off – except now the turf and the ball were wet, and the play was even worse.

Only Gascoigne really stood out now and then, sharp and light in the middle of things; Barnes had disappeared completely. I sat hunkered on my haunches behind a pair of demented Colombian radio commentators talking nineteen thousand to the dozen – God knows what about, it can't have been the game, the game was a dog. Maybe they were letting the folks back home in Barranquilla know in Cagliari they have tropical storms too – they were an amphetamine double act. The lightning raced past over our heads, truly Spielbergian in its scope and drama.

Then, on the hour, Waddle set off from deep in his own half. He skipped past one man, cut in, left another man standing, and got into the area – so Moran simply toppled him. It was a hack to the ankles as obvious as if he'd brought him down with a baseball bat.

Bobby Robson said later it was 'clear as day'.

But we don't get penalties, do we?

In the sixty-ninth minute, Robson took off Beardsley, and sent on Steve McMahon to bolster the midfield – which you might say was sensible enough, in the dismal chaos out there, because he wanted to be sure and hold the lead.

Instead, he lost it. McMahon had been on for four minutes when, with only his third touch of the ball, he lost control of it on the edge of the box. It bobbled off his right foot – Kevin Sheedy pounced, and fired it in first time.

In the next minute, an inch-perfect Gascoigne free-kick, a lovely curling ball, went just a bare yard wide from Butcher's head. And on eighty minutes, a Barnes chip across the box passed a hair's breadth away from Lineker's brave dive.

And that was the sum total of England's riposte. Robson sent on Bull for Lineker with six minutes left – but by then, we were in a ruin of bewilderment.

The tortured McMahon saw red, tangled with McGrath, and got booked.

A minute or two later, Gazza damn near did the same – he came within inches of punching Chris Morris's lights out. But, mercifully, he remembered where he was just in time – turned the wrestle into a hug and a handshake.

And you could say, with hindsight, that that moment of self-collection – on the brink of disaster – was a turning point on the road to maturity for one of the greatest players of Italia '90.

But it didn't look that way then, not on 11 June. It looked, playing the way we were, like we'd get tonked by the Dutch, and in all probability by the Egyptians too. It looked like we'd be coming home in no time, in anguish and in bitterness, to the sound of a howling deluge of recrimination and fury.

Meanwhile the Irish fans went spare, and fair enough:

> *We're on the march with Jackie's army*
> *We're all going to Italy*

The English were silent – misery in the rain.

My soaked monitor had, mysteriously, retrieved a one-inch-wide strip of the picture – it was like watching the game through a fence.

But it had never been worth even squinting at.

England 1, Ireland 1.

ENGLAND IN A SHAMBLES

BOBBY'S BUNGLERS

ARTLESS, CHARMLESS, WORTHLESS

They were absolutely right – it was an abominable display. And yet to be honest, looking at the papers now, the English press if anything were almost tolerant of their team's witless scuffling.

Following Robson's cue, they pointed out that though we may have failed to counter it, we did still all know what the Irish would be like. In Jack Charlton's reign the Irish, after all, had been beaten only five times in thirty-eight. Robson told people to hold the criticism until they'd seen whether the Dutch fared any better against the 'biff-bang' long ball.

And David Lacey wrote in the *Guardian*, 'When it is the Egyptians' turn, they may think back nostalgically to the days when all that afflicted them from the heavens were frogs.'

But blaming the Irish was no excuse. It wasn't just that the football had been awful – but that the whole English approach had seemed gutless. It's all very well saying how stoutly we defended – and, we did, we fought, messy and ugly and tedious though that was – but with the likes of Barnes and Waddle on the park, what the hell were we doing defending all the time in the first place?

When Lineker got the ball, as often as not he was on his own up there – the midfield just sat back and held. But there was no such chickenshit hesitation from the Irish. Sure, they put every man and his dog behind the ball when they didn't have it; but when they did have it, and they pumped it up via the nearest passing stormcloud in the general direction of Tony Cascarino, what did they do then?

They surged up to join him and help out.

I think the problem was this. Bobby Robson had said to me, 'I know the pressure I'm under, I've been through it before' . . . and he was, as we know, a conservative man, with a horror of England losing, and an acute awareness of the rage that would be vented on his head if we did lose. So I think he sent his team into a game that he knew would be a scrap *promoting* caution. And Macca and Gazza would, in effect, say as much the next day.

So what happened? We played cautiously – we played downright badly – and the Irish made the running. Then Robson made a cautious substitution, the substitute made a mistake, and Sheedy said thanks very much and got a draw.

Robson said it would be a different business when it came to playing the Dutch – he said we could play some football then. But on the evidence of the Ireland game, there was little comfort in that. The mind went back to Germany '88, and the devastating Van Basten scoring three times in twenty minutes . . . *that* was football.

And here at Italia '90, we'd had twenty-one goals from the first eight games – we'd had Italy, Brazil, West Germany, Romania, the Czechs and Cameroon, all looking in their different ways like rampant class acts – *that* was football.

Whereas England–Ireland, the first draw of the tournament, had been nothing better than an oafish mêlée.

Dejected, I went to have a look at what the rest of the world was up to; I keyed in the Italia '90 News section of the Databank. But there was no news.

A steward said, 'The news is broken.'

Some time after midnight, I went back into town with Matthew Engel from the *Guardian*. We found the blue lights flashing, the vans all massing – the predictable malarkey.

226

We parked on the Via Roma. A bunch of English were gathered ahead of us at the main entrance to the station; as we crossed the foot of Largo Carlo Felice, a scattering run of *ragazzi* came our way, and then broke up. We backed off a minute; and then went on again.

But nothing much was happening. There was just, instead, this simple problem, which the FSA, the FA, and the embassy had all told the Cagliari police and *comune* would arise, and which had now arisen – because no one in Cagliari had listened.

With games starting at nine in the evening, all public transport had packed up long before the fans were let out of the stadium. But a fair few of England's supporters were staying on campsites out at places like Pula, thirty or more kilometres away – so how on earth were they going to get there? A cab was thirty quid, minimum – so these drenched and discombobulated boys were now marooned as well.

Glen Kirton said the next day, 'We said to them in September, you must put on public transport. We said to them in December, you must put on public transport. We said to them in February, March, April, and May, you must put on public transport. We spoke to them last week and said, you must put on public transport. I sent a fax to the COL two days ago saying, we have been attempting for a long period to get public transport put on to take the fans away from the game – we're getting no response – can you use any influence with the powers that be in Cagliari, to try and get this done? So on this issue it's absolutely not a case of the FA doing nothing – just nil response from the people who could effect it locally.'

Yet they could handle laying on extra ferries to ship the Irish off overnight to Palermo – so why not a few buses to get the English down the road?

The authorities later claimed that, in fact, they had laid on buses – but that at half-time they'd *forgotten to announce it* . . . PASTA JOKE indeed.

Things would be nastier later, come Turin. But on top of the transport foul-up, this was also an early occasion where the intimidating armed presence that encircled the English now offered protection, as well as threat – because one or two local lads fancied testing their mettle on the famed hooligans now gathered so conveniently . . . there was word of one of them swinging a bike chain about.

The minority of English who wanted to make something of it made a surge or two – hence the scatter of *ragazzi* as we arrived.

And the majority who didn't want to mix it (though bear in mind that they were sober here, which definitely did help) – they were backed into the station concourse, with a cold and uncomfortable night ahead.

The *carabinieri* inserted their considerable, riot-ready numbers, and drove off the Sard boys with a surge or two of their own . . . and then we all just stood there.

So what next?

The official Sant'Elia attendance that night had been over 35,000 – not a full house, but not bad – and the game had produced the stadium's all-time record takings, over £1,000,000. And where did the money go? There were twenty-seven officially supplied Cromas and Tipos and Unos and Pandas smoothly ferrying the bigwigs about – but what was there for these boys?

They'd travelled far, and, many of them, paid over the odds into those takings of £1,000,000 via the sharp hands of touts – and yet now, there was nothing, not even a bus home. Just a station platform to sleep on, because their tents were too many miles down the road . . . it was a scene right out of the English game: the money ploughing back into the pockets of the fat cats at the top – and to hell with the punter at the bottom.

And the only people I saw there, actually there on the ground, trying to do anything for them, were Craig Brewin, and Steve Beauchampe, and John Tummin of the FSA . . . someone said Moynihan was there – but where? Doing what? Reading police reports?

And Doug Ellis was there, and David Dein the chairman of Arsenal, and Jarvis Astaire of Wembley Stadium Ltd., merrily confabbing on yachts offshore – while the people who paid their wages sat wet and tired in the small hours on a cold marble floor; or stood and watched the blue lights flashing all around them, and the *carabinieri* hefting their guns.

Kirton said next day, it wasn't true that the FSA were the only people on the ground. The FA had their office in town, they had two security officers out at midnight the last three nights, they had undercover police . . . but these people needed help, not surveillance.

At one point a group of Irish were marched in to join the English. 'For their own safety,' someone said – but the Italians applauded them as they passed.

Engel sighed, 'I don't think the police quite understand the nuances here.'

Then someone said that buses were coming. Beauchampe sighed, 'Yeah – they're just building them now.' Then he added, with an unintentional but ghastly prescience, 'I suppose they'll have to crash a few on the way here first.'

Sometime towards two in the morning, buses did finally come, and the weary boys loaded up to get back to their camp-sites.

That still left maybe 150 to sleep in the station. The platforms and the ticket hall looked like the underground in the Blitz. A bright or lucky few had sleeping bags; others simply lay on the floor, some wrapped in their flags. It wasn't a good night for it.

As I left, I passed one fan articulately berating a high-up plainclothes man in the back of an unmarked car. He said, 'Look, this isn't our fault. There's no cheap rooms here, and no transport – what do you *expect* us to do?'

But the guy only slammed his door, and drove off.

Matthew Engel wrote in the *Guardian*, 'It is not easy finding sympathy for football fans. You cannot blame the Sardinians for being careful; Britain is the only country which sends a government minister round telling other countries how dreadful his fellow citizens are.

'But there is in this the same kind of thinking that precipitated Hillsborough. Obsessed by security, the authorities here have apparently given minimal thought to the simple logistics of moving crowds in and out of the stadium and back to their billets. Or of providing suitable billets, be they ne'er so humble. The scene at the station was pathetic, in more ways than one.'

I asked Glen Kirton about this the next day. The FSA, I told him, was enjoying a rising reputation among the fans – while the FA was widely disliked. (I put it mildly.)

He said, 'I'm not surprised. But the people you're talking about, they're not by their very nature going to accept the FA as a body that has their interests at heart. And the FA, you have to accept, over a period of time, has had very good reason to consider these people as potential enemies of the game. I don't know how many of them would accept this – they believe that they're out there supporting England, and supporting football – but over the years, they've been the people who have actually brought football down. So after Heysel – not just Heysel, but after Luxembourg '77, after Denmark '79 – we've said, please don't go . . . but they still come. And they've become the focus of the press – by their very presence, they've become anti-football.'

But anti or pro, they're there – and they look at the FA and think, the FA's got money (annual turnover approx. £14,000,000), and the FA's making money here in Italy – yet all there is is two ticket desks in a backstreet hallway. And they've got to pay £10 on top of the ticket for a temporary Travel Club membership. Now you could say, They're not our responsibility . . .

'No, I'm not saying that. We're not saying that. We want the Travel Club to *be* a Travel Club – we want to start turning it into a club that gives benefits to the people who join, not just the people here, but the whole range of football supporters – we want to start offering them reasonable travel all across the board. Because if there's been any commercial exploitation here, you know where it's come from. It started with FIFA selling the rights to '90 Tour . . .'

Later, after the Egypt game, I had a word with Pat Smith, the FA's ticket manager. She said tartly of the FSA that of course supporters had a role – but how did I think she came to have her job? Because, of course, she was a fan herself – she'd been a fan since she was eleven.

But she also said that they'd been in daily contact with the FSA – four, five, six times a day. She said they served a need, and that the FA recognised that they did.

And she said it was all very well, the FSA saying the football embassy was the first thing of its kind – but the FA's office was the first time they'd tried it too.

She rejected the accusation I'd heard from fans, that the £10 Travel Club fee was just the fans being made to pay for an under-the-counter ID scheme. It was, she said, £5 to join, and a £5 annual subscription – it was the only way they could organise the ticketing, which didn't come cheap. And, she said, they'd been working in their office since 6 June from 8.30 in the mornings, often until 9 at night – taking half-hour lunches, sorting accommodation, taking one guy to hospital, taking another to a clinic for a rabies injection . . .

There are people at the FA who feel they are unjustly traduced by the fans. Watching them work in Cagliari – and however much they may have been bungling or complacent or inert in the past – it was easy to sympathise with that feeling. All the same – if, as Kirton said, some fans' attitude to the FA is now steeped way too deep in mistrust and hostility, then who else can reach them?

The FSA can.

So if both sides drop their wary postures, and their fearful suspicions over 'politics' – then co-operation could prove fruitful indeed.

Already, in Cagliari, the beginnings were there. The FA, as Bloomfield had said, might not glide into action – but the sounds of its clunking, in Cagliari, were positive. The offices of the two bodies were both firsts – underfunded and ill-prepared, maybe – but at least they were there.

And later, by the time we all got to Turin, the possibilities of co-operation were being recognised even more. So there's grounds for optimism here – because if Kelly & Co. can see it, I don't doubt Kirton & Co. can enact it.

On 11 June, the idea that England might end up in the World Cup semi-finals in Turin was, frankly, preposterous – after the way we'd played against Ireland, you had to question if we'd get to the mainland at all. British football, all round, was the laughing stock of the tournament.

Beneath Matthew Engel's report on the aftermath of England–Ireland on 13 June, the *Guardian* ran a report from the Scottish camp at Rapallo. One of the Scottish players asked, 'Just one thing. Don't say we were as bad as England.'

The Scottish, having blown their best hope of two points against Costa Rica, were now preparing to play Sweden – who had, after all, given Brazil a fair run for their money.

But the Scottish manager Andy Roxburgh said, 'The thing is, we know about Sweden. We know the sort of game they play. It will be more like a typical British match.'

To which the response of the *Guardian*'s man in Rapallo was:

'Those who had watched the England–Ireland game drew hands over eyes and shuddered.'

The local papers next morning said that there'd been no incidents, and sport had been the winner – in theory, at least.

GREAT PARTY, AWFUL GAME

Outside the Bar Svizzera I met a scaffolder from Wimbledon, and a carpenter and a steel erector from Wolverhampton, all heavily tattooed. Also with them was the guy who sold fire protection equipment, who'd been on Stockholm's SHIP OF SHAME – and then a fifth bloke, a Chelsea man. When I asked him what he did he said, 'I dunno what you'd call my job.'

'Fuckin' scrounger,' said a Wolves boy.

He said, 'I work for this very rich person, I sell things for him – antiques, mostly . . .'

One of the Wolves lads said, 'That's gonna look good in his book, innit? Been goin' round with this guy these last couple of days, and now it turns out he's a fuckin' fence.'

These boys had got into Cagliari station from Olbia late on Sunday – the night when there'd been minor *fuggi fuggi* up and down the Via Roma – while the Brazilians and the Germans were winning up north. And in that rumpus one local kid, thirteen years old, had got his leg cut by glass shrapnel from a flying bottle – so now, said these guys, when they turned up, 'There were hundreds of Italians out there, baying for blood. I wanted to get right back on that train, I tell you. And the police were ready just to let us walk straight into it – no way. No fuckin' way.'

They said, with admiration and gratitude, 'Some bloke from the FSA got us out of there – got one of his rear windows smashed doing it – but he got us out, and he drove us to Sarroch.' They would, they said, have been 'ironed out' otherwise.

But mostly, they said, the Sards seemed great. In Sarroch they'd found a bar, and the guy who ran it, 'He was brilliant. We've known him two hours, and he lets us sleep on his floor.

232

Then yesterday in the morning he makes us coffee, and gives us a lift back into town – and he looks after our bags at his place, while we're here at the match. Brilliant.'

A little girl came by begging, and they all gave her money. One said, 'Aw, 'kin 'ell . . . it's only a kid. Bet she thinks it's her birthday.'

And they asked, 'How come the Irish can get a drink, and we can't? We had great crack with the Irish at the game last night – I've not met a bad one.'

But another said, 'They're not perfect. There was twenty at the top here, yesterday afternoon, grouped up and singing IRA stuff. And there was eight of us, we picked up our Union Jacks and walked away, I can't be doing with it. 'Cos I was in the ATC, see, me and five mates at home – and four joined, but not me, I got a job as a butcher. So then two of the four got killed in Ulster – land mine.'

There's good reason, after all, why some people – like Terry Butcher – can't be doing with rebel songs.

I had an idea how awful Steve McMahon must be feeling. Never mind that the football had been dreck – on any other day he could have gone on for those last twenty minutes, he could have held the midfield solid, he could have played the kind of hustling blinder he turns in for Liverpool every Saturday – and then the world would have been a different place altogether.

It would have been England 1, Ireland 0.

Steve McMahon is exactly the kind of English player that the Italians admire, the kind of player of whom Bryan Robson is the exemplar, the paragon – the type of player that the Italians describe, wistfully wishing they had such men themselves, as *duro*. But he'd gone out for his country in the World Cup – and had a nightmare.

I called him up and he said, yes, he'd talk about it.

So I went to the station, and waited for the next bus to Pula.

Outside the main entrance, a battered old taxi sat dented and bruised, and splattered with graffiti proudly announcing, 'Northampton – Old Car – Yes Yes Girls – Tourists Welcome – Very Old Car – Life Is Taxi'.

Life is taxi – but buses are budget.

So we rumbled along the road to Pula, and I read the Italian match reports as we went. They kept drumming it in: *una partita bruta.*

The bus passed through Sarroch, and climbed the slope beyond. Cagliari floated across the bay behind us, a creamy blur in the heat haze; between the vivid blue sea and the cloudless sky the town was a pale hillside jumble, shimmering through the flares of the refinery.

In Pula, a bunch of half-cut English lads got on, heading back for their campsite. They called out cheerfully, 'Drive on, Pedro!'

'Nah, cocker, wrong country. Spiros, innit. Drive on, Spiros!'

'Fuckin' berkhead – Luigi, innit, this is Luigiland. Drive on, Luigi!'

And when we set off:

Here we go, here we go, here we go

I got down at the turn-off into the broiling day. Insects buzzed and whirred as I walked the last couple of kilometres up the side road to Is Molas, and then bantered, gasping, with the police at the gate. They said they liked the English team, they were thoroughly *simpatico* – shame about their football . . .

Macca was waiting with Gascoigne in reception. I wondered if there was something instinctive about that – because when you need cheering up, there's no better boy for it than Paul Gascoigne. He can be genuinely funny, and he's wildly unpredictable – barking out his daft and irreverent comments, bouncing around, stillness quite beyond him – until there's nothing you can do but just watch him and laugh.

But behind the tomfoolery he can be, in his way, very sussed, even sensitive – because no doubt, since September, this boy was growing up.

So he was the right person for Steve McMahon to have about him on a day when you could tell, he was burning up inside so bad, it made the Sardinian sun look like ice. He showed us his chest – he'd torched himself, he was halfway between chocolate brown and brick-red.

I imagined him laying taut and miserable in the fierce glare, going over and over in his head how the ball had bobbed up off his foot – and then that last desperate lunge to retrieve it as Sheedy went round him, and fired it in.

He said the ball had been greasy, and the way it had come to him had been difficult to control; he'd only just gone on, he hadn't got his touch yet, and it was a thing could have happened to anyone . . . but it had happened to him, and boy, did he know it. The way he spoke about it had a pained and furious urgency, ill-restrained.

And it was pig-awful luck, too, to have made that mistake in front of millions the world over . . . but that's the World Cup, and Steve McMahon held his hands up. The fact was the fact; when we talked, he never ducked it.

We walked down to the golf club to get a beer; they readily agreed as we went, it had been a dreadful game. Macca asked Gazza, had he heard? – they were getting 'mullered' back home.

'Mullered', 'mullahed' – I wouldn't know how you spell it, we're in a dictionary-free zone here. But I know a 'muller' is 'a flat heavy instrument of stone or iron used to grind material against a slab of stone' – and whether that's where it comes from or not, you can tell easy enough anyway, from the sound of it, what getting mullered means. McMahon's soul, certainly, was being ground in a hard place.

Gazza said he wasn't surprised, it was fair enough – and Macca said the same. He said he didn't mind gettng trashed, when they'd played a lousy game – what he hated was getting trashed for two weeks solid beforehand, when the Cup hadn't even started.

'It makes you wonder, are these English people? Do they really want you to win the World Cup? Or would they rather you lost it, so they can sell loads of papers?'

Back in April he told me he read the papers, but not the *Sun*. The *Sun*, after Hillsborough, ran a front page saying THE TRUTH – which was basically lying tittle-tattle leaked through South Yorkshire police trying to cover their backs, that drunken Liverpool fans had been riotous and thieving, and had picked the pockets of the corpses . . . the *Sun*'s circulation fell by 200,000 on Merseyside after that.

Now they'd come to Macca, and offered ten grand for his World Cup story. Macca said to Jon Smith, no way. He said, 'My Dad'd kill me. Everyone in Liverpool would kill me. *I'd* kill me.'

As we went, Gazza couldn't walk past a car that had its driver's window down, without reaching in for a quick parp on the hooter.

But when it came to talking of the game, he was both kind and deadly serious, reaching instead for consolation for McMahon. It had been, he said, 'A cunt of a time to get sent on.'

Together they reached for some cause, some relieving explanation for why the game had gone so badly.

Meanwhile, Robson had gone to Palermo, to watch the Dutch playing Egypt. He had a mate with a private plane who was going to fly him around, but he hadn't turned up yet so he'd gone with the press. (Of which Kirton said, 'He's completely daft, isn't he?')

And in his absence, it was a post-match rest day. Other players were on the golf course; I settled down with Macca and Gazza to get some beers in.

People say that footballers are greedy – but I never found it. You couldn't buy a round with these guys if you tried.

I'd said to McMahon, at Anfield in April, that people saw him as a battler, a fighter.

But he told me, 'I don't like particularly to be thought of in that way, I feel as though I do a lot more – I wouldn't get picked for England just for being a battler. You can get someone off the street to do that.'

And the way he played for Liverpool, and for England – he wasn't the man you'd expect to make the big mistake.

But he also did say about Group F, 'Football's so unpredictable . . . they're all going to be very, very difficult games.'

And I'd asked, back in April, if he had any superstitions. He said, 'I always try to go out after the No. 9 shirt. I don't know why, but I've been doing it for years and years. That's the only one.'

But now, in June, he was a man in pain – and any superstition, any little thing that would help put that nightmare mistake behind him . . . it had been, he said, his thirteenth cap.

And before the game, Gazza then said quickly, warming to the soothing balm of that theme, they'd been kept waiting exactly thirteen minutes before going out . . . as soon as you started looking, there were thirteens everywhere.

Way before that though, Gazza said of Ireland, 'They're going away happy – but there's no way I could go happy from a game that's ones all. No way. No matter what match it is.'

I said, we nearly had them . . .

'Unluckily for us,' said Macca, 'we lost the game. We threw the game away. Or if you want, make it . . . if you want to be harsh, I threw the game away. Which is the way it happened. So the Republic go away thinking that they've got a valuable point. 'Cos they were getting beat 1–0.'

'But you shouldn't look happy,' said Gazza, 'if you're a professional footballer, you shouldn't look happy. If McEnroe got beat by Boris Becker three sets to two, he's not going to think, well, I got two sets . . . 'cos I mean, if it was the other way round, and we scored with fifteen minutes left, we're not going to go round saying, *yeeeaah*, we drew against the Irish. We're going to go away thinking, could have had that.'

Macca stopped him and said, 'Yeah, we could have won it. But,' he reassured himself, 'we're happy with the point.'

So I told him how Robson had said, at the conference afterwards, that the team had to take responsibility for it being 1–1 – that it wasn't an individual thing.

'Well, I don't think . . . not really. At the end of the day, it's an individual mistake, isn't it? But it's a team game, and overall . . . I could easily say, if I wanted to, why didn't they make it 2–0, while the team were playing? Why didn't they make it 3–0? But, you know . . .'

They both agreed that it should have been 2–0 – that the penalty was indisputable.

Then I said, Robson at press conferences defended his players, he supported his players . . .

Macca asked, 'In what way does he support the players?'

He backs you up. When the flak's flying he backs you up, doesn't he?

'I don't know. I don't know. Does he? There's times and

places – I think there's times when he does stick up for the players, and that's brilliant. But there's other times . . .'

Did he say anything to you afterwards?

'Not much, no – there's not a lot he can say. I've held my hands up, I've said . . . he come over and he said, "Anything to say to me, son?" And I says, well, yeah, I apologise, I'm sorry, it was my fault, I've made a mistake – and he went, "OK". In other words, I shouldn't need to be . . . I know I did, but I shouldn't have to be apologising to anybody. That was a genuine mistake, I didn't *want* to give a goal away – I didn't go out and say, there, go and have a goal, Kevin Sheedy, let's make it one each. Everybody knows that. It was just a genuine mistake. And the lads are brilliant – that's just the way it was.'

So everybody says, so be it?

'No one's above everyone else. We all play in the same league. Some players individually are better than others but that doesn't matter, we're in a team together, nobody's on a pedestal – or if they think they are, they'd soon get knocked off it. We're all the same.'

And Gazza said too, 'No one in this squad is above anyone else' – Paul Gascoigne said that? He really was learning.

Because when I quoted Tom Finney saying how in his day he was paid to score goals, not to climb the perimeter fence afterwards, then said that he, Gazza, had been criticised for overdoing it after his last-gasp goal against the Czechs – he said, 'I was going to my dad, wasn't I? I knew where he was sitting. And what do they expect from us? Scoring's what you work for all your life, it's what the people come to see.' So of course you go daft.

Then he said another sweet thing; he said, 'You look at professional footballers – every professional footballer *loves the game*.'

And the reason it's sweet, is that it's simply not a true statement. There are professional footballers who *hate* the game – Peter Beardsley had told me there were people even at Liverpool who hated it, hated the pressure, couldn't wait for quarter to five every Saturday afternoon . . . so it wasn't a true statement.

But Gazza would never understand how it couldn't be true – because it was true about him.

And he talked a lot, that afternoon, about 'being a professional footballer' – as if, just turned twenty-three, and playing first-choice for England in the World Cup in Italy, there was a piece of him that still didn't quite believe he really was one.

So he was learning, and he was loving it – because he loves the game. And with Gazza enjoying himself, and a beer or two inside you – it soon enough cheers you up.

Macca said, it had been a bad game, and he'd made a mistake – but he'd still got a cap, hadn't he?

Platt, Bull, Seaman, Woods, Mike Kelly and others came in off the golf course. As people sat down and ordered their beers, Jack Wiseman took time out from watching Belgium score two against South Korea to organise a golf tournament. On the day after the Holland game, he wanted each player and member of staff to play a round against one of their Sardinian hosts – the staff going out first, and then the players later, when they'd got up and felt recovered.

I'm not sure how eagerly people went for that one . . . but Gazza went eagerly for a £50 bet with David Seaman. There was one of the tees not too far off from the clubroom; and then the green for a different hole was, in turn, not much further from that tee. Between the pin and the tee, there was just a steep slope down, and then a smallish strip of water – and the bet was on who, in three shots, could drop their ball nearest the pin.

So we went out on the balcony to watch. Gazza's first shot was a disaster; he barely cuffed the ball, it skidded off along the tee, and rolled away down the slope towards the water. To loud guffaws along the balcony, he leapt into a buggy standing nearby, and careered off down the precipitous slope to retrieve his ball, like something out of the daffier section of a Bond movie. Seaman, meanwhile, dropped his first attempt just a few yards from the pin. Other players grinned; Gazza, they said, could kiss his fifty goodbye.

He veered back up off the slope, pranced out of the cart, and planted his ball on the tee. You watch, said Platt and Stevens, you watch the Gazza twitch. He took up a stiff stance, raising and lowering his club over the ball, knees jerking, body bobbing over the tee each time – and people counted, laughing, nine, ten, eleven . . . then he put the head of the club softly and perfectly through the ball, and dropped it mere inches from the pin. Seaman conceded his fifty.

Butcher, inside, was quiet. He'd shaved, he said, because he was 'under orders'. He had an ugly purple contusion the size of a big coin round his left eye – he'd had, he said, a few 'clashes' with Cascarino.

Macca said, 'Custer's last stand, that was.'

Gazza came back in looking thoroughly cheerful, winding up Platt about his boss at Villa. 'Dougin' Ellis,' he cackled, 'Dooouuhhgin' Ellis.'

Platt said he couldn't wait to introduce them, next time Villa played Spurs.

Gazza mimed out how he'd greet Ellis, with a wildly exaggerated deference and humility.

Others were winding Bull up. There was a poll back home, they told him, people wanted him to play. Nah, said Bully quietly, he wasn't having that – he took it carefully, like he wasn't quite part of the gang yet, and like he knew the pounce was coming any minute.

Sure enough – 'Take no notice, Bully, they're only polling Wolves and Brummies, aren't they?'

Bull said – when people said Genoa were after him – nah, he wouldn't come and play in Italy. Been on pasta three weeks already, it was enough, he was getting a pot as it was.

Macca showed off how tanned his chest was again.

So Gazza felt obliged to look inside his shorts, to see how tanned his cock was.

It was all cheerful, mannish, impenetrable – a football squad, Kirton had said, was 'a self-regulating unit'. They have their own rhythm, their own language, their own names – a shared, sealed, exclusive group cohesion.

And it was, in fact, impressive. They were riding over the disappointment of the draw with Ireland, turning themselves round, getting ready for the next one . . . so I set off back to Cagliari, my hopes a little lifted.

I hitched back; it took four rides. The last was swerving mayhem in a battered farm van with an amiably irascible village man who, to my surprise, started laying into the press with more venom than the whole England squad combined. The papers, he said, were *cattivi* . . . the English and the Irish were fine by him, no problem at all.

240

But McMahon had told me a sad story of how far, now, the hooligan psychosis had gone. Four scousers he knew, nice people, had turned up at Is Molas to say hi to him. He'd got the people at the hotel to help, and they'd found them a cheap place to stay down by the beach. And there were only these four from England, staying in this place – yet every morning, the police turned up to check they hadn't rioted yet.

In town, all the bars were shut – *Aida* was on in the amphitheatre. So I went to the Italia and called Roy Collins's room; he would surely, I thought, be watching Egypt–Holland, that game being somewhat relevant to our prospects.

But it looked to me, when I got to his room, like the man had crashed out – which was a little unfair on the Egyptians, who came very close indeed to doing another Cameroon. Once more, you might say, with African feeling . . . they could have had three before the Dutch scored in the fifty-eighth – and they did get one anyway, with a penalty near the end. It was another really iffy decision – the guy was fouled outside the area, and had to work pretty hard before falling down in it – but it was justice all the same: Egypt 1, Holland 1.

In Cairo, two died in the manic celebrations that followed this excellent performance. And the police officer in charge of that city's deranged traffic said he was pleased it had only been a draw – if they'd won, he said, there'd have been a revolution.

So now each team in Group F had one point, one goal – and while things unfolded all over Italy, no one here on the islands had gone anywhere.

There was, however, this one small difference between the two islands in question: that on Sardinia, we looked like Sodbury Mechanicals could wallop us on an off day – whereas in Sicily the Egyptians looked great, and the Dutch . . . well, they had their problems. But they were still the Dutch, weren't they?

Collins, meanwhile, blearily raged and raved about 'fucking cunting Eyeties'. The COL and Olivetti inefficiencies, and the general reluctance of the Italians to print a ticket for any match that wasn't kicking off in the next five minutes, were getting badly up his nose – and so was the booze ban.

It was a comical thing, all these English journos who'd clamoured for booze bans to keep the dreadful hoolies in line, now finding to their horror that there were indeed booze bans – and that they applied to them too. Collins was urgent about the prime necessity of locating a place that'd give him wine for lunch on the next match day. He said, 'I can go a day without a drink, two days even – but I won't be *told* I can't drink.'

So I took him to the Trattoria La Taverna, where the unendingly friendly couple who ran the place put his dark fears to rest – lunch could be had on the day of the Holland game, and wine could be had with it.

In the process, Collins's wish to learn the languages of the countries he worked in ('beer one' in Seoul now seeming more a dypsomaniac necessity, than a cultural acquisition) turned out to extend only so far as the creation of a monstrous pidgin. His English accent rode through a chaos of random words and syntax – brutishly proud, and lazily unaltered.

Pedro! Spiros! Luigi!

England 1, Ireland 1.

Ghastly press, oafish fans, and 4–4–2 . . . all played out.

It would, I thought, take one of two things for England to get past the dangerous Dutch, and then the splendid Egyptians.

It was either going to take a revolution in the way we played football.

Or it was going to take the likes of John Barnes to wake up and come good.

12   John Barnes

The trouble with Barnesy

John Barnes wears Diadora – they pay him to – and he looks good in it. But then, he'd probably look good in oily rags and a tarpaulin.

No other England player has the easy glamour of John Barnes. It's not that he's uniquely more skilled – Chris Waddle or Paul Gascoigne can each, in their way, be equally electric. But no one else is bewitching like John Barnes – no one else has his lazy pace and grace. And when John Barnes moves – when he approaches his man, then elegantly slips him and speeds away like he did it without a thought, like it came as easy as stepping out in the morning to pick up the milk – that's what the people come to see.

He has a way of running with the ball that makes it seem like gravity's not a problem to him in the way it is to ordinary mortals; a flying, dancing lilt in his stride suggests he can go this way, or that way, and either way it doesn't matter, you'll still be there when he's gone. So defenders tumble before him; he induces a bodily panic, they buckle at the waist and back-track frantically, bent double, their arms spread wide trying to fill the chasms of space he opens all around them – because he makes room where there isn't any, and that's what the people come to see.

And yet, and yet . . . Diadora had a poster in Italy of a naked man caught in a strikingly athletic lunge for a high ball. The slogan was, 'Cover Yourself In Glory'. And covering himself in glory is something that John Barnes, with England, has never really done.

He went into the World Cup voted England's Footballer of the Year (by the Football Writers' Association) for the second year running. And he went into it with fifty-three caps – but only ten goals.

The finest of those came when he was twenty years old, in the Maracana stadium in Rio in 1984. He went on his invisible wings of grace and pace past one man, then another; he cut in, lacing his weightless, drifting way into the area – he slipped a third man, and stroked it away ... he left you, and them, stunned with disbelieving admiration. He'd gone with England into one of the great temples of world football – and scored a goal worthy of Pele at his best.

Not everyone liked it. A fistful of NF thugs followed England on that tour – and though we'd won 2–0, these people (who took the same flight as the squad from Montevideo to Santiago, and barracked Barnes all the way) said the score was only 1–0, because 'Nig goals don't count'.

Fully paid-up members of the human race, however, saw in that goal one of the brightest England hopes of all time. And although since then, as Robson said, we were 'still waiting' for John Barnes – still waiting, six years on – he nevertheless went to Italy as one of *the* great prospects of Italia '90.

In the run-up to kick-off, the Italian papers picked a plethora of 'world teams' from all the stars that were coming their way. Maradona, Van Basten, Baresi – these, of course, were picked time and again. But among England's squad, who did they name? From whom did they expect greatness? Gary Lineker or Bryan Robson, once or twice; Des Walker, not infrequently; and, tellingly, they pointed to Paul Gascoigne now and then. But they picked Barnes pretty much every single time.

So the world waited to see him hit the peak of his career, doing for England what he does for Liverpool every week.

Instead, he was substituted against Belgium, and again against Cameroon – he had a groin strain, and played no further part; he'd not done that much in the previous matches anyhow. It was the saddest of disappointments – and for no one more so than John Barnes.

Gordon Taylor of the PFA told me in Florence that Barnes 'wanted abroad' – that he'd 'wanted abroad' for a good while. But as Italia '90 came to its close, and the Italian papers speculated feverishly in their summer season of transfer madness – linking Walker to Roma, Gazza to Juventus, Bully to

Genoa, Lineker to Torino – they were none of them bothering to speculate about John Barnes any more.

With three lions on his chest it had, in fact, gone very wrong indeed.

So what's the trouble with Barnesy?

In the half-empty bar at Anfield one lunchtime after training, I asked whether Beardsley would be back fit for the semi-final against Palace. Barnes said he was training again – and Peter Beardsley likes to train, he'd train from dawn to sundown if you asked him to. I asked if Barnes liked to train.

He said, 'That depends on the training,' and laughed his easy laugh. Then he said, 'I like to play football – and that's all we do in training here anyway. At Watford we used to do a lot of physical work – but we don't do that much here, we just play football every day. It's great.'

Any takers for a reason why Liverpool keep on winning?

'That's not the sole reason. Other teams do that, just play five-a-side – but the reason Liverpool do well is they've bought well, and they've got the players who suit the system. A lot of teams say it's the way we train – when if they haven't got the players to play that way, they're flogging a dead horse. But teams like Wimbledon and Watford, they've done well because they've realised with the guys they have, they're not going to be able to play the Liverpool way – and they just play to their strengths.'

So when people criticise that kind of 'English' football – harrying, chasing, putting the ball in orbit at 1,000 mph – he wouldn't?

'Not at all. Not at all. Phil Thompson used to play that way. If Wimbledon had the players Liverpool have, I'm sure they'd play the way Liverpool play – but they haven't. If you see Liverpool reserves playing, they play that way a lot – because they've got Phil Thompson in charge, and he believes in playing that way. Just like, whacking the ball up the field and chasing it.'

Then someone in the background (Phil Thompson?) called out, 'Barnesy – tell him it's very difficult to play the long ball.'

It's also very difficult to get John Barnes to criticise anybody, or anything. He's fluent, articulate, moderate, and so laid-back you start wondering what on earth there might be that could actually trouble him. Some say his coming from a stable, disciplined, well-heeled background – his father was a senior man in the Jamaican army – explains why his front is so inordinately calm. So I asked was it true, and was he really that way?

'It's true of a lot of people, in all walks of life. If you ask me, I'll say yes – but what do you want me to say, apart from yes? You walk around here, in the dressing room, you'll see loads of people like that.'

Footballers in England, I said, tended to come from . . .

'The working class. Yeah, that's true. So what?'

Peter Beardsley said he loved his football; and when players like Beardsley or Barnes love their football, the crowd loves them too – so would Barnes say a player who's an artist enjoyed it more than a player who's an artisan?

'Not at all. As an example, I've always used Peter Reid and myself. Because of his industry, people may say – or maybe they won't – that I'm more pleasing to the eye, in my movement, in the way I play. But just as I wouldn't say that Peter Reid is trying harder than I am – he looks as if he is, they always call him hundred per cent because he's a hustler and a bustler, but I'm trying just as hard – so on the other hand, I wouldn't say I enjoy my football more than he does, just because of the way I play. People may say, oh, he just goes out there to enjoy himself, which I do – but I'm sure players like Peter Reid enjoy it just as much.'

Beardsley said he loved his football – but also that there were players at Liverpool who loved quarter to five on Saturday afternoons a lot more. The pressure had taken over from the pleasure.

'I wouldn't have thought I've come across that. Peter may have, because maybe he speaks with ones who live in Southport more than I do, and they say . . . but I really haven't come across that. I mean, I find it hard to accept, because Liverpool are always winning things, and although there's a lot of pressure to do well, Liverpool have always won – more often than not. I mean, I know I always enjoy it – I look forward to every game.'

246

So I asked if it was a be-all and end-all, football – there's plenty who talk like it is.

'I wouldn't think it is for anyone. People may say so, but it's not. Because if all of a sudden they didn't have football any more, I'm sure they wouldn't go out and kill themselves. You say that at the time to get wound up, people think football, football, football . . . and it is at the moment, because that's your job. But when you've finished playing, you go and do something else.'

Did he know what he'd do if he wasn't playing?

'Haven't got a clue. Not a clue. People have asked me that since I was eighteen – in fact, just before I signed for Watford, I was offered a football scholarship at Washington University. I'm sure I could have gone there, just to play soccer, and done something at the university – I didn't have any inclination to go to university, but I'm sure if I'd gone I'd have said, well, OK, I'm going to do this, or that . . . but I didn't really have the inclination. And Watford came in, so that was that.'

Terry Butcher, I said, was the only player I'd spoken to (so far) who expressly said he'd like to go into management. Could Barnes see himself doing that?

'Not right now, no. The closer you get to retiring, then maybe you think, OK, I'd like to coach, or whatever – and some people may not have an option, they can't do anything else, and they're offered a coaching job, so they do it. But at the moment I wouldn't think I'd continue in football. I might play non-league, or coach a school team, or a little local side, something like that – but not professionally.'

I told him about Lineker's idea of going into TV – being a fluent man himself, did that appeal?

'Well, yes and no – because I've done it before and people said, you're quite good on TV. So I've thought about it – but it's not something . . . you see, I'm basically (and he laughed here) a very lazy person. So I really haven't thought what I'd like to do . . . if it came up then I'd do it, put it that way. But it's not something I'd *like* to do. If all of a sudden it came about, and I was doing it and feeling comfortable, OK. And if it didn't, and something else came about, I'd do that.'

You got the feeling, with John Barnes, he'd drifted to where he was in life the same way he drifts down the wing of a football pitch. *Que sera sera . . .*

He said later, about our clubs being banned from Europe, 'I'd like us to play in Europe, but we can't – so it's just one of those things. We're not, so we're not – that's my attitude.'

And he said, 'Graham Taylor, my old manager, he always said how laid-back I was about everything, and how it showed in my football. That was a criticism of me – well, a criticism and not a criticism, because it works both ways – but I think it was a criticism of me in life, rather than in football. Because things happen in life and other people say, *Oh God* – whereas me, I just say, it happens . . .'

Was life really that easy? If it wasn't, he certainly wasn't going to tell you about it – and if it was, then he must be the most relaxed human being on the face of the planet.

And I wondered if that was the trouble with Barnesy, if that was the reason he didn't do it for England – that he was just too damn relaxed. But no – because if it was, he wouldn't do it for Liverpool either. So what was it?

He's a bright and charming man – but talking with him, sometimes, it's like talking to a sheet of glass. You know it's there, but you can't see it.

'We're not in Europe, so we're not in Europe.'

But Graham Taylor, among others, had said Barnes should go to play there.

'So what are you asking me?'

Would he like to go? Was he going?

'Well, if I go, I go – but nothing has happened so far. And I've got another year on my contract here with Liverpool.'

But when you watch a side like Marseilles . . .

'I love that way of playing, whether it be France, Italy, wherever – and obviously, Liverpool play a bit similar to that. But in England you don't play like that every week, because of the people you're playing against. I've always said I'd like to play in Europe, since I was nineteen, twenty – but I'm twenty-six, and I'm still here. So it's one of those things – if it comes about, it comes about. And if it doesn't . . . because it doesn't matter how much I want it. Unless the opportunity is there, unless someone actually wants me to play there, it won't happen.'

*

1. Welcome to Planet Football . . . the opening ceremony in Milan.

2. The Birdman of Bogota? Colombian fan in Bologna.

3. Bull in a Delft china shop . . . Robson sends on Steve Bull against the Dutch.

4. 'The ultimate in joy.' Jürgen Klinsmann scores against the UAE.

5. You cannot be serious ... Ahmed Shobeir booked for time wasting in Palermo.

6. 'It's just bodies. You've either beaten them, or they've fallen over.' John Barnes against the Belgians.

7. Bobby Robson on
the bench in Bologna.
'Winning does mean
such a lot . . .
happiness, elation, a
good feeling for
millions.'

8. And the prize for
best haircut of Italia
'90 goes to . . . Carlos
Valderrama of
Colombia.

9. Rijkaard
and Völler
sent off in
Milan.

10. 'He
jumped like a
salmon' . . .
Paul Parker
goes up
against Roger
Milla in
Naples.

11. Cameroon's gift of joy to Italia '90 – celebrating Kunde's equaliser against England.

12. 'Toto-goal' – Salvatore Schillaci exultant after putting Italy ahead in the semi-final.

13. and 14. The end
of the road. Gazza in
tears, and the big
man, thanking the
fans in Turin.

15. The Final. Argentina's Consultant Ambassador for Sport leads his team by example . . .

16. . . . and they're happy to follow.

Whether in Liverpool or Marseilles, John Barnes and Chris Waddle – these were the kind of players that the people came to see, taking men on and going past them. Was he conscious of that?

'Happens to be the way I play – and I'm sure it's the same with Chris. Because we both have deficiencies – like, I can't tackle very well. If it's a situation where I've got to tackle, I'm probably favourite to lose the ball – same with Chris. We're not tacklers. And I think other players should be given a lot more credit – like Peter Reid, I mean, there we go again – people who tackle and win the ball, and give it to someone who's maybe a more creative player, they don't get the recognition. They do in the game, but only inside it – and I feel for those players, the bread-and-butter players, as Graham Taylor calls them – players who win the ball and give a two-yard pass for someone to beat three players and score a goal. And that person gets all the glory – but without the player who got the ball, he'd never have done it.'

But for himself, what was it like, to be that glory player? What was it like, to beat the man and score the goal?

'Well, my dad's always going on at me to score goals, score goals ... I've got twenty-one this season – played down the middle a few times. But I think even if I do play down the middle, I would never be an out-and-out goalscorer. An out-and-out goalscorer like Gary Lineker would get just as much satisfaction – maybe I'm wrong here, he may get more satisfaction by beating a few players and chipping it in – but ultimately, it's about goalscoring. One that goes in off his arse or his knee, or whatever – it's still a goal, and he's someone who just loves to score goals. Whereas I would feel slightly cheated, if one went in off my knee or my bum, you know what I mean? I would rather have brought it down, and dribbled round a few players first. I don't actually go out to do that, and if the ball comes and it's a tap-in, OK. But I don't think I'd feel as much for the goal, as I would where I'd done something special.'

Lineker had described those few seconds of pure joy ...

'That's an out-and-out goalscorer. Ian Rush is the same, Steve Bull – they're the players who just love the ball crossing the line. Whereas me, if it calls for that and I do it, then I'm delighted – but then afterwards I'd think, well, I've scored. A real goalscorer would go, *yeeaah* . . . doesn't matter what kind of goal it is. But me, beating players and crossing it for someone else to score – I get just as much pleasure from that.'

So I asked him, then, about the goal in the Maracana. Did that stand out for him?

'Well, it would have done . . . but that's another one where I felt slightly cheated, only for the wrong reason – I mean, I don't remember much about the actual goal. I remember taking on a few players, I just remember everyone moving out of the way . . . and of course later, watching it, you can tell what's happening – but at the time, I just saw a lot of bodies and they were just, like, all over the place. But then as soon as I scored, he blew for half-time – I celebrated, we went back, and he blew for half-time. And as soon as the half-time whistle goes, everyone goes, oooph (he mimed a relaxed little slump in the shoulders) and walks off. So if it had been a few minutes earlier I'd have been really elated, saying, *get the ball to me again, I'm playing, get the ball over here* . . . but instead you're in the dressing room, everyone's trundled off the pitch – and it's a long walk back.'

But did he know it was a special goal?

'Not particularly, not at the time. I remember beating a few players . . . but you don't really know what you've done until you see it on television. Even after looking at it, I can't remember beating any particular player – playing, it's just bodies. You've either beaten them, or they've fallen over – you don't really know. You can look at it on TV and you can see, you've put it through his legs, or you've dropped your shoulder – but at the time, you're just reacting. You can't analyse it – you're just doing it.'

I asked, later, how he prepared himself before a game – was he laid-back? Stupid question, really – does the queen wear a crown?

'Very laid-back. Whatever happens, happens. Some players want to be on their own, they have their routines, but I'm not like that. I always have a bath, a hot soak – it's normally cold anyway, when we're playing – but I like to be really warm. Apart from that, there's nothing special that I do.'

No superstitions, nothing?

'There's been times when I've just forgotten . . . I read the programme in the bath, I do a few stretches, and I'm not sure what the time is – and all of a sudden it's ten minutes to kick-off. And I'm like, "Oh . . ."'

And did he notice what the others did? Like Butcher?

'Oh yeah,' he laughed, 'of course, he's running round the dressing room like a lunatic – you can't help but notice him. And some people feed off that, some don't – I don't. I'm just sitting down reading the paper, or tying my boots.'

Laid-back, or what?

'But,' he said, 'I would say I'm just as determined as he is.'

I asked if, when he was a kid – like Steve McMahon, say – he'd wanted to be, or dreamt of being, a professional footballer.

'Not at all. For a start, you haven't got professional football in Jamaica. So before I came to England when I was thirteen, it was never even a possibility, much less a reality. And even then it wasn't a reality, as far as I was concerned. Because although my father played football for Jamaica – and I can remember from when I was five or six years old, I loved playing football – but even so, when we came to England, he was only posted here for four years. So I knew, we were going back to Jamaica. And it wasn't until after my father had already gone back to Jamaica – he'd sold the house and gone back, and I was here with my mother and sisters while he sorted everything out – it was only then that Watford asked me to sign. I was all ready to go back. And it was only when I started training at Watford that I thought, oh, I can be a professional footballer – it's not a thing I've grown up with. I think all kids in England dream about being a footballer – but I couldn't do that. Still, that doesn't mean it was all accidental. What's accidental is that you're lucky enough to be spotted.'

Every player I talked to, I said, sooner rather than later, said they were lucky to have their job.

'Oh yeah. You have to be very lucky, extremely lucky. Because I remember playing at school, when I first came here, with kids who I thought were better than me – maybe they weren't, maybe I didn't know much about football – but I've seen a lot of good kids in local leagues who might make good professionals, and they haven't – because they've not been in the right place at the right time.'

You have to be lucky to get into it – and you have to be lucky to stay in it. Ron Greenwood, in his autobiography *Yours Sincerely*, gives a list of things players can be thrown by: 'Loss of form, inactivity with injury, marital troubles, money worries, business difficulties, gambling debts, bad publicity, changes of manager, transfer requests.'

John Barnes remained unfazed.

'Football's like any other job. And you mention all those things . . . you, what's writer's block if it isn't loss of form? Or your marriage could be on the rocks – everything there just pertains to everyday life. And I don't see why football should be any different. I think loss of form, or confidence, that's the biggest factor for me – so I try not to let anything off the park, outside of football make my form suffer. Because I'd like to think that no matter what happens outside, come three o'clock . . . it may affect you, I dunno, I've never really had anything drastic happen to me – but I just go out there and play. So loss of form, and then loss of confidence from that – that's the only reason why I mightn't play well.'

I asked how or why a man lost his confidence.

'Well, loss of form, like I say. If you look at people who are, like, super-confident . . . Paul Gascoigne. As far as I'm concerned, he's the most confident player in Britain – because no matter what happens to him out on the pitch, no matter how he plays, he's always looking for the ball, he's always wanting it. Now maybe he's like that as a person, I don't really know him – but as a player that's how I see him.

'Whereas me, people look at me and see fifty caps, blah blah blah, Liverpool, Player of the Year – but I've gone through periods where I've thought, I'm a bad player. And it can be because of just one incident, something in one game where I couldn't control the ball – you miscontrol the ball and you think, shit, that was an easy ball, and all of a sudden it's in your mind, asking why you didn't control it. You're thinking, Maradona would have killed it instantly, or Glenn Hoddle . . . any little thing, you can lose your confidence.'

Football's a cruel mistress – one missed touch, and the turmoil sets in. And two months later I remembered that, when I talked with Steve McMahon – because when the missed touch comes in your first game of the World Cup, and the result is the other lot getting a goal ... that's as cruel as the mistress can get. And it takes a brave man to go out again after that.

Barnes said, 'It's so easy to hide on a football pitch. You've got eleven players – and not wanting the ball is so easy.'

After Bryan Robson was injured, McMahon went out against Egypt to anchor the middle in his place – and in ninety minutes he never hid once.

The journalist Dave Hill had written a book about Barnes, and about racism in football, called *Out Of His Skin* – which Barnes hadn't co-operated with. So I asked if he'd read it.

'No. I've read bits and pieces, but not so I could comment on it. Everyone says what a good book it is – I must read it some day.' (Though he said later – 'basically a very lazy person' – that he hardly ever read any books.)

'It's not a question,' he said, 'that I didn't co-operate with it. I didn't say, don't write this book. My agent rang me about it and said, did I want to do this book, and I just said no – because I didn't think it was right for me to be doing a book. I'm only twenty-six now – if I write a book, what do I do about the next six years?'

I liked Hill's book myself – but, at one point, I found it offensive. This was where Hill arrived at the suggestion that, because black players get barracked at some English grounds, they might be less keen when they put on an England shirt than a white player would be – *ergo*, Barnes's disappointing form internationally. The idea smacked to me of a surprising sort of inverted racism, for such a right-on tome – so I asked Barnes if he found it offensive.

But Barnes sets his face against being offended by pretty much anything (except certain sections of the press, who can offend him as much as they like – he'll just whack 'em straight into the nearest court.) So rather than being offended, he just looked as if he found the idea faintly preposterous.

He said, 'I don't think so, I don't think so at all. Getting barracked – by who?'

By some fans, at some clubs.

'So why would black players put on their club shirts then? I don't see that you can tie the two things in at all. If a black player gets barracked at a club game, what's that got to do with England?'

The suggestion was that it might make a black player feel less patriotic – patriotism, as we've seen from Robson and Butcher, being integral to the old tradition of English football.

'Yes, OK – but if I go down to West Ham and I get barracked by the West Ham fans, then maybe I wouldn't want to go and play at West Ham again. But going to Wembley to play Brazil has nothing to do with that – so I don't agree with that at all. Not at all.'

I asked him whether the racist taunting ever got to him personally, England aside.

'Not at all. I think Hill's written this book from a Liverpool perspective – talking about the bananas at Everton, blah blah blah. But I remember being eighteen and playing at West Ham, and bananas came on the pitch left right and centre – and that happens down there all the time. But here, being the first black player to play consistently for Liverpool – they've never come across it. So we go to Everton, and two bananas come on the pitch – big uproar, outrage in the papers, I've got Everton fans coming to me saying they're sorry, really sorry, it's disgraceful ... and I thought, well (and he shrugged) a couple of bananas. So what? West Ham, it's much worse down there, and because it happens there all the time, no one takes any notice.'

Was there any way, I asked, that he could use his position, his success, to do anything about it? Not that he's a man to make an issue of anything ...

He said, 'The way I see it, if someone's a racist – I dunno whether it's racism, or if some people are just ... playing at Everton recently, there's a notorious section where they're giving me all sorts of abuse, where I'm playing on the wing – and one particular instance, I've gone to pick up the ball, and they were all, you know ... so I just looked at them and I smiled, I had a laugh with them. And then they started singing, Johnny Barnes, Johnny Barnes – the same Evertonians. Because I'd had a laugh with them.

'But if it's real deep racism, there's nothing I can do to change that. There was something I could do to change attitudes at Everton – so I don't see that as real racism. Because your real racists, they'd not have started singing

Johnny Barnes – they'd just get even more angry, when they see I'm not upset.'

So there's people at West Ham he'd not bother trying to have a laugh and a joke with?

'That's right. You don't know it until you try. But I've been to West Ham, and I've smiled at it – and it's got *worse*.'

And there was, briefly, an amazed and alarmed look in his eyes as he said that – as if he'd looked up into the terraces of East London, and seen clear into the heart of the beast.

It was one of two times in the conversation when something inside John Barnes stepped out from behind that smooth sheet of glass – when, just for an instant, he didn't seem quite so impenetrably laid-back.

The other time was when we talked about why he didn't play his best for England.

If the notion that he doesn't turn it on with three lions on his chest because he's black won't wash, what will?

I asked what he said, when people said he played better for Liverpool than he did for England.

'Well . . . I've had it ever since I've played for England. So I tend not to say too much, you know – I normally try and laugh it off, because I'm sick and tired of trying to explain it . . . you can't really explain it anyway. But it's much more difficult being a forward playing for international teams, than being a defender – because you look, most international games are either nil-alls, or one-nils, so the defenders are normally on top. So if you ask me what I say . . . what I say is, yeah, you're right. And I laugh it off, or whatever.'

But was it a fair criticism?

Pause.

'I don't think it's a fair criticism, no. If people see it that way, fair enough – and I'm sure it's not a criticism in the sense that they're criticising me personally, because I know they all want me to do well. And maybe it's frustrating for them – but they don't want me to do well as much as I want me to do well. So I think they're making a point, and wanting to know for themselves.

'But take a goalscorer, for example – I don't know anyone with a goalscoring record as good internationally as for his club. So people are never going to say, Gary Lineker doesn't score as many goals for England as he does for Tottenham, because he can't – because it's international football.'

I'd have thought, in fact, his averages come pretty close.

Barnes continued, 'Because of what I've done at Liverpool, people are expecting me to do the same for England – and I can do it in fits and starts – but I don't think I'll be able to do it consistently.'

Robson, I said, described the difference between club and international football as a prodigious leap.

Barnes said he didn't really see it that way. 'Because those players play club football as well. So playing against Ireland, for example – I'll be playing against maybe Chris Morris, who played for Sheffield Wednesday, plays for Celtic, so I'm going to come up against him in club football.'

But that's not the case if . . .

'If you're playing the Italians, OK. But that's down to not playing in Europe – I think that's a factor. I think that if the clubs were in Europe, that would help the international scene – because you'd be used to playing against sweepers, man-for-man at the back, five men in midfield and one up front, which you never ever come across . . . so it's much more difficult to adapt, yes.'

I said the way he was talking implied that he himself felt he didn't play so well for England as he did for his club.

'Oh yeah, I would say so. I don't know any player who could say they play as well for their country as they do for their club.'

You what?

'I think the defenders do, Des Walker, Terry Butcher, I think they do really well – because defensively, although you need much more concentration, I don't think you're under as much pressure as you are club-wise . . .'

You *what*?

'It's much more difficult for forwards, and for midfield players too. Apart from Bryan Robson, who's been superb for England, holding things together, I can't see any attacking player who would do as well for their country, me included, as for their club.'

Gary Lineker might say, internationally, that chances are harder to come by – but I find it hard to believe that he'd

256

conclude from that, that he played better at Spurs. He might just say, he played *more often* at Spurs . . .

Lineker ended the World Cup with thirty-five goals for England in fifty-eight games – a strike rate of 0.6 – or, if you discount four caps won as early substitutions, of 0.65. In the First Division, on the other hand, at the last count he had 104 in 169 – a rate of 0.62. Not a mighty disparity there . . . Asked about the difference between playing for club and country, Lineker said that, sure, you were playing against better players – but, in theory at least, you were playing *with* better players too. Moreover, wasn't it easier to motivate yourself if you were playing for England against Brazil, or whoever, than for your club against the likes of Millwall or Wimbledon?

So could it be that the trouble with Barnesy is, simply, that he doesn't believe in himself as an international attacking player? That the confidence thing's got to him? Because if he meant all this, why bother?

What he'd said, I suggested, was quite some statement.

'Well . . . chances are rarer attacking-wise. The amount of times I would get the ball to attack the full back internationally – I would get it half a dozen times at the most in a match. Whereas you get it every two, three minutes here. So although here I would lose the ball maybe fifty per cent of the time, at least I'll get past him ten times – maybe lose it ten times – but if I'm only getting it six times, I've got to get past him six times. Once won't do.'

This doesn't really square up. How come he's getting the ball so rarely? Because these international defenders are so terrifically relaxed, compared to the pressure they're under club-wise? Relaxed like Terry Butcher's relaxed, going round yelling his face off, head-butting the wall with Iron Maiden on the Walkman? I mean, c'mon, Barnesy . . .

He was plainly uncomfortable talking about this; not as coherent or relaxed as he was in the rest of the conversation. His agent later told me, you could tell when he was uptight because he'd speak quicker, and the pitch of his voice would rise. Listening to the tape, I hear that happening.

And John Barnes doesn't like to talk about this thing, not just because he's sick and tired of trying to explain it – which no doubt he is – but because he knows there's something there to explain.

*

So here's my best shot at explaining it.

It seems to me the trouble with Barnesy is a mix of three things.

First, he's 'basically a very lazy person'.

Second, he's a beautiful footballer – and, in terms of the old tradition, that's not English. He just doesn't fit – not because he's black (a ridiculous idea; Chris Waddle, as we'll see, had much the same problem) but because spiritually, he's Brazilian. And the 4–4–2 trench warfare approach didn't let him run loose to do his thing.

Then third, those two things together add up to the man, when he puts on an England shirt, simply *not enjoying himself*.

I'm not sure if it's a problem of Barnes having no confidence, as much as a problem of him having no fun.

He said to me that every player had 'a wanting' – and, characteristically, this 'wanting' was more relaxed than Gary Lineker's 'absolute desire'. Barnes defined it as players having 'a wanting to do their particular thing – whatever they get most pleasure out of doing'.

Throughout, talking about football, he talked about pleasure much more than he talked about winning. Sure, winning was great, and a good run gave you confidence – but it didn't come over as a motivating force for him personally, in the way that the pure pleasure of playing did. And of course, he said he tried hard. But if he wasn't free and getting the ball and beating men and getting pleasure, then you had to wonder if that was where his effort might start tailing off . . . and a lazy person, presumably, finds it easier to hide on a football pitch than anyone.

Lazy is his own word – but it might be more accurate to say that he's just remarkably passive. He described going to see someone at Granada Television, and how they asked if he'd like to do some sort of programme with them. And he told them, 'Someone like Craig Johnson would come to you, and being Craig he'd say, right, what would be a good idea is we do this, and that . . . but me, you have to tell me what to do – because if it's up to me, if you ask me what I'd like to do, I don't know.'

You got the idea he'd have trouble initiating a cup of coffee. I asked him what paper he read, and he said the *Mirror* (because his girlfriend read it – again, someone else making the decision). Then he said that in Liverpool – where he has a flat, while his girlfriend stays in their house in London – he didn't bother buying a paper, because he was 'too lazy to go across the road and get one'.

And when I asked how he voted, he said, 'I don't. That sums me up.'

Here, in other words, is a man who has to be told what to do – and who has to like what he's told, or he won't bother anyway.

Then, talking about what he likes to do on a football pitch, he laughed at one point and said, 'I don't understand defenders. True defenders must be born defenders – because I can't understand anyone who would *want* to stop someone scoring a goal. I could never be like that. Like the Brazilians, they've got the ball in the six yard box and they'll try and dribble out – because it's in them, they all want to play, to please people, and beat people – they all want to play football. And in England that'll never happen, they'll just get the ball out of there. Terry Butcher, for example, he's a born defender, he gets so wound up about *not letting people pass* – even before going out, he's in there saying, *they won't pass, they won't pass* . . . and that's his job. And I guess he gets as much pleasure out of that as Gary Lineker does out of scoring.'

But John Barnes couldn't get pleasure from it for one minute. Brazil recurred, in the conversation, as the football epitome – and England don't play that way.

And it's irrelevant to say Liverpool play 4–4–2 as well, firstly because they play it so flexibly – and secondly because Barnes is at home there, his passivity is accommodated, and shows itself as the laid-back looseness that lets him play. He doesn't spend his time locked in, tracking up and down the flank, attack, defend, attack, defend . . . and though Robson might tell him (as he'd said at the Charlton–Arsenal game) to 'go for a stroll, take a wander' – he's not an initiator, is he? He needs someone or something around him to give him his cue – and Robson's England set-up wasn't it.

So in the Ireland game you watched him and you thought, he's not enjoying himself – and the guy just vanished.

*

Maybe the best thing about the appointment of Graham Taylor is, if there's a manager in the country who understands John Barnes, Graham Taylor's that man.

13 The Biggest Thing in Our Lives

Italy–USA

'No one gives a damn over there, basically – but it's a great sport. A great sport.'

– John McEnroe

The Americans should never have been at Italia '90.

Elsewhere, minnow nations might emerge from the footballing backwaters – but the USA remains the whale that burped and brought forth plankton.

And that's OK – because for large parts of the world, the very existence of a USA football team is an abiding comic folly, and an object of enormous and consoling satisfaction. Whatever else the Yanqui may do, *he can't play football*.

They were, by any measure, a stupendously inept outfit – though not for want of trying. In the first half of 1990, they seemed to be playing more games than Oldham Athletic, recording historic triumphs along the way over the likes of Bermuda, Iceland, and Liechtenstein. But they were, basically, a bunch of college kids – and what they knew about being in with the big boys could be written on the back of a postage stamp. Their coach, Bob Gansler, had never even been to a World Cup.

But being awful's not a crime – part of the fun of the World Cup's having an affectionate laugh at the whipping boys. If all the minnows turn pike (or at least, a bit more pike-ish) so we don't get Yugoslavia putting nine past Zaïre any more, or Hungary ten past El Salvador – I personally will consider that a loss.

So being awful was no reason, on its own, why the Americans shouldn't have been there. The reason they shouldn't have been there was, rather, that Mexico should have been there instead.

The Americans play in a region whose boss body goes by the hefty acronym of CONCACAF; geographically, the district stretches from the isthmus of Darien to the Canadian tundra, taking in the Caribbean along the way. So qualifiers in this North/Central America zone involve such groovy-sounding fixtures as Antigua *v.* the Netherlands Antilles . . . not surprisingly, Mexico tends to qualify. The only decent-sized country that knows anything about football in the region, they've been to seven World Cups out of ten since World War II.

But come Italia '90, they were disqualified. They'd fielded over-age players in a junior tournament and got walloped with a two-year ban from all competitive international football. Harsh . . . but it helped to make way for the USA.

The qualification of the USA was an outcome devoutly to be desired by the barons of world football. With the States hosting the next tournament in '94, there's no mean investment riding on whether anyone bothers to hop channels from the baseball – so the USA competing in Italy would, in theory, help alert American attention to the game the rest of us play.

As it happened, the Americans went to Rome and played the hosts, and CBS, NBC, and ABC all ignored it. On cable, it got an audience of 900,000. So it's an uphill struggle, boys . . . and Mexico got cleared out of the road for that?

Even with the door wedged handily open, they made a meal out of qualifying. In seven games they only managed three victories, against Costa Rica, Guatemala, and El Salvador. They had trouble getting goals; in three draws, two of them at home, they only scored once. So it went to the tape – for their eighth and last game they had to travel to Port of Spain, and beat Trinidad & Tobago away.

The game, played on 19 November 1989 (twenty days before the draw in Rome) was the 312th and last of the Italia '90 qualifiers – and the Americans scraped a 1–0 victory. A 25-year-old called Paul Caligiuri got the goal – a midfielder who'd played in the West German second division.

But you had to feel sorry for Trinidad & Tobago – a

country a quarter the size of Massachusetts, with a population less than a tenth that of metropolitan New York. They'd only needed a draw to go through – the match was described as 'the biggest thing that's ever happened here'. The Port of Spain stadium, taking 35,000, was full for hours before the kick-off – every soul in it wore red, the national colour. Match day was declared Red Day; in celebratory anticipation over 150 calypsos were written, some remembering the country's last sniff of the big time, when they were robbed by a bent referee in Haiti in 1973 – and everyone who went said it was lovely. A band called Sound Revolution sang:

> *Fifteen years ago in Haiti*
> *Our nation was denied fame and glory*
> *On the road*
> *On the road to Germany*
>
> *Now same breed, different men*
> *Are chasing glory once again*
> *On the road*
> *On the road to Italy*
>
> *Sticks like fire, hot like peas*
> *We're going to bring the US to their knees*

Notwithstanding that last sentiment, 3,000 locals gave the Americans a friendly welcome at the airport – and when the home side lost, they went out and danced to their calypsos anyhow. Sound Revolution added a new verse:

> *Bad luck to the Strike Squad this time*
> *But we are sure to open the door in '94*
> *On the road*
> *On the road to the USA*

As for the Americans, well – apart from Caligiuri's three seasons at SV Meppen, only one other member of the squad that came to Italy played his football abroad – Peter Vermes, at FC Volendam in Holland. After qualifying, a couple did come to try out with clubs in England – but the trials didn't last too long.

They were a home-grown bunch. They played at college, or

in one or other of the ill-organised and fractious US leagues (two of which play indoors – and I mean, who plays football indoors? Scared of a spot of rain, guys?). They played for clubs with daft names like LA Heat, or Tampa Bay Rowdies. And now they were going to Italy.

English journalists who'd seen the Americans said derisively, they were hayseeds. But then, the English need to cherish the superior feeling that Americans can't play football with a particular intensity – because they have always to rub from their minds one of the biggest upsets in the history of the game.

In 1950, when England deigned for the first time to play with Johnny Foreigner in this new-fangled World Cup of his, they went to Brazil for the fourth tournament, and in Belo Horizonte, the USA beat them 1–0.

USA 1, England 0 – a fact like that, it shakes and grinds at the very roots of your culture. It's *unthinkable.*

In forty years since then, the two sides had met four times in friendlies. England won 6–3, 8–1, 10–0 and 5–0.

So the English think – superciliously, and not much – about that clash of the titans in Port of Spain. They think of the USA getting tied up in knots on football pitches by Central American countries which, normally, they run as their personal banana plantations. They think of the qualification of the Americans for the World Cup in 1990 – and they laugh.

But the laugh is never absolute because the English know, like everyone in football knows – anyone can beat you on his day.

Crystal Palace 4, Liverpool 3.

USA 1, England 0.

So I signed on for the Americans tackling Italy in Rome – I figured it'd be fun. I figured the Americans didn't *have* to get skewered, 5–0 or 10–0 or worse – they could always play ten defenders. But I also figured – remember 1950 – that football is football. And what if the Americans won? Because in the land of hysterical fantasy, in the alarming and exhilarating territory of Planet Football, there's no event more stupendous than the earthquake that's an upset.

*

Dawn over Cagliari on 13 June was pink and lilac and orange; the hour's flight to Rome was gorgeous. The mountains in south-east Sardinia were sharp and crystal clear beneath us, a buckled ruck of sparse dry green, and jagged grey rock. Beyond the razor-sharp ridges, the Tyrrhenian Sea was a perfect sheet, textured like opaque glass, with a creamy lance across it of reflected sun. And the new train line from Fiumicino into Rome, compared to the jumbly old bus ride, was *meraviglioso*.

Not, of course, absolutely so – at the station it took you to they were re-doing the metro; so you had to walk up the road through the customary tangle of red mesh and debris to the next stop . . . but never mind.

I thought of Radio Mitch. He had one of those faces where all the features seem a little too big, a peculiarly *emphatic* physiognomy – he was one of those men for whom the world is out there to be delighted with, and his face was well designed to express that. He said Rome was, 'The most beautiful city I've ever seen in my life.' So why complain?

I checked in at the Maxim, my cheap and cheerful *pensione* on the Via Nazionale. Fifty yards off in Piazza della Repubblica, I saw on my way that – on top of the official pasta, the official coffee, the official mineral water (in all, 47 official licensees) – there was even a World Cup porno movie. Called simply, *Mondiale*, 'the hard masterpiece of the year', it starred the Radical MP Ilone Staller, aka La Cicciolina, and her partner in bonking, one Moana Pozzi. So in the name of research, dear reader – wishing to leave no stone unturned in the quest to bring you every aspect of life on Planet Football – I went to see it.

The basic idea was that a couple of Jacobean scheming wop types called in our two heroines to assist the Italian side, by sucking the vital juices (via one orifice or another) from its most dangerous opponents. So first off a Lothar Matthäus lookalike had his scrotum rather routinely evacuated by Ms Pozzi – and then we moved on to Diego.

Now this was just glorious. Maradona was played by this unbelievable fat bastard who spoke exceedingly dodgy Spanish and, when first seen attempting to train, seemed to have serious trouble even trotting on the spot. He had, however, the biggest cock in the history of the human race, and when it came to being a bed athlete, was really quite prodigious – but the brave girls worked long and hard to subdue him. And I wouldn't know if Diego's dinky is really that ginormous – but our last sight of his porno stand-in did have a most stinging aptness: he was left gasping on the floor, kissing his own tool and panting, bravo, bravo.

All this had the required effect on the pitch; so for the provision of what we might call sub-plot bonking, the defeated Lothar and Diego were then provided with consolation ladies by a COL-type official wearing, inexplicably, a toupee like an electrocuted squirrel.

The porno-makers had, meanwhile, predicted an Italy–Holland final, so that Staller & Pozzi could move on to their last and prize target – Ruud Gullit. After another session of humping and slurping they thought they'd done the job on him, but – in line with the crass and gruesome mythology of porn – he proved too potent for one dejuicing to affect his form. So, with giggling feigned reluctance, they set off to the dressing room to dejuice him once more at half-time. He was discovered praying bizarrely to 'the god of victory' on his knees; he was left, their attentions being so thorough, barely able to get off them.

So Italy duly triumphed; and the *Azzurri* were duly rewarded with mass fellatio. You did not, however, see the faces of any of the men in blue shirts – some taboos presumably being unbreakable even for Staller & Pozzi.

Ah well – Gazza joked once that scoring was like coming. And it was worth it, if for nothing else, for the sight of an MP with a banana up her bum. One's thoughts turned idly to certain members of the British government . . .

Me, I turned idly down the road to watch Spain–Uruguay at the Maxim. And at half-time during this game, among the ads, RAI ran a powerful corrective to the 'hard masterpiece'.

Shot in black and white, the only colour was an eerie lilac glow around the boy who shared a needle with his friend in a public toilet – and the lilac glow spread. The second boy picked up his girlfriend in a bar, and at home they made love – and the lilac glow spread. The girl was a secretary, and her boss seduced her in his car – and the lilac glow spread. The boss went home to his wife . . . in the last shot, they walked down a crowded street in their mutual glow of HIV. One last nice touch – another figure, anonymous in the crowd, was also thus invisibly marked as he passed.

266

And a hand set down a condom over the title that told you to take care.

Uruguay were polished and attractive, but like Lineker had said, 'very nicey-nicey, no punch'; while Spain were tepid, and dared little. Their keeper Zubizarreta made four good saves – otherwise, it was a dud. The Uruguayans got a penalty, but Sosa blasted over the bar – Spain o, Uruguay o. It was the first scoreless draw of Italia '90; and the crowd in Udine let them know what they thought of that.

In Mexico, the Scottish had called Uruguay 'violent thugs' – but they'd promised since then that they'd cleaned up their act. Apart from Sosa inadvertently kicking one of his own team-mates in the groin (sparing him, maybe, the dangerous attentions of Moana and Ilone) it looked here, as at Wembley, like they'd done so.

The same could not be said for Argentina.

I went and got some beers down my neck, and then some *grappa* on top. Russia–Argentina, after all, was the thirteenth game of the tournament – but the first where matters took on that special and urgent air of World Cup criticality. The world champions against the losing European finalists, and both had already been beaten – a second defeat for either side, and it was odds-on they'd be going home.

Still, it wasn't for that I got the beers in, but because you fancy a bit of frenzy in the soul when Argentina are on the case. Peter Beardsley said bluntly when I asked if he recalled any side being especially dirty, 'Argentina in Mexico, the two centre-halves were a disgrace – but you half-expect that.' And ever since Maradona scored with his hand in that game you're reduced, against every better instinct, to watching them with a desperate and angry hope that this time, this time, they'll get their come-uppance . . . and Cameroon had done it. So could Russia do it too?

I found me a bar, and leant intently against it right up close to the screen. And how, I thought melancholically, how I love that Russian anthem – that gorgeous, deep, doleful mix of pride and grief and suffering, ending with a note of unresolved yet resolute anticipation as if to say, we'll persevere, no matter how it hurts . . . they were in for another hurting tonight.

Argentina set off scrappy, Russia fluent, looking able on the ball – then, as their first attacks mounted, in the ninth minute Pumpido burst out to cover a low cross, crashed into Olarticoechea, and got a double fracture in his right lower leg. Horrible – in the replay, you could see his shin swinging and wobbling midway down like jelly . . . I was all set to feel sorry for Argentina.

Goycochea came on in goal, and scraped away the Russian corner that resulted from Pumpido's mishap. The second corner came in, got a deft goalbound flick-on from Kuznetsov – and Maradona at the near post stuck out his right hand . . .

So now he can save with his hands as well as score with them? I swore in fury, *you cheating fucking slime*, and the barman looked worried – did he have a hooligan on his hands? So I repeated the accusation in Italian, he watched the replay, and he agreed.

The referee can't have been more than three yards away – and he was looking directly towards the goal. It was clear as day.

And if Russia had gone 1–0 up with the penalty they deserved in that twelfth minute, maybe they'd have found the form that eluded them – while Argentina would more than likely have disintegrated. They'd have gone home, and taken their nasty and cynical football with them – and we'd have been spared a string of matches where you watched the game stained and abused with a sense of ever-rising disgust.

But it ended, instead, Argentina 2, Russia 0.

Floodlight robbery – one Russian was sent off, Bessonov, baffled like Massing and Kana Biyik before him by the arty pace of Caniggia. Three Argentines were booked – including Caniggia, who *smiled*, the mouthy bastard; and then Maradona, who peacocked away from the referee with his shoulders shrugging and his hands held out palms upward as if to say, like he's always bloody saying, who, *moi*? – the Grand Consultant Ambassador for Fraud and Mendacity, running round the park hunting fouls instead of playing.

The Russian manager Lobanovsky said afterwards that non-existent free-kicks were given against his men – but when there was really a foul, the referee had ignored it. He said, 'A referee who doesn't see a handball like Maradona's doesn't have the right to carry on being a referee.'

And he asked, 'Is Maradona untouchable that he can do what he likes?'

His anger was justifiable. But if you want to win in football – whether against people who cheat, like Argentina, or people who don't, like Romania – there's only one way to do it. You score more goals than them.

Still, I felt for the Russians. But if they were the first team homeward-bound, as they almost certainly now were, well – there'd be twenty-two more following them, before the tournament was won. It's a hard road to the final, littered with those who fail.

And me, on that road? – I was half-cut, half-wiped. On Planet Football you were up late at night, watching teams and fans and *carabinieri* do their business – then up early in the morning, catching buses and trains and planes. The last three nights, I'd had thirteen hours sleep.

So I drowned my Russian sorrows, then went back to the Maxim to deal with the Sock Crisis. The laundry in Cagliari had mislaid ten pairs – so I had to wash one of the two pairs remaining every night until they found them again.

It was some time past one when I hung my lone socks on the little balcony of my room; the Via Nazionale five floors below was still a weaving cobbled mayhem. Somewhere out north towards the Olympic Stadium, three searchlights traced erratically through the burnished city sky.

There were two games at five the following afternoon. In Bologna, Yugoslavia beat Colombia 1–0 – Jozic sprinting into the area, chesting it down, and volleying first touch into the roof of the net. Colombia's daffy keeper Rene Higuita wouldn't even have smelt it – but he was good value otherwise. He saved a penalty; and lived up to his loon reputation as the world's premier sweeper-keeper with reckless panache, coming out of his area to head, kick, and dribble the ball away, as if playing with his hands alone was just too boring for words. Still, no one had ever caught him out at that . . . yet.

And down in Bari, enter – with a bang – Roger Milla for Cameroon. Thirty-eight years old, the second oldest player in the tournament after Peter Shilton – and who'd have known it? After their second-choice keeper N'Kono had kept them in the game with a flying save from Hagi's screaming free kick, Milla came on with half an hour to play – and scored two belters. Balint got one back at the death – so Cameroon 2, Romania 1.

Or, as they say in Brazil, another zebra. The Romanians, to be fair, may have had minds half-elsewhere that day – Iliescu'd just sent the miners on to the streets of Bucharest. But still, remarkably, the first team through to the second phase of Italia '90 was now the wondrous Cameroon.

That left Argentina and Romania both needing a draw – while in Group D Colombia were assumed to be out. The Germans would run up a cricket score against the UAE, the Yugoslavs likewise; then the Germans would dispose of Higuita & Co., and leave them stranded on two points . . . oh yeah?

It's a funny old game.

The press centre had a 'press village' complete with tobacconist's, newsagent's, clothes and souvenir shops – even a 'technofitness gym'. I don't know about the rest of the world's press, but the idea of any of the roly-poly English boys getting 'technofit' was implausible indeed . . . we surged back and forth like shoals of fish between the two matches running simultaneously on a million different monitors, and TV filmed us as we did so . . . the media eats itself.

The joyous cheers for Cameroon were loud and universal, as Milla went twice to the corner flag, and did his sexy, celebratory waistline shimmy.

The San Siro in Milan was Ridley Scott science fiction, with a soundtrack from La Scala – but the Olympic in Rome was grand art all the way, with a resonance of the most exuberant national pride. And though it often went manically overboard, I never felt overall, in Italy, that the nationalism that associates with football had that truly dangerous edge or undercurrent of desperation, of hysteric-pessimistic absolutism that comes with . . . well, with one other side one could think of.

So of course they shrieked and jeered at Maradona – but that's a different matter. They are not, in Italy, alone against the world as that man feels himself to be, with such unhappy consequences.

So while there certainly were bad boys about, who'd go out

hunting English with sticks or worse – overall, the atmosphere in the Olympic was demented-festive, rather than undiluted-fanatic. No American need have been scared to go in and watch that game – just to play in it, maybe . . .

A lot of Romans were disgruntled or worse over their new model stadium – not least because the rising cost of the retractable roof, among other items, had sent the total refurbishment bill to something nebulously calculated as near or over £100,000,000. And before, people said, it had been just a big bowl beneath the hills; now, it was an eyesore.

I couldn't share this view. As a Roman cabbie who did like it said to me, the San Siro was *pesante*, but the Olympic was *leggero* – Roman grace winning out over Milanese mass.

You approached it through a clean urban park of straight avenues, hedges and lawns; as you drew near, it seemed tastefully melded into the greenery around, the high black glass walls and the creamy curve of the roof broken by random stands of fir trees round the concourse.

And then, inside – to the palace of desire.

Under the last light of a dirty grey sky, I looked down across the vast simplicity of this sweeping basin of noise and flags. Outside the press box which, unbelievably, filled virtually one whole side of the stadium, every inch of the two curves, and all of the stand opposite, was a shimmering mass of waving green, white and red.

And I thought, if those American boys are in that tunnel down there now, I fear for their souls. The naming of their side was attended by a constant seething whistle – not passionately vicious, in the way they greeted Maradona, but affirmatively hostile – just to let you know where you were . . .

Flares and sparklers and flashbulbs popped and burned round the curves; coloured smoke drifted through the sea of swaying flags.

> *Aaaay – aah – oh*
> *Oh – aaay – ah – oh*
> *EE–TAL–YAH!*

During their anthem the American kids stood looking like they'd all be communally sick at any moment. They had the youngest average age of any side in the tournament . . . off we go. And you think, this won't take long . . .

It takes until the eleventh minute. Pure delight – Vialli hops lightly past a ball crossing low into the area, an immaculate little dummy, and Giannini streaks on to it behind him – he skips two men at speed like it's a walk in the park, leaves them dead on the edge of the area, and pelts it past Meola with venomous precision. 1–0. Seventy-five thousand people have a king-size collective orgasm.

The Ferrari's firing on all six now. Round and round and back and forth it goes – you want the ball, slow boy? Well here it is – whoops, no, there it is – it's here, it's there, it's any place but where there's an American . . . Donadoni scrapes the top of the bar with a free-kick; wastes another header, straight to Meola.

Still, when the Italians advance, the Americans bring eight or nine back. Predictable, and not pretty – but it's determined, and it's working . . . then they blow it.

Caligiuri brings down Berti as he breaks into the box. So Vialli steps up to the penalty cocky as hell, sends Meola definitively the other way – and hits the post . . .

Turning point? With a goal in eleven minutes, they should be murdering them. With a penalty in the twenty-seventh, they should be eating them too – but instead the Americans stick at it, and the Italians go for a walk. They've got the ball, the US virtually never leave their own half . . . and it's going nowhere. The game sticks at 1–0.

And not scoring goals gets to gnaw at the soul. After twenty minutes of the second half, the Americans begin to come forward. A backheel or two – and Tab Ramos, he can do a bit; he beats one man, beats another – then Bruce Murray goes up against Ferri for a high ball. Ferri gives him an elbow to the windpipe, and a bit of face-to-face, and gets booked for it. Welcome to the wild side of Planet Football, Mr Murray . . . and, geed up by this introduction, his free-kick's a blinder. Zenga dives low, and just manages to parry it away – and Vermes is in like a shark on the rebound. Zenga's lucky as hell that he manages to sit on it as the ball flies goalbound; Ferri clears it away as it rolls along the line. We were, there, an inch from the Americans drawing level.

So heads are up; John Harkes can play too. A deflected shot wins a corner; Banks blazes over the top. Now the Italians are giving it away. In the last few scuffling minutes they push back up, trying to save face . . . but the whistle goes; and the crowd whistles heartily with it.

To score nine or ten, you have to break a team – and to break a team, you have to be in the mood, and make the effort. The Italians weren't, and they didn't; the Americans didn't break. Vialli should, of course, have made it 2–0, and then it might have been a different story . . . but he didn't, and it wasn't.

Italy 1, USA 0.

Not bad – not bad at all. For sure, the Italians had all the ball – but still, it might well have been 1–1. As I left the press box, I saw behind me the spooky sight of Vicini's head saying defensively, 'We got two points,' over and over on rank after rank of unattended monitors . . . and I thought, if you don't score goals, my Italian friends, sooner or later someone's going to put you out of this thing.

In the underground car park where the team buses waited, writers and camera crews swarmed round the players. The Americans were polite, intelligent, articulate young men. You went into this thing expecting Lions *v.* Christians – and came out of it reckoning the Christians did OK.

John Murray said, 'In the first game with the Czechs, we learnt you just can't go out against these European teams and expect them to cough up the ball – they'll just laugh and dribble right through you. We were *embarrassed* the other day – but we came here thinking, we're not that bad. So we didn't come here to get beaten 10–0 – I mean, you saw Costa Rica beat Scotland, and on a good day we can spank Costa Rica, we can thump them – you can print that.'

Of his free-kick he said, 'I was disappointed, but hell, they were all over us, so, you know . . . it might have gone in.'

I wish it had, for his sake, and for mine – it'd have been a more entertaining night by far. But he was modest, and realistic – asked if he was pleased, he smiled and said, 'I'd have been more pleased with 1–1.'

He also said, 'We don't have the fan base – I think it'll take another ten years at least. And we'll *never* get the zealots like were in there tonight – they must be the greatest fans in the world, they were unbelievable.'

God knows what he'd have made of it if the crowd had been awake.

Peter Vermes said, 'It was an amazing feeling going out there. We've no experience to draw on, it's difficult for us – we're not involved in this, ever. Sometimes we're taken aback in awe of it; but tonight people will respect what we did. And let me tell you – playing against those people tonight was an honour.'

He said, 'That was the biggest thing in our lives.'

The media bus crawled back to the centre down a jammed Via Veneto. Piazza della Repubblica was a race track. After the Austrian win they'd been out driving round town until four – my man at the Maxim couldn't get home, he had to stay in one of the rooms. It wasn't so crazy this time, but it was still lively enough – people sitting up out of car doors with their flags, hooting, waving, whistling and yelling. And all they'd done was beat the US 1–0 – daft, really.

Making notes over a coffee in a late night bar – surrounded by poor souls staring morosely at their alcohol-free beer – I met two Americans who'd been to the match. They'd been on holiday in Florence with their wives and thought, Italy–USA, that's once in a lifetime – got to go. The tickets had cost them £40 each, and they'd loved it.

They were pleased, of course, that their side, while patently inferior, had done well – but what they'd enjoyed best was seeing the strength and pace and touch of the Italians, and the mania of their crowd. You couldn't say they were converts; but they'd now follow the progress of the tournament – and they'd go to games in '94.

Because, they said, they'd never seen anything like it – Superbowl, World Series, that's huge, but it's only city to city stuff. And like, if that was a no-account first round game – what the hell does it get like later?

Welcome to Planet Football.

14 Revolution

England–Holland

'What do we need this sweeper for?'
   – Bobby Robson, November '89

I flew back into Cagliari with yet another Wolves fan (they were everywhere). He was a bright bloke – and he had a word for Dave Hill on his John Barnes book.

'What's wrong with that book comes out at the end, where he goes back and describes Barnes going past one man, two men again, and he says, Jamaica-style. If he'd have said, Barnes-style, OK. What's Jamaica got to do with it?'

He was, he said, a football fan first, a Wolves fan second. He was in Italy for three weeks and seven games, and reckoning to spend £2,500 in that time. He couldn't afford it, though he had a good job – he ran a video label – but he said by '94 he'd be thirty-four years old, he might have kids, who knows? He'd never done a World Cup, and this was his chance.

It was three out of his year's four weeks' holiday – he'd already spent the rest following Wolves, when they went near to promotion. He didn't go to every game – 'I'm not a trainspotter' – but he had a good time; and now this was even better. No trouble, great country, big pleasure – and just one gripe: tickets.

On Saturday 2 June his travel agent took the cash in person to the FA – and they were shut. She posted it through the letterbox, and called Monday – and they'd sent the tickets in the post. No, she cried, don't, I'll send a bike – too late. He got them three days before he left on 11 June – 'it was bloody worrying'. He'd paid in April.

275

The people he was with didn't get theirs in time; their wives sent them on. He said, to be fair, he knew the Italians had released the tickets very late; and the FA had been very helpful. But you pay a lot of money for these holidays, and this was stuff you seriously didn't need, calling agents all the time, finding the FA office, getting transport into Cagliari – when the place you were staying in was ninety kilometres away.

And he knew, too, of people in his business being offered sponsor's tickets for the semis and the final, who just weren't interested – the 'blue suit and champagne brigade' – when he was out *begging* for these things.

The likes of Mars and Gillette took 2,000 people to Italia '90, minimum; I knew an agent in Manchester who proudly boasted how he had 15,000 bookings from sponsors . . . and he got his tickets all right.

So who owns this game?

Not the millions of poor sods who pay for it, that's for sure.

And of course your truly hard money man could turn round and say, with TV and related marketing, we could play matches in empty stadiums and still come out smiling . . . but it wouldn't be football, would it?

Two pressmen gave me a lift in their cab from the airport to the training ground at Pula. A busload of eccentric Dutch industrial machine reps turned up; they were all uniformed in orange suits and straw boaters, with orange-white-blue weskits and bow ties. Robson had met them in Palermo, and invited them along to get some FA knick-knacks.

But these cheerful souls couldn't lighten the atmosphere in the England camp; the national grid firing up every floodlight on earth couldn't have cast light into the black heart of matters now.

The Hostess Isabella story had broken.

The *Mirror* intimated that three players – unnamed, of course, or the libel wallop would have been mighty indeed – had late night disco and after hours nookie with a local COL stewardess, who'd subsequently been moved from Is Molas to the furthest hotel down the road.

Oddly, the genesis of this bilious malice was a football man from one of the qualities – acknowledged by a colleague to be 'a fantasist' – who'd put himself both professionally and personally in danger, by trying to sell his invention to the *Sun*. Professionally, for the obvious reasons – and personally, because the Hostess Isabella's brother was now muttering darkly about taking the man off into the mountains for a terminal taste of his hunting rifle.

And just to prove the story was crap – the *Sun* turned it down. When the *Mirror* bit instead, the *Sun* were then able to spin round on them with this glorious headline:

MORE LIES FROM FAT MAX
Maxwell, 22 stone . . .

They may be bastards – but they can be funny bastards on their day.

Not, however, if you're the Hostess Isabella. The rotters were hounding the poor girl all over Cagliari – when her only crime had been to speak inadequate English for the job at Is Molas and, anyhow, to be transferred is a matter of routine on the COL work roster. But that's the tabloids for you. One minute your languages aren't up to scratch – the next, you've been out fucking footballers. And like policemen, once they've decided you've done a thing, they'll hound you until they've extracted the confession . . . one Brian McNally, senior sports writer on a Newcastle paper, tried to protect the girl – and, amazingly, was threatened with being reported to the NUJ for 'impeding journalists in the course of their duty'.

The great majority of the football men – including the helplessly shamefaced souls from the quarter of the gutter that printed this muck – tried as best as they could to dissociate themselves from it. Patrick Barclay said he wasn't surprised the players had gone on quote strike – he said there'd been football men who felt like going out in sympathy. (Though another told me later, 'Well, Paddy – he's always good for a reaction.')

But dissociate as you may, it wouldn't do you much good – because from the players' point of view, this was just the biggest piece of shit yet in a long-building tunnel of press sewage. Journalists – they were all the fucking same.

With a weary contempt Robson told the BBC, 'It's pretty

dismal reporting – 'cos there's no truth in it. What are they trying to do? Torpedo the players, torpedo the team? It's a diabolical game to play.'

John Barnes walked back across the training pitch to the bus, turning away questions. 'No,' he said, polite but definite, 'I'm disillusioned, you know? Disillusioned with life, you know what I mean?'

I asked David Bloomfield what had happened; he told me the story, and pointed out the *Mirror*'s John Jackson, known among the press pack as Chief Rotter. Bloomfield said, with bitter irony, 'It was that cunt in the Fair Play T-shirt. Rich, that.'

Tickets for the Mirror Group's reporters had, it seemed, mysteriously failed to appear . . .

Terry Butcher was feeling doubly aggrieved. Not only were the front pages slopping over with toxin; but on the back pages it was BUTCHER AXED, too.

I asked, 'Are you?'

He grinned grimly and said, 'No.'

Something was wrong with the Dutch.

While the English camp was united against their tabloid tormentors, the Dutch camp was, by all accounts, deeply disunited – and had been for months. Ruud Gullit, during his year off injured, said when he saw his national side play, it 'made his toes curl'. Dark rumours of player power – or certainly, of player disgruntlement – seemed confirmed when the manager who'd seen them through qualification, Thijs Libregts, was replaced by Leo Beenhakker of Ajax only weeks before the tournament. Trouble was, the players didn't want him either – they'd wanted Johan Cruyff.

Still, managerial mayhem needn't necessarily screw you over. The Yugoslav Velibor 'Bora' Milutinovic was Costa Rica's fourth manager in two years – and look what happened to them.

But Holland had other problems. Gullit had only played in AC Milan's last two League games of the Italian season; he wasn't match-fit, while his clubmates Rijkaard and Van Basten were match-drained. They'd had an exhausting time of it, winning the European Cup late in May – but seeing their domestic League and Cup hopes blow up in their faces. So was the spine of the Dutch team knackered?

They'd only played four friendlies together, since they were beaten by Brazil in December – they'd drawn with Italy, and lost to the Russians and the Austrians. But then, on 3 June, they went to Zagreb, and tonked Yugoslavia 2–0. The world smiled knowingly; Gullit was back – and internal strife, that was the Dutch way, wasn't it? Didn't they always argue like hell with each other until kick-off, then scorch their opponents, when it came to the real thing, like they were working it out of their system? Look out, we all said – here come the European champions again . . .

On 12 June they worked nothing out of their system: Holland 1. Egypt 1.

Gullit said, 'We were always running, but never with the ball. And I played very bad. The mind wants more than the body, the body isn't ready to do such work . . . sometimes I want to do more than I can.'

And Beenhakker said, 'We all know we have good players in Holland; but we don't have a good team at the moment.'

Robson wasn't buying any of this. For a start, who said Egypt would be easy? He told the Dutch press, 'I've seen Egypt play five, six times – and I've never seen them lose. They have five or six very good players, very good.'

And few knew better than he did how well the Dutch could play. In Germany we'd held the line with them for maybe seventy minutes – then they spanked us 3–1. Van Basten, thought Robson, was 'electric'.

Harry Harris grinned and said we should play Steve Bull. 'Koeman won't fancy some hairy-arsed skinhead charging up his backside.'

The press said Butcher would be dropped, because they knew how badly Robson feared the incisive pace of the Dutch. So how could he make the creaky 4–4–2 less creaky? By playing Wright at the back instead, he was faster – and by playing Paul Parker for the too-orthodox Gary Stevens, because he was fast too, and as good a limpet-like man-marker as we had.

Not that it really mattered. Playing the way we played, if the Dutch woke up they'd tear through us anyway, whoever the back four were.

*

I went on from training to Is Molas, and had lunch with Jane Nottage and Giacomo Malvermi. They had faxes of the latest tabloid bile; in response to Robson's disgusted denials of the Isabella thing, the *Mirror* had now run a self-serving editorial titled, 'Over The Top', in which Maxwell's true purpose was revealed: Get Robson. The piece was a merciless onslaught on his managerial competence – and you thought, we've only played one game . . .

Giacomo Malvermi was a hoot. And you can laugh – Naked Hostess Turned Into Olive Shock, COL Girl Found On Moon Horror – but the atmosphere was wearily angry and disbelieving. Among the players, anyhow.

Malvermi attempted to teach Bloomfield how to say in Italian, 'I am drowning in the perfection of your loveliness,' in case he should chance upon a Hostess Isabella of his own.

Graham Kelly and some BBC types pottered about with tennis racquets. Giacomo said they were crazy, to play at three in the afternoon in Sardinia. Mad dogs and English newspapers . . . and like I say, you can laugh.

But could the families of twenty-two footballers back home laugh? Could Isabella's family laugh? She was reported variously to be twenty, twenty-five, twenty-seven . . . if you can't get her age right, what chance the poor girl's private life?

Outside, Jon Smith cooked in peace by the pool. 'This,' he said, in his postage stamp trunks, 'is the best part of my job.' He'd been busy round Italy, fixing for Argentina to visit Wembley in May '91, then the Germans the following September; and he'd been checking in with the FIFA moguls in Rome. In their offices he heard a torrent of calls coming in, complaining about the refereeing of Erik Fredriksson – the man was being sent home.

And there was, he said, some uncertainty about what might happen with the Russians by the time we came to 1994. Would Lithuania have an independent football team? He joked grimly, 'Instead of playing the USSR, it'll just be the SSR. Or the SR.' Still, never mind – business was booming out on Planet Football.

So was politics. Moynihan was expected in tomorrow for the match, and then for a security meeting Sunday morning to assess what the fans had got up to. Nottage was booking herself into Is Molas for the night, so she could be on hand to help out with the little man's media needs.

'A new Pamella Bordes,' said Malvermi, 'that's what the media needs. Let's shop her – let's get on the blower to John Jackson right now. COL Official Bonks Minuscule For Sport Shock.'

'I give up,' said Nottage, 'I'll ring him myself. The entire England team are in bed with Miss Nigeria . . . I'm having Sunday off. I've fucking had it with those people.'

Bloomfield pulled himself out of the pool, and grinned in the sun. 'What a crap job, eh?'

From the team meeting in the games room came the sound of Robson going through videos of England and Holland, and urgent, uptight little snatches of talk: 'Where were we? There's nobody there . . .'

Bloomfield said Shilton and Lineker, the two men from Leicester who roomed together, were running a book on each match together too; taking bets on who'd win and who'd lose, on scores at half-time and full-time . . . he said Gazza was a couple of hundred quid up. If the boy fell down the toilet, he'd come out smelling of Chanel.

And while we lay by the pool, Bobby Robson – in fear of Van Basten and some other flying Dutchman coming steaming through the middle – planned, almost unwittingly, the revolution that helped make England one of the three best football teams in the world.

After the team meeting, I sat with Terry Butcher in the room he shared with Chris Woods, waiting for Austria–Czechoslovakia to come on at five. They were tiny and spartan rooms, too – just space for the two beds, and leg-room to walk around them.

Butcher reckoned they'd done OK against the Irish; and from his own point of view, given the amount of time he spent heading away high ball after high ball, that was probably fair enough. But he also said, 'Typical British game – there wasn't any football to be played.'

Gullit had excused us for that. He said, 'That's not a normal game – with the sentimental things there, that's just fighting, they don't want to lose. England–Ireland – that's something else.'

Butcher said, 'Against the Dutch, it'll be a bit more cultured.

And I look forward to that more – from a football point of view, it'll be a lot better.'

I asked what Robson had told them to do.

'Win.'

But could we?

'Wouldn't be here if we didn't think we could beat them. The Dutch won't go into the game as confident, perhaps, as they were – the Egyptians played very well – and we owe them a good game after Germany anyway. People look at it and say Holland are favourites, and it makes you very angry, you know – people go on about the Dutch players here in Italy, or Spain, and they've got Kieft going to Bordeaux now . . . but haven't we got good players? We just keep knocking ourselves down all the time.'

Butcher didn't play in Germany '88, he had a broken leg – so he went with his family to America. He said, 'I couldn't have watched it. Not sat at home.'

Then he looked up and said, 'Oi, Woodsy – there's a spider.' He then explained, 'He's a spider-killer,' as Woods flattened the hapless arachnid. Butcher said, 'We have a bug inspection every night.'

'Any little crawling thing,' said Woods, 'I hate 'em.'

The game began; Butcher said the Czechs had been difficult at Wembley. 'They thought because they were big they had the right to walk all over you. They didn't like it when you got stuck into them though – they didn't fancy it then.' But they were behind the Czechs anyhow as a dud game unfolded.

The only goal came on the half-hour. Lindenberger, wearing his acid house zebra crossing again, brought Chovanec down with a fair imitation of a rugby tackle; Woods said, 'I'm not having that.' While Chovanec was carried off to lie by the hoardings, Bilek won the game from the spot. As he took the penalty, he slipped and fell; Woods and Butcher roared at that.

Chovanec was taken away on a stretcher with his thigh strapped, and the cameras followed him down the tunnel. 'kin' hell,' Butcher grumbled, 'they'll be in the bloody hospital with you next.'

Woods made predictions at every free-kick – left foot, right foot, over the wall, or bending round it. 'These new balls here,' he said, 'they really fly.'

Butcher watched in a less technical frame of mind. 'He was going to stay down there. Cheat. Angers me, when people stay down.'

He'd got a phrase book, and it was *buongiorno* all over the place. Like a big friendly bear, he was getting on famously with the staff; every time they did something, it was, '*Grazie*. Top man.'

At half-time we went to get some tea at the bar. Don Howe was sat with Dennis Howell, Labour's Minister of Sport in the distant days before Thatcher – and Howe asked Terry to get some tea for them too. As we went back down the corridor he muttered, 'What's the matter with him then? Did he break both his legs?'

The game dragged on; we lost interest, and talked about the other matches. Woods said, 'Did you see, Maradona admitted the handball this time?'

'D'you think he was under pressure to, or what?'

I told them what a dud Italy–USA had been. Woods said, 'That's like us playing Motherwell though – they all sit back, make it hard for you.'

Meanwhile, the Czechs looked good; the only reason they didn't get more was the Austrians kept upending them (something for the Americans to look forward to there). They had a fair following of fans, too, in this new European home. One had a serious gut on him; Butcher said, 'I bet he stinks. They all fuckin' stink, East European countries. It's, oooph – *omnipresent . . .*'

The Czechs joined Italy and Cameroon in the second phase; and Austria joined the USA and Russia at the unhappy door marked Exit.

Woods ran through the permutations of who might end up where – and there was a chance, if England went through in third place, that we'd end up in Milan. He said, 'I fancy the San Siro. Who'd we get there?'

The Germans.

'Maybe I don't fancy it.'

Butcher said, 'I hate the fuckin' Germans.'

Then Trevor Steven and Gary Stevens came in to get a card game under way; that aura of single-minded exclusivity that footballers can wrap about themselves settled in once again. Twenty-four hours to go until the bus turned up with its escort at the Sant'Elia for the second time . . . so I left, and hitched a ride back into Cagliari.

And at nine that evening the Germans, having put four past Yugoslavia, went out and put five more past the United Arab Emirates. They too were now qualified for the second phase – and they looked by far the best team in it too. Adroit tap-ins, fierce headers, rockets from long range – they didn't mind how they did it, and they kept on doing it. They could have had ten – Klinsmann and Völler were rapier-sharp up front, and Matthäus untiringly powerful through the middle. If they carried on like this, who could stop them?

I watched this massacre with Rogan Taylor and John Williams in the Italia. Then afterwards, we went to check out the eve-of-match festivities – and there weren't any. There were more photographers than fans, and more police than both together. The police had told regular bars they couldn't screen the matches on their TVs any more . . . Cagliari was turning into a ghost town.

And so to another alcohol-free match day . . .

England–Holland was, in theory, the Group F biggie – the head-to-head to decide who'd come out on top. But in theory, both sides should have had two points by then anyhow.

It was the big one off the pitch, too. The press had been awash for months with hysterical tales of English and Dutch ringleaders getting together to draw up their rules of engagement, or of how the Dutch bad boys planned on bringing bombs to the stadium. Hooligan psychosis – the police were ubiquitous, and oppressive.

There'd been 5,000 English, maximum, for the Ireland game; now, for Holland, they expected two or three thousand more. They reckoned on seven or eight thousand Dutch, too – 3,000 coming on twenty-two charters from Palermo; plenty more by boat.

I went to a conference for the rotters in a drab building by the COL offices on the industrial estate; it was held in a barren and echoey little hall, with the dismal feel about it of an unused bus station. The embassy, and the rotters with it, were keeping a daily tally of arrests and deportations – there had been relatively few, and in the villains league the Germans were ahead at that time. Kay Coombes from the embassy, and Moynihan's press man, both tried drumming home to the rotters the difference between detention and arrest – if you were taken in for an hour or two, questioned and released, that didn't constitute an arrest under Italian or any other kind of law . . . but in *Sun* law, it did.

The Home Secretary had given a list to the Italians of about a hundred whose entry they should bar. Several had been picked up on their way through Rome and sent home. Most prominent among these, a day or two back, was the well-known nerd Paul Scarrot, who'd been scraped off the railway lines at Roma Termini with an empty five-litre flagon of wine, loudly blathering about the mayhem he planned to wreak. The state he was in, he couldn't have planned on getting his cock out of his trousers to piss with it – and it was power-fully rumoured that he'd circumvented his banning orders with the assistance of a tabloid. Serious hoolies, after all, do not give interviews, or seek their photographs on the front pages.

A man who'd given his name as 'Mr Kent Sevenoaks', Coombes wryly announced, had been picked up at Olbia with twenty grams of dope, and sent home too.

An English fan who'd been set on by locals was in hospital, with bruising and head injuries.

There had been, last night, just a few minor incidents, and no arrests.

A delegation of photographers had been to see the police, seeking an agreement whereby they'd stop getting whacked as they went about their business. Little hope was expressed that the agreement would hold.

The prefect had confirmed – in response to a letter from Moynihan – that there would, this time, be buses laid on after the game.

The minister's man then said a report that the minister had been refused a drink at Milan airport on his way here was untrue. Firstly, he hadn't asked for one. Secondly, he'd gone via Genoa.

'And he doesn't drink anyway?' a rotter idly inquired.

'Absolutely not. Not during the World Cup, anyway. Just like you boys. Just like all of you.'

I went and had the lunch we'd reserved at La Taverna with

Roy Collins, and two other fine specimens of the genus Chief Sports Writer. As the wine went down Collins said, 'I should write a piece saying the drinks ban should be more stringently enforced. In my case anyway. "Please Stop Me Drinking" . . . but no, I can't do this without drinking. I'd go mad.'

Another of them – unbelievable fat bastard – then came up with a virulent condemnation of Robson's behaviour in his private life. What he found especially disgusting, he said, was that Robson had had the extra-curricular in his own marital bed.

In the next breath he then informed us that he'd had a bit of the extra-curricular himself once, in his family car – as if that was OK. And with crocodile tears he said the guilt (ha ha) had made him sell it. He sniggered grossly and said, 'It was a pokey little runner, too.'

These brave and red-eyed boys, getting ready over the clandestine grape to write clear-headed reports for the customers back home, were sitting already on some serious hangovers. They'd played, as they put it, seventeen holes last night, and got nowhere – until they found the Bar Marius open, and then a club. They'd got pissed enough to argue about being thrown out early – at 5.30 in the morning . . . and the *fans* behave badly?

One of them said he needed a fruit salad, he didn't want to get scurvy.

'That's rich,' said Collins, 'he had fourteen hundred whiskies last night, his liver's exploding – and he's worried about scurvy.'

World Cup Party? *Festa*?

Cagliari was eerie. By three in the afternoon, the town seemed totally shut down. A chopper hung noisy and low in an ugly, lowering sky over Via Roma. There was a cold wind getting up; the two open cafés in the arcade were sparsely populated. Little draggles of fans drifted around looking lost and small. I met a group of Brummies who were staying at the other end of the island, who'd hired a minibus for the eight-hour ride each way to and from the game – it was better that way, they said. Who wants to spend a fortnight under martial law?

I sat drinking coffee and mineral water with some of the boys I'd met before. And then, I thought, a-hah! – here at last come two likely looking lads, two terrifying English storm-troopers, two members of the army of villainous and violent men Jeff Powell had warned the Italians to expect . . . they sat down at the table next to us.

They were both big, strong, tanned, well-muscled and wholly mean-looking guys. One, the bulkier, had a cropped boulder for a skull; the other, taller and broader, sported glinting US bike-cop shades. They ordered Cokes, and topped them up with Jack Daniels from a bottle in their bag. They wore sawn-off T-shirts, with torn strips of blue scarf tied round taut and bulging biceps. The shirts said on the front 'Lean Mean Blue Machine'; on the back, 'Bad Blue Boys'.

A Barnsley lad on my table leant bravely their way and asked, 'You Chelsea?'

'No,' said the guy in shades, with a voice like a rock slide and a clotted Slavic accent, 'we're Dynamo Zagreb.'

I must have laughed the only laugh in Cagliari all day . . .

And still the heavy silence hung over town, broken only by helicopters or the shriek of police sirens – it was like waiting for war. I counted my cigarettes before leaving for the ground (the *tabachi* were shut as well as the bars, prompting one fan to ask, what they think we're gonna do, run apeshit on nicotine?) Nervously, recalling McMahon and Gascoigne's superstition attack, I found I had *thirteen* . . .

On the way to the ground, there were noticeably more girls among the Dutch support than among the English. Everything about them was orange, from T-shirts to shoes; even orange lip-stick.

Four big ferries were stacked up in dock, waiting to get them back out to Palermo.

People were buying tickets off touts all the way along the route; cars would pull up, and tickets be offered out the windows.

I passed a boy with 'Made In Burnley' tattooed on his left shoulderblade, and the England shield with 'Italy '90' beneath it on the right. As we went past two vanloads of *carabinieri*, his mate waved and smiled at them; he said quietly under his breath, 'We see you later, kick your fucking heads in.'

Would it go off then, today? The appalling idiot Chris

Wright – the man in the top hat – was going round making himself feel big again, telling the boys to march on the stadium from the station at six.

At the ground, there were 1,500 police, military, and *carabinieri* – thousands more round town.

And you thought to yourself, I could be partying with Brazil in Turin, or with Cameroon in Bari – it had got to where people joked with relief, now, when they flew out to report on mainland matches: I'm off to the World Cup. Whereas England, we were football in quarantine – and lousy football too . . .

It looked like another thunderstorm was coming. It was humid and windy; through the forest of stubby trees and shiny new yellow lampposts in the Sant'Elia parking lot, the mountains across the bay were just dim shapes beneath a heavy blue darkness. A couple of minutes into Brazil–Costa Rica at five, the monitors in the press centre went down.

And news began coming in that the English march to the stadium had turned into a riot.

There were no Dutch involved. The Italians had met the march with a wall of police, and diverted it on to wasteground where there was rubble to hand. Rocks began to fly, and *whoomph* – tear gas and baton charge. People who'd come from there said it was major over-reaction. An estimated three hundred – seemingly an arbitrary group – were now penned in a gas station. There were worries for these people – journalists had been *sent away* . . .

Meanwhile the TV picture was recovered, and Brazil went one ahead after thirty-three minutes. Costa Rica were unlucky – Muller's strike took an awkward deflection – but this, surely, would now turn into another German-style monster-eats-minnow, spitting out goals like fishbones.

The corner count in the first half was Brazil 9, Costa Rica 0. In the second half too, the Brazilians set up camp in the Costa Rican penalty area – yet the supposed no-hopers defended with a maximum of bravery and effort; they kept it to 1–0 right through to the end.

The Brazilians, it seemed, had the Italian problem, that pretty patterns and fine passes do not alone make goals – that you need a man on the end of your finery who knows where the net is. And the frustration began to show; it was a clean and dive-free game until, near the end, the Costa Ricans had the guileless audacity to start slipping their opposite numbers – so the Brazilians Jorginho and Mozer both got booked, one for hacking at passing knees, the other for an elbow to a passing face.

So we were in for an instructive contrast here tonight ... and while we waited, rumoursome news came in from the riot zone – of cars overturned and burned, of hundreds arrested.

None of it was true.

The fool Chris Wright, we later learnt, was going round declaiming that a fan and a policeman had been shot. The land of hysterical fantasy.

The weather cleared; it was hot and dry again. The sun went down over the bay, a brilliant orange disc between the mountains to the left, and medieval Cagliari on its hill to the right; the helicopters clattered back and forth in between.

In the stadium a Union Jack defiantly stated: Swindon Town Will Never Die. And there they all were, Aston Villa, Bristol City, Rochdale, Salford, Chester, Millwall, Lincoln and Leicester, Coventry, and Notting Hill ... We Are England.

But we're European too. Bobby Robson, like Brazil, was playing a sweeper ... around the press box, people looked at the new back line with a strange mix of satisfaction, trepidation, and disbelief. They looked as if they'd been kidnapped and deposited in a whole new quadrant of Planet Football where the geography was unknown, the ground underfoot unsteady, and the compass readings wild and unreliable.

In the build-up, the headline approach had been the axing of Butcher; people figured Wright would play in his stead. Others, to be fair – not a few others – had scratched heads and thought, maybe he really might do it. But surely not ... Bobby Robson abandon 4–4–2? It was like the queen in a miniskirt.

On the morning of the game, Patrick Barclay wrote that if it were to happen, 'By Robson's standards it would be almost revolutionary ... we must wait and see.' So now we'd waited, we looked, and we saw.

First reactions could be summed up as Laurel and Hardy –
that's a fine system you've gotten me into. Because while the
smarter minority among them had hammered away for some
time for us to join Europe in the modern world, and start
playing this way – even so, wasn't the second and toughest
group game in the first round of the World Cup a pretty
drastic, late-in-the-day sort of time to find out if it would
work?

The guy next to me said, 'It'll work if Holland don't score.'

But it was England who made the first impression – Butcher,
of all people, going forward to release Lineker. I felt too
gnawed with tension to write much; I could only note how
good, how imaginative, how intelligent the football now
seemed. *The ball stayed on the ground* ... and England
looked sharp, winning the first corner after Barnes, this time,
set Lineker free once more with a slide-rule pass that ran
through the middle like it was computer-guided. Then Gascoigne streaked through two defenders; his cross found Bryan
Robson's head, and flew wide. And Barnes was showing his
quality; he won a free kick down the left, confounding Barcelona's Ronald Koeman. Gazza whipped the kick across the
box; both Wright and Lineker failed to get to it by inches.

They were getting through, when it was supposed to be
the Dutch who did that. The back, the middle, the front,
everything linked and flowed – and the English fans were
loving it.

On our monitors, unbelievably, the Scots went a goal up
against the Swedish in Genoa.

And what is football, some days, some nights, but ninety
minutes of agony?

Please please score

The Dutch looped in their second corner.

Please please don't let them score

Gascoigne looked hard and bright in the middle; Gullit
looked soft and rusty. But the Dutch were beginning to make
slim chances, and Gullit missed two; they were linking up,
and flowing as we were. Honours even, by the half-hour; they
were humming now, winning more corners ... then Gazza set
off from the centre circle, beat three men, and was brought
down – not for the first time. He'd have been clear through
otherwise.

There's only one Paul Gascoigne
Only one Paw-uhl Gaaaa-uh-scoigne

Half-time, 0–0.

News came in of seven fans taken to hospital. Three were treated for cuts and bruises, then released. One was said to have a broken leg, after being run over by a police vehicle; two others had been severely beaten – and the seventh had escaped on the way there . . . but it had been (of course) not as bad as it looked. Some fifty or a hundred were still detained.

The Dutch went out strong into the second half, and quickly got two corners. For five minutes, for the first time, they looked in control; but only for five minutes. Then Bryan Robson fired a long shot at the other end – and Gazza went on working through the middle, jinking and passing, going back and coming forward, causing no end of trouble of the very best kind.

Pearce and Parker, too, were steaming up the flanks . . . Lineker had two stabs at goal. The first ricocheted away, the second went in – and was disallowed for a handball, the ball striking his elbow as the rebound came back at him. It was as inadvertent as it gets – he should get a new passport off that nice Mr Menem . . . then, five minutes later, working a delicious one-two through the middle with Barnes, he fired the best chance yet high and wide.

The crowd grew buzzy with excitement, as they realised Steve Bull was coming on for Chris Waddle – we were throwing it at them now. Bull's first touch was a header wide; he was annoyed with himself too. Barnes had started it, Lineker made the cross – England were enlivened.

Press opinion was that the Dutch weren't on their game; but a tactical triumph for Bobby Robson all the same.

Then Bryan Robson came off, limping. He had a bad toe, they'd been cutting the impacted nail away where he'd stubbed it in training . . . ugh.

So David Platt went on – and what a first taste of World Cup, to go on against the Dutch in a game that stood so poised and so fluid, and replace the man who all felt was the pumping heart, the inspiration, the leader; but Platt was up to it.

Voices in the box: 'Who's picking this team? Graham Taylor?'

'He's only doing it to give us stories. Platt and Bull are the only two who talk to us.'

It was a new look England – and it looked just great. Rijkaard was shut down, he had little chance to come forward as he wrestled to contain Gascoigne, Barnes, Bull, Lineker, they were everywhere; while Des Walker at the back had nagged Van Basten into an invisible drift. Gullit was a shadow of his '88 self – there was little doubt who the new name was now.

Gazza left two men standing in stone with an immaculate little turn on the by-line; he was there one minute, then span on a sixpence and was gone the next. He clipped in a quick low cross, and Bull and Lineker in turn both missed it by inches.

'Just wish the little shit'd talk to us.'

Like Bobby Robson said – you'd think they were playing for the papers out there . . .

England were solid at the back, and moving forward well-oiled and deft.

> *All we are saaaa-ying*
> *Give us a goal*

Defying all prediction, Scotland did – in Genoa, they went two ahead of Sweden. The Swedes, much fancied outsiders, joined the Russians and the rest on the road back home – while Scotland stayed in it.

And so did we, with a vengeance. You didn't come much more fancied than the Dutch – and they'd blown it. They were tied back now to Koeman taking speculative whacks from thirty-five yards – there was no way through.

Robson had expected Van Basten and Kieft through the middle, and he'd played the sweeper to contain that. Instead, Kieft was on the bench, Van Basten was alone, and Gillhaus was on the wing – but Gillhaus plays for Aberdeen, and Butcher knew all about him. So now the English back line was a rubber sheet, instead of the brittle wall of times past – and any time they came at us, we just bounced right back.

With sixteen minutes left, Kieft did go on – but Butcher, Wright, and Walker had the middle good and locked up by then; England had enjoyed their new shape for too long going forward, for any change to worry them much now.

Let's all have a disco
Let's all have a disco
La la la la
La la la la

In the last minute, Gascoigne set off again. Headed for the by-line on the right, he was obstructed, and fell. Reward: an indirect free-kick. Pearce lined up, and put the ball in the net with venom; but it didn't touch anyone *en route* ... like Lineker's effort earlier, it too was disallowed.

This was seriously unlucky – because the Dutch keeper, diving, can't have missed it by more than a few inches ... an odd case where the keeper saved by *not* touching the ball.

So we finished England 0, Holland 0.

But like Beenhakker said, in the second half in particular, England were by some margin the better side. The way we'd played, we'd both erased the Irish horror-hoof – and put down our first marker as contenders for the fourteenth World Cup. It was tentative, compared to the Germans – but a marker nonetheless.

Gullit said, 'It was difficult to control them, and we were lucky to get a draw.'

'What do we need this sweeper for?'

The contrast between England and Brazil playing a five-man back line was this.

It was not, as John Barnes had wistfully said (and as most of Brazil was now angrily saying) the Brazilian way to think defensive. But with over half his squad based in Europe (including ten of the thirteen who played the Costa Ricans) the coach Lazaroni had opted for a European back line – then found, when they wore the gold and green, that it didn't suit them.

As for Robson, his expressed opinion about the system had been brusque, and misleadingly Brazilian: 'Why do we need to play *more* defensive?'

But no system *per se* is offensive or defensive. Whatever the system, you can choose to attack with it, or to sit back and hold tight – and which way you go depends, in the end, on how the players are feeling on the park.

So Brazil laboured. Their touch was sweet as ever – but their front and midfield felt undermanned, and they played all out of kilter. Brazil 1, Costa Rica 0.

The effect on England was entirely the opposite. Brazil weren't used to concentrating on defence; whereas England were freed from being obsessed with it. It was when we played 4–4–2 that we'd been undermanned, both at the back and in midfield – but with Wright as a sweeper making three centre-backs, suddenly the heart of the defence felt hugely less vulnerable.

So instead of Pearce and Gary Stevens feeling constrained to hang back and cover on the flanks (so that Barnes and Waddle in turn felt tied back in front of them) Pearce and the nippy Paul Parker were now liberated to push up, in the knowledge that the heart behind them was more secure. Pearce and Parker became 'wing-backs'; and freed up the likes of Barnes to go roaming, and cause damage wherever he may.

Whether anyone had seen it working quite so positively beforehand is a different matter. Robson did talk at the press conference about the full backs pushing up in offence – but primarily he'd been thinking 'sweeper = more defence'. He did it to stop the Dutch, not to kick-start us – after all, he played 5–4–1, not 3–5–2.

In short, he played a sweeper against Holland because, I have no doubt, he was scared of Van Basten and Kieft ripping through his flat back four.

So you might say, his insecurity won out over his conservatism – the same gritted-teeth insecurity that had driven him to hang in there against the slings and arrows of outrageous tabloids – and it made him play the extra safety card against his own professed beliefs.

And yet the defensive improvement, by making things more secure, also made things more flexible – there was more freedom to attack, more room for invention and variety.

Or, to put it another way, Robson played 5–4–1 – but when you've got the ball, defending 5–4–1 converts with elastic recoil into attacking 3–5–2 in no time at all. And then suddenly you're all over them.

It was an ironic turnabout. Robson stood by 4–4–2 as an attacking system, believing in the class of his two wingers; yet 4–4–2 tied those wingers down because playing that way we had always to scramble back and defend. Then he went out and played a sweeper-based defensive system – and, with the back secured, we ended up doing more of the attacking . . .

The man beside me said before the game, 'It'll work if Holland don't score.'

They didn't; England looked regularly more likely to. They were powerfully unfortunate to get the ball in the net twice, and be denied both times. So the reaction at nine o'clock that it was a pretty hairy time to be trying a sweeper turned, by ten forty-five, to approval.

'England did much more than hold Holland, the European champions, to a draw . . . they redeemed themselves, gave heart to their beleaguered supporters, and made a successful World Cup campaign a real possibility.'

If Brian Glanville could write that, we must have done something right. He called the switch to the new system, 'Astonishing.'

But the approval was conditioned, of course, by the fact that we still hadn't actually scored. Two games, two points – and if either Egypt or Ireland won in Palermo the next day, it'd be them who'd be heading the group . . .

It's worth noting, otherwise, that no one got booked – the referee, a Yugoslavian engineer, had a good game – and then, these two points that came out of the press conference. The first was that Bryan Robson, on top of his toe, had now done his Achilles in as well.

And the second was Bobby Robson on Paul Gascoigne: 'He was the best player on the pitch – outstanding. He needs a bit more education, there's a slight over-exuberance – but his contribution was . . . well, I've got to be careful here. But he played very, very well – he made things happen, and he worked prodigiously hard.'

The conference then fell apart in translingual confusion when a journalist from Cameroon enquired mysteriously of Robson, 'Sir – you have said that Barnes and Waddle are the best pistons in the world.'

There's no answer to that.

I left the stadium around midnight and got a ride on the media bus into Rumourtown. At the station, the bedless rump were penned in the concourse with a major police presence, all riot gear and flashing lights again. I tried to sift from fans some picture of what had happened on the march.

People put the numbers from one to two thousand; and the numbers of those who went at the police, when they came on the roadblock, at one to two hundred. One fan spoke of a small group of police up a sidestreet getting 'a fearful pelting'; one police car was surrounded, and another one abandoned by its occupants, who fled.

But, people said, the people wanting trouble weren't ever going to stay ahead of that lot for long. The police regrouped, and came in from all sides; tear gas, rifle butts, batons. Fans trying to get away spoke of frightening crushes in the hallways of apartment blocks, or in garden areas against collapsing fences. One showed me welts and bruises on his arms and back from a beating he thought 'would never end'; another said he saw a girl get a caning, and her hand getting smashed.

And you came away with these questions:

Innocent or not – if you go among people who lob half-bricks at the *carabinieri*, what d'you expect but a beating?

> *Que sera sera*
> *Whatever will be will be*
> *We're going to I-tal-ee*

Fine – but why d'you have to go *in a regiment*? Why d'you have to march?

Assertion, obviously. Then there's others who say (being fearful in an alien land, and short of the old cultural capital) that there's safety in numbers.

But that's a sorry delusion – no one got whacked for going to the stadium in twos and threes. The last thing the police were going to fancy was the lot of you together – whether it made you feel big or not, safe or not.

And why d'you have to feel big anyhow? Aren't you big enough on your own?

I hung around, among Sards doing likewise, watching nothing much happen at the station. A guy from BBC Radio told me how, in Stockholm, he interviewed a fan who seemed the acme of reason and plausibility. Half an hour later, he saw him carrying away his looted stash of brand new bowler hats.

*

The essence of what happened in Cagliari on 16 June is that – again – a small number of yobs got a large number of others mixed up in an upheaval; and it grew larger (albeit fairly briefly) than it need have done because, trembling with hooligan psychosis, the Italian security forces violently overreacted.

What did *not* happen is this:

WORLD WAR!

> Rampaging English soccer thugs turned the streets of Sardinia into a bloodbath last night . . .
>   More than 500 Brits were arrested . . .
>   It happened after 1,000 angry fans hurled rocks . . .
>   The arrested yobs – many of them drug-crazed . . .
>   – *News of the World*

Les Walker, the FA's security man, later told me he estimated the number of hardcore trouble makers at around sixty.

Kay Coombes at the rotter conference the next morning reported five arrests.

The figure of seven English injured was confirmed; it was also thought that five police had been injured.

Moynihan made a statement: 'Orchestrated incident . . . minority of English thugs bring English football into disrepute . . . grateful to the police for swift and tough action.'

'I understand,' someone said, 'that things went well in Genoa last night.'

'Very well,' said a Scottish journalist. 'Jim Leighton made a save.'

John Williams muttered that the arrest figures were small 'because arrest isn't the agenda here. People don't get arrested – they get hurt.'

Brewin, Beauchampe, and Tummin of the FSA took the floor – another sign of the co-operation now beginning to get in gear, that the embassy gave them this facility to put over their views. The co-operation did not, however, go as far as they wanted – Moynihan had refused to meet them. (Unlike Dennis Howell.)

Brewin said the FSA totally condemned the forty or so English who threw rocks, etc.; and that they'd tried to stop the march. But they were, he said, extremely angry about the policing; and totally rejected Moynihan's hasty and ill-considered statement. Does he care, he asked, how people are being treated?

It then emerged, with some embarrassment, that the shit-stirring myth-maker Chris Wright, the self-styled 'organiser' of the march, was an FSA member, elected (unopposed) to their admin committee. He'd phoned Beauchampe and said, if the police threw a roadblock, 'the lads will smash right through it. If they want a confrontation they will get it.'

Brewin said they'd have to check their constitution – but that Wright wouldn't be a member of the FSA much longer. He was, they said, a compulsive liar, and a lonely man – always talking about the lads this, the lads that – and always turning up on his own, entirely ladless.

Then John Tummin gave his account of the evening's events.

He'd left the FSA office at five to six, joined the march, and moved up towards the front distributing copies of their guide-book. There was, at the front, a certain amount of aggression.

When they got to the junction of Viale Cimitero and Viale Armando Diaz, there were maybe forty or more Dutch fans ahead of them on the steps of the big church, the Santuario di Bonaria; police vans blocked the way, to prevent the English getting to those people.

There were two things wrong at this point. Firstly, the Viale Cristoforo Colombo, fifty or a hundred yards south, was broader, unoccupied, went directly to the stadium, and would have been a better, more segregated route.

And secondly, stopping people at a place where you had wasteground strewn with potential missiles to one side, and a half-dug-up pavement ditto to the other, was dim. (Les Walker agreed later – he put it tactfully – that the English police would have handled things rather differently.)

Some fans, said Tummin – he put it at between ten and thirty at this stage – now started throwing stones. The instant resort to tear gas in reply was, he said terrible policing – there was no graded response. They simply upped the stakes immediately, and induced panic and confusion among 1,500 people.

The police charged forward; he saw three *carabinieri* baton-beating a fan on the ground. He was with a group several hundred strong trying to get away, and find a different and safe way to the stadium; he saw three baton charges during this period. There were, he said, hundreds of people running scared and exhausted.

As he told the story, his re-living of it now became – understandably – emotional. He was also shaking a little.

The group he was with was charged again, and hotly pursued into a garage forecourt. He was hit several times by a policeman with a baton. There were now several hundred people crushed into a very small area on the forecourt. They were, he said, utterly terrified, jammed against a wall and a fence. People called in alarm, 'No Hillsborough – No Hillsborough.'

He was hit again. He showed an ugly bruising welt on his upper left arm.

The assistant deputy of the Cagliari police then arrived, one Antonio Pitea. Tummin had met him some weeks back, when they'd been trying to organise things for fans to do in Cagliari. He'd seen him also just a couple of days ago in the street; they'd shaken hands. Now Pitea, he said, came on to the forecourt, recognised him, said, '*Tu*' – and slapped him in the face.

He said, 'I've never seen a crowd so intimidated in my life. I was sitting on someone who was sitting on someone else, it was that crushed.' People were still being hit; people were dragged out and beaten right in front of them. 'People were impotent, they were crawling on their knees.'

No one was allowed to stand; eventually, Tummin was. It took some time to get it calm, and improvise a system to get people away. Then they were let out one by one; they were thoroughly searched, and taken in groups of twenty to the stadium.

It was, Tummin said, counter-productive, and might well prove a prelude or catalyst to more violence later. He characterised one of the later police charges in particular as 'a revenge attack'. Behaviour like this was, he said, only storing up trouble for the mainland; if anyone called policing like that a success, they needed their head looking at.

In the remaining days in Cagliari, I heard a number of tributes from fans – some unsolicited – to Tummin's courage and presence of mind at that garage. People said he had, simply 'saved their hides'.

So I say sincerely, long may Tummin and the FSA prosper – but I also came away from this conference thinking they'll prosper more if they adopt a less confrontational public posture towards the various authorities that they feel are ignoring them, or worse.

For example: horrific though Tummin's experience may have been, calling the policing 'South African' (several times) is over-emotive, and not media-wise at all. They can lock you in the leftie cupboard easy with that sort of stuff – when what the hoolie trouble needs, more than anything, is perspective.

After all, you think England fans have problems? What about the fifty or so Romanian fans who had by now, in the light of events in Bucharest, applied for political asylum? *There's* problems . . . as for 'South African', frankly, my arse. Were they driving Caspars round and firing shotguns at you, John?

And then, how many people really were chucking rocks? The FSA says forty, Les Walker says sixty. The fans say one to two hundred . . . and the *News of the World* says a thousand.

The 23-year-old travel agent from Essex who'd been to Katowice – he'd been on the march too. When I met him three days later, he told it like this:

'It was the biggest mob I've seen outside of England–Scotland in Glasgow. There probably weren't even a hundred real hardcore at the front, actually hand-to-hand fighting – but there were more just cheering, yelling, running, chucking stuff. I mean, most people were in the mob 'cos it's a mob, not doing anything, just running back and forth – just in a mob, it's hard to say why you do it.

'The police stopped us 'cos there were Dutch down the road, but that's stupid, I've been against Dutch before and they're no trouble, they just come for the football, painted faces and that, they're fine, they're fun – they leave their bad ones at home. The papers whip it up, they're making bombs, all that – it's rubbish.

'Still, it was maybe forty minutes of trouble back and forth

– then they come at us from two sides and press us in this garage, they knew what they were doing – they had the helicopter up above. And that was panic, real panic, terrifying, we were crushed in there, hundreds of us, and the people coming at us were your real top nutters, your Italian SPG or whatever – but they'd taken a pelting, hadn't they?

'So you can't complain about police brutality – you can't give it, and not expect it back. I got big long bruises all over my arms and my back, but I was lucky, I only got the truncheons – it was the rifle butts that hurt – but they were bloody angry, it was frightening, the looks on their faces . . . if you lifted your face up it was whack, whack, whack. You had the choice, get crushed, or face the police – probably safer to face the police, it was like Heysel, piles of bodies . . . but you can't blame the police. I've got to be honest, you just can't. You're in their country, you've had a go at them, and that's that.'

He said, 'I don't believe it when they say it's just a minority. There's a majority who don't *come* for the trouble – but if there's trouble they'll join it all right. You can talk about it till you're blue in the face, but it's not a minority *once it's started* – because of the age group. You go down that campsite, it's all eighteen to twenty-five.'

He'd left the Pula campsite and come into town – spending more money in one day than in the whole nine days previous, on a cab and a room at the Italia – because, 'It was like a PoW camp, I was going mental out there. You've got Italians chucking acid at people, English staggering round pissed at four in the morning with knives – I'd had enough. I'm not running the actual camp down, the owner was brilliant, really looked after us, we had a whip-round for him – but it's just a mess out there.'

Then he said, 'There's less and less England going – look at it here. There's twice as many Scots, twice as many Irish. And like, I went for a beer last night (during the Italy–Czechoslovakia game) and all these birds walk in, and they've got their faces painted green, red, and white, and they're wearing green, red, and white dresses . . . you can't imagine the girls back home sitting watching in the pub with the George Cross on their faces, can you?'

England – just no fun any more.

In Genoa, the Scots marched to the stadium behind a forty-piece pipe band, and took the Swedes along with them. Not one Scot was arrested. They were even knocking on people's doors to introduce themselves – because when others get together, it's a party. But when the English get together, it's like a colonial land grab: the fag end of history, all played out ... and if you're ugly and stupid, and you mass together looking that way, then you will – willingly or not – end up in ugly and stupid events.

The travel agent had done Sweden, Poland, Hungary, Romania, Spain, Denmark, and Greece ('wouldn't go there again'). For Mexico '86, he saved up for two years; he said, 'Mexico was so much better than here – it was such an achievement. Arriving at Acapulco was one of the best moments of my life – this rich American playground, and suddenly it's full of England fans. It's all tourism now, but it wasn't so much four years ago ... and I did Germany too – we love Germany, they're so like us.

'But it wasn't a good time – same as here, same old thing – gets boring, sleeping at stations, and them coming in with the tear gas. It's not a break – my holidays every year are with England, and you come back more knackered than when you left. I mean, every time, you say never again – then you go again anyway.

'But it's getting frightening. I mean, someone's going to die – someone's going to die soon.'

I went from the rotter conference to the bus station, and found that the bus I'd used for Is Molas before didn't run on a Sunday.

Outside, three or four English were arguing with a taxi driver. One wore a T-shirt which said on the back, 'England's Finest – Invasion Of Italy 1990 – We Came, We Saw, We Kicked Ass'. On the front it said, 'The Nightmare Returns' over a picture of a bulldog bursting through a wooden wall, like Freddy on Elm Street.

Their idea of negotiating involved shouting and swearing a lot.

The driver took me to Is Molas for near half what he'd been asking of the fans to go to Pula – same distance, give or take. He said, on the way, that England were great, should have won 5–0. Butcher, he said, displayed 'a marvellous hostility'. Terry liked that.

His Italian was coming on. He tested his latest on his new mate the barman, grinning, '*Posso avere uno pompino?*'

It was a new word on me – I tried to think of *pomp-* words. Can I have a grapefruit? A fireman? An Argentinian goal-keeper? Seemed unlikely . . .

'A blow job,' Butcher laughed; his buddy the barman laughed happily with him.

They were chuffed over the way they'd played; but it was beginning to get boring, stuck in that hotel. You trained an hour and a half a day – then what? They'd been in Sardinia twenty-three days now . . . you entertained yourself as best you could. Ireland were playing Egypt in Palermo at five that afternoon – but no one expected that to be much of an entertainment.

I'd gone to see Peter Shilton. He'd won his 100th cap against Holland two years ago in Germany – not a nice way to get your century, watching Van Basten put a hat-trick past you. But last night, against Holland once more, he'd made a far greater milestone – his 120th cap took him past the Northern Irish keeper Pat Jennings to become the most capped international footballer of all time . . . but he wasn't thinking about that much, not now – not yet. He was still thinking about the game, and then the next one. Records, he said, are there for when you finish – on the night, you just want the result.

He said, 'It was a game where I didn't have a lot of work to do, not spectacular work – but it was difficult work, a lot of corners, and shots you expected to save. With it being 0–0, the worst period really was ten minutes to go. We tired a bit, and they were pushing on quite strongly from midfield; I just had the feeling we might give something away. That's when I was really working, shouting, because after all the good work we'd done, we hadn't finished them off – so the pressure was really on at the back not to let one in. From a personal point of view, even more so.'

I asked if he was satisfied, when it ended the way it did.

'I was satisfied with my own performance, very satisfied with a clean sheet, obviously – but I was a bit disappointed we hadn't won. We'd have more or less qualified if we had. As it stands now, we still need another result.'

And the Egyptians wouldn't be easy ... he said, 'I made a complaint to FIFA about the pitch. The actual goalmouths, turf had been put in the goal, just in the six yard box, brand new turf. And it was coming away under your feet – not a big area, but you only need one slip there, it could be vital. You're trying to play in the World Cup ... it was a disgrace. I couldn't believe the state of the goalmouths.'

He was rather more pleased about the fans. 'What impressed me about them was that the atmosphere was very jovial – it was a bit like you *normally* get abroad. There wasn't any bad chanting, or bad language, it was all good fun, good humoured – and they really got behind us. At the end the applause they gave us, it was great, I think they were really pleased with the way we played – and they're the ones that matter, aren't they? They kept singing, let's all have a disco, all that – it was fun. Quite unusual, really.'

So since we're talking unusual – how did it feel, to play behind a sweeper?

'Didn't affect me. At Derby, we played the last two games of the season with the same system, with Mark Wright sweeping – we beat Manchester City 1–0, then we played at Liverpool with it, and lost 1–0. Two of our best performances of the season – and Mark just slotted in, like he did last night. So it wasn't like we'd never done it – it was no problem.'

Then he said, 'As far as I'm concerned, I think all first division teams in England should play that way because it encourages players to think about the game, to make their own decisions. They have more space to create things, they have to play more. I think in England, this pushing up and playing in the middle third of the pitch, and the ball all helter-skelter – that's got to stop. It's not football. It's just tactical warfare, really – managers in England have got to open their eyes. The game is there to be *played* – it's not just picking up three points any old how, it's got to be played as an entertainment – and players have got to be encouraged to develop their abilities.'

But will it change?

'I think it's got to. I think if we do well here, that'll help. But there's one or two managers in England who've got to get the blinkers off and realise, their little world isn't the be-all and end-all of football. There's a big world out there, and we've got to be part of it.'

So would Shilton become a manager?

'I've got it in the back of my mind. Players I used to play with that are managers now, they all say, it's not bad on this side, but you play as long as you can. Because at the end of the day, playing's the best thing.'

Mark Wright was there too, lying in the sun – with Dave Seaman, the third choice keeper who'd broken his thumb in training, and then Dave Beasant, who'd flown out to replace him. Wright said, 'Is he asking were you involved with that hostess?'

Someone said, 'I was, yeah.'

'Yeah, we all were.'

'The whole England squad was. Obvious.'

Wright said, 'Garbage, isn't it?'

I asked him how it had been against the Dutch.

'Very enjoyable.'

Gullit and Van Basten didn't get up to much, did they?

'That's the beauty of the sweeper system. If you've got people who are good markers, and you track them around, and then someone behind who can read the game – it's very hard to play against.'

Beasant asked, 'What category are you then?'

'I'm the reader, Dave, yeah.'

'Just wanted that clarified.'

'I think the sweeper reads, Dave, doesn't he?'

'Takes a book out on the pitch while everyone else does the work.'

'It's harder than what people think it is, the sweeper system. When you stay central, people think you just stay there all the time – but you've got to shut the channels off. You do as much running as anybody else.'

But it wasn't new to him?

'No, like Shilts just said – and when we got beat 1–0 at Liverpool, really, we could have come away with a result. But I was lucky enough to play it two or three years at Southampton, under Lawrie McMenemy – I've had a good grounding in it.'

So when people turn round and say it's a big gamble, that's not true?

Seaman said, 'It's a surprise internationally, isn't it?'

'There's a big difference, playing it at club level, to doing it here against the best. Everything's got to be right for it. So to be fair it was a gamble, on the manager's part – but it paid off, didn't it? We were unlucky not to come away with two points last night.'

What did it feel like, going out against the likes of Gullit and Van Basten?

Wright laughed, remembering Germany '88. He said, 'It's an experience, yeah. He's certainly the quickest player I've ever played against.'

Van Basten?

'No, Gullit – he's sharp, he's fast. From standing start to top speed, he's unbelievable. He's an athelete. And Van Basten ain't slow either. Des had a good battle with him last night.'

They lay by the pool in the sun; it felt mightily better than it had the day after the Ireland game. I asked Wright what he'd be doing if he wasn't a footballer.

'He'd be a window cleaner,' said Beasant. 'That's what I'd be, anyway.'

'Lugging ladders round everywhere.'

'Nah,' said Beasant. 'He'd be a university lecturer. All that reading.'

Wright said he got into football quite late; he stayed on another year at school, to get qualifications to be a PE teacher. 'Only PE though, not fuckin' . . . oops. That's on your tape.'

I said, when you'd been around footballers nine months, you heard a swearword or two.

'Bollocks.'

'Dave Beasant said that.'

Wright said, 'It'd be nice to see that game on the video. Everyone says it was a good game.'

It was, too. And they were confident and relaxed, like they felt they were going somewhere now.

Butcher said, 'It worked very well, didn't it? The way we approached the game, it was positive, we felt confident. We never really talked about it, we'd never done a lot of work on it before. But the players we've got, we adapted quite easily.'

Then he said, 'I talked to some Germans afterwards, they wanted me to criticise the Dutch team, which I wouldn't do. The Dutch could play better than that, sure – but you only play as well as you're allowed to play. Van Basten had probably one of the best markers in the world on him – so where d'you go from there?'

But we could have had it?

'I think we're all disappointed that we didn't. But if we carry on like that, we'll get the goals.'

Was it a revolution then?

'Well, let's not get carried away. We've had one game, we haven't beaten anybody yet – we've drawn 0–0, we've played quite well with it. But it's a start, I think – it's a start to changing a lot of ideas. It's a chance for a lot of first division teams to start using the system – because if everybody's happy with it, it's very positive, it's not a negative system. It makes space – it enables players to do what they can do best.'

So should we have gone over to it earlier?

'Possibly. We've got a great sweeper in Mark Wright – I think he'll emerge as one of our best players – and Des Walker's a great marker. So the more we work at it, the better I think it can become. And when you've got the Robsons and the Gascoignes in front of you – Gazza played well, didn't he? He seemed to mature when the skipper went off. And then the forwards we've got . . . it augurs well, doesn't it? There's a very optimistic feeling now.'

So we'd go out and beat Egypt?

'Bottom line, we must do. We must win. But you never look for a draw in football – unless you're Italian, I suppose. We don't, anyway.'

The Italian papers, I said, kept going back to how Lineker had 'exploded' in Mexico, with his hat-trick in the third game.

Butcher said, 'Any one of the front players could explode. Hopefully they'll all explode together. A mass explosion.'

And looking further?

The Germans, he said, looked far and away the best side. 'Still, people say they're like a machine – and you never know with machines, do you? Every machine's faulty at some stage or other.'

*

I watched some of Ireland–Egypt in the games room with Macca, Shilts, Wright and Dorigo. Shilts was giving 2–1 on Ireland, evens on Egypt or a draw. It was an awful game. Enter Butcher.

Commentator: 'A fine run there by Glasgow Celtic's Chris Morris . . .'

Butcher: 'Blyeagh. Scumbags.' Exit Butcher.

And exit me too, bored witless.

The Irish wanted to win, because they still had the Dutch to face; the Egyptians went for a draw, thinking presumably that they'd do the same against England, and let the Dutch do the rest. So the Egyptians didn't have a single serious shot; and the Irish, not exactly a goal machine themselves, couldn't get through at the other end. Ireland 0, Egypt 0.

Jack Charlton was furious. Asked about the match he said, 'What match? I've never seen a team who haven't created one chance in the whole ninety minutes . . . I didn't like their timewasting tactics. We take a little bit of blame ourselves because we didn't score goals – but at least we tried. We didn't win a match we thought we would, because the opposition didn't come to play.'

But surely they deserved some credit for two draws in their first appearance in the World Cup since 1934?

'They played very well in their own eighteen yard box.'

Sour grapes, really. The Irish fans were great – but the football they were following stank. And if you play like an industrial digger, why shouldn't the Egyptians or anyone else hold you down if they choose to?

So now all four teams in the group were gridlocked on two points apiece, one goal each. Two more draws with the same score again, and they'd be picking the qualifiers from Group F out of a hat. Or, in FIFA's case, a fancy glass bowl.

Back in town I went to the bar of the Italia, and met Rogan Taylor and John Williams – and while Spain were beating South Korea 3–1 in Udine, we watched instead what turned out to be the best match of the first round: Belgium–Uruguay.

Belgium went ahead on fifteen minutes, Jan Ceulemans starting a simple move that flowed wide to the left, perfect cross, Clijsters rose – and in went the header, no questions asked.

Their second was as good as anything we'd seen in twenty-two games so far. Again, nothing fancy – just a square pass, and then Enzo Scifo running on to it for a first-time shot from thirty yards that roared into the net like an express train. A great conga of people went dancing round the moat in Verona, waving their Belgian flags – and in the Italia we were out of our seats.

One guy was excited too much – the goal brought on an epileptic fit, he was rising from his seat like the rest of us but then he started shaking, spraying spittle, eyes rolling . . . beer glasses and an ashtray went flying, as he quaked and slid under the table. We got him out on his back, checked his tongue, the barman bringing a long spoon just in case; but he was all right again in five minutes, and went carefully away – the game was just too much.

A couple of minutes later, one of a small group of England fans who'd been effing and blinding at the back went to his now-empty booth and said, 'Are these seats all right?' Sliding in he continued, doing a horrible mime of a fit, 'There's five thousand volts through here, hyeugh hyeugh.'

He was ignored – but it was easy to ignore anything, watching a game like this one. The veteran defender Eric Gerets was sent off near the break – but the Belgians still came out and got a third. Ceulemans charged through the middle from the centre circle, collected as he arrived in the area, then netted, again with straightforward relish.

Someone asked, 'How old is he now?'

Thirty-three.

'Almost old enough to play for Cameroon.'

It wasn't like the Uruguayans weren't playing, either. There was a lot of Lineker's 'nicey-nicey', dainty ball skills, canny little lacing runs – they spent several periods dancing along the edge of the Belgian area, feinting and weaving . . . nice football, but no punch, after all. At least, not until Bengoechea got fed up, and whacked one in with eighteen minutes left. Then Perdomo tried to emulate Scifo a few minutes later but the Belgian keeper caught the shot as it streaked in, with the kind of leap normally reserved for Carl Lewis.

In the last few minutes we had a quick flash, in frustration no doubt, of the Uruguay we once knew and loved so well. One of them took Scifo's windpipe between his fingers as he walked behind him, and gave him a vicious hard throttling squeeze.

Still, let's keep it straight – Belgium won the foul count 25–8. And they also won the game. Uruguay were good and bright and tricksy, and unlucky too; but Belgium were magnificent.

Only two other footballers in history had played in more World Cup matches than Jan Ceulemans; both of those (Pat Jennings, and the Italian Dino Zoff) had been keepers. And sure, maybe the Belgians were getting on a bit – Gerets and Clijsters both, like Ceulemans, planned to retire after Italia '90. But they'd been semi-finalists in Mexico, and they knew what they were about. Belgium 3, Uruguay 1, with only ten men in the second half– they were the sixth side to go through.

And whoever came up against them next round would have their work cut out, no question.

With Williams and Taylor was Jonathan Foster, a news man from the *Independent* (who'd said on an earlier occasion that the media provocation in Cagliari was the most intense he'd ever seen – worse than the miners' strike). They said now that whatever happened outside, the England fans inside the ground had behaved well.

'Of course,' said Foster, 'they sang 'God Save The Queen' – but what d'you expect? 'Greensleeves'? 'Scarborough Fair'? They're not bloody Steeleye Span.'

As for the *News of the World* saying they were drug-crazed, 'They're all on diarrhoea tablets, is all.'

There was a bloke in his mid-twenties there too, who had promised the parents of his eighteen-year-old companion that he'd look after their son on this, his first England trip. They'd only come for the Holland game – and now he was worried how, when they got home, he'd explain away the bruises.

The England international experience: you pay £250 to get there the day before the game. You end up in a campsite thirty-five kilometres down the road; on the morning of match day, you go to the bus stop to get into town. The police come by and say, no bus, only taxi. So you walk a few kilometres to Pula – and the bus passes you on the way ... then in town, you pay £33 each for £9 seats; you get tear-gassed and batoned *en route* to the ground, and miss the first twenty minutes of the game. Then you can't find the buses back afterwards, because no one tells you where they are – and when you do find a bus, it drops you three miles short of the campsite, at one in the morning . . .

'Still,' they said, 'beats watching Arsenal, doesn't it?'

And they'd be saving for '94 from the minute they got home.

15 Chris Waddle

The Man from Marseilles (with live commentary by Gazza and Barnesy)

If he weren't playing football . . .

'Still be working in the sausage factory, I suppose. I couldn't see me getting out of that – I didn't have the qualifications to move from there. I only knew football, and I was lucky enough to get into it – but I didn't get the break till I was nineteen. Everybody thought I was a bit small – then I got to eighteen and filled out a bit, played a season in the Northern League, and Newcastle gave me a year's contract. I'm twenty-nine now . . . Gazza. Sod off.'

We were sitting on the lawn at Burnham Beeches; the squad had been named, it was the eve of the Uruguay game, and Gazza was chucking grapes at us.

Waddle hadn't thought much about what he might do when the time came to come home from Marseilles. He said, 'If it means dropping divisions, I'll drop divisions, but I want to keep playing – I still get a thrill out of it. And people say when you pack it in, you really miss it.'

When he did pack it in, would he stay in the game?

'It's the only thing I really know. I love watching football, I love the tactical side of it, and I've had good managers – so I'd like to think some day I could put my ideas back into the game, maybe coaching, or scouting. I'd like to stay in it, anyway.'

So I asked about the managers.

'Arthur Cox at Newcastle, I've got great respect for him. I was nineteen, just arrived from Tow Law, and he was strong on discipline; I needed that. And he got me to believe – he thought I had something, and he was determined to make sure I didn't waste it. Then Terry Venables helped me at Spurs, he's got progressive ideas. I was sort of steady, going along, but I think with his ideas, it pushed me into another gear. I think he helped me a lot.'

And Bobby Robson?

'I think it's harder when you come to England, because all they can do is watch League games. And they expect you to do what you do for your club side – but international football's very different.'

'Bollocks,' said Gazza.

Waddle went on, 'I think being the England manager's all about motivating. It's up to the manager to get players to play with the confidence they have at their club – because when players get together here, it takes a while to feel part of it.'

Didn't he feel a part of it?

'Well, now I do – but it's took me a few years. Over the last year or more, I have done; before, I always felt a bit . . . why was I here, sort of thing. You look round and think, I remember watching them on the telly – they're England. And you don't feel as if you should be here with them. Some players, it's different . . . like Gazza here, he lacks a bit of confidence, doesn't he? Once he gets confident, God knows what'll happen.'

I asked how the two of them got on, with them both being Geordies.

'He was an apprentice when I was a pro, I had to beat him up then . . . yeah, we've known each other a few years.'

'Liar.'

'We've got the same ideas, he's just more stupid than me. When he come to Tottenham we had a good laugh, the last season I was there. So we've been the best of mates a while now – but deep down, I really hate him.'

'Cunt.'

I asked Gazza what he'd be doing, if he weren't playing football.

Waddle said, 'Throwing grapes at people.'

Gazza said, 'I've nothing to say.'

'If he hadn't gone for an apprenticeship at Newcastle, there were strong rumours he was going for an interview at the sausage factory . . . he's from a place called Dunston, and I'm from Pelaw, it's only five minutes in the car. And my wife, she's from a place about two minutes from where he lived.'

I asked, did it have any bearing on the way they played?

'I think up in Newcastle, everybody's brought up on the history of Newcastle United, the great players like Jackie Milburn, Bobby Mitchell, Terry Hibbett. Probably round the country all those people aren't legends – but in Newcastle they are. They've always had skilful players, like Jimmy Smith . . . in the north-east, people still talk about them.

'So when you're a kid, the first thing you do when you're on the park, you start dribbling the ball all the time. And it shows, in the England squad now – you've got myself, Gazza, Peter Beardsley, all from similar backgrounds, all skilful on the ball. So there must be something up there – you watch the young ones there, you'll always find there's two or three with exceptional skill. It's just getting them to believe, and play in a team pattern, that's the problem . . . at least, that's what they keep writing about us – saying we can do things, but that we don't play for the team, or that we haven't got defence. Well, we *haven't* got defence. But at the end of the day, the likes of Gazza, Peter and myself, John Barnes – we put bums on seats, don't we?'

Gazza said helpfully, 'Arses.'

'People say we haven't got defence, we don't do this, we don't do that – but if we can do the other thing . . . the other thing's harder to do than defend, anybody can defend. But my job's not to defend – yeah, you got to take your little part, so's Gazza, so's John Barnes. But what are we in the team for, really? To create, and to score. And if we're doing all right at that . . . I haven't got to prove it to anybody. Bobby Robson's the only one I've got to answer to when I'm playing for England. Nobody else.'

So what he said about playing in France the other night, after the Denmark game . . .

'4–4–2's the English system, has been for a long time. And some games it's fine, don't get me wrong, we'll pen teams in, and then I don't have to run back all the time. But when you're playing a class side, you end up defending a lot more. I've spoke to the manager about the times when their full backs keep creating, and I've got to go with them – and he says, That's just our system, you've got to do it. But it'd be great if I could just let them go, and find the space – so when we get the ball they could get it to me quick, and then *he's* out of position. It's all about bluffing then.'

He said, 'In Europe, they buy players to do a job . . .'

Gazza asked, 'Is he going to get paid for this?'

No.

'That's all he thinks about, Paul Gascoigne – *money*.'

Gazza laughed. He said, 'I'm money-daft.'

Waddle said, 'In Europe they buy players to do certain jobs – so I was bought to create goals for Papin, and it's worked out. Now there's certain games where I've had to run up and down, and I've spoke to the coach and said, when I get the ball at the other end I can't create, 'cos I'm going to have to run seventy yards. And he says, OK, we'll change it round . . . they're more flexible on the Continent. They'll change the system from game to game – but England, club sides as well, they'll play 4–4–2 from first game to last.'

So you come back and you think, This is dumb.

'Not *dumb*, no – but we've got a lot of quality players, and if we're wanting to get the best out of them . . . it's like Glenn Hoddle – if Glenn had been French he'd have played a hundred games, easy.'

Then Gazza broke in to say, 'Look at that little kid, look at him, watch.' There were kids in England shirts kicking a ball about by the net on the lawn; there often were, and Gazza'd always go to play with them, more than any other player. They loved it, always – and so did he.

Waddle looked at the kid and said, 'He's nineteen, man. He's got two paper rounds.'

Then he went on, 'People always say, why have we got to change? We had a good record in European football when we were in it, and the national team's gone seventeen without defeat. And they've got a point.'

But it was 2–1 to Uruguay the next day – and Waddle had a point too. 'I'm just saying we should be more flexible. Like, Denmark outnumbered us in certain parts of the field, and it was very hard to get the ball off them. I know it's hard to change the system, because as I say, we've done it all the time now – the only way we'd change it, to be perfectly honest, would be for whoever comes after the World Cup to say, right, I'm going to build a sweeper system . . . but I can't see it happening.'

That was interesting – Waddle assuming Robson would go (or be pushed) at the end of Italia '90. It was three days before the news of the job at PSV broke.

As to playing a sweeper, Robson was asked on the BBC the day after the Holland game, 'At what point did you take the decision to change the system so radically?'

He said, 'Oh, even before I came here. Before we set off.'

Back in the studio in London, Terry Venables looked ever so slightly dubious. He said, 'Well . . . if he had done, I'd have thought he'd have tried it before he'd gone. I think you like to look at what you're going to do.'

I said it was difficult for the national manager, when he was only getting the players a few days at a time.

'Yeah, but what I'm saying is, other teams look at the opposition and say, that's their strong point, let's outnumber them there – and they put players in to do that certain job. Then the flair players are left to go free – you look at the two Laudrups the other night, they didn't chase anybody, they didn't tackle anybody, they just found space to get the ball and create. So they must feel great when they get the ball, they feel fresh – and all of a sudden they're going at you. But when you run seventy yards up and down the right wing, it's very hard for ninety minutes . . . there might come a time in the last minute where you're one on one with someone – and you've got nothing left.'

So the English way stops you playing skilfully?

'It does at the finish, sure, because you get tired. Take him against Czechoslovakia – he had a blinding game, but the last ten minutes his socks went down, because he's done so much work.'

I asked Gazza if he'd been knackered at the end of that game. (Not so knackered that he couldn't score, though.)

'Nothing to say.'

Waddle laughed. 'Well, I don't know why his socks were down then.' Then he went on, 'In 4-4-2, the skill players play wide – but it's very hard to get the ball wide in international football.'

So against Brazil, I said, Waddle had come in.

'I had to. It was three on two in midfield, and I ended up just defending, I must have done more tackles than I've ever done in my life in that game. I was lucky I didn't get a yellow card at the finish, which is ridiculous for me . . . still, it's easy

316

for me to say I should be playing here, or there – it's the English system, and you've got to take your part in it. It's just unfortunate that you have players like Glenn Hoddle, Stan Bowles, Frank Worthington, great technical players, the players people love to watch – and they can't hold a place in the England team.'

Then he said, 'This season, the greatest thing for me in English football has been Swindon. I've watched them play twice now. And we were in the north-east the other day and we said, what was it like with Newcastle in the Second Division? And everybody said – this is Newcastle supporters, mind – oh, Swindon were different class. And the players too, after the match, they said, oh, Swindon were different class. And why? Because he lets them play.'

'He' being Swindon's manager Ozzie Ardiles, previously one of the most attractive players Argentinian football ever produced – yet the FA wouldn't even give him a coaching badge. Then Swindon, having won promotion to the first division, were demoted to the third, for alleged under-the-table payments to players – without details of the charges being made public. A different club, one feels – one that wasn't different class – might not have been so swingeingly punished.

So was the extremity of the punishment revenge for Ardiles being foreign, and playing fancy, and winning? Given the xenophobic greedheads and dunderwits who run the English Football League, it's a suspicion that's very hard to avoid.

The FA's board of appeal, to their credit, subsequently eased Swindon's grief by putting them back into the second division – but what a dim and cack-handed affair it all was. And do ninety-one other clubs all have squeaky-clean hands?

Waddle said to Gazza, 'What are you sitting here for anyway? Haven't you got anything better to do than just follow me around?'

Gazza was chucking grapes in new directions now, and told Waddle to shut up; he was disturbing his aim.

I asked Gazza why he wouldn't talk to the press.

''Cos I fuckin' hate them.'

Waddle said, 'I don't blame him, actually. He's got his

contract with the *Sun*, so he only speaks to one journalist, and he just blanks the rest. Fair enough.'

Later, in Cagliari, when the press–squad relationship was hitting its nadir, I asked Butcher if everyone going round saying they hated the press, but still taking money from them, wasn't a bit . . .

'Hypocritical? Yeah, well – the *Star* was very derogatory towards me, and I'm contracted to them, so I said, right, contract's over. But then, I could legally have fallen down by that – so I had to do more articles. And they're very positive articles, all my articles have been positive – but that only shows how today's news is tomorrow's fish'n'chip paper.'

It's not a satisfactory answer. It's no good saying that when they're bad, they're very very bad – but that when they're paying and you give them decent stuff, it's here today, gone to-morrow.

So I said, given how bad it had got by then, shouldn't the players all just say, stop – no more contracts, no more interviews, no nothing.

'What, with the scandals and that? Yeah . . . but it's good money, at the end of the day, for fifteen minutes on the telephone. And you try to say positive things. If they want sensationalism, they can get someone else.'

But why do you have to be paid to be positive?

Another thing: when they criticise the press, it's blanket criticism.

But they can discriminate all right, when they justify their paid columns by saying the hack who's appointed to do them is OK. One player said his appointed scribbler was leaving his tabloid, he couldn't stick it any more – and that showed his integrity.

I'd just seen the hack in question buying blank receipts for cash from a Cagliari cabbie . . . very bloody integral.

But later, in Naples, Waddle gave a more honest answer to this criticism. He said, basically, that it was great taking money from people that you hated.

I asked what was it like to score a goal – and Gazza forgot his vows of silence immediately. He said, 'It's *brilliant*.'

'D'you want to take this interview over? Well shut your

face then.' Answering the question, Waddle said, 'It's a great feeling. For ten seconds, you just lose your head.'

'It's unbelievable,' said Gazza, 'you feel like shooting your bolt.'

'You do? I never went that far.'

Gazza was caught up in the magic idea now. 'You're all over the place, all over the place, man. Run anywhere. Even if you're 5–0 down.'

'Aren't you slightly exaggerating there?'

I said to Gazza, he was a confident player, so . . .

Down came the clamp again. 'Nothing to say.'

'You'll get nothing off him.'

Someone else told Gazza he should say, no comment, like a politician.

'You don't say, no comment. Then they can put that you said, no comment. But if you say, I've got nothing to say . . .'

'They'll put that you said so.'

Gazza sat there shrugging.

Waddle went back to goals. He said, 'You can't explain the feeling, everything just goes out your head for ten seconds, it's just jubilation – me personally, I'll always sprint for ten, twenty yards when I score. I'll never walk away. I just seem to run and go stupid for ten seconds. At Marseilles, everybody who scores jumps the barrier and goes to the fence, and I'm like that too – in England, you've got to watch that, you might be provoking trouble, but in France you don't. They love their football there – and then, you like to see people go home happy. They go to work or school on Monday, and they talk about it. If you can entertain people like that, it's fantastic.'

Gazza by then had gone to kick the ball about with the kids on the lawn. And he was fooling about – he was entertaining.

Waddle said, 'You either love him or you hate him – but you'll find most people love him. He's cheeky, but he gets away with it – he's got one of them faces. And the way he says things, it always sounds like he's playing funny – but sometimes he's serious.'

I said how everyone joked that Gazza had a confidence problem – and that maybe, on the park, he was that confident. But mightn't he act the way he did because, inside, he wasn't really so sure of himself at all? Terry Venables has said he's a sensitive boy . . .

Waddle said, 'People like that are normally a bit insecure, even when things are going for them. They like to be the centre of attraction, and feel wanted. And maybe with Gazza that might be it.'

But whatever it is with Gazza, he's not telling unless you pay; I'm not sure if he'd know how or what to tell anyhow, however much you paid. And so long as it keeps him playing the way he does, I doubt also whether there's many who'd complain.

'They don't realize you're a foreigner, that you can't speak the language, and you need help. To be fair, Marseilles, they're like the most powerful thing in the city – if the club rings the electricity and says, I want electricity for Chris Waddle, then *boom*, you've got it. Whereas if I ring up, it probably takes a few days, you're on a list, a week or two goes by . . . at the finish I had to say, look, you don't do anything for us, I need electricity, I got problems – and maybe that's partly why I'm not doing so well on the field as early as I wanted – then all of a sudden, the next day the electricity arrives, and the day after that the phone . . . nine times out of ten a club signs you and says, right, get on with it. And if it's an English club fair enough, you haven't got a language problem – but going abroad, it was a nightmare at first. I thought, what the hell am I doing here?'

I asked if he was learning the language.

'Yeah, I've had quite a few lessons now. But because I've been playing Saturday, Wednesday, Saturday a lot, League and Cup, I've not always had time. All of a sudden the teacher'll knock, like, the night after a big game, and the last thing you want is to sit down and learn French. So I've missed out a few – but my wife's stuck at it, she's ahead of me now. Still, I get by – I'm not as good as her, I'll never speak perfect, I end up trying to speak a sentence, and an English word falls in it. But I'm having a go – the lads reckon another year, and I'll be able to speak pretty good.'

And certainly, he was enjoying it enough now – on and off the pitch – that he wanted to stay. He lives up the road from Marseilles in Aix-en-Provence in a rented house; and he talks about it like Lineker did about Barcelona – great people, great food, great weather. He's got a two-year-old daughter who's enjoying it too – she's in the pool every day. He said, by the time the contract finished, if he stayed, she'd be five, and growing up bilingual. It was an idea he liked.

'But then I mean, Marseilles – you get the impression that if you don't do it, you'll not be there. You've got to think, I'm a foreign player, I'm not a French player – and there's only three foreigners allowed. So if he gets his eye on one he wants . . .'

Marseilles had on its books that season Chris Waddle, the Uruguayan Enzo Francescoli, and the Brazilian Mozer.

'At the minute I'm in a strong position, I know I'll not be going. I get on well with the public, I like the spectators over there . . .'

After Italia '90, Marseilles's owner Bernard Tapie sold Francescoli to, funnily enough, the newly promoted Cagliari; and replaced him with Dragan Stojkovic, from Red Star Belgrade. Seeing as he was buying Adidas at the time, swapping a couple of footballers around probably didn't exercise him too much.

I asked Waddle about the money players make.

'You get great rewards – why not? It's a short life. And I'm lucky, I know – well, people say footballers are lucky, but you work hard too. And if that means going to a big club, and playing for England, it's not just luck, is it? If Baggio, say, goes for eight million or whatever, good luck to the lad, he's secure for life, good luck to him – because he's got pressure on him, hasn't he? Especially in Italy. I mean, I was flattered that Marseilles went so high for me – but we've won the League, got to the semi-final of the European Cup and got robbed in it . . .'

What happened?

'We won 2–1 at our place – so we went to Benfica, and if they won 1–0 it was theirs, with the away goal. So it was 0–0, seven minutes to go, the cross come in – and the kid's punched it in the net. It was blatant, everybody saw it.'

Except the referee.

'Unfortunately, yes. That's why I said after the match there – I didn't mean to slag him off, he's under enormous pressure, there's 110,000 there – but it's about time for big games, and all World Cup games, that they have the video replay, like they have in American football. Because for the time it takes to rewind and have a look, after all . . .'

There'd have been no hand of God in Mexico then – or, indeed, in Naples against the Russians.

'Yeah, well, if they'd looked at that, they'd have said no. And I mean, be fair – the player who does that, and then runs away giving it all this (he mimicked the exultation of the scorer), they should send him off – he's just conning the game. How Maradona can say it's the hand of God – it's the biggest load of crap I've ever heard. If he'd have come out after the match and said, yeah, I handled it – everybody would have thought, well, at least he's honest. 'Cos at the end of the day, if Gary Lineker had done the same everybody here might have said, well done – but Gary would have said, I handled it. I would have. And what annoys you is Maradona always says, he didn't handle it – what, is he frightened to admit he did?'

He said, 'There's Gazza, obviously – but I've never really been one to mix with the players off the field. You tend to go with your own friends. Obviously I've drifted away a bit, not being in Newcastle any more . . .'

I asked, was it hard to stay close to people, when you started in a sausage factory, and ended up in Marseilles?

'I know what you mean. I had a row with one of my mates once 'cos he said, it's all right for you, you get the privileges – I remember one night I was in this social club in Pelaw, and me and this lad carried on, and he ended up getting barred, and I didn't. And then his brother come up one night, he's talking to me, and all of a sudden he's just let himself go, he says, it's a joke our kid's barred, and you're not, just because you're Chris Waddle. At the time I thought, that's stupid, we both carried on but he got caught, they thought he was causing trouble more than I was. But then you realise, you do get the privileges – but that's just football, because everybody loves the game. So you do get better treatment.'

And it has its downside.

'Sometimes you don't know people's true personality, they come on false with you 'cos of who you are. There's people want bits of you – everybody's out for something. I'd like to think I've spotted the ones that are just hangers-on – but there's a lot who don't. They don't realise it's the club these people love, or the game, not you – and when you move, say, they don't give a shit about you any more. Or a new player arrives, and they leech on to him instead. At first it starts, oh, you're a great player, fancy a drink, have a drink, blah blah blah – and within a month it's, can you get us a ticket? So you go sure, good mate, I'll get him a ticket. And all of a sudden it's a ticket every game. Then they winkle their way into the club, and they start mixing with all the players, and they love it, that's what their dreams are about – not you.'

In Marseilles, he said, the people were great, sure – but there'd always be people, say, wanting him to go to their restaurant. 'And I know what they're after – they're not after Chris Waddle, they wouldn't have time to get to know what I'm like – it's just Chris Waddle, Olympic Marseilles. Not me. And you have to be careful not to be rude all the time. You have to keep saying, no, sorry – you want to get home, and see your family.'

Was it more tempting, when he was younger?

'Oh yeah. I mean, the friends I was knocking about with, they were on the dole – and all of a sudden I'm on the first team, my money's going up, and there's people offering you free this, free that, free driving lessons ... OK, great. And then all of a sudden I'm in a car now, I've bought an old banger, I got an old Capri for £100. So I can take my mates out during the day – and for a few months, 'cos my missus was working, I used to just drive around ... well, wasting money, probably. But at the time, that was what I wanted to do. I didn't really grow up till I went to Tottenham.'

He said, 'Who's going to stand and get kicked? People say, look at him jumping out the way – but it's not being a coward, it's just using your loaf. In France, you can see a lot of it coming. Brest, they were pulling us, tripping us – they beat us 2–1, maybe to them that was the best way of getting the result. We ended up trying to fight them – and that's not what we're best at.'

He said he'd never been sent off; he'd been booked once in France, and four or five times in England.

'I can't get physical – I'm not going to launch into people

and smash them in half. My bookings have been obstruction, maybe, or telling the ref where to go . . . I like to talk to the ref. If I think his decisions are crap, I'll say so. I got booked once at Newcastle, when I first went back with Tottenham. We were getting beat 2–1 – and he give some stupid decision and I just said, that's a load of crap. So he gives me the yellow card, in front of the Newcastle fans . . . I suppose they liked it. I didn't.'

He said he approached games pretty relaxed, generally. 'People say, look at him, sauntering out – what do they want, they want veins popping out my neck? In our changing room, there's only really Terry who's like that. He's all, *yeah, come on, come on* – but it'd look a bit funny if everyone was like that, wouldn't it?'

'Marseilles happened so quick. We were in Cyprus, and I was talking about the next season, playing with Gazza, and Gary Lineker coming – I was looking forward to it, I thought, this is what we need, a world class goalscorer. Then we get back – and two weeks later we're in Marseilles. It happened so quick, it was just so quick – bang bang crash bang wallop, I was there.'

What would he have done if his wife had said no?

'I wouldn't have gone. The first three months, there were times when I wish I'd said no myself. But I wouldn't change it now – it was a real challenge. Then after Marseilles people say, what you going to do? And I'd like another challenge – probably with a second division club. You look at the big old clubs, Burnley, Blackpool – it'd be nice to see if the support would come back, like when Kevin Keegan went to Newcastle. That must have been a great thing to do. He must have known he could get thirty thousand in there – and he did.'

Then he remembered George Best coming to play against Newcastle, and watching standing in the Paddock, and 10,000 being locked out. He talked about skill players all the time; and he said he always liked playing against the Italians, club or country, because, 'They've got the technique, haven't they? They draw you in, they try to get you nearer goal – but that suits my game. You get into the sort of zones where it's hard to get into, and all of a sudden you're there with ease – and you think, I'm enjoying this.'

Was he a better player then, for playing abroad?

'I feel better, yeah. But it's hard to show you're a better player in the system here – for me to show I'm better, we'd have to play like Marseilles. 4–4–2, it's hard to express yourself.'

We were sat inside with a cup of tea; John Barnes crept up and leant through the window, mock-throttled Waddle from behind, then came in – rolling through the window – to snaffle our biscuits.

Waddle said, 'He's in the same position as me. You get a marker, and you've got a zone – so you haven't got the greatest amount of space to get rid of him. You've got to stick in your zone for the system – so sometimes the ball comes, and you've just got to pass it off. Then people say, oh, he doesn't dribble, he doesn't do what he's doing for Liverpool – but in international football, they're not daft. They say, he's dangerous, get tight on him. If he went wandering away with the ball, what would the bloke do then? If he went into the middle of the park, it's common sense that the full back should just go – but it doesn't work like that. We play such a zone system, you've all got your little areas ... it must be great, marking a player who plays wide for England.'

'If you just stay out there,' said Barnes.

'But then if you go wandering, all of a sudden they're looking to get the ball out there, or the full back does stay back – and you're wrong, 'cos you've left your zone.'

'Also, Chris, I can play for Liverpool, and it's like the continentals – they'll have someone in that zone, but *not necessarily the same person*. So Alan Hansen can go past me, and I'll take his position. But here, if Chris comes off the line, or I come off the line, and no one goes into that position, if the full back doesn't come – then the marker's free. With the sweeper, the full back can go, and the sweeper can cover; or the marker can cover, and the sweeper can mark – you're not caught short anywhere. In England, they place too much importance on position – if you're midfield you're midfield, if you're a winger you're a winger. But a midfielder on the wing, he's not a midfielder any more, is he?'

'But because they're not used to it, they'll quickly run back ...'

'To get to their position, yeah.'

'He could go on a run, or chase somebody, and end up over here – and instead of just saying, all right, I'm here now, you just stay there a couple of minutes until it's sorted out, then we'll swap back around – they don't, do they? They'll run straight back and say, no, no, I'm here, you've got to be there. And for the likes of him and me, it's very frustrating, because we're in the team to create, and do things. And if you can't get the ball, what are we in the team for? People write, we didn't really do anything – it's a load of crap, we work as hard as anybody else when we play those positions – but we're there to create, not defend. At Marseilles, if I lose the ball, I don't have to break my neck to get back – the manager says, you three don't worry about defence, the rest'll do that. And you're not going to tell me seven others and the goalie can't defend. How many defenders do you want? It's just *inflexible* – that's the difference between Europe and us. People go on about Liverpool – but they play near enough European . . .'

'That's why Liverpool have been successful. I wouldn't say they're *as* flexible as the European teams . . .'

'But they're more flexible than any other English team.'

'Yeah. Players rotate, they move around, they're difficult to mark – Glenn Hysen's created goals on the right wing, and is he that kind of a player? But he made two goals against Coventry; he's a centre-half and he ends up down the right, and one of the midfield players drops back . . .'

'It's just common sense.'

'In England you're happy marking your man. But all of a sudden if your man goes somewhere else, you're not happy. In Europe you'd go with him.'

'Because they know they've always a spare defender. So they rotate it amongst themselves – it's very simple. Whereas here, if he goes inside, and then the ball gets knocked out to their full back, nine times out of ten coach'll be out the dugout and it's, *what are you fuckin' doing in the middle of the park?*'

'And then Chris or myself'll have to run back with this full back. And we end up in the left back or right back position.'

'I'll tell you, when you play Liverpool – everybody goes out saying, how we going to stop them? He marks him, he marks him, he marks him – and they still come out winning two or three-nil. You think you do your homework – but they take you into positions which no other English club does.'

Waddle and McMahon later agreed, in Naples, that they'd back Liverpool to beat England two times out of three.

Anyone for 4–4–2?

Asked after the Holland game whether he could contemplate changing back to it for Egypt, Robson said, 'Sure, I could contemplate changing. I've only played it once, I've played eighty-nine times the other way . . . I could contemplate abandoning the sweeper system, yeah.'

I had more sympathy with Barnes now, in May, than I'd had with his more equivocal, stubbornly uncontroversial position at Anfield in April – Waddle's directness had brought him out. Even so, he did revert to the party line towards the end, saying with more hope than belief that we'd be OK . . . but not Waddle.

Waddle said that to be fair, the boss had let him off the leash in some games lately – saying that if he wasn't getting a kick, to come inside. He'd enjoyed Italy, and Yugoslavia.

But then he said, about the World Cup coming, 'Egypt, they'll be man-to-man. And if they mark man-to-man, like, where I go, he goes – then I'll say to the coach before the game, I'm not staying there, I'll go wander. Because I know he's not punishing my team – if they get the ball, he's still not going away from me. And why have I got to stay right wing, if I know this man's not going anywhere? Why right wing, instead of right *side*? It's a half of a half, isn't it?

'You cannot say, for the balance of the team – that's rubbish. That man's staying with me, so if I take him in, somebody's got to be spare somewhere. That's all I'm saying. It'd be nice, if I get a man-to-man marker in the World Cup, if he just said, OK, he's obsessed with you, he's not going to attack – so go where you want. Be flexible.'

That's what you're hoping for?

'I'm hoping.'

And he got what he hoped for, in the end – then proved what he could do with it too, when it turned out to be England who drew the task of mastering the Belgians. Waddle played the full 120 minutes in that game, and was one of the best things we had.

But sadly, John Barnes didn't, and wasn't. He had a good goal disallowed, which was bad luck, and he got a groin strain, which was worse – but he never showed out the way Chris Waddle did.

Changing the system doesn't work any automatic magic – it only helps you if you help yourself.

16　18 June: A Very Long Day

Argentina–Romania

Naples, said Malvermi – hell, hell, hell.

I flew via Rome where, waiting for the connection, I learnt (from *Newsweek*) that Sierra Leone had produced a postage stamp honouring the Cameroon team already.

By saying the magic formula – COL 02447 JXZDOA, easy when you know how – I'd succeeded in retrieving my $500. On other fronts, things were looking less rosy.

I had no ticket for the game. Olivetti said that there was one reserved; but in Cagliari they said, in Naples that means nothing. And I had no room booked either – but then, I'd not be out of the stadium until after midnight – and with the return flight leaving at seven the next morning, I figured I'd do without.

Because you think to yourself, here's a chance to see Maradona play before his adopted home crowd in a match which, if they lose, sends Argentina home . . . and there was a press lounge at the airport. This was worth sleeping a few hours on a sofa for.

Coming in over Naples past the glossy blurs of Ischia and Capri, the green of the pitch in the great ring of the San Paolo looked the brightest thing in town. We got out of the plane – into chaos and heat.

I got a ride in a cab with Barclay, Powell, and Colin Gibson to Castel dell'Ovo – Egg Castle – where they'd housed what Powell called, 'the prettiest inefficient press centre in the world'. The traffic was the densest and most freeform I've seen, outside of Cairo – but then Naples, once the third city of Europe, is more African than European anyhow.

The ticket took two minutes; but placing a phone call was more protracted. The simplest request, in Naples, often requires the convening of a meeting of at least five people. A collect call? Well, let's talk about it . . . and after five minutes they've forgotten you exist, they're talking about something else altogether. Or a map of the city, at the information desk? Mass conferral; frantic heaving open of drawers, rummaging among piles of paper, examination of phone directories and brochures and every kind of FIFA print-out and PR document on earth . . . but no maps.

Egg Castle was a cool labyrinth of damp, dungeony rooms, a beehive of work areas and offices; it was an ochre pile parked on a rock fifty metres offshore from the main five-lane drag along the edge of the bay, opposite the costliest hotels in town. The causeway that connected it to land sheltered a marina with restaurants round the quays; and the views across the water south to Vesuvius, or north to the ramshackle rise of Mergellina, were vivid and bright under a blazing sky.

The ramped jumbles of boulders along the base of the sea walls were bedecked with dark-skinned swimmers and sun-bathers; very much like the over-populated sea defences of Rabat or Casablanca, bodies strewn in the sun in a third world indolence by the rim of the chattering waves . . . further afield, cranes stood stacked along the docks, round frigates and merchantmen. Three rusty freighters waited in the bay with a shining white gin palace, and a *Guardia di Finanza* motorboat. Vesuvius beyond was a lazy threatening brute, a grey mouth gaping ominously at the bleached and featureless sky. Families fooled about in little boats in the foreground. On the Via Caracciolo the traffic raced and hooted; the scooters whined and buzzed, their riders helmetless showmen all.

And maybe to some Naples is hell, hell, hell – for sure, I know I wouldn't want to live there – but it's a great place to visit. I went walking in the packed and narrow streets, and talked with rotten-toothed and rampantly cheerful people; it was easy to remember how, when I was eighteen, and hitch-hiked round Italy for three months, the people here were kinder to me than in any other city in the country.

On the smeared and crumbling walls of the backstreets I saw two posters, in both Italian and English. The English version on one said, 'Water not drinkable, there aren't houses and work – shameful Mondiale'. And on the other, 'If we doesn't have our job, we will boycott Italy '90'.

With Maradona in town, there was little chance of that.

Buses for the media left Egg Castle every half-hour through the late afternoon. Via Caracciolo was theoretically five lanes, one way; Neapolitan style, it accommodated six lanes, inchoate and ill-defined, heaving and weaving. With a police escort going ahead the bus pulled out and then, to our amazement, did a U-turn, and set off nonchalantly straight into the oncoming traffic.

On the bus we talked injuries. Hodge was out, Webb didn't seem match-fit; Butcher had a knee, Walker had an ankle – and now Lineker had a toe, Bryan Robson a toe and an Achilles . . .

'There you go, lads,' said Powell, 'the wheels are falling off. England take on the world with Platt and Bull. An Aston Villa humper, and a second division battering ram. Italy in crisis. Germany in trauma. Brazil all a-tremble . . .'

Gibson said, 'And Platt puts in the cross from the by-line to the near post, Bull rises to head unerringly home for his third goal in the final . . . then you wake up. On a beach somewhere.'

'And you've been there fifteen days,' said Powell.

The police escort worked miracles to get us through the honking, surging mess of the streets to the stadium. As we pulled up, an American photographer was brutally rude to a couple of small Hispanics as they tried to get out of their seats. 'Fuck you,' he said, 'get in my way again, and I'll kick your ass.'

'Maybe,' muttered Gibson, 'he doesn't like your camera case in his face, pal.'

'I just don't like a man getting in my way, mac.' Which is rich, coming from a photographer.

Gibson, a big man, said, 'He'll quieten down when he sees me get off the bus.'

'I'll go first,' said the somewhat smaller Powell, 'give him a false sense of security.'

Gibson grinned. 'Well, don't leave me behind, boys.'

Then we were on the Tarmac, outside the enormous spartan mass of the San Paolo. No Roman fancy here, no Milanese sci-fi fantasy – just a vast industrial barn of a place with functional plastic roofing, and huge hulking walls like some old military fort . . . the poor man's palace in the poor man's capital, pretention-free.

I remarked how in the traffic I'd seen a man in shades shimmying through the cars on a trail bike, with his little girl (both helmetless, of course) just plonked between his knees, hands flat and clutched fiercely to the petrol tank. And with a child of my own now, I'd looked at that horrified – it took the indifference to risk or danger to a terrifying and irresponsible degree.

Yes, said Barclay – but you're in a different country now. When David Miller of *The Times* wrote a book on Trevor Francis, he said that in one game, Claudio Gentile behaved like 'a barbarian'. And an English defender might have been flattered – but northern Italians habitually dismiss south-erners as barbarians; the regional antipathy is so great that hatred need not, sometimes, be too strong a word for it. Gentile, a southerner, was so furious that he sued.

I don't know the outcome of the case – but a Neapolitan took revenge on Miller anyhow. He was stuck in traffic there, and suddenly had his car window stove in by a crowbar. Then, as the shattered glass landed in his lap, in came the thieving hand, and out went the briefcase; so Miller jumped out, in fruitless pursuit. It was, he said later, a bit alarming, and rather inconvenient – bye bye press pass, ID, tickets, wallet, the lot. But what really narked him was chasing the guy down the street, and seeing a police car indifferently wedged in the traffic, just a car or two behind his own . . .

As we talked, yet another immeasurably gorgeous steward-ess led us through the crowds to the media gate. There were Romanian tourist buses – and a man in full flag Romanian regalia, wearing red-yellow-blue robes from head to toe, and carrying a six-foot tall Orthodox cross.

Inside, they even had Italia '90 liner bags . . . and here's Neapolitan organisation for you. I'd not booked in for the post-match press conference – but forty minutes after the deadline by which you were supposed to have reserved your ticket for that, I strolled into the conference room where they were dishing them out. All these press were sat orderly like schoolkids, waiting for their names to be called – so I moseyed up to the desk and said, 'Can I have one?'

'Sure, here you go.'

Naples, *I love you*.

There was a new species of the fauna of Planet Football here too. We've met green for beer already, blue for COL, and red for Coke – but now there was a girl in glaring yellow as well, a Grana Padano girl, Grana Padano being 'the official cheese of Italia '90' ... Cheesewoman. She was of such an unearthly height, she must have had a vertical leap on her to make Oman Biyik look ordinary. I watched her go past through the teeming throngs of press in the bar and the work areas, the way you watch a giraffe towering on an African horizon.

Things, I thought – feeling sticky and dirty after another early morning, two flights, and a long afternoon in this hot packed town – were getting more weird by the minute.

The Databank reported howls of grief and anguish from Uruguay.

'Belgium has deflated the ball of our hopes!'

'A black Sunday for the faded pale blue!'

'A red devil showed us the ugly face of reality!'

In Brazil, they were promoting Lothar Matthäus as 'a candidate for immortality'. And in Germany, after Italy–USA, *Bild* said, 'Only the Brazilians are dangerous – we needn't fear the Italians.'

In Holland, the draw with England was judged, 'a lucky escape'.

We were into the last first round games now, played in simultaneous pairs to avoid fixes (in theory). And from here, it worked like this.

In each group of four, the top two went through automatically: twelve qualifiers. Then, to make it up to sixteen for the second round knockout, the four teams in third place with the best records went through too. Argentina and Romania, both beaten by Cameroon, both winners over Russia, had two points each; so a draw, and another point each, would see them both through.

Russia played Cameroon in Bari at the same time – and for the Russians, parked at the door marked Exit, the last desperate calculation was this: if either side in Naples lost, and they

333

put a hatful past the Africans, they'd get third place in the group with two points, and a better goal difference than the losers in Naples.

And they might still then survive, if the hat they filled against Cameroon was a very tall one; because in at least two other groups, there'd be third placed sides also finishing on two points – Austria after they'd beaten the USA in Group A, Sweden or Scotland or Costa Rica in C, Colombia after defeat by the Germans in D – and anybody at all in gridlocked Group F. All over Italy, people permed the possibilities.

For Argentina, there was another factor in the equation. If they won and the Africans lost, they'd top the group, and stay with Maradona's fans behind them in Naples. Whereas if they drew, they'd have to travel to the Germans in Milan, or to Brazil in Turin . . .

I went into the stadium at 8.30 – and to my dismay, it was half-empty.

FIFA and '90 Tour claimed that over ninety per cent of the tickets for the tournament had been sold. But '90 Tour was only a wholesaler – tickets sold by them to retail agencies abroad didn't necessarily mean bums on seats in Italy.

So now, in Naples, they claimed an attendance of 52,733 – but I doubt it. We were learning – with attendances announced according to the tickets sold, as opposed to the numbers actually present – that there were travel agencies world-wide going to bed with tickets they'd failed to move on . . . and I'd come here for this?

Maradona, what's worse, had an iffy knee . . . but they cheered his name to the blue sky, as the squads came out like ants from a hole in the ground behind one goal.

Diego! Diego! Diego!

The stadium did fill a bit, as the whistle approached; and the blue-and-white of Argentina was everywhere. Banners announced Sante Fe, Banfield, Café El Monoguillo, Snack 78 Cordoba . . . Diego'd picked himself a good second home.

Because after World War II, many of the Italians who went to Argentina came from the south, escaping the ruin and desperate poverty there. In the centre that afternoon, I'd seen a right-wing poster protesting African immigration. It said that in Argentina now, there were half a million Italo-Argentines who wanted to return – to escape the ruin and desperate poverty there – and they should, said the poster, get preference . . . so Maradona couldn't have picked a better town to play god in. It was Buenos Aires on the Med.

Meanwhile, I don't know whether Romania's done anything about its anthem already, after all their grief and uprising – but they certainly ought to. It's *Coronation Street* on qualudes, very Ceausescu . . . at least Naples, predictably, had the fanciest band so far to play it, with king-size gold epaulettes, and dinky red and white tufts flapping on their Napoleon hats. (In Cagliari, we got a bunch of engineers in khaki.) And here we go . . .

Maradona commits the first foul of the game.

Maradona commits the second foul of the game.

The third foul of the game is committed on Maradona, he rolls half-way to Buenos Aires, and Lacatus gets booked. Then, unbelievably, he gets Hagi booked too – by fouling him, then acting up another ersatz death scene when Hagi, flattened and irritated, clips his feet as he passes with a trailing leg. And all this in the first ten minutes . . .

By then Caniggia had already set off from half-way, ridden a tackle instead of diving for once, worked an effortless and immaculate give-and-return at full pelt through the middle with Maradona – and shaved the side netting on the end of it.

Not that the Romanians weren't handy too. Where Argentina's football was rough and jerky, Romania's was complete; they had more possession, incisive passing, strong running on and off the ball . . . and Hagi, 'the Maradona of the Carpathians', was outdoing the real thing, while the real thing just strutted and pouted, the crocked cock of the walk. And as Argentinian drumbeats rattled like gunfire, the crowd began to swing Romania's way.

Their attacks were determined, shapely, and sewn together from front to back. Argentina's, which were fewer anyway, seemed abrupt and ill-considered – spasmodic darts and stabs, the psychotic lunges of an angry but lazy man.

> *Viva Viva Lacatus!*
> *Hagi! Hagi! Hagi!*

Batista brought him down, deliberate, casual, cynical; he

did the same to Balint. And there were sorties spilling in at both ends now; the drums were a constant thud and clatter round the stands. Lacatus came close, rifling it in from the angle that had defeated Dasaev; but Goycochea was equal to it, and equal, too, to Hagi's fierce and curling free-kicks.

So, still o–o at half-time – it was fast, bright, end-to-end, but it lacked the last punch. Maradona was peripheral, all act and no football – whereas Hagi was everywhere, shredding Argentina's clumsy midfield with ease, pulling men left and right, and getting kicked for it too ... Romania were ahead on points, no question.

Word came from Bari that the Russians were 2–0 up, and could have had four more.

Romania came back out, and took charge of the ball again. Hagi got to the by-line, Balint's shot from the cross forcing Goycochea to tip it over the top; another free kick from Hagi found Balint's head this time – but the chance flew high.

I noticed a Romanian offering his hand to the Argentine he'd just brought down – and having it refused ... then Maradona forced a corner, took it himself, and Monzon glanced it in.

It was against the run of play – but never mind, the Romanians had another gear. They came pouring up, Hagi beat two men to force a corner, Andone missed a sitter – and then, seven minutes after going behind, Lacatus crossed, the ball bounced back across the face of goal from Sabau's head to Balint – and his header, this time, was true.

It was greeted with a cheer easily as big as that for Monzon's goal; and boys ran round the moat with that tragic emblem, the Romanian flag with the hole torn in its middle, among them two bearing a banner that read, 'Italy loves a free Romania'. And who cares about Diego, indeed, when they're dying in Bucharest?

Argentina did try to chase the game after that, with the big boys looming to meet them in Milan or Turin; but their efforts were scrappy. They weren't worth more than a point, and they were barely worth that. Romania, meanwhile, were happy to hold the ball, and play out for the point – they had, after all, never gone beyond the first round before.

So they, and the match, ended dull. But the bigger disappointment, by far, was Diego Maradona – he'd not now had one single chance in three games.

And it seemed a long way to come, and a long day to spend — with a sleepless night ahead – to see half a hero, in front of half a crowd.

Argentina 1, Romania 1. So though the Russians ended up with four goals in Bari (against a Cameroon who probably weren't much bothered) it availed them nothing. Powell said Cameroon were knackered anyway – they'd be out of it next game.

I went to the press conference. Hagi was a good-looking bloke, tousle-haired and puckish; Lacatus, on the other hand, had one of those pudding bowl eastern bloc haircuts out of doomy-gloomy movies about hard times in black and white places with grey edges, fog in the trees, and nothing to eat . . . i.e., Romania. Still, he'd just signed with Fiorentina; they'd get him a stylist, no doubt. And the both of them, not unnaturally, looked pleased as punch.

They were asked if events at home had affected them.

Lacatus smiled, with a sad hint of exasperation. He said, 'Certainly, what's happened has left traces in the hearts of our players – we think about what's happening. But we hope it'll be resolved, as we've resolved things in football here tonight – and that equality will prevail.'

So now they'd come second in the group, who would they like to come second in Group F, to meet them in Genoa?

'No preference. Whoever qualifies, we have to play them.'

Emerich Jenei, the manager, said, 'Between England and Holland, I'd prefer Egypt.'

But Lacatus, with his second booking tonight, would be suspended from that game.

'It seems to me the referee gave yellow cards for no reason.'

But of course there was a reason, pal – you were playing Argentina . . .

Was Maradona over-protected?

'Yes indeed.'

Hagi thought it was a real crack, when Jenei said Lacatus was 'one of the greatest of our players'; he sat nudging him, and whispering like a schoolkid.

Then the politics came up again, and the question of fans seeking asylum. Hagi said, 'We're sportsmen, we're not

337

worried about asylum – we are Romanians, we in any case will go home.' Which was easy for him to say – because, being sportsmen, they could now get out. It was Lacatus to Fiorentina, Hagi to Real Madrid, and the market in full swing – the manager of Bari flew to Romania the next day, to enquire after the forward Raducioiu, and the sweeper Popescu. (Though funnily enough, Popescu's ended up at . . . PSV Eindhoven.)

Bilardo, meanwhile, looked more worried than ever. Diego, he said, had 'no one to play with'; and as well as the knee he had an ankle now too, swelling up something rotten. He'd asked to be subbed at half-time; then changed his mind and said he'd play 'if it killed him'.

And all around, Babel – voices in Italian, Spanish, German, French, Romanian . . . some frazzle-nerved jerk from Maxwell's new paper, the *European*, went round hassling anyone who'd listen about what teams might end up where; a bunch of Germans bullied some complacent toad from FIFA about how the draw would be made to pick qualifiers from Group F, if the football couldn't do it.

And thus did quotes emerge from Italia '90, through a tangle of languages; thus did the stories stumble out, mangled in translation, and passed from notepad to notepad by grown men acting like a pack of yowling infants.

Back in town, I had a post-midnight pasta with Jeff Powell and Patrick Barclay on the quay by the Egg Castle marina. And, seeing how the game had been straightforward, Group B was settled, and boiling your brain over who'd play whom where next was pretty pointless, we talked about the press instead.

They were both dismayed by the Hostess Isabella thing. Their attitude was that if a politician of, say, 'the party of the family', got caught offside with a lady other than his wife, then yes, the public interest was valid. But footballers were only public figures in so far as they played football. So if a player wasn't married, it was entirely his business who got into his bed; and if he *was* married, it was entirely his and his wife's.

'We all know,' said Powell, 'they're red-blooded boys. If they weren't, we wouldn't want them out here.' But they'd not been dallying with hostesses – and if they had been, it wasn't legitimate public material.

'Unless,' Powell laughed, 'she got into bed with someone to find out if England were playing a sweeper.'

'We have,' said Barclay, 'the worst disciplined – not the least competent – but the worst *disciplined* press in Western Europe. Just as we have the worst disciplined schools, fans, society . . .'

All played out.

Then they said that if Vicini wrote for the papers, he'd not give you, so–and–so's a plonker, or, so–and–so MUST PLAY. He'd give you a reasoned notion of what any given player would or wouldn't give you in any given formation, against any given opposition.

The implication was, you want intelligence? In English football?

Powell said, 'You think *we're* a rotten press? Have you seen what they're doing to Beenhakker in Holland? Or to Vicini here? He's won twice, and they're doing him for *not winning well enough*. Or Bilardo – Bilardo's got the bloody President on his back. Can you imagine that? "Ah, Mr Robson, it's the Prime Minister here – I think you should drop Terry Butcher."'

Certainly, Powell and Barclay both thought that he should. Powell said, 'His legs are going.'

And then, this not-talking-to-the-press thing – it was all exaggerated. The only two that absolutely didn't were Des Walker and Stuart Pearce – and that was down to Brian Clough at Nottingham Forest. He allowed none of his players to talk to the press, then did it all himself – but only for money. And it was partly, they said, because he'd not want any of them talking about him . . .

And then they asked, as the small hours crept closer and the water lapped against the quay, what I'd be saying about them, in this book.

'It'll be easy enough to find us,' Powell grinned. 'We'll look under W in the index. For Wankers.'

But you don't have to agree with all of a man's opinions to think he's good company anyway.

Besides, there is no index.

*

The press centre was open until four in the morning; I sat slumped in front of the Databank for a couple of hours. I learnt that in the first 400 days of its World Cup coverage, the ANSA news agency had transmitted 2,500,000 words. The globewide chatter of Planet Football . . .

In a magazine I learnt that when it was all over, you could buy a piece of the turf from the Olympic Stadium in Rome, 5 × 6.5 cms in a plexi-glass cube, for £55. Or a piece 13 × 20 in a stadium-shaped container, for £100. Projected sales: $40,000,000 . . .

I got a cab to the airport at 3.45 – and the press lounge was closed. No soft sofas for Davies . . . the airport was a grubby dump, silent and empty. I tried, and failed, to sleep stretched across three hard plastic seats, with a paperback for a pillow; maybe about five, I drifted off. Then at 5.30, a roaring party of Neapolitan holiday-makers arrived . . . the bar opened at six, and I golloped down some *cappuccino*.

Gibson turned up, and Millichip, who – wearing his FIFA hat – had been what he called 'commissar' for last night's match. When I asked him what that meant, he sat twinkling like a gnome as he ran through his awesome responsibilities – making sure that the teams went out on time, that the ref and linesmen were OK, pulling names from a hat for the dope tests, writing a report . . . he said the bookings had all been fine. So he obviously wasn't commissar-ing the same match that I was at.

He and Gibson talked golf; and I sat there feeling, raw tempered, that there was something vaguely wrong, having this smug, 76-year-old, roly-poly scoutmaster-type being unctuously fêted round Italy writing his merry little reports – while the fans who paid his wages got their hides truncheoned back in Cagliari . . . there was word, now, of not one, but three club chairmen's yachts moored offshore.

So, a flight to Rome, another back to Cagliari, then a lift with Gibson to Pula and the training ground once more. We played Egypt in two days . . .

When I got back to La Perla sometime later that day, the excellent Signora Orru took one look at me and said, 'You are *destroyed*!'

But not at all, ma'am, not at all – because we've barely begun . . .

17 Stumbling Out of Cagliari

Bull, Platt, Barnes, and England–Egypt

While the gunmen of West Beirut celebrated Egypt's draw with the Irish by firing volleys into the Lebanese sky – joined, in a rare show of Arab solidarity, by Syrian troops, which just shows the barriers that football can surmount – Jack Charlton, as we know, was being less than courteous about their game.

The Egyptian manager Mahmoud El-Gohary politely refused to respond, and ordered silence from his players too. Dr Ahmed El-Mokadem, however, a professor of economics from Surrey University who was helping to fund Egypt's travel and accommodation, did not feel so constrained. Speaking to the *Independent*, he described the Irish way of playing as 'contagious crap'.

He said it wasn't only the Egyptians that the Irish fans booed after their o–o draw. 'They're fed up with not seeing good football. If that's the way their team's going to play every game, they'd prefer to be getting pissed in the pub.'

He also said, 'Our players get no match fee, no regular income from football, and have no insurance against serious injury. Would you believe our chaps are on $100 for a win here? Their bonuses are peanuts. You would spend it in an hour over the bar. That is the standard by which you must measure their achievement in drawing with Holland and Ireland.'

It was, indeed, no mean achievement – but then, like Robson had said, they had some very good players. In the run-up to Italia '90 they'd got draws against Denmark, South Korea, Austria, and Colombia – they'd beaten the Czechs, and they'd walloped the Scots 3–1 in Aberdeen.

And there weren't too many English in Sardinia who

reckoned getting out of Cagliari against this lot would be easy.

Group D sorted itself out at five in the afternoon of the 19th, though not entirely to form. Yugoslavia beat the UAE 4–1 in Bologna; but in Milan the Colombians held the Germans, until Littbarski scored in the 88th minute. It looked then as if predictions of their demise were accurate; but with the referee allowing four minutes of extra time for stoppages, after a game raddled with fouls and histrionics, Valderrama put Rincon through to equalise in the 92nd.

What, then, to make of these Colombians? They were daft, basically – Higuita made two 'saves' nearer the half-way line than his goal, using his feet and his head; while the outfield players (or, one should say, the *other* outfield players) were a volatile mix of lovely skill, crazy rough-house, and melo-dramatic mock-injury of truly Argentine proportions.

It had been the stereotype of African football that they were extravagantly skilled, and totally disorganised; but Egypt and Cameroon had scotched any patronising notions that the Africans were naive in this way. If anyone was 'African', on the contrary, it was these wacko Colombians – whose tactical formation, theoretically 4–4–2, could in despairing reality be best described only as 11. From Higuita onward, they popped up all over the park with a feckless, disconcerting, and anarchic abandon – and now they were through.

So in Milan and Bologna, there were parties.

Cagliari, on the other hand, was empty – the fans had scattered round the island to get away from the police. We were the morgue of the World Cup.

I ate at La Taverna, where the kindly owners always made me feel like ET: 'Have you phoned home?' Then I went back to the Italia, for the day's second bout of matches in Group A.

In Florence, the Austrians and the Americans kicked each other to a meaningless, tedious, foul-tempered 2–1 win for . . . well, it wasn't ever going to be the USA, was it?

Matters Roman were more weighty and more beautiful by far. The Italians played the Czechs to decide the winner of the

342

group – a prize of huge import to the hosts as the winner stayed in Rome for the next round. But because the Czechs had run up five against the Americans, their goal difference meant a draw was enough – whereas the Italians had to win. Waking up after their American sleepwalk, they did so in style.

Salvatore 'Toto' Schillaci started for the first time, in place of Carnevale. And Vialli was injured – a frenzied debate began over whether the injury was real, or just the result in Vialli's head of not scoring any goals – but either way, it meant Roberto Baggio, at last, stepped up and started too.

The Italians went ahead in the ninth minute, Schillaci heading home for his second goal of the tournament – and they started playing the loveliest football we'd seen so far. Donadoni was electric, Giannini was everywhere, Baresi was masterful; altogether they were neat and fast, one man past another, dazzling and bewildering, graceful and inventive . . . yet *still* they couldn't convert it into goals. Two minutes after he'd scored, Schillaci missed Berti's cross by inches; then Baggio got through twice – and twice Stejskal saved.

So it was beautiful, yes – but when would they ever get deadly?

Baggio had such touch, such imagination – pass after pass released men into space, more often than not Schillaci, who kept racing through with fiery-eyed speed and acceleration. In the 54th minute, he was denied a clear penalty. Then an equally abominable decision at the other end denied the Czechs a perfectly good goal, for an offside that never was.

And it stayed at 1–0 – until Baggio scored unanswerably in the 77th, picking up the ball at the half-way line, beating two men, sending a defender the wrong way, stranding the keeper, and sliding it home. *That* was what Juventus paid near eight million for . . . and it looked like the Italians, at last, had found the dream team up front that they'd been waiting for. Italy 2, Czechoslovakia 0.

The junction of Via Roma and Largo Carlo Felice turned instantly into total hooting dementia. The freighters from Korea and Yugoslavia sat bright-lit at the dock; the tram lines overhead were a glistening net of electricity; and beneath them the cars surged and shoved, manically honking and parping, flags flying from every window, the scooter boys weaving through with their flags waving too – all watched by masses of people poured out from their houses all round town, and now standing on street corners and central reservations, chanting and shouting,

EE-TAL-YAH! EE-TAL-YAH!

Oh-laaaaay, oh-lay oh-lay oh-lay
Oh-lay, oh-oh-lay

It was maximum street party, no beer required. Helpless traffic cops meandered about grinning in the middle of the cacophanous jam; people sat on car roofs, hung out of windows, screamed from balconies.

It was a shame there were so few English left to enjoy it.

You know how it is – you go without sleep for a night, and it's basically OK. Then you sleep seven hours the next – and wake up feeling like a tree fell on your head . . .

I went to the press centre – this is the day before the game now – and there were still no tickets for England–Egypt. I came close to my first sense of humour failure since Florence in May. There was no discernible system yet for second round tickets either, though that began in Naples and Bari in only four days' time . . . but Olivetti, someone said, were bringing new machines. If so, great – new bugs, new glitches, new memory wipes . . .

Nottage was at the centre, looking fraught. Lately she'd been staying in town, at the Panorama; the man in the room next door woke her at 6.30 every morning, with alarm call regularity, by noisily vomiting.

We went out to the training ground, where knots of kids had been let in to gawp. Players, Butcher more than anyone, gave them time and talk, autographs, team photos and badges; he put his arm round people's shoulders for their snapshots, bending a bit so as not to make them look too tiny. You'd never know he'd been dropped.

The only person Butcher wasn't making happy was his contract man, the No. 2 from the *Star*. He'd been told he had to talk, so he was talking – but he wasn't saying anything.

Peter Beardsley, meanwhile, stood alone and apart by the Gatorade table. I always liked Beardsley; he was quiet and modest, and, when you finished talking with him, he always said thank you – which was almost absurdly courteous since, of course, it should have been you thanking him. But being a nice guy never got a man picked.

The biggest throng, as ever, was round Lineker – cameras, scribblers, fans. Even the police wanted autographs.

Robson did the BBC, Sky, and a Mexican crew. Then it was the English press, with the Italian press waiting.

Item one on the agenda was the state of Lineker's toe – they'd been drilling it and draining it, getting out the blood from under the nail . . . yeeucch. He couldn't put his foot in his boot; he wasn't training. 'But,' said Robson, 'we haven't got another Gary Lineker.' It would, if necessary, be a painkilling injection, and out you go anyway.

Bryan Robson's toe, on the other hand, was 'responding' – but his Achilles wasn't. The manager was planning the team without him.

'Who's taking over the captaincy?'

Silence – then laughter.

'You'd have caught me eight years ago. Not now.'

Someone probed, suggesting the selection was bound to disappoint a few.

'It'll disappoint eleven. The players know the team. So if it gets out now, we'll know one of them talked.'

Of the Egyptians he said, 'We think we're due a goal, and we think they're due to concede one. If we get in front we'll be OK – but they have one or two that need looking after. If he gets a draw he'll be satisfied – but I won't be. We need our boys to be world class, not club class. Some threaten, some deliver . . . I wish the skipper was in, I'll tell you.'

At which point it emerged that Bryan Robson had, at his own expense, flown a faith-healer over – one Olga Stringfellow – and also that the *Sun*, at their own expense, had sealed her off in the Exclusive zone.

The skipper, said Robson, was convinced this woman got results. Three weeks before the Poland game last October, he'd had a stress fracture, it had been there on the X-ray. Then he saw this woman and *boom* – no more fracture.

Robson said the Doc and Fred Street would talk with her, and report back. 'But it's me who decides if he's fit. I'll say to him, right, show me. Sprint like hell fifty yards, brake, turn – do that for fifteen minutes.'

Otherwise, he said, faith-healers – it was no story, it was irrelevant. 'What I've been through the last eight years, I'd have needed three thousand of them. One wouldn't be enough, he'd be worn out. Still, the skipper believes it works – how, I don't know. And he's doing it with our knowledge.'

Would Robson himself go to talk with her?

He said, to roars of knowing laughter, '*I'm* not going in her room – and that's off the record. If it comes up, you'll have me down the corridors with a machine gun.' Then he said, 'All right, lads, that's it – and let's keep it to football, shall we? Anybody doesn't, I'll wrap a chair round his head.'

He started to get up – but then Nottage reminded him, there was still the Italian press to talk to.

'Awww nnn . . . yes. OK.'

And round and round we went, all over again.

'To lose to Egypt is unthinkable for us.'

'Like losing to the USA in 1950?

'That's forty years ago – but it would be similar. So I'll play eleven goalkeepers.'

When it was over, Robson went off for a spin in a Tornado from the NATO base down the road. And that at least, one imagines, would clear the worries from the mind, just for a Mach 1 moment or two.

At Is Molas, I learnt of COL people selling their tickets for the Final at £500 apiece . . .

At the bar, Butcher's Italian was coming on; he'd progressed from fellatio to cunnilingus.

Then, as I sat down to talk with Steve Bull, Lineker came in to shake his hand, and congratulate him.

So there was one of Robson's key selections for Egypt. Steve Bull – who'd come on eight times for England, six times as a substitute, and, remarkably, had already scored four goals – was now to start his first competitive international.

Robson had said about him going on against the Dutch, 'Bully found himself in a match out of all proportion to anything he's ever been in in his life. In all his life.' And he came close twice then, too . . .

So I asked – my favourite question – what Stevie Bull would be doing, if he wasn't there, and playing football.

'Couldn't tell you. Last job I had was in a builder's yard, so I'd probably still be there now.'

He'd had an operation on a knee when he was seventeen, and they said he'd never play again – but three weeks later, he was back on the park. He played with a local team, Tipton Town – and when he was eighteen, a scout from the Albion took him there for training, a couple of times a week.

'I thought I'd gone past it by then, eighteen, you know – schoolkids nowadays come in sixteen, fourteen – I thought I'd got no chance. But it suddenly kicked off. They had me on a three month trial, and after a month I'd scored twelve goals, something like that – so they give me a one year contract. Then Ron Saunders had me in one day, he says, somebody's come in for you. And I says, who? – and it's Wolves. I thought, oh – I thought I'd got a future at the Albion, like, I'd had four games, and scored two goals; I thought I had a chance there. But he made it clear it wasn't worth stopping any more, so it was signed and sealed that day. And I've had four years there since – enjoyed every minute.'

He was twenty-five now; and had built up a degree of faith among his fans in his abilities as a goal machine that even Olga Stringfellow would envy. I asked how it felt to be sat on the bench at Wembley and have people screaming through the wire at Bobby Robson to put him on.

'It's a bit embarrassing sometimes. I can't get on there and score goals all the time – they're chanting for me, then I might go out and have a nightmare. But I enjoy it, I enjoy all the publicity, all the stuff in the papers. You can never stop them cheering for you, can you? That's what gets you on the pitch.'

What about when people criticised his first touch – or, more bluntly, just said he didn't have one?

'I think that's a load of rubbish, myself. Everybody has bad first touches – it's on the day, isn't it? Not being bigheaded or anything, but I think I've got as good a first touch as anybody else. You can never stop learning, though – not being dis-respectful to Wolves, but it's nice being here, seeing different class players. The more skilful players, Peter Beardsley, Barnesy, all them – they've got touch everywhere, they're the gifted players – but then, I'm gifted with scoring goals.' He said, 'I'm just an old-fashioned target man, really. I just try and get my head and my foot in everywhere, and score goals.'

I asked what it was like, scoring.

'Unbelievable. Inside your body, it's like a tingling feeling – specially if it's for your country. My first goal against Scotland, I could have cried when I scored that goal, the feeling inside me . . . it's unbelievable.'

Gazza said it's like coming.

He laughed out loud. Then he said, 'It is, actually – like, aaawwwhhh . . . you're a bit drained after it. He's round the bend anyway – but it is a bit like that. A bit relieving.'

So I asked what it was like, playing with Gazza, and he laughed again; he said, 'He's a bit soft, but he's all right, he keeps the spirit going – and he's confident. You need someone just to steady him down, Pop Robson, or Steve McMahon, 'cos he's a bit wild in his head – but his skill is unbelievable, different class. The flicks, the touch, the tackles – it's just nice to watch the things he does. In training he's always practising, flicking it over his head, or whatever – he's always doing something.'

And how did he feel about starting tomorrow?

'Bit nervous. It's everybody's ambition, isn't it? People'd give their right leg to be where I am right now. But I'll just go out and enjoy it, I'll play my normal game. I'm nervous now, you're thinking up to it, you want to get started – the first ten minutes might be a bit nervy. But I'll get into it. I'll just play the way I always play.'

A journalist, I said, had fancied him against the Dutch, because he didn't reckon Koeman'd like some hairy-arsed skinhead charging up his backside . . .

But Bull only laughed again. 'If they want to put it like that, they can – but I'd have enjoyed going on from the start. When I went on for the last half-hour I had two chances, I should at least have put one of them away. So who knows what might have happened if I'd gone from the start? You get a bit of frustration, on the bench – you know you can get on there, you can do what you're good at. And when you see chances missing you think, ohhh God . . . but it's easy said when you're sitting down and watching it. I went on and had two chances, and there'll be other players thinking, oh Christ, look at that.'

I asked whether it wasn't a bit odd, going on for just a few minutes, like he had against the Irish.

'Yeah, it's a bit weird – but it's another cap, isn't it? One minute, two minutes, half-hour, it doesn't matter – it's another cap. You get a cap come through the post, another cap on the wall – it's a bit of pride, isn't it?'

And was it a whole different thing, going on against Holland in the World Cup?

'I've had nothing like it at all. The first experience was coming on against Scotland at Hampden, in front of 60,000 people – I enjoyed it, specially scoring as well . . . but coming on against Holland here, live on television – that's different altogether. I don't know how you can put it in words – Gullit, Rijkaard, all that . . . it's nice to be on there with players like them.'

What about all the media attention – how did he feel about that?

'They go a bit overboard – but I just let them get on with it, it's their job, they've got to do it. I've rung home and told them, but they know what the papers are like. I read them here, I see what they've put, and I think to myself, nah – I never said that. I don't know where they get it from.'

The way he said these things, Bull seemed as good and straight and simple as the way he scores goals. There was, in his decent and uncomplicated fashion, only one way he could put in words what it meant to be there. He said, 'I'm one of the best twenty-two players in the country.'

It was still a new feeling for him –and a very good feeling indeed. I asked how it had felt when he knew he'd been picked.

'It took a while to sink in. It's three or four weeks' agonising, nail-biting – then I saw it on the teletext . . . just great.'

So what had Robson said to him?

'He's not said much. He's just said, I've brought you here to do a job, and I won't be frightened to put you on. That's all. But he's a decent manager, he'll listen to you – and the other players, they've all given me confidence. Being with them a couple of days at Burnham Beeches, you don't get to talk to many people properly. But here, being here for three or four weeks now, you're getting to know them – you get to know the insides and outsides of life. You think to yourself, OK – I'm the same as everybody else.'

Did he miss home, being away this long?

'I keep ringing my girlfriend up – it's nice to hear a woman's voice. I keep telling her now, it's only nineteen days to go, eighteen, seventeen . . . it's a bit hard, like – you enjoy the meals from home. All I'm doing now is eating soup and pasta – when I get back it'll be a good fish'n'chips, and a pint of bitter.'

What about Genoa coming after him?

'Well, I've not had no calls or nothing – but I think I'd tell them no, really. I'm happy where I am. Obviously Barnesy, some of these others, they've got to be on outstanding money, 'cos of the clubs they're at – and I think if any club in Britain came in for me, I'd have to have a serious think about it. But as long as I'm happy, that's all that matters; there's other things than money . . . I know money's a big part of it, it can secure your future – but I'm earning a steady wage to keep me going till I finish.'

And after that?

'I'd like to stay in the game, just playing amateur football – I'm too soft to be a manager.'

Then I asked what he knew about Egypt.

'Not a lot. I know they play five at the back, it'll be hard to break down. We'll see what we can do.'

And I asked what was he like, immediately before a game.

'I try not to speak to anybody, really. I just like to keep my head down, concentrate – get my shinpads on at twenty to three, get taped up and ready. Though since I've been here I've been shaking hands, geeing everyone on as we go out – I don't know if it's changing me. At the Wolves I just sit down, shake my legs, wait to get out.'

Any superstitions?

'Not really. I kiss my shirt three times on the back, I don't know why – I think the first time I did that I got a hat-trick, I've been doing it ever since. And I like to carry the No. 9, I feel strong in it. But wearing 21 here, I dunno – it doesn't matter, just being here'll do, 21, 12, 3, you don't mind so long as you're here. And, touch wood, I've not stopped scoring goals – it's not stopped since I went to Wolves. I scored against Tunisia, last ten minutes, and I've scored four here (in the local friendlies) – so I feel really confident, the way it's going on.'

But what is confidence?

'You tell me ... confidence is just going out there and putting it in the net. That's all it is to me.'

Robson's Tornado, in formation with one other, made two low, window-shaking passes over the hotel. Barnes grumbled, 'Imagine if that was us. It'd be, what you doing going for a fucking ride?'

Some of the players watched Royal Ascot in the games room; I sat with David Platt outside. We talked, as I'd talked with Bull, about how it was to be an England new boy at Italia '90.

Platt had just turned twenty-four, so he was nearly ten years younger than Bryan Robson – going on for him against Holland was his sixth cap, compared to Robson's eighty-three.

The manager said he'd chosen Platt over McMahon in that game because he'd wanted to keep Gullit shut down; but, at the same time, he'd wanted a goalscorer too. Whereas now, against Egypt, McMahon would start, he wanted that tenacity in the middle – so Platt was on the bench.

Platt said when he went out against Holland, 'My concentration took over any nerves I might have had, 'cos I was marking such an influential player. But to replace Pop is important in itself – everybody knows about Pop, he's been there for ten years, everybody knows how important he is. So to go on for him – it was tremendous.'

Platt went to college for a year when he left school, hoping for a couple of A-levels so he could get into physiotherapy. 'That was what was in my mind – though when I look back on it, I don't think I was clever enough to be a physiotherapist. Then anyway, the opportunity arose with Manchester United. I was seventeen, I still had a year to run at college – but it was something I'd always wanted to do. I thought if I didn't make it, I could always go back to studying – but if I did another year studying then, I'd miss the chance in football.'

It didn't work out at United. He did a year as a YTS, then got a year's contract – but six months into it, Crewe came in for him, and United advised him to go. 'Obviously, going from United to Crewe Alexandra was a lot of steps down clubwise – but it was a step up too, because it meant I got first team football.' So he was there three years – then, two seasons ago, he moved to Aston Villa.

When he went out for his first cap against Italy at Wembley 'there was a lot of talk, a lot of publicity, 'cos I was getting the goals – but I thought Italy had come a bit too early for me, I expected to be in the B squad. Then we played Everton live on the telly on the Sunday, and he was naming his squad on the Monday, and I got a couple of goals, we won 6–2 – so I think maybe that swayed it.'

He said of being in the World Cup now, 'Obviously playing at Wembley, there's a lot of attention – but when you come out here, and you play the Dutch . . . I was aware afterwards, not during, 'cos your concentration's so high, but afterwards – that game's gone out to so many people, it's got world attention. Everybody's watching. Like, you go down to the training ground, and all the press that's there – yesterday I've spoken to half a dozen Italian press, and it's unnatural to you, because back home you know your reporters – the most I've ever faced is a dozen. Then all of a sudden it's a hundred, and they're like vultures, it's like flies round shit – as soon as there's something that might be a story, 'cos you've come on against the Dutch, *whoooph* . . . I said I'd speak to one, one I knew from Birmingham, and let him pass it round to them all, 'cos they all look after each other – then it's on his head.'

So I asked how he felt about the Dutch half-hour.

'I feel good about it, obviously. I'm never one to go round saying I've done this, I've done that, not in public – but I'll go back home proud of the fact that I had to stop Gullit, that I had to go out and play in that game. I was pleased with my performance; more than that, the manager was pleased – it means a lot to me. And the press can go on, but it's not just the press, it's everybody back home, they know what I did – I haven't let anybody down. So it'll be nice to look back on it, that I went out in a World Cup game at twenty-four years of age, and replaced the skipper – because in all honesty, I didn't expect to play out here at all. I expected to be just a squad member. I was very surprised, very pleased to be on the bench against the Irish – I didn't think I would be.'

So David Platt would, in the end, be doing far more than he'd ever dreamt of when he got on that plane back on 25 May. Aston Villa had bought him from Crewe for £200,000 –

after Italia '90, they were turning down an offer from Fiorentina worth £5,000,000.

Now, in advance of this unforeseen elevation, he was modest about his place. He said, 'There's nothing I want more than to play from the start, in every game – but you're one of the twenty-two. When the press all come and say I'm going to replace Bryan Robson, I'm genuine when I say I want Bryan Robson to be fit, because I genuinely do. Sure, I think I've come here on the strength of what Bobby Robson thinks David Platt can do – and obviously I'd be delighted to play, now I'm here. But that doesn't mean you want to see players injured. If Pop's fit, then Pop should play.'

But Pop wasn't fit – and it was Steve McMahon who had the midfield place against Egypt, not Platt.

'I can understand the manager's thinking. He's playing with a lot of players who are good going forward, John Barnes, Chrissie Waddle, Paul Gascoigne. Of course I feel confident that I could do a job, and hold the midfield – and that's what you've got to do if you're playing with Paul, because he's very talented, but he's going forward all the time so someone's got to sit in for him. And maybe that's more natural for Steve than for me.'

I asked what it was like, playing alongside Gazza.

'As long as you do hold, it's all right. My tendency is to go forward, so it can be difficult – even in that half-hour I was tempted, I was going up a little bit – and that's my game, I like going forward, I like getting in the box. But in international football if we both go forward, we'll get exposed – so Steve's game's more suited to holding in that way. And I'm disappointed, yeah, but then, you always know he might play Steve. So you put that behind you, and you go out there – because in the first minute Paul, or Steve, or Steve Bull, any one of them could get injured, and then I'm on. I mightn't play ninety minutes, but I might play eighty-nine – so you've got to be concentrating, you can't waste time being disappointed. I know there's players at home at Villa, or Crewe, I've spoken to them – every one of them would sooner be where I am now.'

Just waiting and hoping for his chance . . . which, when it came, he would take with a vengeance.

*

No question about one young footballer who was enjoying himself in Italy ... Gazza spilt gleefully out of the games room and announced, 'On Your Toes, eight to one.'

Platt asked, 'How much?'

'Hundred pounds.'

Lineker the bookie went past, looking gutted.

Platt said he knew about the gee-gees – his girlfriend's brother works in a stable, and he owns a horse himself. But he said even if someone called him and said he could put his mortgage on a horse, he'd still not bet more than a hundred – whereas Gazza, in Platt's affectionately succinct phrase, was 'a daft cunt'. He didn't, Platt said, know the first thing about the horses.

And the firm of Shilton and Lineker didn't need to feel too bad – after all, what Gazza'd won today, he'd lost the day before. He'd gone into the games room, asked Peter Beardsley what horse looked likely in the next race, and then – to a mixture of amusement and horror – put £400 on it. He lost. So then he went £250 each way on the next race ... and lost that too.

But the boredom, after twenty-six days in one place, compounded with the cyclical tension of the games coming and going, and a morose aggravation at the attentions and inventions of the press – was beginning to find outlets in stranger forms of behaviour than Gazza's impulse betting.

Two nights before the Egypt game, Woods and Butcher went to dinner with all their Umbro gear on inside out. They had their coffee first, then dessert – and so on backwards, right through the menu.

Tonight, they planned on having their buddies the waiters fill wine bottles with mineral water for them, and set them out in ice buckets on their table to wind the manager up. And they'd go into dinner in suits and ties, and all the gear – then surreptitiously hand over their trousers to an accomplice on the staff. Half-way through the meal they'd then go, phew, hot in here – they'd get up, walk over to hang their jackets on the pegs, and have nothing on below the waist but their jockstraps ...

Like Butcher said, 'Anything to ease the boredom.'

Gazza bounced around, frantic for someone to play table tennis with him.

In the games room, Lineker idly played trick shots on the pool table.

People played cards for hours, and hours.

Robson came back from his Tornado ride – he'd been fifty miles out to sea, flown at 800 mph at low level, and looked like the happiest kid in town.

Unlike Steve McMahon. He sat alone with a coffee in the bar – and he looked so tense, so coiled up about going out to play again tomorrow, he was virtually gnawing on the table.

John Barnes wasn't a happy man either.

The *Mirror*'d run a groundless and hurtful piece of cod psychological claptrap about him, that suggested he didn't turn it on for England because his mum used to whack him when he was a kid.

So, I asked, was John Barnes disturbed?

'Disturbed by the fucking press, I tell you.'

He'd done an interview for some offbeat Channel 4 programme a while back, and they'd tried to speculate in it that because of the way he was brought up, he was spoilt. He'd said no – if he was naughty, his mum used to slap him like any other kid. So the *Mirror*'d got hold of this, and turned it into, 'MUM'S BEATINGS STILL HAUNT JOHN'.

'They call it a secret video, I mean, really – if you'd have watched Channel 4 you'd have seen it. But that's how ridiculous the whole thing's got. You know that stupid story about the girl – I don't even know what she looks like. Most of the players don't. And they talk about, "at an official disco players mingled with the hostesses" – there's been no official disco bloody anywhere, we've just stayed right here. But it's been dominating our World Cup, this stuff, unfortunately – and it's a stupid situation. Just stupid.'

So I said, let's talk football. Did he enjoy the Dutch game?

'I enjoyed the first sixty minutes. After that they took Chris off. For the first half-hour Chris had a free role, inside right, right wing, wherever he wanted, and I was playing down the middle – and we were causing them a lot of problems. But since we didn't have a left winger, their right back was going forward a lot, unmarked. Now he wasn't causing us that much trouble – but they thought he was, so they moved Chris out left to stop his runs, which was ridiculous. To put Chris out there just to run up and down with this right back and stop him playing, rather than thinking, we're causing them more problems than they are us – Chris's threat was nullified. Then when they took Chris off they put me out there, and my threat was nullified, then it's me just running up and down – and that's not my game. But it's the same old thing. For the first half-hour it was brilliant, I was in a position where I could get involved, and run around, and Chris was free – but rather than being positive and saying, OK, if we're going to have a man free, then they're going to have someone free too, so be it – I mean, you can't have it all ways, you can't have men free, and have all their men marked too . . .'

The manager's too cautious?

'He was in that instance. I think so, anyway, definitely. We could have done more going forward. We still had a spare man at the back, so even if the right back did go forward, there was someone there to deal with it. He was running into a position where all he was going to do was cross, he wasn't going to score. And you've got to realise that teams are going to get crosses in against you, they're going to get free men – but we should have free men too, rather than saying, because he's free you've got to mark him.'

The manager holds you back?

Barnes stumbled for a moment. 'No, not necess . . . it's just, not . . . not physically. Not . . . I don't think he means to. But I just feel . . . I feel the way we're asked to play definitely does. Like Ireland, for example, me and Chris were coming back on Ray Houghton and Peter Sheedy – and a few instances I was looking at us when we're under pressure and I'm thinking, we've got the goalkeeper and nine players defending here – and Gary Lineker isolated up front. And you don't help yourself like that, do you?'

Barnes said he didn't know how it would go against Egypt – but he did know Butcher wasn't playing, and that we were back to 4–4–2. He said, 'We don't know what to expect from them – three right backs, no right back, one right back, no left wing – and that's the problem. 4–4–2, same old thing, static positions – you play these other teams, and you don't know where people are going to run. That's why a lot of them get free – sometimes they only play one up front, so in effect they've got six in midfield. And then because we play 4–4–2 – 4–2–4, supposedly, but it's really 4–4–2 – you've got four at the back marking one, and they're used to staying there, and we're getting run ragged everywhere else.'

Gazza wandered by looking restless – he'd won on another horse, but he wasn't interested in that any more. He started knocking the ball across the table tennis table on his own, a uniquely futile activity. I asked him if he'd been happy after the Holland game.

Barnes said, 'He's never happy.'

'Never happy, me.' He sang, 'Barmy Barmy Barnesy Barnesy,' and tried to hit the ping pong ball into a glass of water from five or six yards. He missed. 'Oh shit. I've got to go and get it now.'

I went back to the Dutch game.

'Paul Gascoigne was man of the match. That's why he's been chirpy all week. Talking to the press and everything – he slaughters them, but as soon as he has a good game, he's their best friend.'

'Bollocks. Paul Gascoigne *never* speaks to the fuckin' press. *Never*.'

'He never talks to anyone if they give him a bollocking. But he plays well, he's man of the match, better than Ruud Gullit – then he's running around being chirpy all right.'

'Thank you, John. Always chirpy.'

Maybe winning on the gee-gees helped a bit.

'He wins money on everything, horses, football.'

Not yesterday.

'Yeah, but I'm up £600 today. That's good.'

He was a grand up on the football, too – he'd backed Cameroon to get 1–0 over Argentina, among others. 'And the linesman denied me £600 last night, that Czech goal.'

'He was offside,' Barnes grinned.

'Was he fuck.'

He started playing solo table tennis with the bat instead of the ball, just chucking it across the table. Barnes and I sat talking about the injustices of life to a soundtrack of clattering wood ... Maradona's handball against the Russians, Maradona getting Hagi booked, that suspiciously disallowed Czech goal. Barnes said, 'Did you see Valderrama get stretchered off yesterday? And five minutes later he just walks back on – fuck-all wrong with him. I don't like it.'

Then he called out, 'No, Gazza, I'm not playing table tennis with you. You can't play table tennis in your flip flops. The manager said.'

I asked one more time about the trouble with Barnesy – did he play less well for his country than his club?

'What I said still stands – even more so now. Look at the Holland game. We're causing problems, and all of a sudden . . . see, had it been the other way round, after thirty minutes I'd have gone to mark the right back. And the rest of the match I'd have been running up and down. But Chris had to do it – so at least I enjoyed sixty, seventy minutes of it. But after that I was just marking, basically.'

He said, 'Take Gary Lineker. His game's about scoring goals. So if he doesn't get a chance to score, you can't criticise him – because whatever else he might be doing, he's not in the team to do that, he's not in the team to be beating three players, or to be tackling back and chasing. He's in the team to score goals. Give him a chance, and he'll score. But me, I'm in the team to create chances, and to do things going forward. And if I'm not given the opportunity to do that, I'm not going to be effective. I'm not in the team to . . . well, as it turns out, that's what I have been doing, tracking back with the right back. But if that's the way the games are going to go . . .'

And the trouble with Barnesy came down to the crunch.

He said, if that was the way it was going to go, 'I think we'd be better off to play someone else in that position, if he's going to run up and down with the full back. It's like asking Gary Lineker to do it. You might as well not have him in the side. And you might as well not have me in the side, if that's all that's going to happen. Like I've said, if a cross comes in, or a ball comes through, there's only one person can clear it out. So how many defenders do we need?'

And how clear can it get? He was, I said, unhappy.

'Yes.' Long pause. 'I'm unhappy with the job I'm asked to do.'

*

It had been harsh and muggy weather all afternoon. I got a ride back into Cagliari with two BBC boys, feeling harsh and muggy myself.

Grim premonitions sat heavy on my heart. We'd woken up against Holland, but it was a false dawn – we were, now, to be sent back to sleep again. Wright and Parker in for Butcher and Stevens, fine – they might be faster, more inventive – but still it was, in Barnes's words, 'the same old thing'.

Bobby Robson is a kind, courteous, and decent man. But he's also a man for whom World War II ran through six central years of his childhood; and a man who, when he started to play professional football as a teenager in the early fifties, would have been coached and surrounded in the game by men who fought in that war. It's the working class who are, after all, the poor bloody infantry – the same people who have football in their blood, and in their souls. And in the steel for the game in his heart, he'd learnt to think of it as war.

And Robson loved skill, he loved class, he stood by Barnes and Waddle, and he kept on picking them – they had over fifty caps each. And he looked with a weary distaste, verging on contempt, at the hoofing mess of the Irish, or of so much of the First Division which the Irish game so much more nearly epitomised than the ball-to-feet quality he wanted to coax from his own men.

But at the core of his wish to play football – to play as others could in Europe – there still lay two insoluble contradictions.

Firstly, he loved to win, he was desperate to win – but he was at least as much terrified of losing. At the press conferences that morning he'd said, Egypt was a game we must not lose. It was a game we had to win – but what he stressed first and most was, it was a game *we must not lose*.

But with Group F the way it was we were, in effect, going into the first knock-out game of Italia '90 – because what use was a draw? Who wanted to risk a Dutch–Irish draw in Palermo too, and see all four sides jammed on the same points, the same goals, and then FIFA drawing lots to see who carried on? (What the good doctor Ahmed El-Mokadem called derisively, 'World Cup bingo'.)

So who wanted to risk that? – especially with the certainty fixed in the hearts of many English, that we and our fans were unwelcome guests, so that if it came to drawing balls from a

FIFA glass bowl, one of those balls would be square, and the English would conveniently be drawn to go home ... how, in these circumstances, could we go up against the Egyptians *fearful of losing?*.

And the second contradiction: that, in the straitjacket conservatism of his Englishness, and of the English game, Robson saw the sweeper thing as defensive, and saw 4–4–2 with two wingers as bold and attacking. Yet then, all caution, he told the players who we needed to be bold and attacking, that they weren't free to do so ... so that Barnes and Waddle were unhappy; and what in theory was offensive, became scrambling-back defensive.

And I could see us losing. I hated the thought, but I could see us actually losing it. Robson was a good man, and his players were good men too – they were generous, they were good company, they fought hard, they gave 110 per cent ... they were, in short, English, and the approach was all played out, and I could see us losing.

Italy, Germany, Brazil – even Belgium, even Cameroon – *that* was football.

Whereas us – we were history.

We were resolute still, perhaps, but we were fearful too. We were padlocked in ways of thinking we knew didn't work any more – yet we were too fractiously, obstinately, nervily bulldog-headed to change, and then stay changed.

The empire was gone, and the world was passed on. The colonies became independent, Europe became a Community – and in 1953, the Hungarians came to Wembley to wallop the founders of football 6–3. And did we learn?

No. We stayed on our island, growling behind our nukes with our thuggish dirty streets, our polluted beaches, our hospitals where the rain comes through the roof, and our schools that can't afford to buy books – we stayed on our island with our fading industries, and our 4–4–2.

In the BBC car we drove over the brow of the hill above Sarroch, down past the steel jungles of the refinery and the chemical plant, towards the causeway across the bay and into Cagliari. The evening had grown muggier than ever; a fuggy haze of grimy grey-blue sat heavily down over the sea, and the town beyond it. There was no line where water stopped, or sky started; Cagliari had vanished.

All you could make out through the bleary murk was the four blazing flares of the floodlights of the Sant'Elia – four eerie spectres hovering on the dim horizon where the Egyptians were training.

Still, what have I got to worry about? I could be a Scotland fan . . . great parties, no question – but then you have to go and watch that unbelievable, that heart-breaking team.

Five times in succession, this nation of five million had qualified for the World Cup – a record that included, this time, getting to Italy ahead of France. Yet after that, they'd never got past the first round – a saga of failure by turns glorious and ignominious.

In Germany '74, they got draws with Brazil and Yugoslavia, and went home unbeaten on goal difference alone.

But in Argentina '78, Peru beat them 3–1. Then they drew with Iran, and only managed that thanks to an Iranian own goal – a national nightmare rendered doubly frustrating by a heroic 3–2 defeat of the Dutch, who went on to the finals.

In Spain '82, they avoided similar embarrassment by tonking New Zealand 5–2, and then had the audacity to score first against Brazil – who, stung, promptly scored four.

And in Mexico '86, after narrow defeats at the hands of the Germans and the Danes, they still had a chance of a third-place passage, when a Uruguayan was sent off after just fifty-five seconds – but against ten men, they failed to take it.

Now in Italy they were at it again, a befuddling mix of bravery and incompetence. Beaten by Costa Rica, victors over Sweden, they needed a point off Brazil – and they held out for eighty-two minutes, with Jim Leighton making a fine save off Romario, before falling victim to the most abject bad luck.

First, Leighton stopped a fierce twenty-five-yard shot from Alemao, but failed to hold it – and Muller tapped in the rebound. Leighton beat the ground with his fists, he kicked the goalpost in rage and misery . . . then, in the dying seconds, Mo Johnston fired a shot from close range that you'd have backed to go in from the second it left his boot. Yet somehow, Taffarel threw his body across it and flung out a hand, got a miraculous touch, and the ball flew wide – it was an awesome save. Johnston lay face down on the turf in an agonised eternity of disbelief ... I felt like I could hear the grief of Glasgow from 2,000 miles away. Brazil 1, Scotland 0.

And you might think it the fiercest injustice, that this small country should so consistently be singled out for such raised hopes, such shattered expectations – but since when was football about justice?

Football's about not getting beat by the likes of Costa Rica ... whose manager Bora Milutinovic knew his job. After a playing career in Yugoslavia, France, Switzerland and Mexico, he'd managed Mexico to the quarter-finals in '86 – but his achievement now was even greater.

In Genoa, it was Sweden 1, Costa Rica 2 – and they joined Brazil in the second round.

All evening it threatened rain; an hour after midnight, the threat was made good.

I was getting into bed – but then I heard the chanting begin again, the raucous belchy yelling, and I got up to go see what I could see.

There was a mobile snack van on the corner of the little park outside the bus station, selling chips and wurst and *panini*. Maybe twenty English were gathered there, stuffing chips in their faces; and they'd been drinking too, though you'd not say they were legless.

Most had their shirts off; they were a sorry-looking lot, with their mottled paunches rolling over the tops of their mutant's puke shorts, and their ill-fitting jeans. Two of them were particularly weedy – really scrawny specimens, noisily leaching manhood off their bulkier breathren. Some had skin-head baldness; others longer and lank, rain-flattened hair. The Chelsea antiques fence was among them; and he was holding shirts and umpiring, or seconding, in a singular and neander-thal exhibition of truly oafish machismo.

Pairs of men ran together and chest-butted each other, arms loose and jerking at their sides, in repeated little sumo-style charges. Rain-drenched guts and shoulders whacked and slapped together, as the others gathered round each slovenly contest to chant,

Chaaahhm - pi - oh - naze

362

They toppled about jeering and bawling, bodies thunking together, flesh plashing against unhealthy flesh. The rank artificial light of the snack bar shone out over them, and on the cracked and litter-strewn paving; Sards and a few police watched, as you'd watch disturbed and lumbering apes caged in a zoo. And all the while the rain hammered down, and vast lightning flashed obscurely in dense clouds. Thunder approached, crackling and booming.

It was primeval, debased, drunk – a scene from the urban apocalypse. It was,

> *Inngg - ger - luh-uhnd*
> *Inngg - ger - luh-uhnd*

All played out.

The next morning there were QPR fans outside La Perla. Why, they asked, had Robson taken so long to play Paul Parker?

'Look, we know we can all pick the team. But it's not who plays, it's how. And I *liked* that system against Holland. But every time the Dutch had the ball, you watch 'em, just watch 'em – the whole lot of 'em drop back. Robson's trouble's he's too bloody nervous – we've got the players, so *why don't we play?* I mean, I can understand, the shit he gets – but *why don't we go forward?*'

'Bold stuff,' said another, 'that sweeper. Bold – or stupid. Thin line . . .'

'The players liked our support last Saturday, did they? Well it was great, the atmosphere – but Gazza's the only one who shows it. He's the only one who thanks us. We pay all this money to come here – they could come over at the end and say thanks, couldn't they?'

'Robson did right though, the way he's brought Gazza in. Six months back he was an immature jerk. He's handled him right.'

Word among them was that Gazza'd gone up to Van Basten during the game and said, 'How much are you on a week then?'

*

La Prensa in Bogota announced, 'Rincon's cry was the cry of all Colombians. We were so excited we prayed, laughed, cried and celebrated.'

Pagina 12 in Buenos Aires was less sure of itself, on matters of national pride: 'The Argentinian team is a fat lady whose lovers will now abandon her.' Of Maradona they said, 'Now it's God's knee.'

In Udine at five, a strangely spineless Uruguay scraped past South Korea 1–0. True, they hit the woodwork in the first minute of each half; but that was about all they hit, even when the time-wasting and tackle-happy Koreans were down to ten men in the last twenty minutes. They finally managed to score in the second minute of injury time, but they barely deserved it – and though they'd twice been Champions in 1930 and 1950, this was now the first World Cup game that they'd won since 1970. Their dubious reward in the second round was a trip to Rome, to meet Italy.

In Verona, meanwhile, King Juan Carlos and Queen Sophia turned up to watch their steadily improving Spanish side win Group E. They beat the Belgians 2–1; Michel's penalty, after his hat-trick against the Koreans, took him to the top of the goalscorers' table, ahead of West Germany's Rudi Völler.

The Belgians had a penalty too, but Enzo Scifo hit the crossbar – and Spain deserved the win. Still, both sides looked good, disciplined and skilful – and as the Belgians were through anyhow, it would have been foolhardy to read too much into their defeat. Guy Thys, the Belgian manager, said, 'I'm very satisfied. We were in command in the second half, with five new players. I don't think we have to be afraid of anybody.'

And whoever topped Group F would find them waiting in Bologna.

The evening of the 21st was warm and dry, the horizons burning orange as the sun went down. The helicopters went round and round overhead. The stadium was half empty; there were only maybe 3,500 English left on the island anyway. But the flags were still there – Blackburn, Burnley, Bootle, Newcastle, Isle of Wight.

One said bluntly, 'Moynihan Is A Traitor'.

And another announced contentedly, 'Greavsie: Sphinx–Nil. You can't say pharoah than that'.

The Egyptian fans were one small block dressed all in white – a shipload of Egyptian navy cadets who'd been given leave, and the use of their boat, to follow their side between the islands until the first round was done.

As usual, they all had a flag to wave. Everyone else, you thought, was so festive, so colourful, and here they were, with their fluttering black, red, and white – while ours sat flagless, because at the searches on your way into the stadium, the *carabinieri* stripped the poles out of the spines of your Union Jack. If you were English you could drape it – but you couldn't wave it . . .

And off we go again.

And Egypt have more of the ball . . .

And who'd be a football fan? The doubts, the anxieties, the fears . . . I wondered again if I could bring myself to write it down any more, as I sat there yearning for us to play, and to win.

Pearce made a good run up the left; Lineker was obstructed, but the referee ignored it. He got through again; we won a free-kick, and it led to a corner. The argy-bargy in the box was sullen and tempestuous.

I was on the edge of the press box; the England fans to my right were in a rage of hope and criticism.

'Get in front of him, get wider, c'mon, *c'mon* . . . who wants it, *who wants it*? Barnes, get *in* man, you poof – where's the support? C'mon Stevie, get in there – you gotta look, you're not fucking looking . . .'

As another pass faded a vivid Geordie voice sweetly sighed, a groan of soft disgust, '*Oh dear* . . .'

It was flat back four again, and another squashed midfield. Lineker and Bull spent long periods spectating – the Egyptians were playing for the draw, just rolling it around, and there were too many back passes by far. As David Lacey put it, their football 'drifted back and forth across their own half like the shifting, whispering sands'. I even began to sympathise with Jack Charlton . . .

It was scrappy and unconvincing, twenty minutes of nothing – the subs were warming up already. McMahon at least was hurrying and harrying; and when Barnes got the ball it was, 'Skin him, *gwooaahhn*' . . . but he never seemed to.

And a man could die of boredom watching this – if it didn't matter so much . . . then, slowly, the Egyptians seemed to realise, if they went forward they might win – they had more of the ball, and they were getting in the crosses. At one scary moment the Geordie next door to me whimpered a little 'Ah', as with the pain and fear of a man under torture . . . and their next attack was scarier yet; Parker slipped up, he let a man free into the box – and the Geordie positively whined with alarm.

But then Gazza brought it away on the sprint – and the whine converted into a groaning roar of desire, '*Do it for me Gazza . . .*'

Bull was trying hard to do it too. Three times he fished half-shots out of nothing, off balance with no real chance – but still he pushed and lunged, just desperate to pelt it in, the bobbling ball flim-flamming in front of him among the knots of defenders, and still he kept on trying . . . and so did Gazza. Twice he beat one man, two, three down the wing – twice he danced through throngs of Egyptians massed on the edge of the area, just standing there bewitched by his swaying, tripping, shimmying little runs – but it came to nothing. There were too many of them, and none of us.

An Egyptian long shot damn near skimmed in, Shilton touching it uncomfortably away. At the other end, Lineker's neat one-two sent Parker through – but his shot was pushed aside. Someone gave Barnes a good hacking, and Gazza near went mental, asking the ref in no uncertain terms, did he need a visit to the optician . . . and we reached half-time, bored and goalless.

In Palermo the Dutch were 1–0 up on the Irish – Gullit, who'd scored, was looking a yard quicker. Out came the calculators and the second round schedules for more frantic perming of the last-ditch possibilities. If it stayed this way Holland were top, Ireland were out, and England and Egypt were in FIFA's glass bowl for the lottery draw between second place in Genoa, and third place in the dens of Germany's Milan, or Brazilian Turin . . .

The second half began with England attacking again. Bull came close from Waddle's cross; Parker skinned two men, and another cross was just barely hoiked away. 'Get it *sorted*,' wailed the Geordie.

And Paul Gascoigne and Mark Wright sorted it. Walker went forward, and was brought down; Gazza's curling chip of a free-kick, perfectly weighted, floated over for Wright to rise and head (as they say) unerringly home . . .

> *We're on the march with Bobby's army*
> *We're all going to Italy*
> *And we'll really shake 'em up*
> *When we win the World Cup*
> *'Cos England are the greatest football team*

But not on this showing they weren't.

Egypt were coming forward now at least as much as we were. The back line was solid, and Parker looked good pushing up; McMahon was everywhere, and Gazza was brilliant – but Waddle and Barnes were invisible again, Bull was struggling for space and touch, and Lineker looked like he was hurting.

The fans screamed at Barnes, 'Express yourself!' But he never really did. And when Waddle lifted a hand at the ref one time instead of playing on, it was, 'Get off the park, you shit.'

In Palermo, Niall Quinn got one back for the Irish – so we had to keep hold of the win now.

Three minutes after Quinn's goal 200 miles away, Peter Shilton made sure that we did. The ball fell to Hani Ramzi close to goal, and Shilton fell like a rock on his quickly snapped shot . . . and the last minutes dragged out in agony, as the fans howled cheerfully,

> *England, England*
> *Top of the group*
> *Top of the group*

Much good it would do us later, if we played like this again. It wasn't as bad as the Irish game, and two Egyptians were booked for time-wasting – they'd come for the draw, and their lack of ambition had undone them. But still, you could hardly say we took it to them.

England 1, Egypt 0. Holland 1, Ireland 1.

Top of the group – and Belgium waited in Bologna.

*

For the first time football, rather than fantasy scandals, took England to the front page – the front page of, who else, the *Sun*:

> ENGLAND GIVE 'EM A PHAROAH STUFFING
> Our soccer heroes shook off the Sphinx jinx and an-NILEated the Egyptians ... as England stormed to victory in Cagliari, Sardinia.

And of course we didn't storm, we just grittily stumbled – but the tabloids went briefly loopy on the glory-glory angle anyway, their jubilation as wildly unrealistic as their past relentless criticism.

> WE'VE MADE IT!

> THAT'S ALL WRIGHT!

> HERO MARK

> WORLD CUP GLORY FOR ROBBO MEN

But once you got past the headlines, more balanced and worried voices could be heard in many quarters.

Harry Harris in the *Mirror*: 'The bitter truth is that until Wright struck, England did precious little.'

Jeff Powell in the *Mail*: 'Had Bobby Robson persevered with his adoption of a modern sweeper system, England might have out-manouevred the North Africans ... but England regressed into their old-fashioned ways.'

And Stuart Jones in *The Times*: 'Rather than the flexible and fluent unit of last Saturday, England appeared to be disjointed and uninspired ... Barnes, once more showing a singular lack of urgency on the left, looked as though he required permission to take on an opponent.'

And I don't see a lot to disagree with there. Sure, the Egyptians didn't make it easy – but it's not meant to be easy, is it? Compared to the Germans and others, it was, in short, a dog of a way to come top, in a dog of a group.

Group F had seen a meagre total of only seven goals scored, and five draws in six games – whereas in the German group there'd been twenty-one goals, and fourteen in three of the others. The best you can say is, England toughed it out – they were England.

But when you looked at what had gone on elsewhere, both on and off the pitch, Cagliari – bar ninety minutes against Holland – had been no kind of party at all.

To make matters worse, one of the coaches in a convoy bringing fans to the stadium crashed; one English boy died.

The FA's good side came out, Kelly and others looking after the boy's parents when they came over; and the FA paid for their accommodation. The players were good too, visiting the fifteen or so injured in hospital.

But right there and then, at the Sant'Elia after the game, the atmosphere was so grim you'd have thought we'd been disqualified, rather than struggling out on top.

I walked down a white-washed concrete corridor curving through the bowels of the stadium, and came to a gaggle of TV crews outside the dressing rooms. In an alcove by a backdrop board bearing the names of FIFA's sponsors, next to a phone and a trolley of medical kit, was a camera position marked Flash Interview. Round the corner, the players ducked out towards the dark, fenced-off bus park; I followed through, and saw a stony-faced McMahon being hassled by five guys with dictaphones as he tried to get on the bus. 'I'm sorry,' he said, 'I've nothing to say.'

'But it's the World Cup,' they pleaded.

'Too right it is. And you treat us properly, you might get stories.'

He vanished into the bus.

It was strangely quiet; it was entirely joyless. We were top of the group ... and stumbling harassed and uneasy out of Cagliari.

When I asked one of the men from the qualities how he felt about it, he said, 'Relieved. It would have been very unpleasant if he'd lost. Especially with that team.'

And the players hunched through like haunted men, journos scuffling in their path for quotes; a BBC crew panted after them too, swinging the light and the camera on each one in turn – 'This one, this one' – and shoving and pushing at the bus door as Rob Bonnet hectically lobbed in his questions, in snatched and accelerated bursts of words.

'Howdidthegamego?'

'Whatd'youthinkofBelgiumnextroundPaul?'

The answers were few and spartan; the bus park had a thrumming undertone of soured relationships – and of men who should have been happy with their progress, knowing instead how that progress had been difficult and ungainly. And anyway, so what, when a twenty-year-old boy had died?

Mark Wright was backed up against a wall by the biggest pack; but then, he'd talk all right, and fair enough – he'd just scored his first goal for England, in his twenty-sixth game.

Robson came out with his arm round the shoulders of El-Gohary, the Egyptian coach – a typically decent and considerate gesture.

I asked Rob Bonnet later what he'd got and he said, 'Very little.' He said he'd tried to get Robson, to ask about the bus crash – he'd wanted, he said, to get a quick, 'Good-result-on-the-night-but-sad-about-the-news-of-the-accident-Bobby'. . . which seems to me a pretty base and invasive sort of question. What on earth could Robson have said, except yes on both counts?

But there you go, that's football management 1990 – you carry the hopes of the nation, and become a universal spokesman in times happy, and times sad.

Back in the press centre, the monitors showed FIFA's general secretary Sepp Blatter do his 'clean hands' act again. As he'd done for the draw in Rome in December, he supervised the placing of plastic balls in glass bowls – then called to the bowls a nervous stewardess, who allotted second place to Ireland, and third place to the Dutch.

And no matter if their football was about as attractive as a pack of warthogs running riot in a mud bath – for Ireland to have got there at all, for the first time in their history, was achievement enough. But to have qualified now too, that was remarkable – and when did Jack Charlton ever care about points for artistic impression? He said, 'Palermo tonight will have the biggest party it's ever seen.'

But not Cagliari – not policed-to-silence Cagliari.

I went outside to catch the media bus back into town. The white tent of the press centre sat, faintly aglow, on the other side of the emptying car park; two months ago, all this had been bare dirt.

But now for Cagliari it was over, on a hot night, in a light sea breeze. The BBC truck pulled out with the last taxis and hired cars – and the phone booths stood bright-lit and empty. No one was calling from Cagliari any more.

Nice town, shame about the football . . . I turned to get on the bus, feeling sad; then I thought, fuck it.

We came top of the group, didn't we?

18 Win Or Go Home

Cameroon–Colombia, Brazil–Argentina

Eight squads went home; four had lost all their three matches. Of these, it was no surprise that the USA and the UAE were the fall guys of their groups; and the same goes for the South Koreans who, with eighty-six fouls, eleven bookings, and one expulsion in three games, would not be missed.

Egypt's departure wasn't unexpected either, though they might have done better than get two draws – but they had only themselves to blame, for the paucity of their ambition against England and Ireland.

As to the other countries whose interest was now ended, the demise of Scotland, poor luck notwithstanding, had a doomy inevitability about it – but Austria, Sweden, and the USSR were different matters altogether.

The Austrians arrived with some handy results behind them, including defeats of Spain and Holland – but they blew it.

They didn't blow it as comprehensively as the Swedes, though – the fourth side who lost all three games. Many had expected Sweden to surprise and alarm the best – instead, the only surprise was the alarming magnitude of their failure.

So what happened to Sweden and Austria? At the risk of beginning to sound like a man obsessed, would it be too much to point out that they both played 4–4–2? . . . and even Scotland didn't do that any more.

Still, the bigger surprise by far was the Russians, tipped for the quarter-finals at least – but what can you say?

They was robbed, is what.

Robbed, failed, or just plain no good, those eight all went home – leaving sixteen to get down to the serious stuff. Because now you either won – or you went home.

And the second round looked like this:

23 June –	Naples, 5 p.m.	Cameroon–Colombia
	Bari, 9 p.m.	Czechoslovakia–Costa Rica
24 June –	Turin, 5 p.m.	Brazil–Argentina
	Milan, 9 p.m.	Germany–Holland
25 June –	Genoa, 5 p.m.	Ireland–Romania
	Rome, 9 p.m.	Italy–Uruguay
26 June –	Verona, 5 p.m.	Spain–Yugoslavia
	Bologna, 9 p.m.	England–Belgium

A Yugoslavian journalist wrote a piece accusing their manager Ivica Osim of drinking seven bottles of whisky a week.

No such nervy rancour in Dublin, where 'a rhapsody in green' was proclaimed: 'Hip hip hooray, the result puts us on top of the world. They are all heroes . . . we can get as far as the Final.'

Thus does reality go out the window, as we reach into the wild far regions of Planet Football.

I flew to Rome on the 22nd and went out that night, among English and Irish, for some quality Guinness in the Druid's Den – and the contrast between their stories was telling.

The English told how, maybe ninety minutes before the Egypt game kicked off, there was no more room in their section for Union Jacks to be hung along the rim – so a few Italian police and photographers started laying out the remaining flags on the grass by the track. But then some officious official came along, and kicked the flags up into balls to take them away. 'It nearly caused a riot, that – it's a disgrace, to kick another country's flag.'

Adrian Titcombe, the FA's equipment manager, went to sort it out, and laid them all back down to grateful applause.

The Irish, by contrast, told of a noisy and uninhibited party at La Favorita in Palermo – where, they said, Gullit and McCarthy plainly signalled to each other that with England ahead, they could play out the last fifteen minutes together, and settle for 1–1.

In the stands, in seas of orange and green, the fans all sang together, 'You'll Never Walk Alone' – and no one messed with *their* flags . . .

I was with a group of four from the Maxim. They were from Bromborough on the Wirral; Sean worked for the post office, and his Irish girlfriend Marina worked at the Halifax. Eddy was a hotel chef (though if England got to the Final, he said, 'It's P45 time'); and Kend, who at twenty-eight was the oldest of them, was a crane driver.

Eddy and Kend had been in the travel agent, when Marina saw them from the bus stop outside. So she went in, found out what they were up to – and Sean got home that night to find he was going to the World Cup. He went ape for a minute, because they'd just bought a flat; but only for a minute, it wasn't hard to win him over . . . and anyway, their holiday was extraordinarily cheap.

For flights to Milan, and a coach ride back, they'd paid £77 each; then they'd bought 3,000km rail rover tickets to get them round Italy for £68. Their apartment on Sardinia cost £60 each for a week – and somehow, don't ask me quite how, they'd cadged the second week free. They talked gleefully of meeting other English who'd paid £900 or more for their Sardinian fortnights. 'But they weren't scousers, were they?'

They stayed seventy kilometres out of Cagliari, and hired a car to get in and out for the games – that way they'd steer clear, if any trouble went off. They were Liverpool fans, but told people they supported Tranmere Rovers, just to be on the safe side – and they took clothes bags to the Sant'Elia, so they could wear England colours in the ground, then change out of them before they left.

And they admitted, in general, to a fair degree of nervousness as to how things might go – but said, in fact, that the Sards had been great; they'd seen cars in the party parades after Italy won with the Italian flag out of one window, and the Union Jack out of the other. One Sard offered them a meal in his house – and when they tried to white-lie their way out of it by saying they had to get to Palermo, he offered them a ride in his yacht instead.

And these are the good times, these are the friendships that football can make – but those, also, are the plans and precautions that the smarter England fan has to make, if he or she wants to enjoy watching England abroad . . .

They were good people. So I only hope they survived the attentions of the police in the two weeks that remained –

because there'd be places now where discrimination between the good and the bad would be so non-existent as to make Cagliari look friendly.

They said one other thing: 'Why do they keep giving it to Barnes stuck out there, when there's always two or three men on him? We watch him every week, we know how good he is – but he's not a magician.'

> 'There's no way Cameroon will get stuffed in their next match. They could play Italy and they might go out, but there's no way they'll get stuffed. Against Russia, they knew they'd qualified – but you saw how they played when they had to, against Argentina and Romania. There's no way anyone's going to stuff Cameroon.'
>
> – John Barnes

On the 23rd I took the train down to Naples, and found that the official cheese was taking over the world. A huge metal Grana Padano sat on a dais at the station; another was towed round town on the back of a truck.

I walked through the sun-baked and teeming heart of the city to Egg Castle, where I learnt on the Database of troubled souls in Montevideo: 'To Rome we go, full of anguish . . .'

Naples, however, was an anguish-free zone. I got the media bus to the San Paolo; and even in a half-empty stadium, the Italia '90 theme tune playing loud on 790 monitors in the press box as the TV coverage began, the three helicopters in the blazing sky, the little banks of African and South American flags, all added up to vivid colour and certain knowlege: it's a new game now.

And the point about this particular new game was, if England could beat Belgium – which was no small if – then their next stop was here in Naples, to meet this afternoon's winner in the quarter-finals.

The band played Cameroon's jolly tiddly-pom-pom tune, and then the Colombian anthem, another five-act Gilbert and Sullivan affair positively awash with fancy little melodies . . . and the second round of the fourteenth World Cup got under way.

Colombia got the first corner – and Higuita went to the edge of the centre circle to watch it. As it was taken, and the ball came away, he stood bent over with his hands on his knees; then, nonchalantly, he backed towards his goal. A minute or two later he was out again, joining his back line to make a pass or two . . . and given that the prize was a place in the last eight in the world, it was a strangely indolent affair. But this, of course, is where over-zealous critics of hectic English hoofing have to watch their step – because all the skill and fancy patterns in the world don't mean a thing, if you don't make a game of it.

Fans entertained themselves with drums and cowhorns and whistles; you found yourself looking away at the scrambling clumps of apartment blocks on the dusty green hillsides, idly wondering who might bring Italia '90 to life – because for all their colour and promise, it didn't look like these two would. And the game drifted in a skilful lethargy towards the goalless end of ninety minutes.

Colombia started the first half of extra time with a brief bright flurry – then we were back to more footling around in the centre circle. You found yourself thinking, well, if we get past the Belgians, we'll murder either of this lot . . . such are the dangerous delusions of Planet Football.

Higuita had a good long throw on him, he hardly ever kicked it out – unless he was dribbling out himself, leaving the goal empty to join his back line and pass it away . . . and Colombia continued looking just a tad more urgent – but it was a matter of small and fine degree, like fifteen mph instead of ten. And it got to the turn-round, fifteen minutes of the game left, still marooned at 0–0.

Then straight after the kick-off, Roger Milla pounced on a short pass through, beat one man, hurdled the tackle of the next, and whacked it in. So now we were getting somewhere – Higuita was out dribbling again – Colombia pushed more men up front . . . and Higuita was pushing up too, the maniac. He joined the back line, passed the ball out, had it passed back to him none too wisely – and lost it to Milla who was on to him like a shark, round him, and racing to the empty goal with this huge grin on his face, while Higuita flailed in his wake.

The grin said, I'm too old, son – he was fifteen years older than Higuita, after all – to waste my time watching you play your daft little tricks . . .

So they went two ahead in the space of three minutes – and the amazing Roger Milla joined Spain's Michel at the top of the goalscoring table. He headed for the corner flag, hips wiggling in triumph until his team-mates arrived, and then vanished under a jubilant pile of bodies.

As for poor Higuita – well, pal, you may be fun, but this is the World Cup, and *you just got roasted* . . . he lay face down on the turf, wishing no doubt that it would split open and swallow him whole.

And did Cameroon sit on it, to see it out safe?

Do goldfish smoke cigars?

Up they came again, eleven smiling men, two-nil up with eleven minutes left, and still attacking. There was a buzz of happy chatter at these enlivened and suddenly glorious Africans . . . whereupon Redin went one-two with Valderrama, slipped through, and got one back. Crazy game – 105 minutes of yawnsome cat and mouse, then 15 of Formula One.

Cameroon started thinking safety now all right – four minutes to go, and they backpassed the kick-off straight from the centre circle to N'Kono. One of them got booked, for the time-wasting – a Colombian went close, but not close enough . . . and it was over.

Cameroon 2, Colombia 1.

The Africans celebrated, running to the little patches of their flags in the stands with a kind of straggly, bewildered, heat-drained, exhausted, and disbelieving amazement.

Still, four of them got their second bookings here – so they'd be suspended, when England or Belgium came to town. And with their first choice side thus depleted this was, surely, the happy end of their brave story.

Milla said, 'I never foresaw what would happen to me.'

In Yaounde, Cameroon TV renamed their studios after him, and called for the establishment of a fund to build a monument to his achievement.

And the Colombians walked off slowly, their heads hanging down.

The Colombian manager said, 'Football is human, and it is human to err. This will help Higuita to grow. He is only twenty-three.'

The plucky Higuita himself faced the press, and frankly admitted, 'It was a mistake as big as a house.'

So bye bye Colombia – roll on Cameroon.

Naples – the only city in the world where even railway station announcements have an operatic and hysterical air . . .

On the metro from the stadium, a yelling throng of boys and girls gathered round a Brazilian father and his teenage son to cheer them and sing for them and, in the case of the girls, to sit in their laps and cuddle them. They looked slightly shy (if being Brazilian and shy isn't a contradiction in terms) – but imagine being mobbed just for wearing green shorts and a yellow shirt . . . they got the kind of close-gathered and fascinated attention the white man gets from children in remote African villages – greetings from Naples!

And cheerio, Naples – for a few days, anyhow.

The overnight train to Turin takes ten or eleven hours; I shared a compartment with two Egyptians, a Somali, a Malaysian, and a Scot in a £300 kilt.

The Jock was twenty-three, a Hibs fan from Edinburgh, and entirely charming. And how, I asked, could anybody possibly spend £300 on a kilt?

'It's for a lifetime, isn't it? It's an *investment*.'

Being from Edinburgh, he hated Rangers. 'I could stay up all night thinking of reasons to hate Rangers. And then I hate Celtic too, only just a wee bit less. But they're both so arrogant – and so much prejudice, too, every piece of them that's not wallet is bigotry.'

He was a travelling man, this 23-year-old, setting off in two weeks' time for New York, and then a year heading south through the Americas. He had a qualification for teaching English as a foreign language to get by on – and then, for his second year's wanderings, a year's work permit for Australia. But his favourite city to date (after Edinburgh) was Budapest – he'd been to Hungary four times.

That was mostly because he just liked it – but once, the best time, because Hibs played Videoton in European club football. 'We beat them 3–0 there – eight hundred Hibs fans made more noise, by the end, than the rest of the thirty thousand put together. We scored early, eighth or twelfth minute – I ought to remember, I must have taken 400 pictures of the scoreboard – but it was a magic night.'

Coming back from Hungary last summer through northern Italy, he was on a Turin-bound train, and got talking with an Italian from that city. They couldn't speak each other's language – but they both spoke football, and that was good enough. The Italian was, of course, a Juventus fan – and Juve'd walloped Hibs 4–2 in Edinburgh once, back in the days of Scirea and Altobelli. This, and the language of the round ball, was enough to start an hour's conversation until the Italian got off in Turin – and, the way you do when you're travelling, they swapped addresses, not really thinking that anything would come of it.

Then, in February, the Jock got a postcard from this man, saying that as Scotland were playing Brazil in Turin, why didn't he come and stay? So he did – and they'd put him up for three weeks.

I said, that's really good.

'Yeah, people say, that's really good. But let me tell you, it's fockin' unbelievable.'

As eleven passed, and we pulled into stations here and there collecting the last late-night travellers, I leant from the window asking for news from Bari.

'I think,' said the Jock, 'I can sleep without knowing the result of Czechoslovakia–Costa Rica.'

But a guard on a midnight platform eventually told me, it was a 4–1 thumping to the Czechs – no surprise there. Tomas Skuhravy got three to add to his American brace, going top of the goal table ahead of Milla and Michel – so in Genoa they'd be happy. They'd just bought him that morning from Sparta Prague.

Otherwise, nice one, Costa Rica, and bye bye to you too.

Inside and outside Turin station the next morning, my first sightings of Brazilians in large numbers – a man in the toilets playing a trumpet while I shaved, another on the concourse with a tambourine – men and women of all shapes and sizes and ages in the gold and the green – with rare souls in

Argentina's blue and white moving among them, shaking hands sorrowfully as if bitter defeat was theirs already, eight hours before kick-off.

The range of their hats especially was brilliant and daft – bright yellow seed caps, vast green sombreros, plastic top hats, flat and be-ribboned black gaucho discs – already it felt happy just to be there, to walk down the street with the first flag-waving cars streaking past down quiet Sunday avenues, music thumping, horns parping: Brazil–Argentina in Turin – for colour and soul, for heart and life, does it come any bigger? Because today, with Germany–Holland down the road, was the core of the eighth-finals.

Two big teams were going home after tonight – and this was football, this was joy, this was *festa* – with two big dollops of great sadness lurking, for when the referees came to blowing their final whistles . . .

Newly built at a cost of £80,000,000 – and finished, of course, at the last minute – the Stadio delle Alpi in Turin was the best of them all.

Set into an artificial hill, from the outside it's as boldly, gracefully, electrically sci-fi-modern as the Guiseppe Meazza is menacingly so. You can't see the mass of it from the outside – just the silver sweep of the roofing, suspended from a spider's web of cabling hung off a repeating circle of upright, brick-red double girders – it's like seeing the Golden Gate bridge in a hall of mirrors, with a shimmering gauze of metal draped off it under a geometry of wire and steel . . . and then you go in, and, inside the hill, the enormous three-tiered oval of the stands all around and below you opens out like a cavern, a temple in a mountain of tense and still air; it's like the architecture has contained for you, and 67,410 other people, one vast held breath of expectation.

Central government chipped £24,000,000 into this – the total national spend on just twelve stadiums was half a billion. So, a memo to Westminster: if we in the UK ever want to host the World Cup again . . .

On the horizon to the north, the Alps rose buckled and stern in a cloudless haze – while in the car park the Banda Beijo played on the roof of a half-bus, half-truck affair, to an audience of thousands. The band was an indeterminate number of souls clattering and plink-plonking away on an indeterminate number and variety of percussion instruments, while the bass melted your hips, the singer melted your heart, and two girls of positively illegal shapeliness, dancing frantically on the roof of the cab, melted everything else. The crowd danced too, under a sea of gold and green flags swaying in the brilliant sun. Everyone, it seemed, was Brazilian – Scot, Swede, and Piedmontese all joining the real thing, and becoming honorary Brazilians for the day. So, the myth confirmed: being Brazilian is *fun*.

Being rich and Brazilian, anyhow – because you'd not have made it to Turin from the *favelas* of Rio or São Paulo, from the parched flats of Bahia, or the eco-war zones of Amazonas or Rondonia . . . but there you go, that's Brazil, insouciant as hell about everything – let's have *samba*, let's party, let's wallop those dour Argentines and go win the World Cup again . . . it was like nothing else so far – pure and utter party, in an air of joyous expectation.

'Brazil are still my favourites to win the World Cup. Argentina look very lucky to have qualified. With Argentina in the past, I've always thought once the knock-out starts, they'll be there – but I don't have that feeling now. They've struggled in all their matches, and I can't see them getting any better – I can't see them all of a sudden doing anything to really frighten anyone. But I didn't fancy them this year from the start. Maradona hasn't been as influential, and because of that they haven't been the force that they were – he's not as sharp as he was.'

– John Barnes

'Maradona? He's a pygmy.'

– Careca

There was general agreement in the press centre that this was the last big game we'd see Diego Maradona ever play.

And on the Database, I learnt that Argentine grumbling had arrived at a new proposition. Since 9 May when they arrived, Bilardo'd been saying over and over that it was hard to get his team ready and organised with the best part of his squad playing in Europe – so now President Menem, who was snuggled up inside FIFA in some capacity or other, was saying clubs should have to release their foreign nationals sixty days before the tournament ... fat chance, pal. Would you pay Maradona-sized wages, then wave goodbye to him weeks before your season's finished? No way.

And sure, eleven of Bilardo's twenty-two played in Europe – but so did twelve of Lazaroni's men, and did you hear him asking for sixty days? Did the Italians get together for sixty days, or the Germans, or the English?

So let's face it – like *Pagina 12* said in Buenos Aires, the Argentine side was a fat lady, and her lovers had moved on – there was no amount of griping could hide it.

FORZA BRAZIL!

Inside the stadium the intensity, the deep ferocity of the booing and shrieking that greeted the announcement of Maradona's name was in a whole new league; it was a torrent of relentless hatred, every piercing whistle meant right from the bottom of every raging and envious heart ... it was too much. He is, after all, a footballer – not Lucifer.

As the announcer moved on, the crowd fell strangely silent, as if with all passion spent against this sorry little man – and my own dislike faded in the sadness that his talent seemed faded too, kicked and abused, injured and worn. I'd gone to see him twice – I'd slept (or rather, not slept) on hard plastic airport seats, just because I figured that to see him would be worth it ... and he'd done little or nothing in either game bar dive and protest, and go hunting for fouls; while the skill had merely flickered like an ember.

But you can boil at his gamesmanship, you can despise the way he comes on so innocent and arrogant – there's still no one on earth could play football the way he did in Mexico. And it was that you went to see, only to find that it wasn't there any more – and then to decide that he didn't deserve, in the end, this dread magnitude of hatred.

The grim moment passed, and Brazilian party took over again – the drums beating, the bells ringing, the whole place lined with a constant background susurration of maraca and tambourine. The crowd was a sea splashed with yellow – then in the stand opposite, the crowd unfurled a simply vast sheet of striped green and gold cloth, so fanatically vast that the entire middle tier the whole length of the pitch vanished beneath this great undulating spread, this ocean of national colour . . .

Brah – zeeuhw! Brah – zeeuhw!

Confetti scattered down like a rain of diamonds; the band stepped away to the running track, the photographers scattered to behind the goals, the stagehands hoiked off the floral arrangements of the two flags and FIFA's logo, and the players fanned out to play.

Brazil were magnificent. Careca went through in the very first minute, bursting past Simon, side-stepping Monzon – but Goycochea was out just in time to shut down the angle, and fend off the strike. The noise of anticipation was like no other crowd I've heard, a wholly sexual moaning, sighing, gasping, screaming . . . I thought, we're in for a feast and a half here.

Simon, beaten, went down mock-injured to delay the corner. And when the first foul went in against an Argentine, Maradona was squealing to the French ref right away – but you couldn't see it doing him any good. Brazil seemed to be always on the ball, always flowing gracefully forward; they won another corner in the eleventh minute, Branco curled it in, and it slithered past Ricardo Rocha's lunging toe by millimetres. So how long before they scored?

They rolled forward with long loping strides, passes always running smooth to their targets, leaving tackles slipped like the blue and white just weren't there . . . unless, of course, in crude desperation they made you *feel* they were there with a boot to the gut, or a leg across your shins. And you felt, if Brazil got one, they'd get five or ten – and all around the stadium, the men and women in the green and gold howled in lust for that first goal . . . but it wouldn't come.

The women in the crowd to my right keened at a piercing high pitch, frantic for consummation.

Maradona and Caniggia trotted back and forth with nothing to do, nowhere to go . . . Argentina weren't on the same pitch. And one goal, just one goal *please* on the end of all this finery, would surely unleash an avalanche.

Monzon got booked – one bone-crunching tackle too many. Brazil played pitty-pat with the ball, off knee and head, off thigh and toe, like, who do I fancy giving it to now? And

Giusti got booked too – there seemed no other way to stop them.

Brazil's fifth corner sailed inches over a rising head – and still it wouldn't come. The passing was so clean, they were slicing through Argentina like a bandsaw through blotting paper . . . but as time went by, the absence of goals brought down a strange, urgent, yearning sort of silence. It was football as coitus interruptus.

Maradona was beginning to look a haunted and desperate man, coming deeper and deeper to try and find the ball, and putting his hands out as if to say, what can I do? What can I possibly do here?

Brazil got their sixth corner, as we arrived goalless at half-time.

The second half began, and we picked up were we'd left off. Galvao got booked for a brutish bodycheck on Maradona; but otherwise, normality – Careca streaked down the left, looped in a teasing cross that had Goycochea in a terrible stretched turmoil, just tipping it off his fingers and away off the far post. The ball, hectically cleared, fell to Alemao; his twenty-five-yard shot tipped once more off the leaping Goycochea's fingers – and glanced away, off the identical piece of woodwork, for Brazil's seventh corner.

They got their eighth; the crowd's pain and displeasure mounted, as it came to nothing again. Their ninth – why can't they finish it? Their tenth . . . it was the same problem they'd had against Costa Rica, against Scotland – Brazil didn't know where the goal was any more.

And I began to think, this is another game going nowhere here – there certainly wasn't a lot of lambada about now, as the ninety minutes drew goalless towards their end.

Crosses went in, but found no one on the end of them. They played lovely football, sure, they always had a man spare – but never a man spare up the front where it counted. And why?

Because it used to be that Brazil didn't care if the other lot scored, they'd just score more themselves. But now they'd abandoned that faith, they'd put less into the last piece of the field where they were best – and more in to a Euro-system that, by its very solidity, seemed to have set a grip of constriction on their natural insouciance. They were, like Uruguay, nicey-nicey – they were as nicey-nicey as it can get – but they were punchless.

With ten minutes left, Maradona found Calderon. He laid it off to Basualdo, surged forward into the area, accepted the return – and only a magnificent tackle by Ricardo Gomez prevented Calderon from striking.

The ball came out, and was played too quickly forward to a Brazilian who got caught offside; a free-kick to Argentina, on the edge of their own area. And there were eight minutes of the game left – when Maradona did what I'd waited for through 262 minutes of crude and unappetising Argentinian football.

The free-kick came to him on his own half of the centre circle, his back to the Brazilian goal. He set off a yard or two in no particular direction – then jinked and turned, and burst into fierce acceleration that left the first Brazilian dead on his feet behind him.

Out of nothing, suddenly, he was sprinting for goal. A second Brazilian pelted up behind him, throwing his legs out, and cracked him in the right ankle; but somehow he rode it and continued full out, the tackler flat on his back in his wake.

Still there were three between him and the goal – and he drew the lot of them. In a panicking line, as if they all thought as one, *look out for Christ's sake here he comes*, they fanned out ahead of him – and they forgot about Caniggia.

But Maradona didn't – and his pass was impossibly perfect. The first Brazilian in the line of three, a far bigger man than he, put his hand firmly on Maradona's shoulder, literally squashing him earthwards as, still, he continued to run at that pumping, bullet-like pace; and yet, even as he was being flattened, he slipped the ball through the running legs of the second man, who crashed in bewilderment into the back of the third ... while Caniggia hared free towards Taffarel, committed him, rounded him, then finished with unanswerable venom and precision.

But if the finish was fiercely clinical, the creation was astounding. In a few short seconds, pure football burst out of that battered body – strength, speed, utter control – it was worth waiting three games for.

And word has it that Mozart was a brattish shit too – but

you don't care, do you, when you listen to the music? Likewise now, so what if Maradona seems often to have a bad side as big as a house? Because he's not there to run a charm school, he's there to play football – and on his day he can do that like nobody else.

He ran to the corner flag, and lay in joy on his back in the sun. Then, when he got up again to play out the last minutes, there was suddenly something about him, like, *yes, I've got it, that's it* – and the whole of Argentina was lifted with him. Basualdo surged through clear on goal, and all Ricardo Gomez could do was crudely hack him down from behind – quite rightly, the referee sent him off. Maradona took the free-kick and it was a blinder, forcing an exceptional save from Taffarel as it curled round the wall, and sailed for the top corner.

A brave Argentinian fan ran back and forth with a vast bunch of blue and white balloons before a massed bank of enraged and grieving Brazilians. One man attacked the balloons with his flag pole, until another frantically calmed him down. Out on the pitch, Maradona squirmed through three to the by-line; they hacked him down. Then the deftest of lobs put Calderon through again – and they tumbled him over with a boot to the chest. They were desperate, and it showed; and their last chance summed up their afternoon.

The ball looped over into the Argentine area, Muller ran on to it – and hurriedly slashed his shot hopelessly wide.

Argentina 1, Brazil 0.

It was the first time in four attempts that Argentina had beaten Brazil in the World Cup; the first time Maradona had ever beaten them anywhere. But make no mistake – love him or hate him, it was him who beat them. Unless, of course, you consider that Brazil beat themselves . . .

Lazaroni: 'This is the way football is. It's made us very sad. Argentina had one chance, and they scored.'

Bilardo: 'This was a premature final. Argentina are now playing at fifty or sixty per cent of their capacity.'

Brazilian fan, Rio de Janeiro: 'I'm rooting for Cameroon now – they're much more of a team than our bums.'

Maradona conceded that Brazil had bad luck – they hit the woodwork three times – but they missed a hatful of chances too. And if you don't score goals, you go home ... the stadium was full of men and women in the green and gold just weeping, just crying their eyes out. And the cameras zoomed in on the tears, now, of the beautiful woman who'd been smiling so wide only ninety minutes ago.

Outside a huge man beat his flag, rolled up on its pole, repeatedly on the ground in front of him. A mother comforted her crying son. And a crazy black man with an Argentine cap and the face of god on his T-shirt went among them screaming, *Maradaaaaahhnna, Maradaaaaahhnna*.

Which was maybe just a tad foolhardy ... but Brazilians aren't bad losers. They accept defeat with a few stunned and terrible days of mourning – then they say, what the hell, we'll whip your ass next time.

Because it's never the end of the world in Brazil. Not unless you're burning down the Amazon ...

I got the tram into town, and then the 7.53 to Milan.

Germany–Holland was well under way when I arrived; there was little point trying to get out to the stadium, so I went to the Casa Rossi instead. My friends Marco and Maria-giulia were out – but they'd left their keys for me in a local restaurant, so I went to collect them, then stumbled into a bar just in time to catch Klinsmann put Germany one ahead of the Dutch, five minutes into the second half.

It was a fierce, fast, and passionate game, and very open too – which wasn't surprising, as it turned out Völler and Rijkaard had both been sent off after twenty minutes, the two of them on the brink of rearranging each other's faces. Rijkaard didn't do his image a lot of good here, twice gobbing copiously on the German forward's head.

The Dutch might have had a couple in the first half; while Germany certainly would have been ahead by more, if not for some stupendous goalkeeping by Van Breukelen – but Brehme's second goal six minutes from time was a scorcher, a brick wall wouldn't have stopped that one. They did like whacking it in, these Germans ... with two minutes to go, the Dutch got one back with a penalty – but it was academic.

A lot of people rated this one of the games of the tournament – I put it fourth best, myself. The quality was marred by the

Dutch queuing up to hack down Matthäus; but still, Klinsmann was outstanding. He and Völler now stood third equal with three goals apiece; they looked a front pair fit to scare anybody.

I'd seen only one full game involving Germany – against the UAE – and taken the rest of my news about them from highlights, from the papers, or from others who'd seen them. I almost couldn't bring myself to watch them, knowing they'd always been my favourites to win – so their progress felt somehow like a looming shadow, like a grinding noise in the distance of some ominously well-oiled and unstoppable machine marching on Rome while I raced about elsewhere, looking for someone who might beat them . . . but on their Group F form, it couldn't ever have been Holland.

So it was Germany 2, Holland 1 – and four of the eight quarter-finalists were decided.

On the Dutch–German border, opposing fans fought a minor private retread of World War II . . . and at the final whistle, I fled the bar for a shower in my friends' flat in the Casa Rossi. I'd been in the same clothes for forty hours in four hot cities, sleeping crumpled fitfully in the seat of a stuffy overnight train – and I didn't fancy someone alerting me to my personal hygiene problem.

Tomorrow was Bologna; and the next day, England–Belgium.

19 Tension Time

England–Belgium

On the train from Milan to Bologna I learnt from *Corriere dello Sport* that England's captain Bryan Robson had flown home. The inflamed Achilles had not responded, to Olga Stringfellow or anything else, and surgery looked likely.

After Robson scored two goals to beat Yugoslavia in December, Hugh McIlvanney summed up in the *Observer* what the player meant for England like this:

'His immense quality declares itself not, as with other supreme footballers, in stunning flourishes of grace, but in the persistent application of a powerful armoury of high skills ... he may not always look like one of the giants of the game, but that is what he is. At his best, he is a class above anybody else now plying the same trade in this country!'

And now we had to do without him. Bobby Robson put a brave face on it – but let no one doubt the hole this tore out of the heart of the England squad. Ask any one of the players who our key man was, and you'd get the same answer – even from the supposedly irreverent Paul Gascoigne. Indeed, I think Gascoigne harboured a deep fund of respect and admiration for his captain that would greatly surprise all those inclined to think that the boy is never serious ... but now, all the same, we had to do without him.

Still, he was thirty-three – sooner or later we were going to have to learn to do that anyway. And it might not have been the best time for that – but for Robson personally, it was a disastrous time. Injury forced him from his second World Cup running in a career marred by injury throughout. He'd had four leg fractures, plus groin injuries, shoulder dislocations – without all that, he'd unquestionably have won well over a hundred caps.

And the shame of it is, you couldn't meet a more decent man – there's not a player in the country less deserving of such ill fortune.

He'd told me in May, 'Ever since I was a young tod playing on local greens with my father or my schoolmates, I've always enjoyed my football. And I miss it when I'm out injured – when you're not involved, that's hard. You've go to be in earlier to go to the treatment room, so you miss the banter of the lads when they go out training and you're in the room looking out the window, or you're down in the gymnasium by yourself doing exercises. Then you go downstairs and the lads are changed and they're away, they've gone home – but you, you're back in the afternoon for more treatment. So you miss the routine – then the lads'll be travelling for an away game and you can't go, because you can't miss your treatment. So you miss the coach trip, staying in the hotel, the game . . .'

Or, indeed, you miss the World Cup.

He'd said about being captain of England, 'You feel proud. It's from when you look back – I felt the thrill of watching Bobby Moore lead them out in 1966, and what it meant to my family. In our own environment, in the house, watching that on the telly – when they won it, the enjoyment that was in our house . . . to me when I play now, with our lads, if we win an international match, I can imagine the thousands of families all sitting there, like, the father's having a beer, the kids are sitting there – and they're all excited when we win.'

When England won the World Cup in 1966, Bryan Robson was nine. And all his playing life was about trying to do again what Bobby Moore did then – but now, for the second time, it had been taken away from him.

So for England, it was life without Bryan – and bring on the new boys . . .

I got into Bologna, and found at the station that there wasn't a cheap room left in the city. I decided I'd be a commuter for the day, and go back to Milan that evening – the trip was only a couple of hours – and for the night of the game, I booked a room in a three star hotel for the unearthly sum, for me, of £40. But I thought, at least I'd get a mini-bar for once in my life – it'd be like being a journalist . . .

England were staying at the Novotel in Castenaso, a place twenty minutes' bus ride away on the edge of town. It was a businessman's hotel – a featureless concrete box in a field. I walked out there from the bus stop and, in the humid and glaring heat, found a kind of pre-reception set up at the gate – a table on the sun-softened Tarmac with a telephone, a COL girl, and a pair of police.

A small and sparkily pretty girl from some London ad agency was waiting there with a friend, seeking admission. She was on a 'sponsored breakout', the idea being to get someplace and back in a given time, theoretically for nothing, and bring with you when you returned some proof that you'd achieved your destination – for which, if you made it, £1,000 went to charity. And the proof the girl sought was a picture of herself with some England players.

Given how good the players are about doing that kind of thing, it had to be the easiest grand that ever went to charity. In the hotel I told Bloomfield they ought to let her in, she was gorgeous – the bland and dim foyer could have used a bit of brightening. He grimaced, and muttered ironically that it'd have been safer if she'd not been so attractive ... but of course they let her in anyway, and she got her picture.

The players roamed about, a fair few of them looking restless and taut beneath their habitually casual demeanour; some waited by the phone booths, keen for words from home. But Gazza, of course, was still smiling. I asked him, was it true he'd asked Van Basten what he got in a week?

'Nah. It was the centre-half, what's his name? Koeman. He makes this lovely little chip and I says, cor – what they pay for you then? And Rijkaard says, a hell of a lot – but I was never near Van Basten. I bet he's on plenty more than me though.'

Not many smiles from Bobby Robson. I'd asked Kirton earlier about speaking to the manager that day; but when I approached him, the message hadn't got through. Looking distracted and tense, he muttered with some irritation about having things sprung on him. Then – courteous as ever, despite being so coiled up – he agreed anyway.

And, obviously, the certain knowledge of the vicious flak coming his way if we lost to Belgium would have made most men tense – but there were other reasons why the man was so wound up.

Two days earlier in Saturday's *Independent*, Patrick Barclay had a piece headlined, 'ROBSON'S TACTICS CREATE RIFT WITH PLAYERS'.

The piece began, 'England's reversion to a back four on Thursday night was against the wishes of most senior players, and even Don Howe, Bobby Robson's assistant, is understood to have asked the manager to use the sweeper against Egypt.'

When I'd asked Barclay on Saturday in Naples where he'd got this from, he naturally wouldn't say; but Powell, in grinning and gnomic attendance, said, 'He's a very nice man. But I'd not want him as my assistant.'

Now Waddle and Barnes sat in the foyer of the Novotel, and complained articulately about 'the same old thing'.

'We aren't being allowed to get in their half enough – so we're playing like full backs. And we've said that, in so many words – and he probably understands now.'

So would they go out and attack?

'Hope so,' said Waddle. 'He's not said the team yet, so I don't know if I'm in it.'

He said, 'We've got to have a licence. They don't say to Baggio or Hagi or Gullit, we want you back defending. They don't say to Völler or Littbarski or Klinsmann or Scifo, you can't run about, stick in your zone. They go where they want, they make options. Even against Holland, we didn't stick at it long enough – after half an hour I'm back cancelling out their right back. So we end up with three centre-halves, two full backs pushed in, and goalie makes six. Two midfield men makes eight; me and Barnesy run back too, that's ten men defending – and then they say we can't attack. Of course we can't, we're seventy yards from goal . . . and they want us to go zip-zip-zip all the time – but with three men on us?

'The trouble is,' he then said about Robson, 'he's not used to it. He's used to thinking 4–4–2, he's used to thinking English English English – and he's worried about people not doing what they're used to doing. But we need the freedom . . . I'll tell you, and Gazza said this – one of the first sensible things he's said – it should start, systems like we want, when you're young. But you go to county trials, you watch (and the way he said this suggested bitter experience) the guy'll name the biggest squad. Always the biggest – not the best.'

Barnes said, 'You look at England Schoolboys, they're bigger than everybody else. And they might win, because they're stronger – but when the little French or Italian kids grow up they're better, aren't they? And where's your advantage then?'

'In the English First Division,' said Waddle, 'you can play 4–4–2 'cos they all do. But this is the world here – and if I was the England manager (a thought that made him laugh) I wouldn't play that. I'd play 3–5–2. And defenders defend, attackers attack – because to be perfectly honest, we've got the players in this squad who can win this thing. Back, middle, front, we've got it all. And everybody can see it, all the players can see it . . . but at the end of the day, there's a man employed to pick the team. Not us. We can have our little point of view – but at the end of the day, he might not have listened to a word I've said. Like, "It's my team, I pick it." And sure, a manager lives by results – but how many games have we won *away*? 0–0 in Sweden – they played 4–4–2 as well, and was that a boring game, or what? And then Poland, they didn't play 4–4–2 – and they played us off the park. And now here – you're not in your home yard here, are you? Take Scotland – sure, they've gone home – but I was pleased to see them try to play continental. The system wasn't quite right, but who did they beat? Sweden – and what do Sweden play? Then their other two games, they were unlucky – but I bet if you talk to a Scottish player he'll tell you, cor, you get some freedom playing this. See, the only effective 4–4–2 is Ireland – and will they win the World Cup? People said Ireland–Holland was class, so I got a video and watched it – and how was that a great game? And people say Ireland played – but first half, Holland played them off the park. It was pure power that got them back, that's all. Romania'll be thinking after twenty minutes this afternoon, *what is this?* Me, against Ireland – I never dreamt in my life I'd end up standing on my own eighteen-yard line chesting it down, then just booting it upfield – and afterwards I thought, *what am I doing?* At least if we weren't caught between two stools and just played out-and-out 4–4–2 really hard, the ball'd be hefted up and we might get it free upfield like Sheedy does, or like Barnesy did at Watford . . . but us, it's rigid instructions. Look at Brazil – was Alemao sitting? Was Valdo sitting? Dunga sits, Dunga's the anchor, Dunga's the axe-lad – the others go where they want. At Marseilles it's the same – Tigana sits, me, Papin, Francescoli, we move. But us, we get shown on a bit of paper, more or less – "this is where I want you to play, this position, this role". He'll never say, "You're here, run there, run back and get it, go left, go right, come in, go wide." And the Belgians – they're a good attacking side. There's so much movement, so many options. Scifo's centre-mid, left, right, forward . . .'

Then he stopped, run right out of his steam and tension. He said, 'But who's to say I'm right? Every system's there to be beat – and it's all opinions, isn't it? That's why it's such a great game . . . anyway, people might say I'm making excuses. I mean, your book'll end up making like I'm knocking the English game – but it's effective, club level. It's just, at world level . . .'

He said, 'I always like watching Ireland, 'cos it's always interesting to see how the other side cope. I wonder if Jack'd play like that if he was the England manager – be interesting, wouldn't it? Though God knows what the crowd'd think.'

We went back to talking about the time we'd been away now; he was missing his daughter, who'd turned two in May – I was missing my son, Joe, who'd been six months on the day I left home.

'He says, what's six weeks away? People were away five years in the war.' Then Waddle grinned and said, 'But they didn't have to play 4–4–2 in the war, did they?'

Robson took Waddle outside, and asked him how he felt. Was he tired? Could he play like he had against, say, the Italians in November?

Waddle said he could.

So Robson said, well, do, 'cos I'm playing you. 'Cos people like you and Barnes can win this game . . .

When they came back in Robson called me over, and we went up to his room to watch the first half of Ireland–Romania. He said of the Romanians, 'Bet they pick up a lot of injuries, these lot. The Irish don't half get into you.'

He had injury worries of his own; Lineker's toe was still painful, but improving – and Des Walker, who'd had his leg clattered again by an Egyptian, would worry him right up to the moment he announced his team.

What had it been like, I asked, to leave out Butcher against Egypt?

'Very, very tough. But it had to be done, there's no sentiment – I know what it meant to him, what he's done for us – but sentiment, that can get you unstuck, I couldn't afford it. And he took it so brilliant, he's such a good man – he took it on the chin. He's an example to others. He said, that's fine, it's your decision. I asked him how many caps he'd got – seventy-four. So I said, we must get you the seventy-fifth. Oh, don't worry about that, he says – I'm grateful to get seventy-four.'

About his reasons for dropping him he said, 'We played against Holland with three centre-halves. But against Egypt we'd be overloaded doing that, it'd be three on one, so we went back to 4–4–2. And some people have this stupid opinion it's outdated – but AC Milan play it, Belgium play it – it's a very good system. Is Liverpool Football Club outdated? In Europe next season, how would they play? Some clever concoction? When people talk to me, it's outdated – are they talking about Liverpool?'

He talked fast, with his mouth tight and angry. If Barnes and Waddle, I suggested, had a little more freedom . . .

'It's down to the player, it's not down to the system. It's tougher here, it's harder, there are no loopholes, there are no bad players on the pitch. There are bad players in the First Division, there are bad players in France – but these are the best out here, take Egypt – those are the best eleven players in Egypt. And I tell them to play like they play for their clubs – but sometimes better players don't let them. And yes, they've got jobs to do, to get past people and put crosses in, to get in scoring positions – but they've got a duty to the team too. They've got to make defensive runs. So these free roles . . . free to do what? Free to disappear from the game? Free to always be in space? If you're a good player and you go free, they'll mark you. Look, I can demand, encourage, motivate – and if that doesn't work, I can leave 'em out. Drop 'em. People expect the manager . . . but at the end of the day it's up to the players, isn't it? What d'you fuckin' pay them for? You can't control them by remote control, can you? You can't sit there with the little buttons saying go there, tackle, go there, press, drop back, pass him . . .'

It was a strange situation – Robson defending a system, a way of playing, that he'd played and believed in all his life –

395

on the eve of the game in which, with England at least, he'd finally abandon it.

He said, 'Players make systems, systems don't make players. So don't blame the system – if someone's not picked, blame them, blame their performance. But,' he then said, 'you have to adapt here – tournament football's different to running the England team. You have eight or ten matches in a year – then here you've got five or six or seven in four weeks. And the further you go, the harder it is. So you have to adapt.'

Which he certainly was doing. I asked, what did he say, when people said he was too cautious?

'I don't care if they think that. What do they mean, too cautious, anyway? I've played more bloody wingers than any other manager in the history of the English FA. Caution – what are they talking about? I think they like the sound of their own vocabulary. I played two wingers against the Irish – and Waddle and Barnes aren't hard men, are they? They're *gifted* – and we knew it'd be a hard slog – but I played them. What are you talking about, cautious?'

On the television, Hagi was working his magic – but Irish hoof and Irish heart weren't letting him get anywhere. When he or another Romanian did get somewhere, down they came; and then there was Pat Bonner, solid as a rock in his goal . . .

I asked about the captain's departure.

Robson said, 'The inflamed tendon wasn't responding at all to rest or treatment. And this here has only a couple more weeks to go – but he has an injury that's more than two weeks. So he can't do any good for us here, and it's important to get him diagnosed as quick as possible. Of course his absence will be felt – on the pitch he'll be missed, and in the squad he'll be missed. See, Barnes and Wadddle may not play as good internationally as they do at their clubs – but with the skipper it's the other way round. Gascoigne, Wright, they've played better internationally – Gascoigne's the only player we've had in the team who's actually got the ball and run at people consistently, in all three matches. Even against the Irish . . . oh, that's a foul, look at that. That's the third time he's done that, that McCarthy – he's a dirty bugger. If he's not booked he's lucky.'

And McCarthy did it again, turning another Romanian into splinters. 'Look at that. He's not even *looking* at the ball.'

Still, he said he'd like an Irish win. 'I wouldn't mind that, sure. Be nice for our football – put a bit of pressure on us, maybe, but there's that anyway.'

He certainly looked like there was pressure – but his good manners, even when a question angered him, never left him.

There had been, I said, reports suggesting rifts between the players and himself over tactics . . .

'Make-believe. Innuendo. Rubbish.'

At half-time, Ireland–Romania was goalless. The Romanians were clearly playing the better football – but then, they weren't the first to try playing football against Jack Charlton's Ireland . . .

Robson went to see Don Howe. In the corridor I said thanks, good luck and do well, and he said, 'Yeah, we hope so. OK, Peter, bye now.'

And he found a smile from somewhere. Because even here – plainly uptight as hell – he remained, simply, just a very nice man. And let's face it, not a bad manager either – since, having held out one last Egyptian time for the old ways he'd just defended, he was nonetheless now preparing, as he put it, to 'adapt' – and play the sweeper again . . .

Why? Firstly because he was worried, presumably, about the Belgian front men Ceulemans and De Gryse, just as he'd been worried about Van Basten and Kieft. De Gryse, he said, was a darting centre forward who reminded him of Lineker . . .

And secondly because, basically – *pace* Robson – Barclay's story wasn't 'make-believe, innuendo, rubbish' at all. Robson must have heard his players and his staff, and recognised – as a good manager should – that it was time to move on to the new ways.

Down in the foyer Lineker said of the sweeper system, 'All the players want to play it, we're more comfortable with it. Before, Bryan Robson would talk with him – there's no sneaking about, no rebellion, no we're-going-to-do-it-our-way-sack-the-manager business – but we talk amongst ourselves, and the captain talks with the manager.'

So I'm speculating here – but as Butcher was now the captain, this raised the odd scenario of Robson's favourite son – who he'd just dropped, and who'd said less than three months before that England were more comfortable playing

4–4–2 – now going to Robson to promote the new order . . . but maybe that never happened. More likely it was, in fact, Bryan Robson's last service to England before leaving, to put the merits of the system – and the players' belief in it – to the manager that he'd been with eight years. After all, what did Manchester United want to do with Bryan Robson, now he was thirty-three, but play him as a sweeper himself?

Lineker said, 'We all think we should play it. I don't think there's one player in the squad who thinks we should play 4–4–2 – because the winger situation doesn't work, they're too easy to mark. But like I say, there's no rebellion – he's the manager, and it's not come to undermining him or anything, there's nothing underhand – and if he plays 4–4–2 you respect it. It's him who lives or dies by it – and players just suffer along the way . . . but we're relaxed enough, I think. The manager's what you might call a bit intense – I think his head's going to blow off before the end of the tournament. But you live with that, don't you?'

Earlier he'd joked that the England camp was now a smile-free zone; that smiling was out, under orders . . .

As to the game, he said he'd put his head on the block: 'I think we'll win. I think we're good at the back, I think we'll play the sweeper system, and I think we'll score. Do I think I'll score? – no, I never say that. I think we'll score, and I *hope* I'll score. But as long as we score one more than they do, I'm not bothered.'

We went to watch the second half of Ireland–Romania; the daffy violinist Nigel Kennedy wandered in, beating the drinks ban with an ITV beer, which he then knocked over. He cackled and said, 'England Players Mess Up Fucking TV Room Shock.' Then he said he was going out for some fresh air, so someone could score.

I said yeah, it was always that way – you went to the loo, and immediately missed someone getting a goal.

'Right then – I'll go drop a few monster turds, and that way we'll get some action.' Players laughed; Kennedy's appearances were always enjoyed, like he was unofficial camp muppet, some kind of alien comedy turn.

And we gazed glazed at the football; Lineker wondered idly if the Irish were on a fiver for every time they hit the roof of the stands.

398

He asked if I'd seen Lothar Matthäus getting booked last night – the German captain had run on after the whistle had been blown, idly netted the ball on the end of the run, and then been cautioned for it. But his play-on had been innocuous, and the booking was ridiculous – after the game, Matthäus had an angry run-in about it with the referee.

Lineker sad, 'I've got a problem, haven't I, if they're going to start booking you for putting it in the net.'

But if we beat Belgium, it was Cameroon in Naples; and if we beat them, and assuming the Germans beat the Czechs – then it'd be us and the Germans in the Turin semi-final.

So Lineker said, 'I think he deserves to be booked all the same. On the grounds of being a German. And being a bloody good player – I mean, Christ, he's got some engine on him, hasn't he?'

We sat meanly hoping that Matthäus might collect another booking against the Czechs, and be suspended for Turin . . . if we got that far.

And Ireland–Romania charged passionately, chaotically on. On the record, England players wanted Ireland to win, absolutely. Off the record, they didn't at all – on aesthetic grounds.

And on aesthetic grounds – on the grounds that while I hoped the Romanians won, I was more interested in watching Italy–Uruguay with my friends in Milan – I gave up when the ninety minutes ended goalless, and the game went into extra time. I went, instead, to get a lift into town with Jon Holmes, Lineker's agent.

Then, as we were waiting for the cab, who should I see meandering palely like a ghost in the foyer of the Novotel but – unbelievably – Dick Wragg . . . but I don't suppose there was a doctor in England who could have held the man back. Even so, it was utterly crazy – he looked bloodless and shaky, and had a slight but plain slur in his speech. An ITV man joked, with nervy bravado, that it must have been the Sardinian wine that did for him – and Wragg gamely said he'd better try a few more bottles to find out. For spirit, you couldn't fault him – for common sense, however, you really had to wonder . . . I mean, people talk about the fanaticism of the fans, and how stupid they were coming out here with no money, no tickets – yet this old guy was coming back out here when he'd been sent home once already, and with half a likelihood the trip could kill him.

Holmes said on the way into town, 'Christ, the atmosphere's bad.' He represented Barnes, Webb, and Shilton, as well as Lineker – and you could tell, he said, that Barnes was well uptight. As for Robson, he was walking about wild-eyed, *wild-eyed* . . .

I'd noticed in his room that Robson was reading a Sidney Sheldon novel – beats taking tranquilisers, I suppose . . . and he'd seemed to me, yes, tense as hell – but not out of control. Because if he couldn't handle it, he'd have jacked it in long ago – he'd not have lasted those eight much-maligned years. And the more I thought about the way he'd talked, with a lid of clenched restraint just about containing the paranoid feeling that he was all alone, in a world of vicious criticism – the more I thought about it, the more I wondered if, perversely, Bobby Robson wasn't *enjoying himself* . . . here in tension camp Novotel.

But Holmes said he reckoned he was out of his depth. 'I think they're all going mad. Look at Swales, walking round like a football yob . . .'

Peter Swales was another senior FA bod – another man too old, like Millichip, to be going round in complacent disconnection with reality, dressed absurdly in shorts and England shirts like lager louts on holiday – while the national side that was supposed to be in their charge had a manager on his nerve-ends, working a last-ditch 'adaptation' that went against the grain of his whole football career – and players, meanwhile, fenced in a tetchily resigned laager of anti-press, anti-4–4–2 discontent. England under siege . . . from which we'd either burst out against the Belgians – or blow up.

Still, you know what they say about the English – always best with their backs to the wall . . .

It was a relief to return to Milan, sit down with Marco and a beer, and watch Baggio and Schillaci working their magic again. Uruguay managed to hold out for sixty-five minutes against the tide of the *Azzurri* – but then Schillaci, set free by the deftest flicked lay-off from Serena, volleyed first time from thirty yards. There wasn't a keeper on earth who'd have stopped it. And Serena, who'd come on as a substitute on his thirtieth birthday, then celebrated again, by scoring a second with his head . . . Italy 2, Uruguay 0.

Schillaci joined Völler and Klinsmann in third place on the goalscorer's chart – while Vialli was deemed fit enough to sit on the bench. Vialli had said, 'I am not a liar. I have an injury' – but the doctors couldn't find it.

So a team spokesman responded, 'As far as we're concerned there's nothing wrong with him – though he still seems to be feeling pain.'

With or without the mysteriously crocked Vialli, it was now the Italians' turn to work out how to deal with the un-compromising march of the big-hearted Irish. You might not like their football, but you had to hand it to them – they didn't let anyone or anything put them off just being them-selves. They'd hustled and bustled the Romanians and, after 120 goalless minutes, held their nerve to win the penalty shoot-out. Bonner, having kept the Irish in it with saves during the game from Hagi and Raducioiu, then saved the Romanians' last kick – and O'Leary made no mistake, to put the Irish through 5–4 with the deciding penalty. So Ireland had scored only two goals in four games – but they'd made it to the last eight in the world all the same.

And it was the first unresolved game that needed settling with the ersatz excitement of the penalty lottery – but there'd be plenty more of that. Indeed, far too much more . . .

Not that anyone was worrying about that in Milan just now. I went out with Marco, and we hared round the streets for a while with what seemed like every other citizen of the city, in another deafening Formula One rally of victory celebration.

A short night's sleep after the Milanese party, and then back to Bologna – a splendid city, sumptuously mercantile and bourgeois, with over forty kilometres of covered walkways lining the wealthy cobbled streets of the centre, and all manner of architectural treats from the middle ages lurking round every other corner.

But it was also broilingly humid – so bad you could have showered five times a day, and still ended up stinking. And then, that England feeling was with us again – the town half shut, a latent tension in the air. It had all the festivity, after the joys of Turin and the party in Milan, of a bad day in a bread queue.

I went to the stadium four hours before kick-off. There seemed more Belgians there than English, sprawling stunned in the heat, motionless in whatever shade was to hand. They sported caps and shirts that said either *Diables Rouges*, or *Rode Duivels*, depending on whether you were Flemish or Walloon – and they were an ugly lot, physically indistinguishable from the English, except that there were among them more moustaches, and more women. One appalling slug who'd got in the bus on the way out there wore nothing at all bar a filthy pair of shredded shorts, through the rents in which both buttocks could be seen gruesomely jiggling beneath the grey mesh dishcloth of his antique Y-fronts; Italians beside me gaped in disgust. You could see the skid mark up the crack of his arse.

The press centre was the same as any other, though with the one refinement that you couldn't smoke in it – a rule ignored in corners everywhere by furtively puffing journos. Also, the Cheesewoman here was even taller than the one in Naples – did Grana Padano pick them from a basketball team, or what? By the time we reached the Final, would they be eight feet tall? She towered in her blazing yellow suit past the skulking mere mortals of the world's press.

One other difference was that the sandwiches at the bar here – Bologna, after all, being the gastronomic capital of the known universe – were the best in all of Italia '90. But it was small consolation for the fear and gloom that hung over some quarters of the press. Either we'd lose, or we'd riot, or both.

In Dublin, police and security had danced in the corridors of the EC summit there on hearing of Ireland's win; in Genoa, thousands of Irish fans had shushed each other through the Romanian anthem, and applauded it afterwards. The mayors of Turin and Genoa had thanked the Scots for their excellent behaviour; in Rome, they were now preparing with pleasure for the Irish to come down . . . and from Rimini, 246 English had been deported.

Though as ever, English villainy wasn't so straightforwardly villainous as the tabloids would have you believe.

THE SHAME GANG

BATTLE OF RIMINI

GET OUT YOU ANIMALS

According to one English journalist, by the time it went off, the press had all left for Bologna; there'd only been one radio man and two press agency guys there to watch what actually happened . . . and the War Correspondent told me he saw it like this: Italians, celebrating their win over Uruguay, had taunted the English who were drinking in the bars. In one bar, the Rose and Crown, a hard core of maybe thirty boozed-out scum took this as their cue to start chucking bottles and whacking people – and the police in turn took this as their cue to wade in and detain every Englishman in sight. There had been, said the War Correspondent, English begging for shelter in houses and bars as the tear gas flew, and the snatch squads roamed . . . so that yet again, a small number of the poisonous minority had catalysed the hair-trigger policing into maximum response, and indiscriminate street clearance.

The FSA – with the aid of Dennis Howell – has subsequently lodged appeals with the courts in the cases of seventy-one of those deported, seeking compensation on the grounds of wrongful detention and deportation. Perhaps embarrassed by what a legal action might reveal, the Italian authorities have rescinded banning orders on the people they deported.

And why 246? Some of those deported had previous convictions – but not the majority of the 246. So just pause and ask youself, how many seats on an Airbus? I think you'll find it's about 246 – and it looks rather as if they had a plane at the airport, and filled it to set an example . . .

In Verona, the Yugoslavs rode their luck against the Spanish – who twice hit the post – and Dragan Stojkovic scored two delicious goals, the second in extra time, to win a tense and tight game 2–1.

But it'd take a bloody good game to cheer us up in Bologna. Harsh views among English journalists varied from the English in general – 'We pollute the tournament' – to the team in particular, 'I just want to see the bastards get done.'

They had a weary dislike of the leaden air of the cities we played in; and then, a good few of them by now just hated our football and the team that played it anyhow.

All played out?

The English players came out and stuffed it down their many critics' throats. They, and the Belgians, didn't just give us a bloody good game – they gave us the third best game of Italia '90.

The Renato Dall'Ara was a nice little stadium, tight and neat, a small simple bowl updated for a mere £25,000,000. Outside, in Matthew Engel's words, it resembled 'a Victorian mill turned into a theme park' – the redbrick walls meshed round with tiers and stairways of blue and yellow iron. And inside, Terry Butcher'd got his seventy-fifth cap after all.

Robson played the same side as against Holland with the one forced change of McMahon anchoring the middle in place of Bryan Robson. Not that it looked like it'd help us much at first ... nightmare: in the opening minute Butcher gave the ball away to Scifo – Ceulemans and De Gryse both went blasting through the middle – but somehow Gazza raced back between them to salvage it. Then Versavel got through, Shilton just got a hand to his fierce low shot – and Wright made it back in time to clear the free ball out of an open goal for a corner. The Belgians got a second corner, and a third ... great start.

But we did look better this way. Gazza was everywhere again; and Waddle looked bright too. There was, in his own word, freedom – he was going left, right, back, wherever he wanted. Early on, he skinned De Wolf and got it in to Barnes, who won a corner; he turned him a second time, raising cheers – at last *this* was Chris Waddle, fast, tricky, making it look easy with that shambling, shuffly run ... then at the other end, Ceulemans hit the post. An instant TV close-up on the bench showed Robson looking like a man who'd just swallowed a cold fish whole at a wedding.

And though we looked better than in the past, still, with the initial two alarms, some pulsatingly efficient forward movement, and now Ceulemans's wolfish strike, the Belgians had an edge ... but at least England looked like they *liked* to play

404

this way – and steadily the Belgian edge was pared down to the width of a Rizla. Even Barnes was in it at last, looking to trick one man, then another, twisting, turning, shimmying so they couldn't see the ball, even when he was right there with it at their feet and in their faces . . . a Pearce free-kick whistled wide by two yards; Scifo shot a volley high at the other end. It was anyone's game now, and whoever won it would deserve it – but it was great to watch either way.

Even Butcher got free; he pushed up the wing once, with Pearce and Barnes inside him, almost to the corner flag. Then Des Walker took his turn to take it up, drawing a defender, giving it to Barnes – and what was this but the Liverpudlian pass-and-move Barnes had wanted so long? It was beyond revolution – it was *liberation* . . . Waddle was running at the Belgians on both flanks, and through the middle too; Butcher was now here on the right, now there on the left; and then, *wham*, Lineker netted it . . . but was called, dubiously, offside.

Still, the Belgians had been denied a penalty appeal just before; and, immediately after Lineker's goal, they went through, only to be closely called offside themselves. It was action at both ends. Wright rose, a replay of the Egypt goal, and headed just wide. Waddle was fouled, chipped in the free kick, Gazza lightly lofted it on, and Pearce's header this time fell just too far on to the roof of the net. Then a Belgian attack poured up to the other end, made it into the area, and only the last pass went astray; and back it went down the field, Pearce crossing to Barnes going clear on the edge of the area – but his shot was weak, and Preud'homme gathered easily.

Waddle now was coming back central a lot, sitting in front of the back three like he couldn't wait for someone to give it to him, like, *just give it to me here right now, I'm going places* . . . he found Lineker in space, Lineker crossed – and Barnes this time wasn't weak at all. He fired a searing first time volley, *whoomph*, catch that if you can, Mr Preud'homme – a glorious replay of his Uruguay goal at Wembley – but again, the goal was called offside. The replay showed no way, no way was it offside . . . were we getting robbed here, or what?

Waddle went through two, and chipped it across the keeper – but there was no one there. All the same,

Let's all have a disco
Let's all have a disco
La la la la
La la la la

Half-time, goalless. It might have been two to us, it might have been two to them – either way, it was shaping up better than any game I'd seen so far.

After all, I'd been wondering since Saturday who'd light up this tournament in the second round – and here we were in the last game of that round, with England and Belgium between them not just lighting it up, but threatening to set it on fire too . . .

Scifo picked up the second period with a bang, whacking in a glorious curling shot that cannoned back into play off the post. At the other end, another break by Waddle sent Lineker haring free, doing his fighter-plane impersonation as he took off into sprint mode – but the ball just ran a yard too far ahead of him, and the keeper got there first. Play coursed back down the pitch, to a Belgian free-kick which rebounded for Demol, whose shot from outside the area went only a yard or two wide. The Belgians were pressing now – a Scifo cross shaved across our goalmouth; their passes were working, ours were running lose – then Gazza tried to dance through four into their area, and very nearly made it.

He was looking puckish and lively; England came together again. We won a corner, a free-kick . . . still nothing. The crowd started asking for Bull.

The Belgian fans had their flags out now; they were backing theirs, and we were backing ours – and the tension rose, as the game surged back and forth. Van der Elst came off, Nico Claesen came on – and two minutes later he damn near scored, getting by Walker, then shooting tight across the face of the goal.

With nineteen minutes left McMahon came off, and Platt went on; two minutes later, Barnes pulled up with a groin strain, and Bull went on. It was the worst possible news for Barnes, and for England, just when he and they together looked like at last it was clicking . . . but still, were we attacking now, or what? It was win or go home – and like the man said, 'What are you talking about, cautious?'

Corners came at both ends – but the most dangerous man on the park was now clearly Enzo Scifo; and if anyone was edging it as the last minutes raced by, it was the Belgians again – certainly, Shilton was the busier keeper. Butcher took a clattering tumble, then Walker too – both had injured legs already, but there was no going off now, both subs were on. So they wrestled on – but the Belgian fans were noisier by far, they felt it swinging their way. Platt was working hard, Bull was running and running – but we weren't approaching their goal with that fluid movement any more, and they still were – it was getting hairy out there and Gazza must have felt it, because he threw in a crunching tackle that got him booked, as extra time loomed – and how he'd pay for that in tears, in eight tense days' time . . .

Walker was limping badly. But there was more work yet to do – because full-time came, and still it teetered at this thrilling o–o.

And you run and you run and you run – and if neither side gets lucky, the rules say then you have to run and run some more . . . this wasn't ever going to be easy. But another thirty minutes of football out there now would be hard as hell.

The RAI statistics came up on the monitor, saying that over sixty-eight of the ninety minutes had been actual playing time – a wearingly high percentage, and a credit to the clean quality of the game played by both sides . . . and then the heart sank, to see trouble in the stands.

There was a sudden charge upwards, a hideous ant-like scurrying of bodies up over the mercifully backless seats – and a great hole opened on the terrace, a gaping horror-mouth in the crowd . . . there were English at the bottom, Belgian at the top; but the police plugged the hole fast, a filling of force in a cavity of fear. And later it turned out that nothing much had happened – some Belgian hard core had been gobbing on the English beneath them, but it settled down fast enough . . . though for a few minutes at the time, as England kicked off the extra period, the mind was gone, the ugly worry rising – until Platt volleyed narrowly wide, the seats slowly filled again, and the moment passed.

And on the field it was back and forth again, back and forth – weary-legged maybe, but Waddle for one was still passing people, still feinting and jinking . . . Versavel fired wide by inches at our end; Scifo went through – then Platt did likewise to win a corner – and who was going to crack this? They were older than us, and maybe more tired – it was looking a bit like Poland in October, they couldn't get in the area, if they scored it'd be a long shot; while Preud'homme in the Belgian goal was covering every ball we sent in. England were pressing, but every run in, they pressed us straight back off it. Gerets shot high and wide . . . the first fifteen minutes passed, and still it was o–o.

The last fifteen began. How Walker was carrying on, God knows. Gazza was looking knackered and peevish, turning round and round on the ball in the middle, with no one to give it to. But then everyone looked knackered; and from the back they were just hoofing it away . . . the guy next to me said, 'It'll be a miracle if they win this now.' But still Platt was running everywhere, still Waddle was beating his man . . . Bull combined with Pearce to take a powerful shot, forcing Preud'homme to push it wide for a corner – at the other end, Butcher headed away Scifo's cross, for a corner to them. And time was running out – England were hugely jeered and whistled as they played it round the back, at this of all times, shorn of legs and ideas . . . could it really slump, after all that fire, to the stupid heartless bingo of penalties?

Then Gazza picked it up on the edge of his own area, and just went, suddenly – like he'd not been playing two hours of football at all. Could he do it, as the clock ticked away? You prayed as he advanced . . . and he was fouled. Free-kick. Everyone poured desperately forward; Gazza stood over the ball, looked up, and looped it over the heads of the Belgian defenders to where Platt had surged through. He had his back to goal – but spinning on the spot he struck it first time as it fell, whipping round to lash it in the back of the net, just picking it out of the air and *wham* – and as they say in South America.

GOOOOO – OOOO – OOOAAAAAHHHHHLLLL!!!

There were just thirty-two seconds of the game remaining. Gazza was kissing Robson on the touchline; Robson was urging him back on, for those last few seconds. They played them out – the whistle went – Gazza circled the ground applauding the England fans, and, cruelly, playing a mock-violin to the Belgians – and Waddle and Butcher went with huge grins on their faces to do their daft little dance in the centre circle, to say thanks to the fans. Let's all have a disco . . .

England 1, Belgium 0.

It was a magnificent game of football; it had everything, not just class and pace and action but – at the bottom line – persistent bloody-minded guts as well. And, of course, a really cracking goal . . .

In front of 250 journalists, Robson said straight away that it was 'very cruel for Belgium'. And he said, 'Platty's pleased to give the goal to Bryan Robson.'

And England, for the second time in Bobby Robson's term of office, were in the last eight in the world.

The quarter-finals looked like this:

30 June –	Florence, 5 p.m.	Argentina–Yugoslavia
	Rome, 9 p.m.	Italy–Ireland
1 July –	Milan, 5 p.m.	Germany–Czechoslovakia
	Naples, 9 p.m.	England–Cameroon

The Bologna COL seemed, however, only to be offering tickets for Florence – which, if you were English, wasn't a whole lot of use. I went to the information desk to check this out and was told, 'We have no information.' I gawped. Just to make sure I understood, they said, 'We're only the information desk.'

But all round, the left hand at the Bologna COL seemed seriously detached from the right. Back on a packed staircase of thwarted journalists barred from an interview area, there'd been hysterical police manhandling the press; Bloomfield had been argy-bargied by COL stewards, and even David Platt almost physically shovelled out into the bus area. It was, you might say, a total *bolognese*.

Nottage was in a frenzy of temper over this – and it got worse. She was in a hotel costing nearly £200 a night – Italia '90 block-booked rooms for its people in the best hotels in every city, God knows what the total bill was – yet when we got to this place, near two in the morning, there was no bar, and no room service. She threw a terminal wobbly, and some choice Italian at the indifferent staff. The No.1s sat there loving it: WORLD CUP GIRL IN LATE NIGHT BAR BUST-UP . . .

Back in my own hotel, I found they'd been so scrupulous about the drinks ban that they'd emptied my mini-bar of everything but two Campari sodas. So much for paying out for the privilege of a journalist-style liquor supply for the night – though in fact, the alkie faction of the sports press had taken to staying in other towns altogether, then driving in, stopping at restaurants *en route*, so they could keep themselves in booze – the wily stratagems of Planet Football . . .

I lay there smoking and drinking coffee in the small hours. Sleep felt by now like a knack lost long ago – I watched Italian MTV, and thought over and over of the ball hitting the net . . . and of how the pairing with Cameroon, depleted as they were by suspensions, was widely considered the easiest route to the semi-finals . . . 3 a.m. went by, and 3.30 . . . Paul Young, the Blow Monkeys, Madonna, John Lee Hooker, who mixes this lot? . . . funky telly, sweaty carcass, clogged lungs, and the prospect of a semi-final against the Germans in Turin, Juventus town, the city of the Heysel victims . . . there were awful possibilities of deep violence . . . and then, ay-ay, the possibility of winning, too, and going to Rome to the Final . . . England–Italy? Or what about England–Argentina, now *there* would be a showdown . . .

We were in the last eight in the world.

And thinking further than that was dreamland . . . there was Cameroon to get past first.

I slept for three hours.

Next morning I got a ride out to the Novotel with Nottage in a local COL limo. In the foyer I bumped into David Lacey while we milled about waiting for a press conference – and he said he'd seen Gazza at Spurs back in April, and that Robson had been there too. There'd been a free-kick in a similar position, and back then, Gazza'd just blasted it – and the ball wafted away . . . so Lacey'd said to Robson, would he like the boy to try that for England, just on the off-chance?

No, was Robson's answer – complete waste of a free-kick. And Gazza had listened, because he hadn't wasted it last night. He was learning, fast, getting better all the time . . .

Not that the press conference was about any of that. It was, instead, about the now yawning chasm in relations between the press and the England camp. We're in the last eight in the world – and look what we're talking about.

After training on the day before the game, the players had blanked the press, and got straight on the bus. But Parker stopped on the steps to talk to them – and Gazza, inside, had lobbed a cup of soft drink over him for his breaking the ranks. So Woolnough and Clarke, the No. 2s at the *Sun* and the *Mirror*, had turned this into a story of national disgrace, a pelting, a showering, a whole hail of yobbery – more mountains out of molehills . . . and though the incident was plainly childish enough (but what d'you want from Gazza? Wittgenstein? Mother Theresa?) Robson told me what the tabloids made of it was 'obnoxious'.

Robson told the press that day that the difference between England and others wasn't that their conferences were less business-like – though the FA's organisation on this front did, in fact, leave much to be desired – but that, 'The English press don't seem to be *with* the national team.'

On the morning of the game Barclay wrote that this was, 'balderdash'.

But it wasn't – because as Barclay knows well, there were journalists enough who'd not have minded England losing at all.

Instead, however, we'd won – and now it was time to air the paranoia.

Why was it so badly organised? Why were we kept waiting for an hour, in the boiling dusty heat? The Italians get let in – but when we get in, the players are on the coach already. And if they won't talk to us, that's the surest recipe for misquotes scratched together at second-hand, and bad reporting in general . . .

Robson and Kirton sat looking glum.

Gazza, they went on, gets four questions on a piece of paper from foreign journalists, and all he answers back – on a piece of paper – is, 'No, no, yes, no'.

Yet Völler talks to the press fifteen minutes after he's sent off. The Germans are available at twelve every day . . .

'We don't enjoy this, Bob. We'd like to share in the team's

success, and be part of it.'

They said the players couldn't have it both ways. They were being surly and childish – why can't they grow up, and be like footballers from the rest of the world?

Robson had a little run-in with Clarke then, angry about his writing up of the Parker incident. It just wasn't true, what he'd written.

'I write what I see.'

Another guy complained, 'I was nearly arrested last night, for trying to do my job – and that's ridiculous, after that game. It's not funny, being intimidated by the *carbonara*.'

Carbonara is, in fact, an egg and bacon sauce on your pasta – but let's not split hairs here . . .

'Why can't they be as professional as you, Bob? You do it, often when you don't want to. Why can't they?'

Robson sat staring, saying next to nothing. Kirton mumbled about the problem being endemic to the whole of English football.

Then it came to what they really wanted from all this – and what they needed, to be fair. After all, they've got jobs to keep . . .

Can we see David Platt?

Outside, a ruck of rotters thronged and waited . . . and John Jackson leant in and asked, smirking, 'Can the bad boys come in?'

When it got to the football, Robson said he'd given up on getting a result. Gazza'd gone negative five or ten minutes before the end, he was shattered, treading water . . .

When he kissed you, was he thanking you for your advice on free-kicks?

'I was complaining about his aftershave, that's for sure.'

Injuries were getting worse, with only four days to go to Cameroon. Barnes's groin, Butcher's knee . . . but Walker's leg was worst – he'd not be doing any training.

Cameroon, Robson said, looked very strong mentally and physically. I don't know how they're doing it, but they're doing it. Against Argentina with ten men, they were superb . . . though to be honest, I've not investigated them.'

Then they got what they wanted. Platt came on – a very

composed individual.

Was it a special feeling, to get his first for England?

'Now, yes – not yesterday. But you realise now, sitting in front of you lot.'

And I have this one little problem with some of these journalists sat here asking to be treated fairly, because they're running stories calling the players heroes now – THE GLORY BOYS.

And that problem is, do they expect people to forget how just the day before, they were calling these heroes a disgrace to the world?

Besides, whatever the football writers here might do, there's always the yobs at the top desks of the *Sun*, the *Mirror*, and the *Star* back in London, busy hatching more headlines ... as a guy from BBC Radio said, 'Put a bomb under that lot, and the problem would go away.'

Meantime, once the conference was over, what's happening round the Novotel, at the bar, in the foyer, in the garden? What's happening is players – Platt, Parker, Lineker, Wright – all talking to those journalists who they trust ...

So if you – or your paper – doesn't have that trust, *who's to blame*?

I asked Barclay if he thought the airing of grievances would make any difference – and he said no. The England organisation's approach, he said, was so *ill-mannered* ...

Rob Bonnet told Kirton in the foyer that they (the BBC) had film of the Parker incident – and that Parker had indeed been 'pelted' ... with one cup. But the film hadn't been shown, 'by the grace of God' – or in fact, by the 'grace' of the IRA's bombing of the Carlton Club, which had squeezed it out of the news.

Even so, one cup or a thousand, it hadn't looked good. Gazza'd thrown the cup hard ... but when does Gazza do anything softly? And it had been 'clearly designed' to stop Parker talking ... but is anything Gazza does, outside of a football pitch, ever clearly designed?

So what are we to make of all this?

First off, if Gazza wasn't the way he is, he wouldn't play the way he does.

But second, if you want him – or other players – to have the multilingual social grace of a Ruud Gullit, then you have to change the environment that produces them. Would Gazza be any different, after all, if he didn't happen to be a footballer? He'd still be English, wouldn't he? He'd still be Gazza – probably following his team, drinking beers on the Via Roma, and sleeping after games on Cagliari railway station . . .

So again, it comes back to parents and to schools – and in the case of players, crucially, to clubs – it comes down to all of us, in the end, having a responsibility for any shortcomings of ill discipline, of gracelessness, of stupidity . . .

And if we saw the light and changed things now, maybe in twenty years' time our players, our fans, our journalists, our tourists, our businessmen, our politicians, might all start coming through as paragons of cultured moderation and virtue.

But until then, we are what we are.

English.

And one of the best eight teams in the world with it, too.

Chris Waddle came into the foyer, looking pleased with life. He smiled and said, 'See – it's the system. I went where I wanted.'

And he said, yeah, Gazza's legs had gone by the end.

But then suddenly, I said, in the dying minutes, Gazza'd still made that run . . .

'Yeah, but it's funny, in football – you can always run again, when you get the ball. It's when you lose it it's hard.'

And he said he'd been dreading the penalties. 'I was on the list, wasn't I?'

After I'd left the Novotel at lunchtime, I'd gone to the press centre at the stadium, and got tickets for two quarter-finals – Italy–Ireland, and England–Cameroon – with no difficulty at all, in about sixty seconds flat. The place was empty, they were sweeping up and shutting down – it was another city for which Italia '90 was over.

And now in the evening (my train didn't leave until one in the morning) I went about sumptuous Bologna, and the town as a whole seemed normalised – de-Mondialised. All the well-dressed people moved smoothly through their well-preserved environment, everything was open and relaxed again – tension time was over.

A nutter in a pink sleeveless T-shirt, pink cords and pointy boots roamed down the Via dell'Indipendenza, and from there on to Via Rizzoli, with a huge boogie box which he set down whenever the mood took him and then danced, self-absorbed, juddering and tottering. People passing – all seeming so young, so good-looking – would do a few dance steps too, as they went by.

At the far end of Via Rizzoli from the Piazza Maggiore, the tall twin medieval towers, Garisenda and Asinelli, loomed up yellow-gold against the darkening sky. The nutter disappeared through the traffic, into the wide brick spaces of the Piazza. The African vendors in the archways packed away their stores of sunglasses in their paper slips; girls sat on the crossbars of their boyfriends' bikes; clean new buses rumbled past . . . bye bye, Bologna.

I went to collect my bag from my hotel's reception; the porter said Waddle had been *fortissimo*. But you know the England player who'd always pleased him most?

Glenn Hoddle.

20 As Good as Brazil

England–Cameroon

'No one on the African continent could remain indifferent to the battle waged by the Indomitable Lions against the English . . . Roger Milla and his comrades have permitted us to vibrate to their rhythm for three weeks, taking us on board with them for this wild adventure.'

– *Fraternité Matin*, Ivory Coast newspaper

I got into Naples about 8.30, went a stop too far on the metro, and found myself walking back towards Egg Castle along the bay in heat that was blazing already. The horizons shimmered under the bald disc of the sun; Vesuvius was a grey blur in the searing haze. I didn't feel too alert after another night sitting on a train – but you soon become alert enough on a Naples pavement. They're not really pavements at all, just extensions of the road – scooter lanes.

By the time I got to the Excelsior – one of the fancy hotels opposite the press centre – I was dripping so much sweat I must have looked like I'd fallen in the bay. What with that and the stink on me from the ride, it was no surprise when the snoot merchants at reception wanted my passport before they'd let me in. Five star, see – that's another country.

In Nottage's room I had a shower, an inordinately expensive breakfast, and left my ghastly laundry for the lucky washerfolk of the Excelsior – all on Italia '90. Cleaned and fed by the lady's Mondiale largesse, I felt like King of the Wanglers – but then, what's a few pairs of my crispy socks, in a budget of billions?

416

Nottage had a car booked to get her the sixty kilometres south to Vietri sul Mare and the England camp; but this being Naples, no show for a while. When the car did turn up we got in, the driver got in – then the driver got out and went away again.

The car was like a sauna. After ten minutes I was pouring new Niagaras of sweat again, and began seriously to consider cadging another shower – after all, there was bound to be time. The driver'd probably gone off to have a long and convivial meeting somewhere about the rules and regulations involved in turning the ignition key.

I watched a zillion scrambled lanes of Neapolitan traffic wedging fiercely past my window, while Nottage went off to locate the driver. She was away ten or fifteen minutes in turn, before the two of them reappeared with a basic outline of our problem – no petrol.

But authorisation to buy some filtered down through the system eventually, and we set off.

On the way, we learnt that our driver – another of the local military boys, pressganged into ferrying World Cup people (and wanglers) about – was actually from Bedford. His mother was Calabrian, his father Polish; so his surname was one of those glorious Polish names that are all c's and z's and y's and w's, the linguistic equivalent of a train wreck – while his christian name was Franco.

He had dual nationality, the relevant passports, and the choice of national services that came with them – two years in Poland, or one in Italy. Which would *you* take? And, he said, Italia '90 was great. One minute you're in the army – the next, you're driving the likes of Henry Kissinger about . . . or, on a bad day, the likes of me. Still, takes all sorts, Planet Football.

We whizzed down the terrifying death-track of the two-lane *autostrada* and Vietri sul Mare, when we slipped down the exit ramp, was a stupendous revelation of jagged green hills tumbling into the crystal sea.

The actual town – an Amalfi Coast resort just up from the port of Salerno, which you could see across the bay as a sprawling haze of brick and ochre – was scattered in higgledy-piggledy layers over the crests and ridges of the steep shore. The England base, the Hotel Raito, was just outside it, along a vertiginous lane snaking round the fierce contours of the slopes.

The hotel was a white wedding cake of a place, a jumbly tier of architectural confectionery stacked up against the hill over the sea. And the foyer seemed, indeed, to be one perpetual wedding reception – massive families roamed the terraces in their nuptial finery, every one of the women looking like she'd stepped straight from the starring role of some plush opera, resplendent in flounces and ruffles and drapes of silk and satin in bird of paradise colours, shiny black and dazzling scarlet, emerald green and searchlight yellow – under the brilliant blue sky, looking out over the brilliant blue sea, it was like walking on to a movie set.

The squad had the first floor sealed off to themselves, and were eating lunch. Nottage had given them a few copies of her novel, *The Italians*, which was due to be published in August – they'd located the naughty bits immediately, and were reading them out loud to each other, to her considerable embarrassment.

A TV-AM crew came up to do a Gazza interview. He cheerfully complied, and sat answering questions like he was on holiday – not in the last eight of the world at all.

Asked by the BBC back in Sardinia what image he wanted people to have of him, he'd just said, 'Meself.' Now, asked if he wasn't feeling some tension as the games grew bigger, he said, no – 'It's just eleven of us and eleven of them kicking a little white pill about.'

Underneath, of course, he cared with a raging determination as absolute as any member of the squad – but it never stopped him smiling. And stardom suits Gazza – he's a natural. Watching him talk with this happy insouciance, I realised what it is about his face that's so loveable: he looks like Michael Palin . . .

Asked about Cameroon, his grin cracked wide and he said, 'Well, they're tanned, aren't they? So they'll be used to the heat.'

Paul Gascoigne, like the QPR fans had said outside La Perla, might six or nine months ago have been an 'immature jerk' – and he could still be pesky enough on his day – but the way the atmosphere was sometimes, with the press and the pressure, that England camp would have been a dour place without him.

*

418

Forty-five per cent of the population of Belgium had watched the game in Bologna. The team went home heroes – they'd played superb football, and as Robson readily conceded, it was a cruel way to lose. Mark Wright – now being named by the Italians the best sweeper in the tournament, which was ironic, given that twelve days earlier England didn't have a sweeper – said they were the best side he'd ever played against.

Scifo was generally considered to have outshone Gascoigne; if his vicious curling shot from twenty-five yards after half-time had gone in, instead of hitting the post, it would have vied with Schillaci's goal against Uruguay – or his own against that team in Group E – as the goal of the World Cup. (Though Matthäus might want a word about that, after his pair against Yugoslavia.)

Still, England had the luck – and they'd been denied themselves, after all, when Barnes's goal was disallowed. And they also seemed now to have another, equally vital quality – what Barclay called, 'stickability'.

When it came to Cameroon, luck and stickability would be needed in very large measure . . .

The Irish, meanwhile, went to Rome and had an audience with the Pope (who, in his younger days in Poland, had been a goalkeeper himself). And they might all come from Glasgow or Liverpool or Wales or wherever – but every player was a Catholic, and the words of the two heroes from the Genoa shoot-out summed it up. Bonner said, 'It was a fantastic moment – one of the really special times in my life.'

And O'Leary said likewise, 'It was the most memorable morning of my life.'

After that, they cancelled training . . . and after four matches in fifteen days and a meeting with the Pope too, who's surprised?

There was, however, one Irishman who couldn't afford to relax. Frank Fahey, Dublin's Sports Minister, flew to Rome to raise urgently the issue of Ireland's ticket allocation. The Olympic Stadium took nearly 80,000 people, and there were nearly 20,000 Irish now marching merrily on the Eternal City – yet they'd been allotted a mere 2,000 tickets.

Before he left Dublin to see FIFA Fahey said, 'I won't come back without a good reason. We should have at least 15,000 tickets . . . in my three years as Sports Minister I've never come across such an organisation as this. We've been treated very badly.'

Another man in need of a little tension relief was Glen Kirton. He'd flown to Rome to collect the FA's share of the ticket receipts so far from FIFA – and been handed it over *in cash*. Flying on to Naples with a six-figure sum of banknotes in his briefcase had felt, he smiled wryly, just a touch unnerving . . .

Income for the teams that reached the Final would be, he estimated, in the region of £2,000,000 each.

As for the players, with four days to recover from their exhausting two hours against Belgium – a game played in a temperature at kick-off of thirty degrees, and in forty-five degrees of humidity – they badly needed some relaxation as well. Some of them went out shopping, while Gazza, Bull, Waddle, and McMahon got permission to go down to the beach – so Franco took them down there in Nottage's Croma.

Then Nottage had a mother hen panic attack – they'd be mobbed, they'd get lost, they'd get caught drinking by the rotters – so we rounded up Malvermi and went after them. But they were, or course, just fine – after all, they're big boys now – and they had a couple of police as unobtrusive minders in the background anyhow. So Nottage and Malvermi cleared off, fretting – and I stayed. I looked about and thought, unreal – beer, beach, sand, sea, sunbeds, parasols . . . it was like stepping off Planet Football into normality again – and I felt like I'd forgotten what that was all about.

The people on the beach didn't mob them, either. While we lay about talking, at first, the players did sign a few autographs – but then they asked politely if they could be left alone to have some peace and quiet, and the locals considerately complied.

Later though, with a beer or two inside us, and the great feeling of demob relaxation filtering through, a small but growing group of Italians did gather round. And between my Italian, and the competent French Waddle spoke with one of those who came to sit with us, we had the friendliest afternoon of Italia '90 – talking football in the shade by the sparkling sea, as time slipped away uncounted, just for once, by referees and officials.

The four players were unfailingly courteous; one of the Italians told me he just couldn't believe that there were, as he put it, 'four champions on our beach'. Italian players, he said, would never be so approachable.

One of them asked McMahon – somewhat nervously – about the Irish goal. Was it his fault? Macca just held up his hands and said yes.

Alarmed that he might have raised a touchy issue, the Italian then said, 'But the ball was difficult to control.'

'Sure,' said Macca. 'But it was still my fault, and there you go.' Honest, or what?

On the subject of a less honest player, when someone asked if it was true that Marseilles were going to buy Maradona, Waddle said grinning that if they did, he'd leave.

It was during this afternoon that I asked Waddle, as I'd asked Butcher at Is Molas, whether it wasn't hypocritical to be taking money from the tabloids, at the same time that the feeling towards them was one of such hostility.

He said for him it was particularly embarrassing, as he had a contract with the *Sun* to speak to Woolnough – who, after the way he'd written up the Parker-pelting incident as a national disgrace, was the last man on earth he wanted to talk to.

On the other hand, the way the contract worked meant he was obliged, if required, to do a given number of pieces, and he'd not done that many so far – so he was stuck with it. Still, the further they went in the tournament, the higher the fee – the money went into the pool – and in the end, getting it off the hated tabloids was great.

Because, he said, it wasn't like he was telling them Bobby Robson was a wanker, or he hated Steve McMahon's guts, or Paul Gascoigne was the ultimate prat of all time – he was just sitting there getting paid to say everything was fine and dandy, and it was great to be in the last eight in the world. It was money for jam . . .

One of the Italians asked if they liked it, in Italy – to which they replied sincerely that they did, very much. But obviously, all the same, they missed home more and more. Bully said he was calling twice a day now – but it wasn't doing him any good. And Waddle said, with an air of some desperation, that his sack was hanging down to his knees, he had balls like John Wayne's saddlebags . . . I didn't bother translating that.

Asked about Cameroon they said, obviously, they wanted frantically to win – not least for Pop Robson's sake back home. The idea of getting beat by Cameroon ... Waddle and Macca had a debate about that, then defined the possibility as a disaster, but not a disgrace. It would, they said, be a *personal* disaster – no disrespect, but it was unimaginable, basically. Even so, they'd not discuss a semi-final against the Germans in Turin – McMahon in particular was exceedingly emphatic.

'This is cup football – so don't anybody ever talk about *when* we beat Cameroon. *If* we beat Cameroon, we go to Turin and that's great – *if.*' Look what happened, after all, to Liverpool against Crystal Palace, in the FA Cup semi-final – they'd got beat 4–3 by a no-hope side that they'd beaten in the League earlier in the season by a thumping 9–0.

Waddle recalled his disbelief, when he'd heard that result – but that's cup football ... still, he said, 'If we get an early goal, they're there to be walloped.'

And they were working hard not to underestimate the Africans – but compared to the tension time before Belgium they were, now, unavoidably more relaxed and confident. Waddle said if we scored good and early, it surely had to be ours. 'They don't know how to come out, they're very defensive, very physical – ask 'em to *play*, and they're doomed.'

But as I'm sure he'd agree – just how wrong can you be?

Gazza, meanwhile, was working his way through a seemingly limitless repertoire of impressively executed tricks with cards and coins and glasses, to the huge delight of the Italians all about him. Fame and talent emptied the little beach, as evening came down; kids gathered around excited and smiling, to be charmed and entertained. A pair of cheery old women asked what numbers they wore, so as to know who to look out for come Sunday night.

So are these the surly and childish men of press legend? They sent a small crowd of people home very happy that evening – because for a few short hours they were free to be themselves, friendly and unassuming.

At the Ratio next morning, Robson gave a conference on the terrace. He said, naturally, we were always going to be apprehensive about Argentina in the quarter-finals in '86 – but this now was 'something we feel we can handle'.

They're a bit physical though, these African boys . . .

'Doesn't worry us. I hope they knock us down all evening. Especially round the box. And,' he added presciently, 'in it.'

England were now third favourite for the Cup, someone said.

'Doesn't matter. That's for the punter.'

Any message from the PM?

Silence. Kirton looked about, mock-searching for words of encouragement, or acknowledgement . . . other countries had kings and presidents going round with their teams – and we had Moynihan getting up and calling fans 'the effluent tendency'.

Any word from him, maybe?

'He says, why don't you play Bully?'

I went down to join the players by the pool. There were maggots in their freshly squeezed orange juice.

The eccentric Doc Crane floated past saying, 'There's nothing in maggots. I eat them out of cheese all the time.'

I had a word with Les Walker, the FA's amiable security consultant. While Moynihan was winning brownie points with his boss for slagging off England fans, Walker said that, actually, things were going rather well.

I raised what the good lady mayoress of Turin had just said, that she didn't want the English in her town if we got past Cameroon – that she wanted the semi-finals switched round.

He said she was *creating* a public order situation, with statements like that. 'It's crazy, saying it now. It gets the young Italians going – it's like giving them public backing. And it's very foolish to raise the stakes at this time. People should weigh more carefully what they say . . .'

In three weeks in Sardinia, Walker said, there'd been forty-four arrests. With 5,000 young men lying about, that was good – not wonderful, but good. And Walker said he reckoned Moynihan was being more positive now – that he and Thatcher had learnt from Stockholm.

The coverage of that, he said, had been unbelievable. 'So many things would be easier if it weren't for the fucking press, excuse my French. But if anyone ever writes a history of football violence, a lot of the blame can be sent their way – 'cos these villains, they do like their publicity.'

But overall we had a good conversation, and a hopeful one. He stressed, 'We *are* making progress. I know the fans don't trust anybody – not the police, the FA, nobody – but when you've been whipped enough you don't, do you? They think we don't care – but we do. And with luck and time, that'll get through.'

As to Naples, he said the drinks bans were a help – but you'd never stop a city of 2,500,000 people drinking, especially not Naples . . . and there was, in the end, very little trouble there. Naples might be, in the pithy language of the fan, 'a khazi' – but it was a friendly khazi. The city had a decent fan camp laid on, with decent supplies of food and water that fans could buy there – and, in general, it had decent people. Mad, but decent . . . so fans were treated better here than in any other town – with predictably happy results.

There was an accumulating undercurrent in the Raito not of tension, as there'd been in the Novotel, but of *constraint*. Players lay reading by the pool – the latest Ludlum was doing the rounds – while the manager sat for hours with Bob Harris on the main terrace above, doing their Italy diary thing. Outside, the tech men fussed round their computer-laden trailers, sending blips and gobs of news back to London. *Carabinieri* stood watching, in featureless incomprehension. Back in the lounge, other players watched a tape of the Belgium game.

On the beach the day before, one of the Italians had asked Bully what he'd thought of Enzo Scifo.

'Who's he?'

Time came round to go training at the San Paolo – motor-cade time again. There were two police cars, a police Land Cruiser, the team bus, an Italia '90 kit van, and me and Nottage in an Uno at the back. We snaked through Vietri, with laughing local boys in hot pursuit on two scooters and a trail bike – then we hit the *autostrada*, and roared up through the gears until the convoy was travelling at a truly terrifying pace.

It was pell-mell weaving mayhem all the way, sirens and

blue lights and terminal speed addiction – it made the Sardinian cavalcade look a model of decorum. Every car and van on the A3 tried to join us; all these maniacs jinking in and out between us, as we swarmed up the two lanes like a SWAT team *en route* to some serious bit of uproar. I tried to read some more of *The Italians* – but Nottage could have written chapter after chapter of orgies involving the entire Fiat workforce, it couldn't take my mind off what was, unquestionably, the scariest hour in a car I've ever had in my life.

Vesuvius loomed ahead in a terrible yellow sky ... and then, absurdly, the whole panoply of security this crazed charge was supposed to provide broke up anyway when we got to the toll gates to leave the A3 and get into Naples – because all the vehicles had to go through paying just like everyone else.

Once in Naples, we hit four lanes of total jam; so the sirens howled and we swerved and veered through, trying frantically to keep up with each other. It was like the dodgems, it was horrendous – people would be spilling alongside you not looking where they were going, and calling out to the driver to ask what it was all about. I mean, how can you have a conversation at fifty miles per hour through Neapolitan congestion? No problem ... when we hit tunnels, the lights and sirens became blinding and deafening. Everyone you went past joined in on their hooters, just to keep up with the spirit of the thing; a local police car tagged on to our tail for a while, but then opted out, deciding presumably that it was too dangerous by far.

Naples freeways clamber through and round each other in a jungle of concrete stilts; it makes Spaghetti Junction look like a village crossroads. The place is an enormous, perpetually unfinished sprawling mass; and as the disintegrated motorcade meshed through the hysteric surge and seethe of the traffic, I thought, this is Futuretown – all cities will be like this some day ... but no.

No place will ever be like Naples.

It was strange waking up in my *pensione* the next morning and realising I could take an extra hour's lie-in.

My head was all jumbled – the dreamland within and the

dreamland without merged in the hot light of dawn . . . I kept thinking, I've got to run out and ask how the Czechs did – but that was days ago . . . I'd been three days without football. In the second round now big holes were opening up in reality – when you weren't in a stadium you were half-life, mysteriously suspended . . . drained and drowsy, I didn't know where I was, or when I was, or how.

But a look in my wallet and out the window got me straight. Today was Italy–Ireland in Rome; and outside was Naples, with the Via Caracciolo mercifully quiet, early on a Saturday morning. The sheet-flat sea lay burning already, under the fierce climbing sun.

The training ground was at Cava dei Tirrena, the next little place along the road from Vietri. While Mike Kelly whacked in crosses across the keepers, and players signed autographs for the packs of local kids in the little stand, Robson announced that Butcher's knee was fine, that Walker was ninety-five per cent, and that Wright and Barnes had groin strains – which might, in the latter case, be serious.

Of his final preparations as the game approached Robson said, 'It's ninety degrees here. Everybody keeps in the shade from now on. We'll look at Cameroon. We'll rest. We'll tie Gascoigne to a chair . . .'

On the day of the Belgium game, Gazza'd played tennis in the sun for an hour – daft as a brush. But you forgive him, don't you? Robson did. When Danish journalists had asked in Sardinia if they could speak to him, Robson explained how things were with our tabloids, and how the players felt – then he said to them, 'But he's a lovely boy. Lovely boy. Really, a lovely boy.'

He said now, 'If there has to be an improvement it's in the front positions. We've looked impregnable at the back – one goal in four games, and that was a mistake. It's our forward play needs to be better – but we made quite a few good chances against Belgium. If Barnes's goal had stood . . .'

Would he play the sweeper system?

'I'll play eleven fit players.'

Were we pacing ourselves better than the Germans? Hadn't they gone off at a bit of a rush?

'I'd like to have beaten Holland 4–1.'

What we did have on Cameroon was experience. Nine of

the squad were involved against Argentina four years ago. And to win now . . .

'It means a lot to all of us. It'd give all of us a marvellous feeling – it'd be a very decent achievement. We've got to where I felt the team could get to, we're good enough to be in the last eight – after that, it's down to the draw. Last eight's not bad, it's acceptable – but it's not where we'd like to be. But then, when you think of Parker, Wright, Gascoigne, Platt, Walker – they've had no European experience, no education in that way, just English football every Saturday – so if we get to the last four, at this level, in this heat – it'll be a great tribute to the players.'

And after all his tribulations – and his vacillations too – it would also be an almighty tribute to Bobby Robson, in the last days of his time as the manager of England.

Because apart from when we won it at Wembley in 1966, England had now been to the World Cup nine times – and seven times we'd made the quarter-finals – and we'd never gone further . . .

We went up to Rome in the squad's Iveco van – me, Nottage, Malvermi, Stefano Arrica from Cagliari, David Bloomfield, and five others. It was a party ride; we had a cassette deck, two portable telephones, and a malfunctioning TV on which you could, occasionally, make out how Argentina were getting on against the Yugoslavs in Florence.

So how would Stojkovic make out against Maradona? It was difficult to tell – the Argentinians spent most of the game decorating his legs with stud marks. Yugoslavia were down to ten men after half an hour – but Argentina, their football still looking as iffy and rocky and rough as ever, couldn't make the advantage count. So it went to extra time, and then to penalties . . . and Stojkovic hit the bar.

With the score at 2–1 to Argentina, as we pulled into the car park of the Rome Hilton, Maradona went up to take his kick. Malvermi frantically put the hex on him, waving crossed fingers at the screen – and Maradona's strike was saved. Savicevic scored; Troglio hit the post . . . and surely Argentina were going home now.

But then Goycochea saved from Brnovic, Dezotti scored,

427

and Goycochea saved once more from Hadzibegic . . . so, 3–2 to Argentina and on they went, beating a superior side yet again. And these penalties – what a stupid, stupid, stupid bloody way to sort it out.

Ireland has a population of 3,500,000. It was estimated that 2,750,000 of them would watch the game . . . and that £12,000,000's worth of drink would get sold that night. Jack Charlton, also, was being touted to stand for President of the Republic.

But while Italy loved the Irish fans, their English manager was a sight less popular there than he was back in Ireland. His boorish demeanour at press conferences – 'I'm not going to discuss what I'm thinking about. It's nothing to do with you. I've no thoughts about anything' – reportedly caused some Italian journalists to walk out in disgust. It was a stark contrast to the long-suffering good manners of Bobby Robson . . .

And his team weren't too pretty either – but still, the happy little blocks of emerald green made themselves cheerfully heard, amid the sea of Italian flags. Frank Fahey had pulled more tickets from the FIFA hat . . .

OIRE-LAND! OIRE-LAND!

The stadium was a total sensory overload. On the monitors and the huge scoreboards, RAI's Italia '90 title sequence rolled – a football flying through Renaissance graphics towards the flag of the European Community. All the three-quarters of the great bowl that wasn't taken over by press stand was a roaring mass of red, white, and green, the colours waving in frenetic and lusting agitation. The naming of the new god Schillaci brought forth a boiling surge of apocalyptic noise – the place was beautiful, and terrible. There were so many flags it was almost as if there were no people, as if the crowd had become one vast frenzied sheet of the national colours . . . but then the game now was that basic, that deep – colour, song, mass, a ball, twenty-two men, and 80,000 yearning hearts. You got flooded with emotion in a stunned, heart-seized way; you bled tears, as if your body was being compressed by the sheer volume of all that noise and desire.

428

The Italians kicked off in a scattered dazzle of flashlights – and no question, they were pacier and more skilled – but it wasn't them who were attacking. The Irish fans refused to be out-shouted, and their team refused to be out-played. And in quarter-final country, after all, anything can happen ... the Irish were even passing it through the middle.

The Italians were hustled into error; ten minutes in, the Irish won a corner – and barely a long ball yet to be seen. But at the other end Donadoni put Schillaci through – his acceleration was ferocious – and when the Italians had the ball, the Irish 4–4–2 turned into 5–5. Get through *this* if you can ... and the Italians began to do so, Baggio and Schillaci flicking it between them like conjurors. So now the hoofing began after all, as if the moments of trying to play them properly had been a passing delusion, a brief madness of impossible ambition ...

Then McGrath crossed, Quinn towered up to head in, and Zenga flew across his goal at an astonishing altitude to save. The stadium screamed in agony; the steward behind me was whimpering, a girlish sound of horrified shock, the unthinkable right there before his eyes ... then Schillaci glanced wide of the Irish goal, and the same guy was banging his fists on the table in rage. Schillaci, by now, was getting seriously angry at the heavy-handed attentions of McCarthy ... and Maldini put a header on the top of the net; then Baggio went through and netted – but was called offside, to universal outrage.

And still the Irish made a game of it ... but the Italians were too good for them. Bonner parried a scorcher from Donadoni, and Schillaci was in like a knife to send the loose ball into the empty net. The roar of triumph burst out to echo round all Italy; Schillaci was on his knees in orgasmic abandon by the corner flag.

And that's how it ended: Italy 1, Ireland 0. Schillaci sliced an awkward shot high before half-time, and had a free-kick come down off the crossbar only inches from the line in the second half; but the Irish never gave up, and there were many nervous times for the Italians, as they were harried and pressed. And the Irish got seriously fed up with the referee. Knocking people about was their way – but it wasn't smiled on here.

Still, they played their hearts out, and kept getting it in the box – Baresi by the end looked worn and weary – and the roar at the end was a roar of relief.

So it was 1–0 to Italy – but the Irish won anyway. The way Bonner smiled at the final whistle said it all – like, hell, it was great crack anyway, lads, so let's all go have a beer and feel good about it.

So now Italy had to play Argentina . . .

To try and prevent the celebration of their arrival in the semi-finals turning the centre into a racetrack again, the police had blocked off a lot of roads – but the only effect of that was to jam everywhere else up twice over. The media bus ground to a halt – so I got out and walked.

Outside the Maxim in the Via Nazionale, two tractors went past waving flags, their hubcaps painted green, white, and red. Knots of Irish walked by, weary at the end of their long adventure – and Italians in their cars slowed up, leaning out to shake hands with them and tell them, well done and good luck.

And other Italians turned their minds now to the next game. Two boys went past me singing contentedly.

> *Mara – dona*
> *Vafan – culo*

Or in English: Maradona go fuck yourself.

Back in Naples, there was a heat haze so bad even the sea was smogged over – Vesuvius rose purple-domed from the bilious murk. I walked along the bay to Egg Castle, where a quick flip into the global press round-up on the Database revealed the ongoing anguish in Belgium.

THE GOALPOSTS WERE ENGLISH

WE SHOULD SHOOT OURSELVES

In the rather happier city of Yaounde, the *Cameroon Trib-une* announced blithely that Cameroon were the favourites . . . and the prospective TV audience was estimated at two-thirds of the country's population of ten million.

Their four suspensions had deprived them of first-choice players from both defence and midfield – a bit like England losing Wright, Walker, Platt and Gascoigne – but were they worried? English journalists coming back from their camp outside Brindisi reported a really happy bunch of guys.

Barclay said Roger Milla'd given more interviews this week than the entire England squad combined. 'I'm a footballer,' he'd said, 'it's my job to give interviews.'

In the Egg Castle café, we watched the Germans play the Czechs in Milan – the Germans pouring forward with ominous style and efficiency once more. Two Czechs got booked for their desperate attempts to stop them – and Matthäus scored from the spot, after Klinsmann was brought down on his way to goal.

Klinsmann was excellent again, and the Germans relentless. The Czechs were rarely much in it, especially after the absurd expulsion of Moravcik with twenty minutes left, just for kicking his boot in the air after it had come off in a tackle. And the Germans didn't score again – but 1–0 was good enough.

So they went through, as expected, to face the winners of England–Cameroon.

Michelle Lineker had interviewed Roger Milla too for ITV – he was, she said, a charming man. She'd tried to get him to do his hip wiggle – but he said no, he'd do it for her at the game when he scored.

She said, 'I'd rather you didn't.'

I asked if she fancied herself as a TV person; she said she'd probably like it, then laughed. 'I don't think Gary would be too impressed.'

She and Lineker had grown up together in Leicester; she said she always went to watch him play, she always had – apart from when she was at college and had a Saturday job at Habitat.

As time ticked away in the bowels of the San Paolo before the game, I asked if, watching, she worried about him getting injured.

She said, 'Sometimes I cringe in the stands when a defender's following through on him, but touch wood . . . maybe if I was

Bryan's wife I'd be on the edge of my seat, like, *don't touch him* . . . but you try not to think about it.'

She'd have to try pretty hard, with Cameroon on the case. After the game, Lineker would describe one incident in which he pushed away from the exceedingly large Benjamin Massing – and next thing he knows he's flat on the ground with his chest feeling like someone just ran a car into it. Massing stands over him and growls, 'Don't touch me . . .'

Inside, some decent soul had put up a large banner saying, 'Napoli Welcome English People'. But it was the Cameroon anthem that got all the cheers; and, let's face it, they might be hard – but they were vibrant and happy too, and the whole world was with them. Before the kick-off, they ran over to the England players and gave them each a Cameroon badge or favour of some sort, a nice gesture – 1–0 on the PR front already . . . but then, if you scored goals for PR, England needn't have bothered turning up.

The sky was a heavy slate-grey; the humidity was intense, it was really sticky in there – and the opening was slow, iffy and tentative. England had all the ball; Cameroon made two messy approaches, but went nowhere in particular. Parker was looking good down the right; Waddle once found him with a pass of pin-prick precision from our half, right to their corner flag. And Gazza went dancing through, picking up where he'd left off against Belgium . . . then, suddenly, a chaotic crumbling of the English defence – Pagal dummied, Walker went flying under both the man and the ball, and Omam Biyik was free. Shilton raced out to save, standing up well, but the rebound flew out to Mfede, who fired it right back – and it didn't go far wide. Jesus, guys . . . and they were in it now.

The England boys were singing, but the crowd was Cameroon's. Gazza still looked bright and dangerous in the middle, and you were thinking of him, Barnes, Waddle, c'mon, you can go past these people – and sometimes they did – but we seemed so poor at keeping possession. The Africans, on the other hand, were beginning to string passes nicely together. They got the ball back in our area, and it bobbed about alarmingly on heads, until another shot went over the top – but not before your heart was *boom boom* in your mouth again. And another shot – into the side netting, this time. Butcher was looking hard-pressed; he was lucky bringing one man down not to give away a penalty. And Wright came forward, and Gazza pushed up . . . but we lost it, we kept on losing it. Robson on RAI looked like he'd been swallowing cold fish whole every minute since Biyik first went through . . . and no question: Cameroon could win this.

Then Butcher sent Pearce away neatly down the left. He beat his man, sent in the cross, Platt arrived at speed – and he rose and just buried it, an unstoppably direct header whacked down under the keeper.

Twenty-five minutes gone: 1–0 to England.

> Let's all have a disco
> Let's all have a disco

And like Waddle said, Cameroon had to come out and play now . . . but the trouble was, they'd been doing that already – and rather better than us.

Lineker got fouled; Massing got booked. Gazza went tripping his little private light fantastic again, through three or four men packed on the edge of the box . . . and you thought, uh-oh – if they start clouting Gazza and he loses his rag, we're in trouble – he had one booking already . . . Makanaky pushed him over from behind, and he got up looking peeved.

Again, slowly but steadily, the rhythm of the game swung Cameroon's way. In the thirty-eighth minute Mfede put a cross on Libih's head – too close for comfort once more. Butcher kept getting it at the back – and kept giving it away. Then Maboang's clipped pass put Mfede through – and I sat there thinking, c'mon Gazza, stop talking to the ref . . . the crowd gave England's slips and blunders the bird, while Cameroon came forward again, Maboang going down, looking for a penalty – and now Roger Milla was warming up.

What a state to be in. 1–0 up over Cameroon – and worried witless about a 38-year-old guy with a shaved head in a red tracksuit top on the running track in Naples . . .

Barnes was invisible again. Not a good time to have a groin strain, OK – but if you're on, you're fit, *so do something* . . . or at least someone, for God's sake, do something somewhere – because it won't stay 1–0 much longer if you don't.

Half-time came. Gazza came off looking loopy, players getting round him to try and calm him down. Michelle said, 'He better cool his jets.'

I was in serious fear of how the second half might go. It started with Barnes off, Beardsley in his place, and Milla on too ... the talisman. And on it goes – who said these boys were clumsy?

And in the back of your mind lurked the knowledge that if we survived, then played like this in Turin – with the touch and pace the Germans had, they'd murder us.

Gazza tried to go through four again – but I couldn't write it down any more, the anxiety was too great. I sat with my gut turning over, my chest thumping ... a Lineker shot shaved over the top. But it was a rare burst in a game that, otherwise, seemed to be away up the other end the whole time. Unless maybe Gazza could get the thing by the neck – he skipped through two in the middle, passed out to Waddle, to Pearce, in came the cross ... and Platt went tumbling down over N'Kono.

No penalty. But we don't get penalties, do we? In ninety-one games under Bobby Robson, England had had just two ...

The ball came out – and Gazza brought Milla down at the other end. I howled, fool, fool, fool. Because Cameroon got the penalty all right – and fair enough too. So the sweeper Kunde strode up calmly, and wellied it past Shilton.

Sixty-one minutes gone: 1–1.

All right, England – what are you made of? 'Cos we can see hot and bright as a Naples day what Cameroon are made of ...

Makanaky streaked through, and fired a roaster that damn near put them ahead. Tiring, Mfede came off, and Ekeke came on. Then, two minutes later, a lovely chip from Milla – Ekeke on his fresh legs raced in and he *did* put them ahead.

Howls of pain, grief, and rage rose up from the English contingent; a glorious tumult of approbation poured down from 50,000 others. Cameroon were a pile of bodies by the corner flag: N'Kono ran the length of the pitch to join in.

Sixty-four minutes gone: 2–1 to Cameroon.

I'd agreed with Nigel Kennedy before kick-off that it'd be 3–1. But to who?

Butcher downed Milla, he gave him a real thump – there was two sides mixing it out there now. Pearce took out Makanaky, and got booked for it. The crowd was wild with outrage and support – and why not? The better side was winning ... Butcher came off, and Trevor Steven went on. Fifteen minutes left – sweeper and all, I'm sorry, but we were *all played out* here now.

I thought, God knows what the press'll do with this – and they must be dancing in Turin ... Wright came close to having a punch-up with N'Kono.

Then Gazza put Platt through – just a lovely pass, split 'em right open. Platt missed his shot by a bare few feet ... and Milla was getting angry with Wright now. Ten minutes left – the monitors were going weird in the press box, giving out this soughing, weeping noise like dying whales ... Omam Biyik all but scored *with a backheel*, for chrissakes. The ball bounced away off Peter Shilton – but how cheeky-classy can you get?

And this was *not* the unimaginable – Cameroon were just different class. My desk in the press box was falling apart, the metal coming away from the concrete beneath my feet; and out there on the field, England were falling apart too.

But still they attacked now, no one could say they weren't trying ... and Cameroon's rough methods let them down. Wright's flick sent Lineker through – he was pulling back his right foot to shoot – and Kunde sent him crashing over.

It was one penalty you could never in your life have failed to award. It was England's first since February '86 in Israel – and Bryan Robson took that one ...

Now, Gary Lineker put the ball on the spot.

Roy Collins said next to me, 'He'll miss it.'

But he rifled it in like he took penalties for England every day of the week. Butcher was up off the bench screaming at them to get back and restart, come on, *come on* ...

Eighty-two minutes gone: 2–2.

And this is football – pain, fear, effort, joy, relief ...

> *Let's all have a disco*
> *Let's all have a disco*

Wright and Milla clashed heads; Wright came off, spilling blood from a gaping head wound. England were down to ten men.

> *We shall not*
> *We shall not be moved*

Cameroon got two corners. Wright had one eye swelling

purple, he looked like he'd met Mike Tyson in a back alley. Parker went into the centre with Walker; Steven dropped to right back.

> *Walk on, walk on*
> *With hope in your heart*
> *And you'll never walk alone*
> *You'll never walk alone*

Extra time was looming again . . . Shilton made a blinding save low from Omam Biyik; Wright came back on, with a fat wad of bandage over the gash on his head.

> *We love you England, we do*
> *Oohh, England we love you*

The players' wives were waiting back home to set off to Turin. People had talked about going to some health club near Dubrovnik for a holiday once our story was all played out – there was a pool, a gym, tennis, lots to keep Gazza busy.

So where were they going? Dubrovnik? Or Turin?

Wright went out on the right wing; with a head wound like that, he was no use in defence. And here we go again, into extra time . . . I really didn't feel like I could handle another thirty minutes of this – it was one amazing game of football.

The men in green were stroking it about again, and burning forward. Shilton saved on the line from Omam Biyik again – he was the best thing on the park. He went past Platt, and whacked it narrowly over the bar; then Makanaky crossed, and the ball spent another agonising moment bobbling about in the face of England's goal. Another shot sliced high; they had all the ball, all the running . . . while us, knocked about and forced out of shape by Wright's injury, we just didn't look like a team any more. Gazza's socks were down; we looked knackered and busted, duff passes spraying and sliding about to nowhere and out. Unlike Milla – going one-two so deftly into the box again . . . so were we done for?

No. And it was, who else, Paul Gascoigne again – just as it had been with his fifty-yard run to win the free-kick against Belgium. Suddenly he just looked up, set off – and freed Lineker on goal with a pass of knife-edge precision. N'Kono and a defender sandwiched the striker without mercy, and down he went . . . so that after two penalties in ninety-

436

one games, now we'd had two more just in this game alone.

N'Kono was booked in the middle of Cameroon's protests; Lineker whacked the spot kick past him anyway.

A hundred and five minutes gone: 3–2 to England.

We're on the march with Bobby's army

Heads were high again. Gazza went through three, and put Lineker in once more; his shot scraped inches wide. Gazza's socks were back up.

There's only one Paul Gascoigne
Only one Paaw-uuhl Gaaaaa-uh-scoigne

And still Omam Biyik kept going; but Parker took it off his feet. He was outstanding, playing out of position now, but getting everywhere, to everything; and Trevor Steven likewise, having a right go at the exhausted Beardsley at one point, geeing everyone on. Lineker and Walker were both limping, Waddle looked half-dead; but Cameroon looked wiped out too. We'd taken all they could throw at us and, finally, with a ramshackle defence cobbled together *in extremis*, come bravely stumbling through. Stickability . . .

Not that it was over yet . . . a Milla strike went away for a corner; he got booked, and was furious about it too. Then Steven went through two, planted in a lovely cross, and Platt and Lineker took turns to miss the easiest chance either side had had all night . . . and the whistle went.

England 3, Cameroon 2.

Gazza embraced Robson. He told one of Cameroon's men, sure, he'd swap shirts – but first he had to go and thank the fans. So he went and gave them a little dance – while the Cameroon players did a lap of honour, under a torrent of applause and admiration.

Because it had been very, very good football – and most of it had been played by them. They were, these no-hope minnows, as good as Brazil.

On the beach a few days ago Macca and Waddle, refusing to predict victory, had said that in cup football the best side didn't always win. Well – tonight it didn't. Cameroon had nearly twice as many shots as we had . . . but, battered and misshapen, England had hung in there. Shilton had made the saves, the defenders had made the tackles – and going forward when we needed it we'd had the class, and the composure, to make three chances count.

The Africans, on the other hand, had finally fallen to their naivety. As they'd shown from the start against Argentina, they could do great things going forward – but at the back they could be clumsy and rough. And Gary Lineker's dangerous enough at any time – but give him two penalties, and you're asking to lose.

With three goals, he went third on the scoring chart. And who else was there with him in third spot? Klinsmann, Matthäus, and Völler . . . all waiting in Turin.

'Blood, sweat, and tears,' said the War Correspondent. 'Churchill would be proud of it.'

Too right. Top four in the world, whatever it takes – England were there.

To get there, we'd played in the third best game of the tournament in Bologna – and in the second best tonight. But the best was still to come – and would involve us yet again.

Bobby Robson: 'We're naturally delighted to be in the semifinal. It's unbelievable – well, it's not unbelievable, we believe it all right – but we got in a searching match there, and at one time I thought we were on the plane home tomorrow. They were a very good side, and they're unlucky to be out. We got in front with a good goal, a wonderful goal – but at the time they were the better team. And when they went ahead, they were the better team. But we pulled it out of the fire, I don't know how sometimes – we were depleted, Wright, Walker . . . but the two midfield players worked marvellously hard, they ran for miles. Lineker did well to get knocked down twice, and he showed great composure to get back up and score twice. Parker and Trevor Steven did very, very well, Parker jumped like a salmon, tackled like a ferret . . . Wright's got a very nasty cut, it needed stitches we couldn't give him – I think it's seven stitches now. We couldn't play him at the back – one more header, and it'd have been fifteen.'

You had to remember, he said, that they'd had an eight-day break; we'd only had five. And now there were three days to go to the semi-final. 'But we've just got to get up now, and get on.'

And the Germans?

'We can all but try – which we will. They're very impressive – but you've seen what we're made of. It'll be some game.'

Someone asked how England had won. Was it luck? Tradition?

'Tradition has nothing to do with it. I didn't see anyone called Tradition play out there today. We've got good players, players who fight. And yes, we had luck – you need luck. But it's about players and they had some good players too. They did to us what we thought we'd do to them. So we've been party to an outstanding game – and I applaud them. They were excellent. Everybody had a bit of sympathy for Cameroon today – I know I did. When I saw them beat Argentina I was delighted for them. They've done very well here, like Morocco four years ago, and Algeria eight years ago – African football has to be respected. *And they will get better.*'

It was great to see the man so happy. He was bubbling – and he couldn't resist a little dig, either. 'We were told to go home after the first match. Well – I believe the country back home is dancing in the streets now. It's quite marvellous – and we're so pleased for them at home. Because we're in the top four in the world in 1990 – we've lost once in twenty-four games – and now we're here with Argentina, Italy, and West Germany. And I'm proud of that – because I stand up for our football.'

A question went in to David Platt; he said, 'I can only echo what the manager's said.'

Robson grinned, 'That's him in the team next time.'

And what was Robson going to do now?

'I'm going to bed for two days. Then come and ask ... we're going to enjoy it. We'll worry about Germany in good time. They're very good, we know what confronts us – and they know what confronts them. So get your ticket, it'll be worth it.'

I'd had four hours sleep in Rome the night before – and now it was two in the morning again. When I got off the bus in town, I started to go to Egg Castle, I don't really know why – but halfway across the causeway my legs turned suddenly to jelly with fatigue, I found myself stumbling, and almost falling, as if drunk, or not entirely conscious. So after I'd propped myself up on the wall a little bit, I went back to my *pensione* instead.

In bed I found a strange, aching depression in the inside of my left elbow, as if muscle and bone inside me were beginning randomly to evaporate.

My room shared a feature with some of the rooms in the Maxim back in Rome – that if heavy traffic passed, the whole place shook, floor to ceiling. But it didn't seem so funny down here, in earthquake land – and there'd been a small shake not so far off from Naples in May, when I'd been in Florence. A couple of people had been killed.

I had a paranoia attack, and lay naked and spilling sweat like a fever victim – I had buckets of the stuff coming out all over my scalp, collecting in my eyebrows, gushing down my face, while my torso covered with a clammy sheen of attraction for the large and strangely silent Neapolitan mosquitoes . . . typical. The only thing that doesn't make an ear-splitting racket in the whole damn city is the thing that flies up and bites you . . . and the land of the last minute became, now, the land of slow minute after minute idling sleeplessly past in the small hours.

And I thought, the team are all right – it's bloody *me* that's all played out . . .

21   The Beautiful Game

England–West Germany

I was reduced to a badged creature, a being labelled in plastic by Olivetti, Fuji and Nedap, Holland. I was down to the bare essentials – notebook and pens, the day's *Corriere dello Sport*, a ticket for the game, a thinning book of Eurocheques, a passport, and a plane ticket home. I wandered Planet Football booking beds I barely slept in, or riding trains through the night into the arms ... of the Turin police.

I woke at 10.30 on 2 July on sweat-soaked sheets. At the station I checked my bag, then entered into the Neapolitan ticket-buying fray among groups of fans of inarticulate but considerable resource. The trains straight through to Turin were booked solid; the way to do it was get to Rome, and get a sleeper from there.

Three kinds of ticket were involved – the basic, the supplement, and the bed – and to get them, we span a merry-go-round whirl from the Green Disco booking room via two ticket counters to a room mysteriously located in a car park out the back, then back to the counters again ...

Word among the fans, as we gawped at vouchers and malfunctioning computers, was that Turin would not be safe. They planned, on arrival, to ride local trains right out again, staying away until the evening of the match. And what might happen after the game, well ...

In Rome between trains I propped up bars, and discovered the interesting new phenomenon that I was no longer able to tell how far away my feet were from my head.

There were still loads of Irish about, making holiday now – and they'd heard of a dozen Chelsea lads who were, they said 'meaning to kill someone'.

441

They said, 'It'll be war up there.'

Heysel town . . . from Rome to Turin was my third night journey in nine days – and the last thing you need at the end of days like these is to be, in effect, arrested.

I got into Turin station at about eight on the morning of the 3rd – and the police were out in force. All the English coming in were separated from other travellers, sat down on the platform, and surrounded. Then, when the others had gone, you were stood up and marched through the concourse, between lines of armed and baton-wielding police, towards buses waiting to take you to what they called a campsite.

I wanted to check my bag in left luggage, get breakfast, and find a hotel. I took out my press pass, and, indicating it to a bulky and unshaven policeman in shades and a beret, made to drop out of the group.

The guy grabbed me violently by the upper arm, and threw me back in with the other fans. He had his stick out, and looked happily ready to apply it. Exhausted and furious, I said in Italian – or snarled – 'I'm not an animal, and nor are these people either.'

Reluctantly, they let me go.

And these were the people who were 'protecting' us . . . Turin had hooligan psychosis like no one else.

Back in Naples, Maradona was talking up a storm. He tried to get the people of his adopted city to support him instead of the *Azzurri* on the grounds that 'the Italians are asking Neapolitans to be Italian for a day, yet for the other three hundred and sixty-four days in the year they forget all about Naples. The people do not forget this.'

Consultant Ambassador for Sports or not, these were neither wise nor careful words at all . . .

Toto Schillaci, meanwhile, was the man of Italy's moment. He was, inevitably, being widely compared to Paolo Rossi, whose goals won the World Cup for Italy in '82 – but the fiery-eyed little Sicilian would have none of it. 'Rossi was a champion,' he said. 'I am an ordinary, modest guy. I just hope I can go on doing what I've been doing.'

And Vialli announced, 'Yes, I am ready.'

At the England camp they said, after two two-hour matches

442

played hard and fast in sweltering humidity, that they weren't going to bother training any more. Lineker, in Naples, had lost near a stone in weight . . .

Robson of course would be playing a sweeper again in Turin with Völler and Klinsmann to deal with – though whether it would be Mark Wright, with seven stitches in his head, wasn't too certain. Paul Parker could do it, if Wright couldn't – and Trevor Steven would come in as the attacking full back.

But Wright said, 'I'm confident, I've played with cuts before. All I could do is make it worse, maybe . . . but I don't want to miss a World Cup semi-final.'

Robson also made the point that we finished against Cameroon – though we'd not meant to – playing 4–4–2. Once Wright's injury had 'fractured' the line-up 'it was our back four that got us out of trouble.'

Or maybe it was 4–2–4 . . . and you can bang on about sweepers and systems all you like because in theory, and on the pitch too, any opinion can work up to a point.

But you go beyond normal points, once you venture this far into the turbulent and pressured heart of Planet Football – and all that talk goes out the window. More than ever now, like Robson said, it's not about systems – it's about players.

It's not, in other words, about how you line them up on the park – it's about how much heart and gut they've got when they get out there.

And with heart and gut, with luck and stickability, England had gone further in the World Cup than they'd ever done on foreign soil before.

The Germans, however, had got this far, or further, five times in the previous six tournaments. In the last two, they'd been finalists – and getting past Holland and Czechoslovakia here in Italy, they hadn't needed any extra time either.

So they were favourites – but Franz Beckenbauer knew, more than anyone, how little that meant now. The German manager – ironically, the first and greatest attacking sweeper ever – said, 'England never give up. They are always difficult to beat. And,' he said, 'I have learnt to have a great regard for Gascoigne.'

*

England stayed in Asti, south-west of Turin. Coming back from there in the afternoon, I decided this time to go along with being herded – and, something that doubled the fans' anger and aggravation, to go along with being filmed and photographed by swarms of the world's media in the process.

With other fans, tired, intimidated, grumbling, and appalled, I got on the waiting bus outside the station. We were escorted away by a vanload of police, with lights flashing and sirens blaring . . . truly, it was unbelievable. To follow England here meant submitting to the effective deprivation of your liberty – it meant being treated like some sort of prisoner of war, on the most limited of paroles.

When you got off the bus you were bodysearched, and your baggage minutely scoured, item by item. There was no courtesy involved, either. They tossed your belongings about – but it was you who had to put them back together again afterwards.

The campsite was just a ragged pitch in a weedy, crumbly old stadium. There was nothing there, no refreshments, no nothing. And you could leave, in theory – but having given you little option but to go there in the first place, they then gave you no help to get away. So the fans sat about, disgruntled and disgusted – and there was more than just the physical treatment they were getting to disgust them, too.

Between those who'd followed the team all the way from Cagliari, those who'd joined in along the way, and those coming over now for the semi-final, there were at least 10,000, possibly 15,000 expected in Turin. Yet the initial allocation of tickets to the FA was less than 1,000.

Kelly, Kirton, Bloomfield, Nottage, Les Walker, Pat Smith and Brian Scott – all these people had been out busting a gut on the phone and round Turin, trying to extract more tickets from FIFA, from the COL, from '90 Tour, from somebody. And while they did this, a steadily more angry crowd of several hundred fans gathered in frustrated and urgent desperation before a pathetic little booth in a fence, with three little grilles – but no tickets to pass through them.

Behind the fence, on the driveway of a sports hall, Scott, Walker and others talked hurriedly on their portable phones. It was getting late in the afternoon – and many of those waiting there, in the crush before the booth, had been waiting since ten in the morning, or earlier.

The FSA's Steve Beauchampe was in amongst them, trying to calm people down, trying to get them to move back – which, in the hot and short-tempered press of bodies, involved (as with Tummin in Cagliari) a degree of physical courage. The fans wanted information but, basically, there was none – the FA would have liked some too.

But the FA with its history, and the fans with theirs, didn't make for any likelihood of communication, at this flashpoint, being received with faith or trust – so it was here that the role of the FSA, as a conduit of information and assistance, could vividly and visibly be seen. Because the FA were helpless on one side of a fence, and the fans were enraged on the other . . .

Word did come, eventually, that more tickets were on their way – and Beauchampe went among the fans, trying to pass that word on.

Fans who don't believe the FA does anything for them might note, however, how these thousand or so new tickets were obtained. They were £33 tickets – yet the FA was obliged by the official Italian agency in Turin not only to pay £65 per ticket but also, incredibly, to pay cash up front. Here we were, in the semi-finals of the World Cup, and what were we, not credit-worthy?

Besides being pretty powerfully insulting, this also involved a bothersome and – with those fans waiting through the angry afternoon – potentially explosive extra wasting of time. Because rounding up £65,000 from an Italian bank isn't the quickest or simplest of matters . . .

The mark-up was justified with the claim that the tickets came with some meaningless 'package', a 'World Cup kit' – bag, hat, T-shirt, that sort of stuff. But no one either got or wanted any of this junk – and the FA, naturally, sold the tickets at face value to the waiting fans anyway. In other words, they subsidised them to the tune of a loss, in one afternoon, in excess of £30,000 . . . it was a disgraceful farce. I mean, come on, Italia '90 – it was just plain *greedy*.

And in terms of fan control, it was also quite phenomenally stupid.

Herding them out to this dismal park with siren-wailing escorts, like unwanted criminals, was bad enough. But then making it so hard for them to get tickets too was just asking to turn them into the maddened and riotous beings you so feared in the first place . . .

445

Add in the spreading word, Rumourtown-style, that the Germans had 40,000 tickets – and what you had here was big combustibility.

'They want £75, £80 for a ticket on the street out there. I've been here a month. Who's got £80?'

People pressed against the fence in rage and need. When the new tickets arrived, Pat Smith and her helpers sold them from the booth as quick as they could; rough hands fluttered hungrily through the grilles with sterling and lire and Travel Club IDs . . . it was a refugee scene. On this parched and dusty back lot of a place, the poor and the abused clamoured for access to the stadium, as people fleeing a war clamour for visas at transit points and customs posts . . . but then, what was a ticket, after all, but a pass through the gates of heaven?

So this was, really, just one hell of a depressing day – and when Argentina played Italy, it got worse.

Back in town, Malvermi lifted me an invite from the COL to a big mayoral bunfight.

The Mayor of the City of Turin
Mrs Maria Magnani Noya

the Alderman for Sport and Tourism
Mr Lorenzo Matteoli

and the President of Circolo della Stampa of Turin
Mr Bruno Perucca

have great pleasure in inviting you
to enjoy the 'World Cup Menu'

Any old irony . . . in the first place the lady, after all, didn't want us here anyway. And in the second, here we were getting wined and dined with the quality – while outside there was a two and a half day booze ban that the lady probably signed off herself. And those poor buggers at the camp down the road could have used a canapé or two, let me tell you.

Before dinner there was sparkling wine and Italy–Argentina. And at half-time, there was the biggest Cheesewoman yet, a gigantic, a positively Amazonian blonde in her blazing yellow suit, wielding a cheesecutter with fierce and muscular digs

446

into a wheel of Grana Padano two feet or more across – so what did they have waiting in Rome? The Colossus of Rhodes?

And would Italy get there? They had been, with the Germans, one of the tournament's two outstanding teams – while Argentina had been scrappy, dirty, dishonest, and lucky . . . even their progress this far was bemusing to many observers, who searched in vain for a word to explain it – all they could manage was 'gritty'.

But while we watched the game, with our wine and our Cheesewoman, on TVs parked on stands round the gardens of the press club, it became slowly apparent that there was more to Argentina than we'd seen so far – and less to Italy.

In sum, Argentina played their one half-decent game of Italia '90 – while Italy blew up. Home advantage had always had the look about it of a double-edged sword – and the frantic weight of expectation now proved too heavy on their shoulders.

Moreover, as a Brazilian later put it to me, 'Bilardo put Vicini in his pocket.' The Argentine camp may have been raddled with paranoia – Maradona all but came to blows with the police at their base, when his brother was stopped and questioned over a car he was driving – but holding it together at the helm, they still had one of the world's great managers.

Vicini, on the other hand, made unaccountable decisions. First, he played Vialli, and left Baggio on the bench. Yet what had Vialli done? He'd missed a penalty against the USA, and not played since . . . then, when he did send on Baggio, he took off Giannini to make room for him – and gutted the Italian midfield. Argentina made the most of it.

They attacked from the off – in both senses of the word. There were five free-kicks in the first three minutes . . . and Italy didn't put a move together until seventeen minutes were gone. But then, what a move – Schillaci started it, De Napoli and Vialli flicked it on, Giannini took it into the area, Vialli volleyed, and Schillaci, finishing what he'd begun, shot in the rebound with his now familiar appetite.

So Schillaci had five goals in six games – he joined Skuhravy at the top of the table. And with Italy ahead, a look of complacent contentment settled on the quality supping at their trough in Turin.

But in Naples Italy didn't seem to know what to do – to sit

on the lead, or to push up and maximise it? No such dilemma for Argentina – it was attack, or go home – and in the second half especially, they did.

Fifty minutes after Italy had scored, Caniggia brought it level with one fine-tuned glance of his flying blond head.

Tempers rose – in went the fouls, out came the yellow cards – until in extra time, Giusti was sent off for bundling over Baggio. But Italy were too tired and shapeless to use the advantage; it was Argentina who came nearer to scoring, before the two hours ended – then the semi-final became the third game of the tournament to go down to the lottery of penalties.

And Goycochea worked a miracle again. He saved first from Donadoni, then from Serena – and Italy were out. It was a national disaster, but one entirely of their own making.

Still, even for non-Italians, it was depressing as hell. A beauty of a team had failed, and an ugly dog of a team gone through.

It did mean, however, that for the English and the Germans, the path to the Cup was clear – because for whoever should win in Turin, the prospect of Argentina waiting in Rome was tantalising. The Germans would surely let no nervousness hinder them as the Italians had done – and if they played in Rome as they were able to, they'd sweep the blue and white away like a broom does dust.

As for the English, of course, a Final with Argentina was an opportunity urgently, grimly, passionately to be desired – we owed them one for the hand of God.

To make it more appetising still, Argentina had paid a heavy price for the methods that took them to the Final. They'd collected more bookings than Cameroon, twenty in six games – and they'd be deprived, in Rome, of the services of four suspended players. Without Giusti, Batista, Olarticoechea and, most damagingly, Caniggia, what hope could they realistically have?

Moreover, Maradona by now was so kicked and crocked, he was virtually playing on one leg ... there was, in Turin, everything to play for.

The quality in their fine clothes sat eating glumly by the

clubhouse pool. It was, of course, a splendid spread – but the best buffet in the world couldn't dispel the gloom of defeat. I sat with the War Correspondent – and then the news of trouble came in.

Pausing only to pick up our freebie promotional cookbooks, we hared out to get a ride with other Italian journalists into the centre of town.

Over at the campsite, five hundred Italians had gathered round the English; some of these attacked, throwing bottles and stones. The police went in with tear gas.

In the centre, meanwhile, it was the same old bloody thing – except this was Turin, and it was bigger and nastier. Perhaps a thousand very pissed off *ragazzi* were gathered along the Corso Vittorio Emanuele II, and around the front of the station; they chanted that Maradona and the English, or both, could *vafanculo* – and they chanted that they wanted to break English heads, fronting up in an eddying mob against the usual mix of police and *carabinieri*.

The law was also spiced here with some really evil-looking bods in plain clothes ... and what a stupid and meaningless scene it was. There were few English inside the station to be protected; they were either staying wisely elsewhere – or herded out at the campsite, getting bricked and gassed. So it looked like the police, here, would be whacking their own. The eerie lights turned, the boys surged and shouted – and we watched, in weary dismay.

One Englishman in his thirties told me the next morning how he'd been locked by the owner into the restaurant where he'd been eating with his friends – while a group of Juve boys outside pressed their faces to the windows, and ran knives significantly across their throats . . .

And among the journalists, the feeling and the tone was just plain sick and tired – four weeks now of these witless, mock-machismo stand-offs. As one of them put it, he'd be filing City Of Fear, Part 695. I broke my rule of silence, and did an interview for someone from BBC Radio about how the English in the main had behaved well – and the Italians likewise – but how still, everywhere we went, this dumb shit kept landing in our faces, this desire to confront our reputation . . . I expressed my anger about the ticket situation, and the heaviness of the policing, and the provocative crap in the papers.

449

The guy who interviewed me described arriving at Naples airport with his radio gear, and a taxi driver spotting him and saying, as he offered his open car door, 'Hooligan camp?'

And he described, mimicking the thwacking down of truncheons, the way the English were greeted at the station in Turin.

'Get on bus – *boing* – get on bus – *boing* . . .'

At the stadium on 4 July, Italia '90 News on the Database had gone into a tailspin, presenting helpful reports dated 2 June about the Romanians training under the olive trees at Telesa Terme . . . confusion and time slippage reigned, as the end drew nigh. The press centre was a jammed morass. The telly said the temperature was thirty degrees, the scoreboards said twenty-seven – we didn't even know how hot it was any more.

Outside in the parking lots there was not a note of music, not a jot of the party feeling there'd been when Brazil had played here – it felt sullen and tense. Tickets changed hands everywhere, on car bonnets, at stalls, even at the entrance gates in full view of stewards and police – of whom there were 2,000. The fans were searched again. I shook my head and stared, feeling the world gone quite beyond belief or reality, at the sight of an English boy being ordered to unpick the lettering that named his club from his Union Jack . . . supporting England, for the young and the broke, looked set fair to be the ultimate joyless rip-off.

Yet in the end, it wasn't. Supporting England, in the end, proved against all the odds to have been worthwhile, thanks to the one central thing that mattered more than all the rest – the team and the players.

Because they, and the Germans, were about to give us the best game of Italia '90.

Inside I wondered, where the much-rumoured 40,000 Germans were. Large sweeps of the lower tier, and great gap-toothed chunks of the upper two, were empty . . . ticketing incompetence and greed, combined with the hooligan psychosis, had made this semi-final an absurdly under-attended event. But then, what was new? The stands had had gaping vacancies in them in many of the twelve cities all down the track – the only thing that was new here was that the number of helicopters chattering low overhead had increased. But never mind – those who'd endured were rewarded.

The English singing was loud and proud, out-noising the Germans. And the players stormed into the game, as if these opponents were no more to be feared than the UAE. Mark Wright was playing – could you ever have stopped him? – and Peter Beardsley was in the hole between Gary Lineker and midfield, with John Barnes's sad injury finally denying him any last hope of redemption. Otherwise, it was the new England we were coming to believe in – with Terry Butcher sweeping, Des Walker alongside Wright in front of him, Paul Parker and Stuart Pearce outside, and David Platt, Chrissie Waddle, and Paul Gascoigne to run the middle.

So it was hot, the sky was bright blue, the Alps looked ravishing to the north – and we were away. The fans roared out 'God Save The Queen' – and I thought, there may be some ugly and stupid dimwits among them, and, no doubt, a few scum and villains too – but *they are England*.

They get no party, just antagonism; they get no joy, just searches and batons; but they get their football – and here and now, that'd do.

England won the first corner straight off in the first minute, and from the clearance coming out, Gazza fired in a rocket of a volley that looked to be just curving wide – but Illgner lunged to push it away anyhow, and we had a second corner. And then we had a third . . . our football was surging and relentless – we were playing like the Germans did, and the Germans didn't like it. Bruises and knocks, sore joints and worn limbs, forget it – there's no end to the magic hope can work. Wright had Klinsmann under wraps; Waddle released Parker, Beardsley went through once, and then again . . . Hässler took the Germans' first serious strike, and it deflected away from Pearce for their first corner – but Butcher towered up, and headed away. Then Wright picked a through ball off Klinsmann's feet; the German looked angry and rattled. You could feel their pace, their threat – but still we had them, and the first phase was all England.

No question: England could win this.

The press box was buzzing. Gazza tangled with Brehme; he got another shot in, then broke to the left corner, won a free kick . . .

Let's all have a disco
Let's all have a disco

It was more than a disco, it was history – Butcher of all people played a nifty backheel; Gazza nutmegged Matthäus ... half an hour gone, and it was England, England. The Germans just couldn't find their way, they were trying so hard, but they were pressured so much. You'd never know Wright had a head wound – while Beardsley was running and running, he went through, gave it to Waddle, the cross shaved off Lineker's head, and just past Platt. Gazza worked another opening, and Pearce fired wide. Then Walker ran back with Völler, who he'd been marking off the park, and the German striker fell – he lay wounded on the sideline, and they were down to ten men.

Waddle showed a touch of magic now, when a free kick had been blown against Platt – he saw Illgner off his line, and chipped him with power from thirty-five yards anyway. The German keeper scrambled back to tip it against the bar – it wouldn't have counted, but that didn't matter – scaring them like that did no harm ...

It was wonderful football; we were first to everything, and Gazza made Matthäus look ordinary. But Riedle came on for Völler – and the Germans were forcing their way back in. Shilton saved low from Thon; I felt my chest constricting under the terrible tension of the beautiful game, in this beautiful cavern of a stadium ... as Shilton pulled off a magnificent save from an Augenthaler free-kick, fingers just stretching to edge over for a corner. Beardsley was back tackling; and the Germans were playing fine football themselves now, pass and run, pass and run – another corner, another proud leap from Butcher – and suddenly it was all Germany.

Who says our defenders can't play? They were playing now – they bloody had to. Gazza and Brehme tussled again, on the brink of half-time ... but came out of it smiling, Gazza ruffling Brehme's hair. As the whistle blew, I felt like I breathed out for the first time in forty-five minutes.

The second half began – and twenty-two men picked up where they'd left off. Beardsley released Pearce, and we won a corner; it came out, Thon broke upfield, and Shilton saved. The German attacks were looking faster and more coherent, they seemed fresher – Matthäus was coming ominously to the boil.

Pearce downed Hässler for a free kick on the edge of the box; the English wall formed up, Paul Parker a yard or two wide on the right-hand end of it. Hässler touched the kick square, Brehme drove the ball in and, as Parker advanced, the ball ballooned up off him, the deflection looping beyond the reach of desperately backpedalling Shilton – and into the net.

Shilton sat in his goal in disbelief. Parker had done the right thing, going to charge down the kick, and it was hideously unlucky – no deflection, I think, would have meant no goal – but then it was, to be fair, with the run of play at this stage.

So, fifty-nine minutes gone: 1–0 to Germany.

Platt ran back to pick up the ball, and get us going again – and the England fans roared their deafening support. It was time to ask what we were made of again.

And they dredged up the energy they needed, from somewhere where normal people would have none. A Gazza free-kick glanced just wide off Pearce; Illgner saved from Wright. Then Gazza put Waddle through, with a gem of a ball; and a surging run by Pearce ended in a clattering sandwich on the edge of the area, for another free-kick.

Twenty minutes left. Butcher came off, Trevor Steven came on – and had a shot straight off. Nice first touch ... we'd closed in to four across the back, with Steven going up wide on the right. It was all or nothing, do or die, burning deck, into the breach ... 'God Save The Queen' rang out around the ground.

Brehme went down, and the Germans kicked the ball out of play so they could see to him. From the throw-in, Pearce gave it back to them; they in turn kicked it up for Shilton to restart, all fair and evens – it was that sort of game.

It was, basically, the real World Cup Final ... with only ten minutes left, and the Germans one ahead.

Parker fired over a long cross. Kohler failed to deal with it; Lineker caught it neatly on his thigh as he ran in at full speed and, harried and bumped, swept voraciously past the flailing Augenthaler, past Berthold too – and then fired, with immaculate precision.

England were level.

Lineker looked frenzied, he looked mad with joy, eyes

bulging wide and staring all around as he sprinted away, fists and teeth clenched . . . and the support of the boys singing in the stands was fantastic. They'd blundered and shoved and banged and barged their single-minded and sleepless way round Italy for a month – and still they were there.

So screw the venom-headed minority – and screw it if even those who don't mean harm can be charmless and boorish and stupid. Because the good and the dim together, they'd been spat at and shot at and shat on all round, they'd been sat down and stood up, they'd been herded over here and marched over there – and still they were singing – because this was their time, in this great bowl of light beneath the Alps, in this raging cavern brought to life against all the odds, against all adversity, by the England football team.

> *When you walk through the storm*
> *Hold your head up high*
> *And don't be afraid of the dark*
> *At the end of the storm*
> *There's a golden sky*
> *And the sweet silver sound of the lark*
>
> *Walk on, walk on*
> *With hope in your heart*
> *And you'll never walk alone*
> *You'll never walk alone*

Ninety minutes: 1–1. And who goes to applaud them before the restart? Gazza . . .

Walker saved us with a flying last-gasp tackle off Klinsmann's feet; I had to stand, I couldn't take it sitting down any more. Now Shilton saved us, a reflex reaction to Klinsmann again. It was all Germany, attacking, attacking . . . Klinsmann went clear through yet again – and missed by inches.

At the other end, another razor-sharp pass from Gazza went to Beardsley – who lost it. Bully and Macca were warming up on the track; and then Gazza was booked, for the most innocuous of fouls. He'd gone for the ball – but Berthold made a meal of it, diving and rolling; and the German bench were up in noisy protest, making the foul look worse than it was . . . it was Gazza's second booking, he was out of the next game – and the next game might well be the World Cup Final.

454

He looked mental, torn up, cut to the heart and the knife twisted hard. Lineker was tapping a finger to his temple, warning the bench that Gazza might have lost it – it was the harshest injustice.

> *We love you Gascoigne, we do*
> *We love you Gascoigne, we do*
> *We love you Gascoigne, we do*
> *Ohhhh, Gascoigne we love you*

He didn't lose it – he threw himself in more fiercely than ever. And Chrissie Waddle hit the post . . . Jesus. You couldn't bear to watch it – and you couldn't tear your eyes from it.

Fifteen minutes left; turn-round time. But the song was still the same.

> *There's only one Paul Gascoigne*
> *Only one Paaw-uuhl Gaaaaa-uh-scoigne*

Every piece of me was frozen bar the heart that beat and the hand that wrote.

Brehme crunched Gazza, ugly and hard. The English fans rose in a tumult of outrage. Brehme was booked instantly – and Gazza got up, and shook the German's hand.

He'd been threatening to grow up all this time – but there was the moment, booked himself and heartbroken, that he proved that he'd done so. Six months ago he'd have hit him, and got himself sent off.

So whatever happened here now, England could go home knowing that we had on our hands a player who'd come of age, at twenty-three promising to be one of the world's greatest in the 1990s . . . and from the free kick, Platt put the ball in the net.

Offside, offside . . . it was disallowed. No matter – Beardsley went through two, and came within an ace of releasing Lineker. It was all England now, forward, forward, finding speed to run and strength to play in their sixth game in twenty-four days, their third extra time in nine days – it was a performance of matchless pride. The fans sounded like they filled the whole stadium.

And we deserved to win this. We'd fought hard, and our hearts were big. Who says they were better than us?

But then, it takes two to make a great game of football – and what I've just written could just as well be written of the Germans.

Shilton saved from Thon; a shot from Brehme went rocketing close over the crossbar; Steven went searing through on a lovely lay-off from Beardsley, and crossed to win a corner; then at the other end, Buchwald hit the post just as Waddle had. So no one deserved to lose here. But after two hours, we'd battled to a standstill – and no one did lose. The score was 1–1 – and we had to settle it on a duckshoot instead.

Applause rang out round the whole of the magnificent arena, pure and wholly merited by both sides. In the centre circle, players from both sides shook hands, put arms round each others' shoulders, and exchanged congratulations on the game. Gazza was crying; Robson took time out from organising the penalty takers to console him. And in London, Bryan Robson said from the heart, 'They should take the camera off him.'

In the VIP box Kissinger watched with Agnelli, the latter wearing the fattest kipper tie on earth.

And the keepers went to the goal; the players sat down in the centre circle.

> There's only one Peter Shilton
> Only one Peter Shilton

But he didn't make any saves – though he did go the right way all four times. And thirty million English people watched this game; we all know the cruel way it ended.

The penalty shootout's a heartless piece of ersatz TV drama, irrelevant to the game of football ... ah well. Lineker, Beardsley, and Platt all scored; Brehme, Matthäus, and Riedle ditto. Then Pearce fired it straight at Illgner, who, diving left, saved with his legs. Beardsley ran to Pearce as he walked back, and Lineker – but what could you say to him? And Thon scored; then Waddle fired his kick over the top. 4–3 to the Germans.

Nightmare. The black pit of loss opened wide ... and the sound system immediately blared out, 'All English fans are kindly requested to remain in your seats for fifteen minutes. You will then be escorted by security to where your buses are located. All English fans ...

1984. I mean, how dare they, *how dare they*? It was staggeringly, brutishly insensitive. And there were people with little flags forming up a silly bloody Ciao on the pitch in some naff Turin closing ceremony . . . a decent period of silence and respect was called for here. And look what we got instead.

Gazza was crying in the big arms of Terry Butcher. And I was crying too; from a tight chest and an aching head, the tears had been threatening since they sang, 'You'll Never Walk Alone'. Robson, putting the bravest imaginable face on it, gulped down his sorrow, and subjected himself to the instant interview. He said, 'This is a cruel situation, but we just have to accept it. We played a big part in the tournament.'

We certainly did, sir. We certainly did.

A Scottish journalist going out, I don't know who he was, saw me crying, staring out blindly over the huge emptying stands. He said, with the softest kindness, 'It's hard for you. It's very hard.'

And it was. Our story was all played out – but how bravely, in the end. How very bravely.

I went down cavernous corridors to where a scrum of press and TV crews waited to be let into the interview area. The COL limit was twenty-five each from England and Germany, twenty Italians, and ten agency men. So what Ecuadorian TV was doing down there I don't know . . . but that's Planet Football for you; a jostling ruck, getting sweaty under the hot lights of camera crews.

The War Correspondent pushed through, and we shook hands. He just said, 'The best, the best' – it seemed all he could say, he seemed wordless – and though right then I felt the worst, the worst, I knew also that what he said was right.

Because football is Pele's beautiful game – and with the Germans we'd played it beautifully – with strength and speed, with courage and skill, with honesty and honour.

The two team buses waited in a dim-lit and cavernous space of concrete. The bulk of the press went, naturally and mercifully, to the Germans. Macca asked me to translate a crucial request to the bus driver: 'Where are the beers?' And out came the Becks from the cold box – I hope they drank a fountain of the stuff.

Beardsley came through, silent, looking cut in half. And as Gazza came then, head still shaking at the ground in anguished disbelief, just wanting to get on the bus, Rob Bonnet shovelled the mike in his face as he got on the steps.

He asked, 'Whatareyourfeelingsonthegame?'

What a stupid question. And what an awful bloody job, for an intelligent man to have to ask it, at this time of all times.

The bustle and squeeze milled about, question and answer echoing dully off the bare dark walls. There was a mob around Platt. Butcher came, smiled, and we talked quietly for a moment, standing a bit apart. It was like, on the bench, he'd had time to work it out – he was thirty-one, it was his third World Cup. And he knew – though it hurt awful to be out in this way, at this stage – that it was still the best, the best.

He joked, 'Every time they bring me off we score. Maybe they should have brought me off earlier.'

Seventy-seven caps; an almighty contribution. And six weeks later, as the new season started with Rangers favourites to win the Scottish League again, Terry Butcher announced his retirement from international football.

Les Walker said, 'It was a good result for English football, and a good tournament for English fans. They've been good as gold in there. I think it's the start of a new era – I really do.'

Robson arrived – the man who'd brought the old era to an end that few had imagined might be so magnificent – and one crew after another was on him, from England and Brazil, from Germany and Ecuador. And even here, now – with the bus waiting, and his highest hopes so cruelly stolen – still he talked, and signed autographs for people from the other side of the world. He said, 'It's the biggest match we've played in twenty-four years.'

Gary Lineker ended one last interview backing away, looking just bleakly, desperately sad. He'd been once to the quarters, once to the semis – he was twenty-nine. Would he still be there, in four more years? He shook his head, no, no more words – speechlessly sad.

And Platt was all interviewed out – but he did another, and another – until finally, politely and helplessly, he just asked, 'Can't you get it off somebody else?'

Les Walker watched Robson still talking, and smiled with a

fond incredulity. Would the man ever stop giving himself to them?

But most of the players and staff were on the bus now, with Stuart Pearce last on, someone keeping him company to try and salve the pain of the missed penalty. And now the German bus was leaving, and the press and the cameras too.

I backed away, against a rough grey wall; one of the last few there, though I wasn't there really, not fully – I was still back in the beautiful game, still watching the weave and weft of the play, the patterns and the passes, the missed chances and the goals, the hope and the grief – still crying and cheering in the stands where the ordinary folk go to watch the men who've got gold in their shoes.

On the bus, the staff were at the front, and the players in their own compact world at the back. Gazza, when he'd got on, had been still barely over his tears; he'd sat down, and for a short while looked silent, and bitterly miserable.

But what the hell, a beer and a sing-song, it's all over now – and it was Gazza who started them singing. Lineker looked back at it, and looked away – then he smiled too – and before long they were all joining in, working some daft little routine with their arms to the song, as the bus pulled away. Because we may have been edged out of this one – but there's always another game down the road, and another season, and another goal to go for.

The last thing I noticed was Bobby Robson standing in the aisle near the front, leaning slightly forward with one hand on the back of a seat, and the other over his eyes. It was the posture of a man drained and shattered – the posture, perhaps, of a man in tears at journey's end.

And in the empty bus park, the small simple words of the War Correspondent came back. Because what had it been like, to follow England to the semi-finals of the World Cup?

It had been the best – just the best.

22 Aftermath

Escape from Planet Football

In the afternoon before the game, English drunks had fought with plainclothes police on a train coming into Turin from Genoa. Groups of Germans ambushed other English in the streets around the station. Minor skirmishes between English, Germans, and Italians ran on and off for an hour or so; one young German got a 12-inch stab wound in the back and was taken, seriously ill, to intensive care.

So Les Walker may hope for a new era – and in football terms, it's possible to hope that he's right. But the drunkenness, stupidity, and violence of all too many Englishmen won't go away overnight just because our team did well, or because the great majority of its followers behaved themselves. And I really don't know what you do about that.

I do know that the policing of the English at Italia '90 – oppressive, aggressive, and provocative – was depressingly misconceived; that it was a paranoid over-reaction to media and ministerial prophecies of doom which, effectively, criminalised Englishness for the duration of the tournament.

But the thought still nags that we brought that on ourselves – that we get the media, the ministers, and the policing we deserve. And those who want to be thought innocent can't complain, as long as they tolerate the guilty among them.

So sure, for a couple of hours in the Stadio delle Alpe, it was possible to relish the best in the bulldog – but that was down to the players, that was Planet Football.

In the real world outside, there were bad manners, a sullen xenophobia, a wide inability to get on with a smile in a different culture – and a lousy dress sense to boot. While other nations made *festa*, in short, being with England too often meant seeing an ill-disciplined, ill-educated, uncaring narrow-mindedness that won't easily be extirpated.

Because it's social endgame, the rancid end product of history – it's the lost and left-behind who loom up when you're lashing round in the dregs of vanished empire . . . it's what you get when you're all played out.

And we could have won the World Cup – but would it have made us any smarter, or more polite?

Nor is it any consolation that we're not alone with these problems . . . I went into Turin with the War Correspondent – and there was a bigger Italian mob outside the station than there'd been the night before, milling around hoping for a punch-up. English fans were penned in the concourse; it was riot helmets and blue flashing lights again . . . and I couldn't be dealing with it any more, least of all right then.

I went back to my hotel, and broke the drinks ban with the proprietor and a friend of his until four-thirty in the miserable and disbelieving morning. We, like the Italians, were out – it was a stunned, shocking feeling. It was simultaneously an unanswerable fact, and yet impossible to believe. We wished half-hearted curses on Maradona, and numbly consoled ourselves that the true final would now be the play-off between England and Italy in Bari.

While we sat talking, English lads arrived breathless and sweating in twos and threes. They'd paid £75 each for tickets from touts marked clearly FIFA Poland, or FIFA Trinidad & Tabago – then, afterwards, they'd been blocked for two hours in the station, and decided in the end just to run for it. It had been, they said, very hairy indeed.

They were all fine, these boys – bar one older and thuggishly rude Chelsea man who left the next morning with a bill of nearly £70 unpaid. But it's always the same – you meet good lads . . . and then some bastard lets you down.

The morning of 5 July was hot; I woke thick-headed, depressed, and uncertain what to do. The traffic thrummed and burred, thin and disconnected and distant; everything seemed broken and out of kilter. A tobacconist who had stamps wouldn't sell me them, he was on some obscure form of stamp strike; then I went to a bank for money, and they didn't know how to cash a Eurocheque – they were, they said, a new bank, and started phoning superior branches for instructions.

I reeled away into the street in a dumb and irritated haze, and sought directions for a bank that might actually function like one; but the directions led nowhere. Turin seemed surreal, stunned and vacated, like the site of a neutron bomb test – where was everybody? What had happened here? I roamed the strangely silent backstreets, swigging hits of black mud coffee here and there to try and bring myself alive – but all the coffee brought me was the sweats and the shakes.

And what to do? A grim and final recognition that the story was over grew slowly, like the onset of bad indigestion; and with it there grew, in the hot and empty streets, a dim determination to escape from Planet Football.

Because who cared who came third? The play-off between the losing semi-finalists is a meaningless game, and FIFA should abandon it. As for the Final, I hoped the Germans really tonked Argentina, but I didn't need to be there – it was a Final that nobody impartial had wanted; without Italy, it was a gutted event . . . so I made my decision.

Tomorrow was Friday. I had a bag of notes and tapes and papers back at La Perla; my charter flew out of Sant'Elmas on Friday week. So if I could get back to Cagliari today, surely I could work one final wangle, switch my unswitchable cheap ticket, and get home on tomorrow's flight a week early . . . I found a bus to the bus station, and another from there to the airport.

At the booking counter they said all the flights to Rome, and from there on to Cagliari, were full. No chance, they said, no chance – but I waved my groaning plastic, and bought standbys anyway. Because remember, this is Italy . . . and full or not, I got flights out of both cities all the same.

The Airbus to Rome was OK – but I really don't know how I got on the second leg, from there back to Cagliari. It really was full – at the standby counter I smiled, I spoke Italian, I explained how it was pressingly urgent that I should get back to Sardinia . . . but it wasn't any charm of mine that wangled it. On the contrary, it's them who are charming, it's them who can always find a way – Italians are masters at producing, out of the indescribably chaotic, an unexpected happy ending.

So I wedged myself, wasted and aching, into the mass of supplicants at the boarding gate. The engines whined and whistled outside; the harsh metal glare of the orange evening sun lay heavy on the livery of the Alitalia jets on the Tarmac, and the service vehicles buzzed like frantic drones between the queen bee planes. Into the bleak dusk of the sweltering day after defeat, I rode the squat fat bus across the pan to another plane, another ride, and another step closer to home.

Scrambling up the steep steps between the DC-9's engines I thought, is this thing safe? It was my twelfth flight since leaving Luton on 1 June; and you never worry about it when you're outward bound – but the nearer home you get, the more you fear not making your destination. In your worn and bleary head you see your home, your wife, your baby – and you see pilot error, engine failure, metal fatigue, improperly sealed cargo doors . . . we rose up towards the sea.

The miracle of flight . . . eating up the ozone, burning up the atmosphere. And what will things be like thirty years from now, when Joe is my age? Will we still jet about so casually? Will we still play World Cups?

Fatigue brings on terrible fears . . . but then life, like football, is a game of ninety minutes. You get your span allotted, you do your best – and at the end, you're all played out.

And though that end be cruel as hell, there's no one can fault you for trying all you can until it comes.

After thirty minutes, Sardinia rose again out of the Tyrrhenian Sea, black and jagged in gold waters under the last red sun. The island was a misty silhouette, jewelled with the diamond-bright traceries of its thin and rare streams.

One last *vongole* at La Taverna, one last tour of the bars, one last look at where England's story began . . . and looking back on that story with the waiters and the barmen in the Cagliari cafés, they were keen to make sure and tell me before I left that the English were fine. They sat together with Sards, they said, they caused little trouble, and they paid. It was only, they said, when photographers came . . . but perhaps, I said, they protested too much; the English weren't angels.

No, they said; but nor are we.

In the morning, courteous people in a travel agency and at the airport fiddled my ticket, free of charge, to let me fly home. The plane was five hours delayed; waiting, I met young Englishmen from the NATO base down the road whose families were coming in for holiday. And they loved it on Sardinia – so they weren't running the place down when they told me this story. They had, they said, done security duty at the consulate during the first round – and one day an English fan came in and said, 'I think I'm drowning in my own blood.'

He'd been whacked in the chest with a crowbar in a back alley the night before . . .

Violence is just violence. It isn't football's problem – it's a Europe-wide shadow, scuffling and bawling round the edges of the great events. And as long as they're out there and angry, you can police those events as heavy as you like – but the anger and the violence will still rumble blackly on.

I went home, and slept for eleven hours.

For the record: in Bari on 7 July, England and Italy played a fine game of football. Italy had been beautiful throughout Italia '90, and England brave – and the best of both came out in a match the pointlessness of which was forgotten as the two sides did themselves and football proud.

The fans, at last, had a party (or a disco, indeed); and after Italy had narrowly but deservedly won 2–1, the players did a lap of honour together. Only the referee and the linesmen disgraced themselves with some atrocious decisions – but with few exceptions, the refereeing had been dismal from the beginning, so there was no surprise there.

The goalscorers were, appropriately, Baggio, Platt, and Schillaci – the latter converting a penalty to take his tally to six and become, as Lineker had been four years ago, the tournament's leading scorer.

Lineker ended with four, Platt with three – and England were given the Fair Play award for the least-booked and best-disciplined side in the tournament. I believe, myself, that that means a great deal, especially when the players are so much criticised – and when you look, then, at what happened the following night.

In Rome on 8 July, Argentina were responsible for turning the game's great occasion into the worst and lowest-scoring World Cup Final ever seen. They seemed from the outset to be void of ambition; they played entirely negatively, as if they wanted this to be their third game in a row to go to penalties. The Germans dominated throughout, but seemed themselves to be enervated by the occasion; in the face of Argentina's cynical hacking and diving, their finishing was spineless, and they ended up diving about pretty unforgivably themselves.

It was, all in all, a grotesque display. Argentina had come to the Final with a record of a foul every four minutes – and they carried on just the same.

Germany's first shot was the result of a free-kick, after Serrizuela fouled Völler in the second minute. Three minutes later they shoved Littbarski over, and Dezotti was booked for protesting against the award of another free-kick. And on it went from there . . . they had only one attempt on goal in the whole first half, compared with Germany's twelve.

The second half kicked off just the same with a brutish bodycheck by Troglio on Matthäus. And then, in the sixty-fourth minute – but you could see it coming a mile off – an Argentine became the first player in history to be sent off in a World Cup Final. But Monzon's tackle on Klinsmann was near psychotic – so he got the disgrace he deserved.

Worse was to come. With six minutes left, the only goal of the Final came when Völler, challenged by Sensini, fell over in the penalty box – so it was, appropriately, in this lousy finish to a poorly adjudicated tournament, a dubious decision that settled the result. Troglio, protesting the penalty in a pack of frantic dissension, was booked; Brehme scored.

Two minutes later Dezotti tried to strangle Kohler, and got sent off too. Maradona was booked as the filthy-tempered protests continued – the referee was inexcusably pushed and barged and jostled and before the gruesome charade could end, he had to add on three minutes' extra time, as much for the time-wasting and the expulsions as any injuries. The Germans had had twenty-two shots at goal – Argentina, just one.

The tabloids loved it: ARGIES SHAME WORLD.

But that's about right. So I'm glad I watched it at home – and my only regret is, I never found out how big the Roman Cheesewoman was.

*

In the Inca capital of Cuzco in Peru, Christmas 1984, I met a charming Argentinian with whom I talked carefully – the Falklands-Malvinas war being still then quite recent – until I felt we were getting on well enough to ask what he thought about that conflict.

He laid immediately into the generals, and the way they'd used military action and crude nationalism to get the country behind them – it was, I said, a familiar-sounding story.

His father, he said, had been a well respected war correspondent; he'd been in Indochina, Central America, and elsewhere. In spring '82, he'd gone in with the Argentine invasion from the beginning; he'd been on the islands throughout. And when he came home to Buenos Aires after the defeat, he was so appalled at the cruel and incompetent management of the conflict, that he began to write a strongly critical book on it. One day, as the book progressed, he left the house – and was never seen nor heard of again.

The young man who told me of his disappeared father got up, and hurriedly left the room with sudden tears on his face. And I have nothing against Argentina – because I know what the people of that country have been through, and what they're going through today.

So if Argentina have been the villains of this book, let no one for a minute imagine that there's any nasty jingo nationalism involved. On the contrary, for all I care they're welcome to the Falklands – they can sail their awful football team out there, scupper the boat, and leave them nothing to foul and dive over but the sheep. They've been the villains of this book because, pure and simple, their football was a disgrace.

But why? Why do teams sometimes turn up with such a desperate, paranoid rage to win?

At the conference in Florence in May, an urbane Uruguayan called Rafael Bayce described the difference between Brazilians, as against Argentinians and his own countrymen. Brazilians, he said, go through life feeling good about it. Their flag says, 'Order And Progress', and while Brazil may not in fact be the world's most orderly place, her people do still tend to believe that they're progressing – they're optimists. Hence the joy in their approach to life, and to football. So when they lose it's a drama for a day or two – then they shrug and say, 'Oh well, there's still no one who can play the game like we do – and we'll be back.'

466

Uruguayans and Argentines, on the other hand, said Bayce, feel that theirs are countries in decay. Like the tango, they tend to fatalism, passivity, nostalgia – and with all else crumbling, every hope left is urgently, yearningly invested in football.

So maybe that's why Maradona wept the way that he did at the end, so uncontrollably – because he didn't just want to win, he *needed* to win. He'd said at the press conference in Milan on the eve of the opening game, not that he was defending the World Cup for Argentina, but that he was defending Argentina in the World Cup – defending the last pride and prowess she had left.

And it got to them – winning became more important than playing. They drove with a maddened, gutsy, violent resolve towards a Final that, on merit, they should never have been in – they used whatever means came to hand, sometimes literally – and, in the end, they paid for it horribly.

But understanding it can't ever excuse it. After all, there's probably a fair few people in Cameroon who haven't got too much going for them, but their team smiled all the way, and we loved them for it. They could be rough – but they weren't cheats.

So looking back now, I think the worst moment of the tournament was the mysterious failure of the egregious Fredriksson to give the Russians the penalty they so blatantly deserved for Maradona's handball after twelve minutes in Naples. If the Russians had found their game, and Argentina had gone home when they deserved to, we might have had a better tournament by far.

Still, that doesn't mean I am, like Chris Waddle, in favour of instant TV replays. The referee's the referee, a participant in the show – take away the finality of his authority, and he might as well not be out there. And then, we want our football to be as just as possible, OK, but it's not *about* justice, it's about drama – and the drama requires villains.

And boy, those Argentines – did we get us some bad and resilient villains there, or what?

Argentina aside, in football terms it wasn't a great tournament. Three of the four semi-finalists were very good teams – but Brazil disappointed, and only Cameroon brought to the party something genuinely fresh.

All the same, it was a thrill and a privilege to follow England. You can say that the best side in the tournament won it, or that Germany and Italy played better football than England overall – but England's was the best story. Because with due respect to Germany–Holland and Belgium–Uruguay, England's progress out of stumbling indecision in Cagliari produced the best three games of the tournament, each one better than the last. Who would have said on 25 May, when the WORLD CUP WALLIES were being jeered on their way, that thirty million people would be watching them play their hearts out in Turin all of forty days later?

So Bobby Robson finished eight years in the hardest job in English football having achieved more than any man in that job before him bar Alf Ramsey – and Ramsey, of course, did it at home. Robson's record reads,

Played: 95
Won: 47
Drawn: 30
Lost: 18
Goals For: 154
Against: 60

Along the way, he took us once to the last eight in the world, and then to the last four; and he did so often under torrents of wholly unjustifiable venom and vilification. So maybe he wasn't the greatest manager in the world – but when it counted he mostly made the right decisions, and he got the right results – and what more could be asked? So it was good, in the end, that he went out triumphant – because it couldn't have happened to a nicer man.

As for the players, we know what they did – and we know that now, of course, they're doing it again. At the time of writing, Lineker has been appointed the new England captain; Gazzamania's raging, and he recently scored his first hat-trick. Elsewhere, Barnes and Beardsley and Macca are bubbling again at Anfield, Waddle's Marseilles are at the top again in France, and Butcher's Rangers look unbeatable in Scotland.

Peter Shilton, having announced his international retirement in Bari, is coming on to Graham Taylor's new England coaching staff. Bryan Robson, sadly, is having yet another operation – but does anyone doubt that he'll end up managing Manchester United? And Bully's still whacking them in the net up at Wolves.

But the greatest legacy of Robson's eight years is that – apart from his adroit handling of Gazza – England now have players like Platt, Wright, Walker, and Parker who've been blooded at the top, and come out proud.

So we can look to the European Championships in Sweden in 1992, and beyond that to the fifteenth World Cup in the USA, with the highest of hopes. Robson and his twenty-two men gave us more than a fine performance in Italy – they gave us something to look forward to as well.

The one downer about following England was the way that sour relations with the press hung like permanent bad weather over the camp.

The squalid inventions, the loutish claptrap, the illiterate hysteria of the tabloids needs no further rehearsing – but the players aren't guiltless either. When the Hostess Isabella story broke, there was a lot of sympathy among the football writers for the way the players felt. That sympathy was dispelled, however, when the players – not all of them, but too many – failed to discriminate between rotters and football men, and between tabloids and qualities.

But more generally, there's the question of their contracts – Waddle's 'money for jam'. Because it's really no good saying, 'I hate the press' then taking the *Sun*'s dirty money. It's been going on long enough – the practice is mentioned in *Only a Game* – and the players take the situation (and the money) as they find it.

The argument, however, that theirs are short and precarious careers, in which they should earn what they can, is an inadequate justification here. They have every right to their wages, and any commercial income they may generate is entirely legitimate – that's professionalism. Professionalism, however, also involves talking to the media – *it's part of the job*.

Contracts with clubs in some American professional sports include express stipulations that players shall not earn money from interviews or 'exclusives' – and that's the way it ought to be here. Of course it would help if we didn't have such base newspapers, with their chequebooks ever ready – and if the FA could manage press relations with some higher degree of professionalism itself. 'The hierarchy,' said one journalist, 'is out here for a holiday. The international committee's come out of this looking like a bunch of drones. I really don't know what their function is.'

So in general, my sympathies are more with the players, than with their yobbish detractors, or their indolent and complacent employers – but taking tabloid money all the same is just wrong. The players should be available for clearly limited, well organised periods – to the football writers only – and be happy about it.

And if some gutter scumsheet still comes up with the libellous toxin, then you just lock out its writers and sue. Or, if a particular writer comes up with opinions you don't like, either criticise him rationally to his face, or blank him – but don't blank everybody. Because, like Waddle said, 'People like to read football,' and 'I hate the press' is both simplistic and fruitless, and a disservice to fans.

Two last issues arise in the aftermath of Italia '90.

Firstly, what use is anything players or managers might achieve, in Italy or elsewhere, if the English game continues to be run by such a lot of complacent, short-sighted, self-interested, greed-crazed clots?

And secondly, will any of us care anyway if FIFA ends up turning the game irrevocably into a circus for the moneymen?

The Football League has recently decided that in the next season after this one, the First Division will go back to having twenty-two clubs, instead of twenty. The FA, to Kelly's credit, opposes this dreadful decision – but will they do more than just mumble about it? Their flabby record to date gives little cause for hope.

FIFA, however, makes the people who run England's clubs seem models of modest and sensible ambition.

I like the USA, and I like football – but I really doubt whether, come 1994, the two will mix.

Attempting to make them do so, FIFA President Havelange's

suggestion that football should be played in four quarters, so the telly can run more ads, is grim evidence that money matters more to him than the game.

But if that's the direction we're headed in, me and millions like me will stop going. Because this is *our* game, this beautiful game – it doesn't belong to Coca-Cola or JVC, or to Mars or Gillette, even if my freebie new 'shaving system' is very nifty.

So keep your hands off, greedheads.

It's a game of two halves – and we like it that way.

Picture Credits